T0380437

NORTH AMERICAN BIPOINTS
From the First Settlement of
Prehistoric Americas to Contact

Wm Jack Hranicky RPA

Blackwater Draw, New Mexico

authorHOUSE

AuthorHouse™
1663 Liberty Drive
Bloomington, IN 47403
www.authorhouse.com
Phone: 1 (800) 839-8640

Dedicated to:
>**George Carter – It's Earlier Than You Think.**
>>**He was the first to argue a "great" antiquity for humans in the New World.**

According to Carter (1980) for the Americas:
>*My claims concerning the antiquity of men have been far out of step with the field – 100,000 years, not 10,000 years…*

Cover: All three bipoints are from the Pleistocene era in the U.S.

Published by AuthorHouse 01/24/2019

ISBN: 978-1-5462-6696-9 (sc)
ISBN: 978-1-5462-6695-2 (e)

Print information available on the last page.

Preface

This publication is a re-write and update of ***Bipoints Before Clovis (2005)*** which has a vast amount of data and information that was not available for the earlier version. It discusses and illustrates world-wide bipoint technology. They are presented in their historical contexts and presented with their physical attributes. The major focus is U.S. bipoints of which two bipoints have Before Clovis dates. This bipoint technology as found on the eastern U.S. Atlantic coastal plain has varying dates from 50,000 years to European Contact and the U.S. Pacific coast with dates to 18,000 years with Alaska supporting a 35,000 year date. For both U.S. coasts, there were major emigrational events around 16,000 years; and the bipoint was part of it. In presenting this prehistory, the Virginia Cinmar bipoint (22,760 YBP) and the Florida Marion County bipoint (16,400 YBP) are illustrated and discussed.

The author in the 1980s suggested that humans were in Virginia 16,000 years ago and, naturally, few archaeologists even considered this possibility. This date was based on projectile point typologies, which stand today as representing considerable antiquity in the Middle Atlantic area. Now with early site dates from Cactus Hill and Saltville in Virginia, the concept of ***early man*** has new meanings in the East.

With good/bad dates for extremely early sites in the New World being common place (for one 36,000 years example, see Watanake, et al. (2003)), the prehistory picture is left open to everyone who wants to forecast a historic calendar. With this perspective, the following discussion provides insights to the Asia-Euro-Africa connections for the Americas.

A Bipoint Morphology Model (BMM) is argued which includes basic attributes and properties. And, classic bipoints are marked with this symbol. The symbol implies a prehistoric legacy, which are divided into three classes.

The bipoint is a legacy implement from the Old World that is found through time/space all over North America. The bipoint is defined and basic manufacturing processes are presented along with bipoint properties, shape/form, resharpening, and cultural associations. This publication illustrates numerous bipoints from the Atlantic and Pacific coasts (and within the U.S.) and presents some of their inferred chronologies which are the oldest in North America. Several morphologies between American and Iberian bipoints are compared. It concludes that a Solutrean occupation did occur on the U.S. Atlantic coastal plain.

Once the bipoint was established on the East Coast, it spread westward to join up with the bipoints that were introduced on the West Coast. The bipoint is found in the U.S. from the Paleoindian era through to the Woodland era. This publication reports bipoint dates on the Atlantic coast from 35,000+ to Alaska at 20,000+ years.

This study represents 35 years of collecting bipoint data and photographs. Numerous papers were submitted to journals which argued the bipoint as a single technology that precedes Clovis in the Americas; these papers were rejected by numerous journal editors. This technology was brought into the New World when the first Americans entered it. Bipoints were manufactured and continued … after non-European Contact.

This publication follows Clarke's (1968) ***Analytical Archaeology*** where he comments:

> ***...in the belief that the future of archaeology depends upon the further clarification of its concepts in order that powerful, modern techniques may be employed to the utmost capacity of their potential.***

Even though his publication is over the so-called magic 40 years old in archaeology, Clarke's publication still has an effect on world-wide archaeology. This and other, older publications have their merit in archaeology, especially classics that started the discipline. And importantly, Don Crabtree once told the author: *there are just so many ways to make stone tools.*

In other words, flintknapping is the process of transferring energy from the hand into stone; with a simple 50 mm knife, civilization was created. The bipoint was only one of thousands of different tools used by early humans.

While a bipoint technology per se, this publication also attempts to suggest and define the origins of the Clovis lanceolate technology which produces subsequent point types, including the bipoint. This biface lanceolate technology is suggested as technology starting among the European Mousterians 60,000+ years ago.

Alan Bryan's (1965) *Paleo-American Prehistory* was the first publication to identify a bipoint tradition in the Western world which he considered as a prior-to-Clovis technology. His early work is continued here. And, the term "**PaleoAmerican**[1]" is now used in American archaeology.

Finally, this publication assumes a lithic tool continuum for all humanity. Technology produced the first material culture in human history. While non-material aspects of society, such as social, political, and religious practices, were developed before the discovery of technology, numerous forms of this lithic technology were transferred to the New World and become the major focus in American archaeological analysis of human history.

Wm Jack Hranicky RPA

Jasper may be the preferred stone in the Pleistocene era of the eastern U.S. This broken jasper specimen is thin (6 mm) for its estimated length. It has cortex remaining on one face and has large, thin flake scars. It is assumed here to be pre-Clovis.

Jasper Biface, L = ?, W = 86, T = 6 mm

Reverse Face

---

[1] PaleoAmerican – any time before Clovis in North America.

Table of Contents

SECTION 1 – INTRODUCTION 1
Is It A Bipoint? 2
The Bipoint's Ancestry 5
Bipoint Acquisitions and Curations 5
Research Rules for American Archaeology? 6
Defining Lithics as Applied to Bipoints 9
Bipoint Morphology Model (Model) (BMM) 12
Bipoint Model Factors 13
Physical Bipoint Axis 13
Archaeology Terms and Divisions 15
The Basic Bipoint 18
Lithic Technology Continuum 30
Identifying Bipoints 31
Basic U.S. Bipoint Manufacture 32
Bipoint Shape 33
Blade Bipoints 34
Pure Blade Bipoints 37
Transverse Bipoint 37
Lithic Tool Organization 39
All Tools – All Dates 40
Legacy Requirements 40
Legacy Bipoint Stones 41
U.S. Bipoint Timelines 41
Bipoint U.S. Areas 41
Clovis and the Bipoint 42
Bipoints and Folsom Points 43
Expended Bipoints 45
A Bipoint Bit Theory 47
Example Bipoint Model 48
Bipoint – V-Stemmed Knife – or a General Tool 51
Lithic Tool Organization 59
SECTION 2 – RESHARPENED BIPOINTS 60
Bipoint Resharpening 61
Bipoint Resharpening Stages 62
Legacy Reshapening 62
Resharpening Standards 65
SECTION 3 - BIPOINTS AND PREHISTORY 66
Early American Archaeology 66
Dates for Early Sites 67
U.S. Early Chronology 68
Early Eastern U.S. Historical Framework 70
First U.S. Ports of Entry 72
East and West PaleoAmerica 72
Pacific Occupation Area 73
U.S. Atlantic Occupation Area 76
Atlantic Coast Artifact Examples 80
Bipoints on the U.S. Pacific Coast 81
South American Bipoints 82
African Routes for the Bipoints 82
SECTION 4 - NORTH AMERICAN BIPOINT SPECIMENS 84
4-1 Time Lines for Late Bipoints 84
4-2 Alaska Bipoint Specimen 86

4-3 Florida Bipoint Specimens 86
4-4 South Carolina Bipoint Specimens 90
4-5 Georgia Bipoint Specimens 91
4-6 North Carolina Bipoint Specimens 97
4-7 Virginia Bipoint Specimens 103
4-8 Maryland Bipoint Specimens 115
4-9 Delaware Bipoint Specimen 120
4-10 Rhode Island Bipoint Specimens 120
4-11 New Jersey Bipoint Specimens 121
4-12 New York Bipoint Specimen 123
4-13 Connecticut Bipoint Specimen 124
4-14 Pennsylvania Bipoint Specimens 124
4-15 West Virginia Bipoint Specimens 128
4-16 Ohio Bipoint Specimens 129
4-17 Tennessee Bipoint Specimens 134
4-18 Kentucky Bipoint Specimens 138
4-19 Missouri Bipoint Specimens 142
4-20 Iowa Bipoint Specimen 144
2-21 Illinois Bipoint Specimens 144
4-22 Mississippi Bipoint Specimen 148
4-23 California Bipoint Specimen 149
4-24 Nebraska Bipoint Specimen 150
4-26 North Dakota Bipoints 150
4-27 Colorado Bipoint Specimens 150
4-28 Oregon Bipoint Specimens 151
4-29 Nevada Bipoint Specimen 155
4-30 Texas Bipoint Specimen 156
4-31 Alabama Bipoint Specimens 157
4-32 Indiana Bipoint Specimens 158
4-33 New Mexico Bipoint Specimens 159
4-34 Wisconsin Bipoint Specimen 161
4-35 Arkansas Bipoint Specimen 161
4-36 Idaho Bipoint Specimen 162
4-37 Canada Bipoint Specimen 162
4-38 Mexico Bipoint Specimens 163
SECTION 5 - BIPOINTS IN THE AMERICAS 166
Bipoints in American Archaeological History 166
A Lithic Technology History 169
American Bipoint Age/Chronology 170
SECTION 6 - OLD WORLD BIPOINTS 173
Bipoint Origins 173
Bipoint Firsts 174
The Mousterian Factor 175
The Solutrean Factor 177
Solutrean and Transatlantic Migrations 181
Indented-Base Bipoint 182
The African Factor 182
Aterian Tool Legacy 183
The Magdalenian Factor 185
The Asian Factor 187
Southeastern Asia 188
Old World Bipoint Dates 189
Classic Bipoint Forms 190

Bipoint Bit Resharpening...191
Establishing Bipoint in the U.S. 194
Bipoint Patination...197
SECTION 7 – EARLY VIRGINIA BIPOINTS **198**
Environmental Factors 198
Virginia Paleoenvironment for Bipoints 199
Virginia Early Bipoints 199
The Dismal Swamp of Virginia and North Carolina 203
Pre-Clovis Lithic Tools..207
SECTION 8 – EARLY NORTH CAROLINA BIPOINTS **210**
The Rights Cache, North Carolina 210
SECTION 9 – EARLY FLORIDA' BIPOINTS **212**
SECTION 10 - SOUTH AMERICAN BIPOINTS **217**
El Jobo Ancestry 219
Chile Bipoints 219
Andean Bipoints 219
SECTION 11 - BIPOINT MECHANICS **220**
Bipoint States and Modes 221
Bipoint Morphology Production 221
Bipoint Knapping Methods 222
Bipoint Preforms...224
Asymmetrical Procedure 224
Bipoint Symmetry 224
Bipolar Procedure...224
Haft vs. Bit Area 224
Lateral Chassis Margins 229
Thick Bipoints..229
Bipoint Resharpening 230
The Iberian Curve...232
Mega Bifaces...234
Bipoint Quality 234
Bipoint Size 235
Bipoint Lithic Materials 236
Bone Bipoints 237
Bipoint Hafting 238
Biface Bipoints...240
Expended Bit Shapes and Styles 240
V-Stemmed Anomalies...242
Expended Bipoints 243
SECTION 12 – BIPOINT CONCLUSION...**244**
Hypothesis on the Americas..244
50,000 Years and Counting...245
African Content in American Prehistory 245
Now for Clovis 246
Late Prehistoric Bipoints..246
Conclusion: Technology – Coincidence or Legacy 247
Eastern Atlantic Coast of Yesterday..248
Finally – A Conclusion..249
APPENDIX A – PROPERTIES AND CONCEPTS IN TOOLMAKING **250**
APPENDIX B – RAMAN LASER-INDUCED **252**
APPENDIX C – NORTH CAROLINA BIFACES **254**
The Rankin Cache..254
APPENDIX D - ROUNDED-BIT BIPOINTS **257**

APPENDIX E - MORROW MOUNTAIN RESHARPENED BIPOINTS 260

Savannah River Bipoints 264

APPENDIX F – QUANTUM STYLES IN LITHIC TECHNOLOGY 265

Style – Quantum Classification Method 265

POSTWORD 266

REFERENCES 267

INDEX 300

**America's oldest known artist may have been an Ice Age hunter in what is now Vero Beach, Florida,
it is a 13,000-year-old bone etching.
(Purdy, et al. 2011, Purdy 2012, and Smithsonian Institution, Washington, DC**

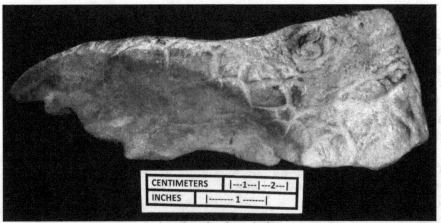

**Another Ancient Artist
Fossilized Ivory Condor Head Figurine, Arkfeld Site, Frederick County, Virginia**

The Marion County, Florida Bipoint

A SURFACE FIND IN FLORIDA HAS PRODUCED A DATE OF 16,400 +/- 325 YBP. IT COMPARES FAVORABLY WITH FRENCH SOLUTREAN SMALL BIPOINTS; THIS BIPOINT IS THE SECOND BIPOINT SPECIMEN FOUND ON THE ATLANTIC COAST WITH A BEFORE CLOVIS DATE. NOTE ITS BOLD, THIN FLAKE SCARS WHICH ARE AN ATTRIBUTE OF SOLUTREAN TOOLMAKING. IT HAS A RESHARPENED DISTAL END.

Ocala Chert Bipoint, Marion County, Florida
(L = 72, W = 37, T = 12 mm, R = 23.35, E = 1.95, g = 27, M = 5YR8/1, g = 27).

The term _pre-Clovis_ is a misnomer in American archaeology. The term implies that before (all) lithic technology leads to Clovis technology. This technology assumption is completely false; all Before-Clovis technologies have various time spans, distributions, and/or completely disappear prior to Clovis. Or, they remain in the background of Clovis. If archaeologists continue arguing that Clovis is the principal technology with no antecedents, their picture and interpretation of prehistory are very misleading. Therefore, terms such as Early Man, Paleo-Amerind, Early American, Expanded Paleoindian, PaleoAmerican, or pre-Clovis are found in the literature and have little validity today. The preferred term is Before Clovis, and, for the present, the term has a beginning date of 13,000 YBP in the U.S. Its time period is generally called the PaleoAmerican era. This era ends with the advent of Clovis pointmaking.

The Virginia Cinmar Bipoint

THE CINMAR BIPOINT WAS DREDGED UP IN 1970 BY CAPT. THURSTON SHAWN FROM THE WATERS OFFSHORE FROM HAMPTON, VIRGINIA. IT IS NAMED AFTER THE CAPTAIN'S SHIP. IT CAME UP WITH A MASTODON SKULL WHICH PROVIDED THE RADIOCARBON DATE OF 22,760 +/- 90 RCYBP (UCIAMS-53545). THE DEPTH OF THE FIND WAS FROM 38-40 FATHOMS IN THE ATLANTIC. NOTE ITS BOLD, THIN FLAKE SCARS WHICH ARE AN ATTRIBUTE OF SOLUTREAN TOOLMAKING. AND, IT HAS NON-INVASIVE RETOUCHING ALONG ITS DISTAL MARGINS RESULTING FROM RESHARPENING DULLED EDGES. IT HAS THE LOWEST LWT RATIO IN THE U.S.

18.5 cm

Rhyolite, Cinmar Bipoint, Off-Shore Virginia
(L =188 mm, W = 54 mm, T = 6 mm, R = 20.88, E = 3.48).
Photograph courtesy: Dennis Stanford and Bruce Bradley (Smithsonian Institution)

For a countering argument, see (2015) Eren, Metin, Matthew T. Boulanger, and Michael J. O'Brian _The Cinmar Discovery and the Proposed Pre-Glacial Maximum Occoſation of North America_. Journal of Archaeological Science: Reports, Vol. 2, pp. 708-713.

Transverse Bipoint

THIS VIRGINIA BIPOINT WAS MADE USING AN OLD WORLD FLAKING TECHNIQUE CALLED TRANSVERSAL STONE KNAPPING (HRANICKY 2018 AND VERTES 1954). THIS METHOD WAS USED TO REMOVE A BLADE FORM A CORE. THEN THE BLADE WAS FLAKED INTO A BIPOINT. FORTUNATELY FOR ARCHAEOLOGY, THE KNAPPER LEFT THE STRIKING PLATFORM ON THE BIPOINT; OTHERWISE, IT COULD NOT HAVE BEEN IDENTIFIED BY THIS METHOD. THE CHERT STONE USED IN THIS BIPOINT IS NOT FOUND IN THE POTOMAC VALLEY.

Transverse Bipoint from Virginia (Platform – upper left margin)

THIS IS THE ONLY BIPOINT IN THIS STUDY COLLECTION THAT WAS MADE THIS WAY. EVEN THE FLAKING IS SOMEWHAT DIFFERENT FROM OTHER AMERICAN BIPOINTS.

BIPOINT FACTORS
1 – Bipoints are found worldwide and all over the U.S.
2 – Bipoints are found throughout late Paleolithic human history
3 – Earliest date for the bipont is 75,000 years in southern Africa
4 – Bipoints are the oldest continually-made tool in human history
5 – Bipoints are among the oldest stone tool made in the U.S.
6 – Bipoints are dual-pointed knives
7 – Bipoints were resharpened until expended and then discarded
8 – Bipoints were introduced to the U.S. at 35,000+ years
9 – Bipoints were introduced to South America 30,000 years ago
10 – V-shaped stem of a bipoint dates to the Old World Acheulian age
11 – Resharpening bipoints conforms to Old World bipoint methods
12 – Early U.S. bipoints are made off a blade using high-quality flaking
13 – Resharpened and expended bipoints are difficult to classify
14 – Bipoints have multiple size morphologies
15 – Bipoints are the first tool class introduced into the Americas
16 – Bipoints have associated microtools which make up the bipoint toolkit
17 – Bipoint's platform end is the hafting end
18 – Folsom toolmakers produced the earliest and best Holocene U.S. bipoints.

The Suffolk Bipoint

THE FOLLOWING RHYOLITE BIPOINT IS SUGGESTED AS HAVING A CONSIDERABLE ANTIQUITY IN VIRGINIA BUT LIKE THE BIPOINT IN GENERAL, VIRGINIA'S BIPOINTS DO NOT HAVE SOLID LAND-BASED DATES, NAMELY AN EXCAVATED DATE ASSOCIATION WITH DATABLE ORGANIC MATERIALS. THE SUFFOLK BIPOINT WAS FOUND IN THE TIDEWATER AREA OF VIRGINIA; THUS, ITS NAME. ITS REPORTED AS A FIND LOCATION WHICH IS NEAR THE DISMAL SWAMP AREA IN VIRGINIA. IT IS A SWAMP MOSTLY OF CYPRESS FOREST TODAY. AT PRESENT, THIS BIPOINT'S SHAPE IS UNIQUE IN THE MIDDLE ATLANTIC COASTAL AREA; IT IS A NARROW BIPOINT WITH AN OFF-SET TIP AND INDENTED BASE. IT MATCHES BIPOINTS F. BORDES' 1965 TYPOLOGY. ITS FLAKE SCARS ARE VERY FAINT AS IT MAY BE A WIDE UNIFACE FORM.

Suffolk Bipoint - Slate (L = 100, W = 36, T = 13 mm, R = 36.11, E = 2.78, g = 48)

THE STORY OF THIS ARTIFACT DATES TO 1966. THE AUTHOR WAS WALKING A FIELD ON A FARM IN THE DISMAL SWAMP AREA OF VIRGINIA. I FOUND THIS OBJECT AND SHOWED IT TO BEN MCCARY WHO WAS WALKING WITH ME. IT WAS MY EARLY DAYS IN ARCHAEOLOGY AND BEN WAS SHOWING ME THE "ROPES" OF ARCHAEOLOGY WHICH WAS THEN "WALKING FIELDS LOOKING FOR ARROWHEADS." HE SAID HE DIDN'T THINK IT WAS AN ARTIFACT. I, OF COURSE, DID NOT KNOW WHAT IT WAS AT THE TIME, BUT...FOR SOME REASON, KEPT IT. I HAVE BEEN BACK TO THAT FARM MANY TIMES...FOUND POINTS AND BLADE TOOLS. I BELIEVE THERE IS A PLEISTOCENE SITE THERE, BUT MUST DIG TO PROVE IT. NOW, I BELIEVE IT TO BE THE OLDEST ARTIFACT FOUND IN VIRGINIA. IT DATES APPROXIMATELY 35,000 YBP.

A Solutrean Jasper Bipoint

THIS JASPER BIPOINT WAS FOUND IN DAUPHIN COUNTY, PENNSYLVANIA. THE TIP WAS BROKEN AND RESTORED BY GARY FOGELMAN. IT MEASURES: L = 70?, W = 30, T = 4 MM. IT HAS FOUR CROSS FACE FLAKE SCARS. THESE FOUR THIN SCARS ON A SPECIMEN ONLY 4 MM THICK IS CERTAINLY SOLUTREAN FLAKING.

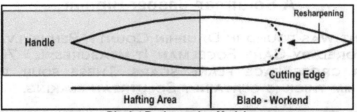

Bipoint Resharpening Model

Note: Once a bipoint was resharpened, it seldom is called a bipoint in American archaeology.

Bipoint - reference to a bipointed biface or blade; it is not a named type. It is a knife that was frequently resharpened which causes it to be mis-classified. Resharpening eliminates the second distal point.

Definition: The bipoint[2] is a laurel-leaf (foliate) knife form that usually has dual pointed ends, made from high quality stone, has excurvated lateral margins, and has a thin and D-shaped (blade) cross section and occurs as a uniface- or biface-worked specimen. It has a well-defined long axis and has a bilateral symmetry on the long axis. One end serves as a chassis (handle/stem) and the other as the bit (workend/blade). The basal end can be: pointed, rounded, or clipped (straight). The bipoint's bit tip can range from acute to an obtuse ($\approx 20°$ - $45°$) angle and does not have to be exactly pointed. The proximal-distal shape usually has a slight length-wise curve; however, post-Paleoindian bipoints have straight or convex profiles. It usually has a remaining platform or cortex remaining for the chassis end. One lateral margin usually has invasive retouch.

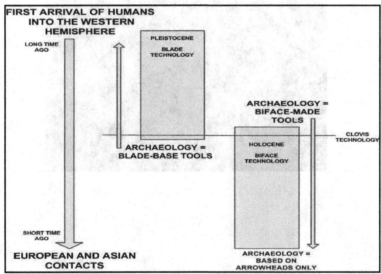

Suggested Overall Western Hemisphere Chronology. New World humans' Years Before Present (YBP) vary among archaeologists; probably, there will never be an agreement among them.

Earliest Reference to the Source of American Indians
... they arrived by boat.
*I conclude then, that it is likely they first came to the Indies (*New World*) was by shipwracke and temest of wether* (**Jose de Acosta 1599**).

---

[2] Bipoint technology is a general reference to the way they were made; it is considered a class in prehistoric lithic implements. They cannot be used as culture markers or timemarkers in the U.S. The morphology of the Solutrean bipoint may be the exception.

Section 1 – Introduction

This section provides a basic bipoint overview, including definition, concepts, archaeological operating rules, tool organization, tool design, and terminology. A bipoint timeline is presented which introduces the bipoint legacy proposition in antiquity. Basic bipoint metrics and methods are suggested as analytical approaches to the study of bipoints which are presented as a Bipoint Morphology Model. As argued here, bipoints are found all over North America in both time and space. This section argues that the bipoint is as common as America's arrowheads - all lying on the ground remaining to be found archaeologically.

Lithic Technology is a single, pan-human continuum[3] that starts at Olduvai Gorge and ends with the metal age of humanity. Once hominid primates learned to manufacture tools, they became human -- the toolmaking species. Most stone tools are simply legacies of earlier forms. Human prehistory has specific chronicles based on recording and classifying cultural materials by archaeologists which are based on specific usage of selected parts of the continuum.

North American Bipoints surveys the bipoint as this technology is found through time and space around the world. The bipoint's history of its technological origins, first distributions, and its *coming* to the Americas are discussed. It is defined, and numerous examples of its various morphologies are illustrated. A discussion argues how the bipoint was transported around the world. As a catalog on Western Hemisphere bipoints, this publication shows the geographic range and cultural chronologies for them. An environmental study shows possible causes for human long-range ocean migrations. The boat is argued as the principal form of transportation for these migrating populations, and they carried lithic technology with them. Dates are provided for bipoints with an emphasis on the Solutrean cross-Atlantic movements bringing the bipoint to the U.S. Does this introduction of bipoints lead to Clovis; an answer is suggested. Or, does it lead to a single American bipoint technology and bypasses Clovis altogether?

The bipoint implies a before Clovis technology in the U.S. that continues to Contact. And, the idea of early bipoints on the North and South American continent has been extensively studied over 50 years ago by Alan L. Bryan (1918-2010) who published his finding in *Paleo-American Prehistory* (1986). His publication was used as a starting reference for this publication which, overall, suggests the highest frequency of bipoints is the western U.S.

▶ This bipoint book provides:
- Overview of Mousterian, Solutrean, and Magdalenian ancestral technologies
- Illustrates bipoint examples from all over the world
- Defines the bipoint, including its resharpened forms
- Describes manufacturing methods used for making bipoints
- Presents a timeline for bipoint chronology
- Argues cross-ocean migrations into the Americas
- Provides 500+ bipoint examples from various U.S. states
- Presents world-wide environment conditions for bipoint prehistoric users
- Illustrates major bipoint finds in the U.S., such as the Cinmar, Norfolk, Suffolk, and Marion County bipoints
- Argues origins for Early Americans at 50,000 years ago
- Provides information on mammoth-associated bipoints.

The idea of Before Clovis[4] (commonly called pre-Clovis) has had a rather apprehensive acceptance in American archaeology. As a cultural time period, professional archaeology has numerous problems with it, namely Clovis is viewed as a single population making a fluted lanceolate projectile point. Evidence is presented that argues people were in North America prior to Clovis and producing a knife that is called the

---

[3] This lithic technology continuum follows a cultural transition philosophy (see Champs and Chauhan 2011).
[4] Numerous journal editors from Maine to Florida refused to publish parts of this publication; the Clovis police have struck again. And, there is an elite group of ivory tower professors and museum archaeologists that present a single viewpoint on Clovis origins and technology; it can be called the Clovis Club – members only.

bipoint and making other microtools. The American lithic technological time period covers 50,000 years before present to Contact. As presented in this publication, the bipoint is argued as having an Eurasia-wide distribution by 75,000 Years-Calibrated Before Present (YBP) which includes Africa.

Further, this publication argues that bipoint technology is neither a blade nor biface technology exclusively. It is a third technology that can simply be called bipoint technology, or perhaps…a world-wide laurel-leaf tradition. The key to bipoint technology is point resharpening. See Plate 1.

Is It A Bipoint?

Figure 1-1 shows a jasper[5] specimen was found in central Alabama. In its examination, does it have all the qualities to be classified as a bipoint? With the jillions of stone tools found in the U.S., identifying and classifying them still after hundreds of years of archaeology remains simply an opinion of the person studying them. While countless study hours in academia have occurred, years of personal experience, and millions of pages of archaeological publications, there is still no agreement among archaeologists on archaeological methods, terms, procedures, attitudes, reasons for preservation, and probably just one problem – too many prehistoric artifacts – none of which are exactly the same. Regardless, the following bipoint technology has these factors:

- It is a narrow, long object
- It has a flat distal-proximal profile
- It has marginal invasive retouching
- It has a small patch of cortex remaining
- It has an over-flaked medial axis
- Its bulb scar is usually removed by its knapper,

If platform is present, it probably has a thin bulb scar remaining.

- It has several flake scars that cross the medial axis
- It has hafting that shows where the blade's workend begins
- Its basic hand-held size
- It has symmetrical lateral margins
- It has a small ruminant platform
- It is made from high-quality bipoint lithics
- It has parallel features with Old World bipoints.

Figure 1-1 - A Classic Jasper Bipoint (L = 139, W = 37, T = 7 mm, E = 3.76, R = 26. 397, g = 53)

(Continued on page 5.)

---

[5] Jasper is the most common stone in bipoint technology.

Plate 1 - Main Focus – Survey of Bipoint Morphologies

Bipoint Technology - a knife form that is found all over North America[6]. Once the prehistoric form had extensive prehistoric usage, it is difficult to classify it to the initial bipoint form; thus, it is the most mis-classified implement in American prehistory. It was brought into the Americas by the first immigrants and was continually manufactured at Contact.

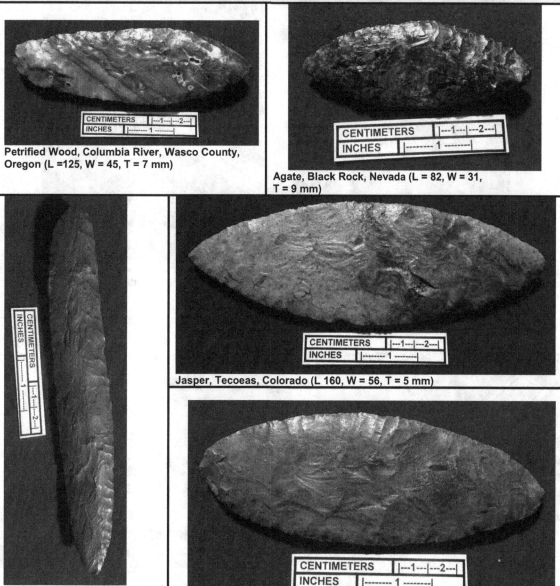

Petrified Wood, Columbia River, Wasco County, Oregon (L =125, W = 45, T = 7 mm)

Agate, Black Rock, Nevada (L = 82, W = 31, T = 9 mm)

Jasper, Tecoeas, Colorado (L 160, W = 56, T = 5 mm)

Flint, Humboldt County, Nevada (L = 180, W = 30, T = 10 mm)

Jasper, Meagher County, Montana (L = 127, W = 47, T = 5 mm)

---

[6] These bipoints and their data were supplied by John M. Selmer of Virginia. He was very helpful in suppling western bipoints.

As mentioned, over 700 bipoint specimens were used for this study and publication. As such, the author selected the best, most eloquent, and what could be considered a major classic bipoint from the United States.

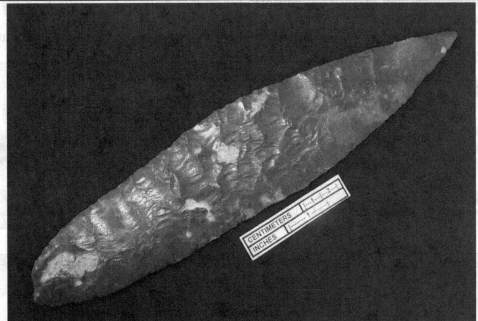

Pleistocene Era Bipoint, Edwards Plateau Chert, Heat Treated, Texas (L = 272, W = 57, T = 6 mm, E = 4.77, R = 28.63). It has no knapping errors, remaining spots of cortex, thin flake scars, no bulb scar, and the platform was removed. It is the best bipoint in this study.

Richard Austin[7]. Chair, G.I.R.S.'s 2018 Artifact Show.

---

[7] Mr. Austin keeps computer records for all his artifacts. Books for each case are provided which lists data for the general public and professional archaeologists to look up information for each point on display and in his collection.

Continued from page 2.

These are just a few of the properties and attributes that are used to identify the above bipoint. Someday, its quarry source will be found. The following book-text provides a study of bipoints which includes their compositional basics. The bipoint industry is a standalone technology which is associated with numerous prehistoric human activities. This specimen is among America's oldest stone implements. What makes it so special? This bipoint's major properties are:

- Remnant platform
- Invasive marginal retouching
- Remaining cortex patches
- Thin flakes scars
- Blade-sourced manufacturing
- Hand-held size
- Cross center (medial axis) flake scars
- Straight structural axis
- Off-center functional axis
- No flake scar henges
- Blub scar removed
- Bipoint shape - morphology.

The Bipoint's Ancestry

For all North American bipoints, their ancestry has "to be" the paleolithic worlds outside North America. As reported herein, the bipoint's ancestry dates 75,000 BYP; thus, there is adequate time for it to have spread worldwide. Hranicky (2005) argued Solutreans into the Middle Atlantic area. This was followed by Stanford and Bradly's 2012 publication which argued the Solutrean connection from the U.S. to Spain's Solutrean bipoints. Plate 2 illustrates relationships among certain European implements. Does the bipoint morphology get modified in the Holocene? Yes, it probably becomes the so-called turkey-tailed points.[8] Figure 1-2 shows two possible bipoint modifications.

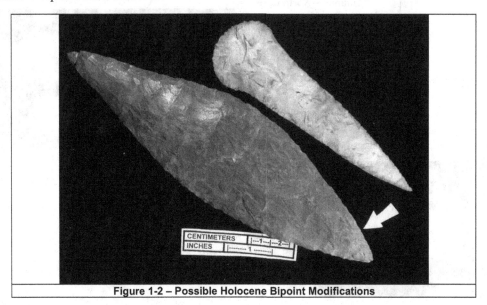

Figure 1-2 – Possible Holocene Bipoint Modifications

Bipoint Acquisitions and Curations

The nation-wide frequency of bipoints remains totally unknown. This is due to the specimens that were collected and the non-availability of data on these collection. Also, there is the problem of classification of collected specimens, namely complete vs. expended bipoints. One of the major factors is the discontinuance

---

[8] Turkey-tail preform – tip badly restored.

of large area surveys by agencies and institutions. However, collectors continue to "hunt" and, as such, probably 90% of known bipoints are in private collections. As a consequence, this study relied mainly on private collections and the data and information obtained from them. For this study, over 700 biponts were studied.

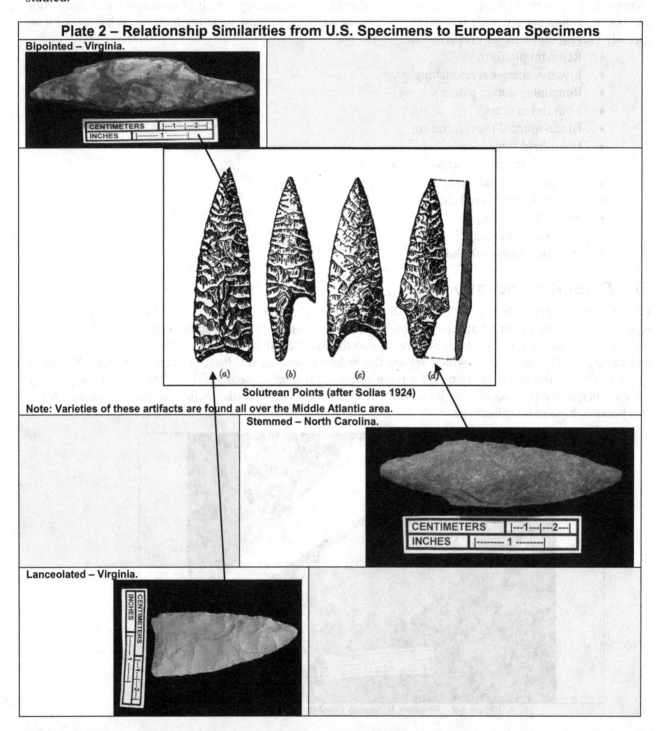

Plate 2 – Relationship Similarities from U.S. Specimens to European Specimens

Bipointed – Virginia.

CENTIMETERS |---1---|---2---|
INCHES |------- 1 -------|

Solutrean Points (after Sollas 1924)

(a) (b) (c) (d)

Note: Varieties of these artifacts are found all over the Middle Atlantic area.

Stemmed – North Carolina.

CENTIMETERS |---1---|---2---|
INCHES |------- 1 -------|

Lanceolated – Virginia.

CENTIMETERS
INCHES
1
2

Research Rules for American Archaeology?

When Lewis Binford introduced the *New Archaeology* into professional archaeological practices, the discipline changed greatly (as in Binford 1980 and 1983). However, many of the old-way archaeological practices and methodologies are still being practiced. For example, many American archaeologists believe that the bow and arrow was invented by the American Indians around 1000 AD. Nonsense, the device dates

5,000+ YBP in the Old World; and, it was carried by the so-called Old World's *Ice Man* in Europe. All toolmaking technologies were transported into the New World; all of which suggest numerous trans-oceanic migrations to the U.S. The main problem with this analysis is lithic vs. organic technology preservation. For another example, the atlatl was brought into the Western Hemisphere from Europe.

Archaeology needs a refocusing as the cut-and-dry arrowhead orientation is still prevalent in the discipline, such as Adovasio and Pedler (2016). If you take projectile points out of American archaeology, you have nothing, except perhaps chronology. Human history, stone tools that is, is a long line of technological inventions/discoveries that eventually are replaced by metal tools. And, the functional nature of tools was discovered millions of years ago, namely tools could be used as: human functions (or as a mode – physical actions) as:

- Cutting – became a specific tool form with a specific function and usage
- Pounding - became a specific tool form with a specific function and usage
- Punching - became a specific tool form with a specific function and usage
- Penetrating - became a specific tool form with a specific function and usage
- Abrading - became a specific tool form with a specific function and usage
- Chopping - became a specific tool form with a specific function and usage
- Scraping - became a specific tool form with a specific function and usage
- Drilling - became a specific tool form with a specific function and usage
- Shaving - became a specific tool form with a specific function and usage
- Polishing - became a specific tool form with a specific function and usage.

Each industry has a tool logic associated with its tools. These industries represent a specific tool state, or specific tool initiation form when manufactured. Additionally, each function is composed of a specific toolset which was manufactured from a specific state, such as from a blade, biface, or macroform, namely the axe, celt, etc. Old World archaeologists have 50-75 names for tool a in the above functional categories. The basic tool is a composite of mental images based on primitives (see Appendix A and Hranicky 2004).

And, numerous other lithic technological industrial functions are within humanity, many of which have been lost in prehistory. These categories, as they were learned, were incorporated into a technology continuum which was passed to each succeeding generation. The technology then spread worldwide as humans migrated. Various groups may have varied the tool designs in each industry, but the technological principles remained. While some societies discontinued various tool forms, overall humanity pasted all tools forms into the various societies in time and space.

As tool technology was invented, discovered, and borrowed over human history, the knife served as the first principal tool. It was a simple sharp edge on a broken rock which eventually became a V-shaped stemmed implement which fits the human hand. This technology led to the bipoint which is the standard cutting implement in prehistory.

Few site reports analyze the functional differences of the various artifacts found during the excavation. Other than Clovis, it is difficult to find a projectile point with an identified associated toolkit. The projectile point only identifies the site; little analytical work follows, especially wear and residue studies. Once pottery is found, the focus is on the ceramics – what type of tools goes with them is frequently missing from reports.

This bipoint technology publication has numerous facets, conditions, properties, and terms which are defined as:

- A **lithic continuum** – a pan-human toolmaking tradition that starts at Olduvai Gorge and ends worldwide with the metal age. The continuum is divided by archaeologists into arbitrary divisions which are usually self-serving, and rarely mention prehistoric people or culture make ups.
- Choice of **lithic materials** – once blademarking was discovered, knappers wanted high-quality stone for bipoints to make better and longer blades. Fine grain stones were generally used, namely jasper.
- A **blade** – it is a piece of stone that was struck off a prepared core or parent rock that is several times longer than it is wide. It also has workend or cutting part.

- A **flake** – generally it is toolmaking debitage, but can be a spall-like piece of stone that can be manufactured into a tool. It is also sometimes referred to as a tool type or lamellar.[9] It is generally pointed and usually has a striking platform remaining.
- A **legacy** – toolmaking methods and techniques are practiced the way ancestors did it and passed on to future generations, via language.
- A **toolkit** – a collective group of stone implements that are made by working stone into a blade or flake implements. Style or morphology may vary, but the tools are basically a pan-human design and have an African legacy.
- A **composite tool** – functional parts of tools are grouped into a single tool, such as the bow and arrow. Once discovered, this form can be called a mechanical device. Once hafted, bipoints are composite tools.
- The tool **function** is the intended or actual use of a bipoint.
- A **bipoint** is a blade-produced, dual-pointed knife and was rarely thrown as a projectile.[10]
- The **stem (chassis)** is the hafting part (handle) of a bipoint.
- The **base** is the non-working end of the bipoint.
- The **bit (workend)** is the cutting edge or work-end part of a bipoint.
- The bipoint **state** is the initial form of a basic bipoint which has variable attributes. Its principal forms are: straight, round, and pointed.
- The bipoint is a **synthethic form** (synthetotype[11]) element in the pan-human use of lithic technology.
- The bipoint is an **antholithic form** element in human thinking (cognitive) of technological structure.
- **Retouching** is any modification after the artifact was manufactured to its first usage stage.

In essence, the bipoint is a collection of variable physical attributes and properties which are consistent over time; the problem is which ones to assign to cultures and at what time. Furthermore, the bipoint is a collection of variable attributes which are consistent throughout the entire prehistory of the class/industry. This aspect is what makes the bipoint difficult to assign to specific cultures…and chronologies.

Old World vs. New World Archaeology

There will never be an agreement in archaeology's methodology between the Old World and New World practice of the study of prehistory (Table 1-1). While both worlds have collectors/archaeologists, and of course, their philosophies about how to study and classify artifacts differs greatly (Binford 1969). When it comes to tool typology, American archaeology has little resemblance to the Old World practioners, especially, the use of the term " tool type." For Americans, if there is not a point type on the area under investigation, it will never be called a site. Archaeologists do not recognize the differences in the cultural world between the Pleistocene and Holocene eras, namely blade vs. biface technology.

Table 1-1 – Old World vs. New World Archaeology Methods		
Operations Based on: Binford and Sabloff (1982)	**Old World Archaeology** As in Bordes (1963)	**New World Archaeology** As from Krieger (1960)
A - Lithic Technology	Blade and Core	Biface and Core
B - Framework for Observations	Type List	Attributes
C - Basic Unit of Observation	Assemblage	Artifact Type
1 – Criterion for Recognition	Principal of Association	Principal of Continuity
2 – Observational Framework	Recognizable Depositional Stata	Multiple Occupations in a Region
D – Method of Description	Quantitative Arrays	Grouping of Types
1 – Method of Presentation	Cumulative Graphs	Trait/Attribute List

---

[9] French term for blade-like artifact.

[10] It is impossible to compare bipoints from one geography to another; however, a relative date based on resharpening methods can be determined.

[11] Synthetotype was coined by Laplace (1968:158) as tools that combine to make a culture set.

8

2 – Artifacts	Each as Individual Entities	Grouping of Artifacts
E - Unit of Synthesis	A Culture	A Culture
1 – Criterion for Recognition	Principal of Similarity	Principal of Association
2 – Observational Framework	Different Site Assemblages	Repetition of Types
3 – Technological Systems	Lack of Artifact Redundancies	Repetitive Artifact Forms
4 – Tool Manufacture	Chronological Continuity	Horizonal Distributions
5 – Artifact Usage	Mechanical Function	Subjective Function
F – Cohesion Measured By	Similar Quantitative Patterns of Constructions Among Artifacts	Qualitatively Defined Types at Different Places
G – Defining Axes	Function vs. structure	Basic design styles
H – Stone Identification	Laboratory analyses	Laboratory analyses

Bipoint: Knife or Dart?

The Kennewick skeleton from Oregon argues a bipoint aspect that has not been discussed archaeologically. The Kennewick bipoint's function as a tool was probably projectiling. The imbedded point in that skeleton suggests that the point was thrown. However, this publication argues for the knife function for bipoints as no specimen has been observed with an impact fracture. One specimen does not make a generalized case for projectiling, but we must remain open for this possibility.

Defining Lithics as Applied to Bipoints

Often referred to as material culture, lithic-made objects occur throughout human prehistory – only to be identified and classified as archaeological objects. Humans produced macro- and micro-tools of which the latter group is the concern. These lithic micro-implements can be divided into large groups (industries) of:

- Bifaces
- Blades (Unifaces[12]).

In defining North American lithics in archaeology, the major problem that occurs is that American archaeologists are obsessed with the projectile point. Quite simply, the point does not occur in the so-called pre-Clovis times, namely the Pleistocene era. As a proposition, we are not generally dealing with blade tools in the Holocene nor are we dealing with bifaced tools in the Pleistocene.

Figure 1-3 shows the basic overview process of basic stone toolmaking and their divisions in archaeology. The initial form of any human modified stone object is its state from which any type of lithic artifact can be subsequently made and used in a prehistoric society. The figure presents a high-level classification in archaeology, of which the bipoint is only one technology category. Any specimen is called its state or preparatory form from production (Hranicky 2004) and has the following Pleistocene definition:

The state for bipoints is an initial blade-produced and unifacially flaked-reduced piece or stone object that has dual pointed or rounded ends and an overall elongated shape. This object can be sub-flaked into the classic bipoint (laurel-leaf) form or as a preform from which numerous microtools can be manufactured. State refers to an initially modified stone object or its preparatory form. These states are then transformed into a bipoint. After its initial manufacture, the bipoint was often resharpened until the tool was exhausted in length. Facial flaking is not always present on a bipoint.

---

[12] Uniface bipoint is a dual pointed implement with no second/back facial flaking.

9

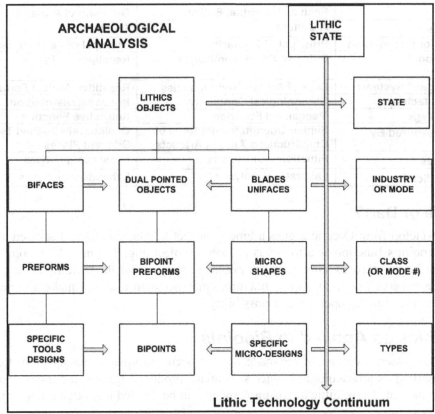

Figure 1-3 – The Lithic State of Human-Made Micro-Objects. Bipoints can be considered a middle-of-the-road in prehistoric lithic technology's continuum, but as a class – it is the oldest in the prehistoric world.

It is generally accepted that people were in North America prior to 13,000 YBP. Of course, the assumption is: they made and used stone tools. While some implements were bifacially produced, most are products of the Old World's blade technology for this era. The problem lies on the ground, what artifacts are actual tools and what artifacts are post-Pleistocene flaking debitage? Figure 1-4 shows artifacts that are classified here as Pleistocene tools and blade drawing. A true PaleoAmerican blade usually has a minor remnant platform remaining, thinness, invasive single margin retouching, bulb scar, and remaining patches/areas of cortex (Hranicky 2018). Each specimen below meets these requirements.

West Tennessee River, Alabama >>>>

<<<<<Platform and Cortex

Figure 1-4 – Flake Stone Tools/Knives – now Called Blades.
Note: Once this artifact was flaked on each face, it is usually referred to as biface while it was initially a blade. The following tool was produced using blade technology. Most archaeologists would classify it as Paleoindian, but they would fail in showing it on Clovis sites. It was found in Limestone County, Alabama and has invasive marginal sharpening. It is a Pleistocene era tool.

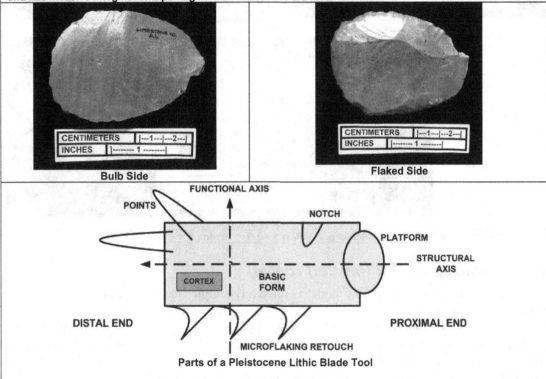

Bulb Side

Flaked Side

Parts of a Pleistocene Lithic Blade Tool

The attributes[13] or properties in the drawing are basic for any Pleistocene flake/blade tool, which are:

- Bulb Scar – evidence of percussion on the back (inside) face
- Base[14] and Platform – starting point in the tool's production
- Point – the final part of input energy that produced the tool or flake
- Front Face – cortex side of the tool or outer face
- Retouch – any edge/margin chipping
  - Invasive edge flaking
  - Evasive edge flaking
- Back Face – face closest to its parent rock
- Body – bulk of the flake or tool
- Top – from the proximal end, the interior face's right side is the top
- Bottom – from the proximal end, the interior face's left side is the top
- Structural Axis – direction from which it was stuck from the parent rock
- Functional axis – direction of human action in using the tool.

---

[13] The term "trait" is a subdivision of attribute. The term property is used in the publication.
[14] White, Binford, and Papwoth (1963) were the first to use the term based on a flake.

11

These factors, of course, apply to the bipoint's manufacture. Remember, resharpening is the key to understanding bipoint technology. Again, it was often resharpened until it was an expended implement. Plate 3 shows a classic North American bipoint. These factors constitute what is term herein and the Basic Bipoint Model (BBM)

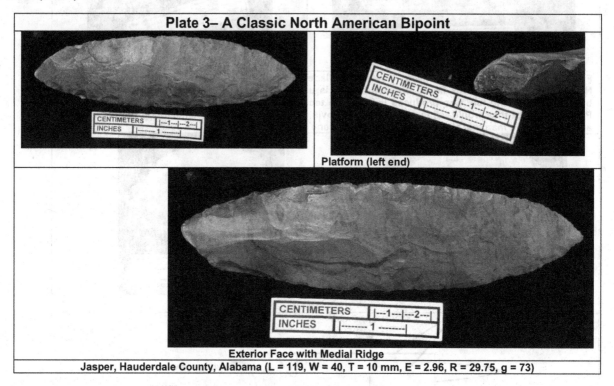

Plate 3– A Classic North American Bipoint

Platform (left end)

Exterior Face with Medial Ridge

Jasper, Hauderdale County, Alabama (L = 119, W = 40, T = 10 mm, E = 2.96, R = 29.75, g = 73)

Bipoint Morphology Model (Model) (BMM)

As shown previously, the shape of a bipoint model is relatively simple; the implement is composed of **two pointed ends** and dual cutting edges. It has excurvated blade edges and a convex or D-shaped cross section. It is made from a long blade, but large flake-constructed specimens occur. Also, rare but biface reduction forms occur. This pattern occurs on most bipoints; thus, the Bipoint Morphology Model (BMM). Figure 1-5 shows the basic bipoint structure with resharpening and basal styles. While not proven, the bipoint is usually hafted. Importantly, it is not necessary to have an exact pointed tip at each end to be classified as a bipoint. Other than the Solutrean, the point's end style varies within societies making and using bipoints. These variations are what Clarke (1968) calls multistate attributes.[15] The BMM is based partly on Clark (1967 and 1970), Brantingham, et al. (2004), and de Heinzelin de Braucourt (1962).

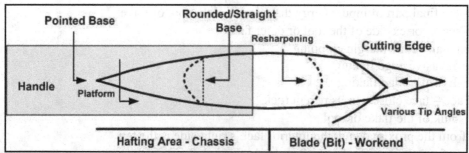

Figure 1-5– Basic Bipoint (V-Shaped Stemmed Knife) Bipoint Morphology Model.
Note: Bipoint: 50% = Chassis and 50% = Workend.

---

[15] State – attribute state; alternative values or qualities of an attribute which may be found at the attribute's locus (Clarke 1968). Or, a bipoint can have various forms and maintain its state of being a bipoint. State can be called continuous variables.

The BMM is essentially an Operation Model, as from Clark (1972: 10-42) which represents a class or state of specific artifact. As a possible hypothesis, non-basal pointed forms are earlier in prehistory and can be classified as true Solutrean bipoints. Table 1-2 presents the basic principles for the BMM identification requirements of world-wide bipoints. Probably the most common bipoint property is its maintenance of symmetry.

Table 1-2 – Bipoint Morphology Model Principles
First Principle – Pointed (or semi-pointed) Distal and Proximal Ends
Second Principle – Excurvate Lateral, Symmetrical Margins
Third Principle – Length Dimension is Three (or more) Times the Width
Forth Principle – High-Quality Flaking in Manufacture
Fifth Principle – First Manufacture Dates 100,000 YBP
Sixth Principle – Under 15 mm in Thickness
Seventh Principle – Made Cross-Culturally Through Time and Space
Eight Principle – Distribution is World Wide
Ninth Principle – Distal End Resharpening
Tenth Principle – High-Quality Lithic Materials
Eleventh Principle – Structural/Functional axes are the same.

These succeeding bipoints (secondary forms) are legacy bipoint forms. Legacy is defined as a heritable continuity which resulted in a culture transmission from generation-to -generation in toolmarking, as in Clark (1968) and O'Brien (2010). Naturally, there were cross-culture associations.

Bipoint Model Factors

This symbol represents legacy bipoints in this publication which is discussed. The classic bipoint is argued as above as Bipoint Morphology Model (BMM) which is used throughout. The BMM includes consistent:

- Manufacturing quality
- Lithic material
- Shape and form
- Resharpening (microflaking)
- Structural axis
- Functional axis
- Legacy in toolmaking
- Universal time period.

Physical Bipoint Axis

Any prehistoric Pleistocene tool has a structural and functional axis (Dibble and Dibble 1994). This is the basic requirement to classify an object as a tool. For the bipoint, the structural axis is from point-to-point. Its functional axes is not easily defined, but is simply its V-shaped bit or workend. In other words, both axis are almost the same in the tools. This feature or property is what separates the bipoint into a separate industry from its parent industry (Figure 1-6). Marginal microflaking is called the secondary functional axis.

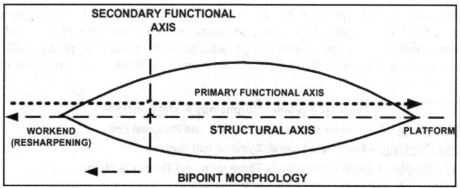
Figure 1-6 – Bipoint Physical Axes (Axis) – Structure vs. Function

Bipoint Torque Operations

The physical operation of a bipoint is the amount and place on the tool where force was applied. It is classified as operational torque. The basic assumption here is that the average bipoint is divided into two equal parts and the workend part is where force is applied:

- Workend part (50% of its total initially manufactured length)
- Hafting area (50% of the remaining area used for hafting).

50% Hypothesis:
The Pleistocene bipoint was a mentally and physically stone implement that was split into two parts: the working end and the holding end. For a newly prehistoric manufactured bipoint, these parts started at mid-point or each had 50% of the tool's area. It was the working angle or leverage of the implement where force (torque) was applied into a target area.

Figure 1-7 shows the basic torque applications or operations in using the bipoint. Upon wear, the bipoint was resharpened creating new torque areas of operations. Once resharpening reached the chassis area, the bipoint was discarded.

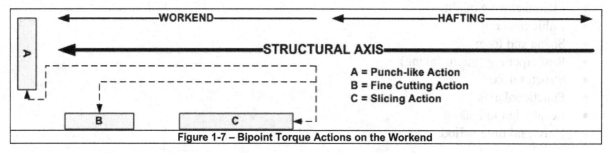
Figure 1-7 – Bipoint Torque Actions on the Workend

The drawing shows the angular force (torque) in using the bipoint. In physics, torque is measured in the International System of Units (ISU).[16] For the bipoint, it is the amount of pressure and angle of applied force, as:

---

[16] The International System of Units is the modern form of the metric system, and is the most widely used system of measurement. It comprises a coherent system of units of measurement built on seven base units. It defines twenty-two named units, and includes many more unnamed coherent derived units.Torques are given newton metres. In the U.S., foot-pounds force are also commonly encountered.

14

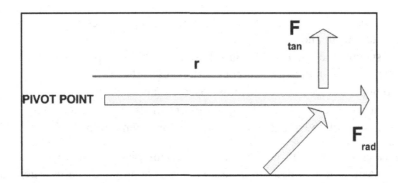

whereas:

is the torque vector and is the magnitude of the torque,

r is the position vector (a vector from the origin of the coordinate system defined to the point where the force is applied)

F is the force vector,

Most bipoints were resharpened until the reaming blade reached the mid-point of the tool, or when 50% of the blade was expended (Figure 1-8). Then, the bipoint was discarded and a new tool was produced. This size V-shaped implement is the most common artifact across the U.S. Most of these expended bipoints have similar final resharpened bit shapes – usually a rounded form and follow the 50% rule. Different implement sizes have different foot-pounds which Early Americans knew. No torque studies have been performed in archaeology.

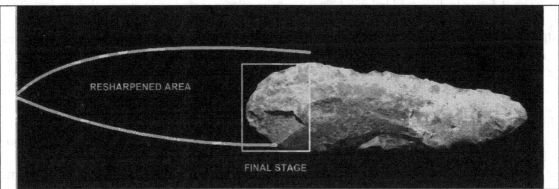

RESHARPENED AREA

FINAL STAGE

Figure 1-8 – Operational Expended Part of a Bipoint. Slate Bipoint is from Stanly County, North Carolina (L = 97 mm). Its estimated length was 150 mm. Box shows the final stage of resharpening.

Major Questions about Structure:
• **Is the bipoint assumed to be a dual workend tool?**
• **Is the bipoint always assumed to be a hafted implement?**
• **Did the bipoint technology carry into other hand-held implement designs?**
• **What function did the bipoint tip-point perform?**
How many foot-pounds of torque do various knappable stone take before they fracture and break?

Archaeology Terms and Divisions

Additionally, all lithic objects can be used simply as large knives, scrapers, perforators, etc. as in hominid's first toolkit in the New World (Hranicky 2007). Once this tool form is further modified, its original state is difficult to determine archaeologically. The process is from the state which is transformed into a useable-expended implement. This initial stage can be considered as a preform; however, the stone toolmaking process is considered as analytically constituting:

- **State** (Initial Manufactured Form (IMF)) – a specific set of primitives as concepts (see Appendix A) that goes into the manufacture of a bipoint; its first struck form. State can also refer to the generalized form of a bipoint.
- **Stage** – degree of bipoint resharpening (one to five stages).

- **Mode**[17] – the constructive nature by the flintknapper in the design of a bipoint; mode implies a heritage of the state form and general function.
- **Industry** – a specific set of tool designs based on the knapper's mental template and intended functions/structures within a major society – a division of tools.
- **Class** (Work object) – a specific set of tools based on a consistent design for a specific function.
- **Type** (Tools) – a specific set of tool designs within a class; its morphology.
- **Artifact** – an entity showing a legacy of the above conditions from the Old World.

While the above categories vary in usage among archaeologists, especially between the Old and New World's professions, a basic tool organization based on an archaeological analysis generally does have some consistency across the discipline (Hranicky 2004). From flakes to blades to bifaces, American archaeology tends to be site-specific and projectile point-orientated; thus, terminology varies from archaeologist to archaeologist. A higher level is needed for any tool category.

Once a toolmaker breaks a first (primary) piece of stone, his/her intentions can constitute the manufacture of an infinite number of tool forms. As suggested, this initial form is called the state in making a bipoint and other tools. Four biface state examples are shown which are numbered for identification purposes. Each specimen has structural (long) axis which clearly defines its state. Figures 1-9 and 1-10 show two bipoint states that have different functions, neither of which would be called the classic bipoint as discussed here. Figure 1-11 shows a state bipoint. Figure 1-12 shows the elongated state. All their states are bipoints; however, functions and knapping intentions are different. Note the high R factors for the preform specimens. The R factor is discussed below. As each specimen's knapping state approaches its intended tool structure, the R (width/length ratio) factor becomes smaller. This sample is for biface reduction, blade (large flake/spall) is entirely different; however, the R factor is the same. The argument: there are several ways to manufacture a bipoint. The basic methods are neither a biface nor blade reduction; they can be either technique. These methods in the U.S. have a chronological history; an analyses which is not attempted in this publication, other than on a high level of bipointmaking. These physical or structural differences are noted throughout the text.

If lithic technology is treated as a continuum, then, once it is transferred to the Western Hemisphere, it becomes common to all cultures, such as Clovis, Maya, Adena, etc. The question is still: the *where/when* did hominids bring lithic technology into the Americas.

There are other state forms for bipont technology; these are suggested as a starting place to identify a state form. The basic argument here is that they have a legacy in Old World bipoint technology, which includes both blade- and biface-manufactured specimens. Bipoint technology is neither a pure blade technology nor a biface technology; it is basically an in-between manufacturing technique. If one of these states has to be identified as a *first legacy*, then it is State Three above. The rounded end is argued throughout the publication as a bipoint state. The mechanics of the state forms is discussed in the Bipoint Mechanics Section 11.

---

[17] Mode is a technology division initiated by Clark (1969). The term is used here as the behavioral intentions of the bipointmaker's form and usage. Mode is used as the artifact form that is produced from a state's initial form.. It involves the maker's mental template of the intended tool. See Appendix A.

Preparatory Biface State Forms

State One Example:

Figure 1-9 – Ocala Chert, Bipoint State, Northern Florida (L = 157, W = 65, T = 21 mm, E = 2.42, R = 50.72, E = 2.41, g = 236, M = 10YR8/1). It represents a possible preform for the reduction into a bipoint. Its date is 2045 YBP.

State Two Example:

Figure 1-10 – Bipoint State, Ocala Chert, Bipoint, Marion County, Florida (L = 142, W = 76, T = 21 mm, E = 1.87, R = 39.23, g = 245, M = 7.5YR6/2). It was used as a knife. Its date is 2010 YBP.

Note: The degree of analytical separation for these artifacts is a matter of semantics. They date to Clovis (or earlier). For an example, State One is found on the Phil Straton Cumberland site (as in Gramly 2012).

State Three Example:

Figure 1-11 – Ocala Chert, Bipoint, Lamont, Florida (L = 162, W = 64, T = 18 mm, E = 2.53, R = 45.56, E = 2.53, g = 181).

17

State Four Example:

Figure 1-12 – Elongated Bipoint State, Ocala Chert, Dade County, Florida, L = 185, W = 48, T = 24 mm, R = 90.61, E = 3.85, g = 217). For many archaeologists, this specimen is simply a long biface. Its legacy may suggest something else.
State Five: Ovate Biface; State Six: Tear-Shaped Biface, etc.
These forms can be identified as a state in bipoint technology. For U.S. prehistory, they account for all forms of the bipoint. Even biface-made bipoints have these states.

Bryan (1978) comments on bifaces:

The old idea of the biface could then (his book) be seen from a new perspective. Rather than a rough hand-held implement of general utility, it was conceived of a preform for producing a strong, sharp projectile point (or a combination knife/projectile point) with a specific shape, which could be fitted securely onto a shaft. As different people had by that time developed different techniques for hafting their bone and wooden or minimally retouched flake points onto their projectiles, ultimately several distinctive forms of bifacially flaked stone projectile points (i.e., bulled-shaped, willow leaf-shaped, tanged, fishtail, fluted, stemmed, and notched) developed independently in various parts of America between about 14,000 and 10,000 years ago.

Again, major questions: The elongated bipoint state starts in the Mousterian era and probably has a date of 50k years or greater. Numerous rounded-end elongated specimens are found worldwide…the suggestion here is: this state leads to the bipoint. Figure 1-13 shows African blade specimen with round distal/proximal margins. Somewhere, sometime, out of blade technology comes the bipoint. For these example specimens, there is even a *touch* of Clovis to them. *How did these humans get from blades to bipoints in the Americas? And, where and when?*

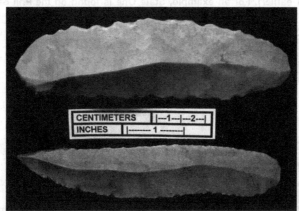

Figure 1-13 – Flint, Elongated Blade Bipoint Forms, Northwest Africa. They date to the Aurignacian era in Africa and are members of the lithic continuum of humanity. Morphology has local shapes, but overall, blade technology is the same throughout the Pleistocene era.

The Basic Bipoint

Figure 1-14 shows many of these problems in defining a bipoint because of its various forms. A major problem is after the bipoint was resharpened, what is it called? Few archaeologists would classify it as a bipoint. Thus, the text argues for a bipoint (V-shaped stem) legacy in American prehistory. Varieties do occur, but the variation is generally due to bipoint resharpening. The generalized shape (form) of a bipoint is called here its ***state-derived*** form. The V-shaped bit is an infinite wedge that occurs on numerous prehistoric implements, starting with Acheulean age.

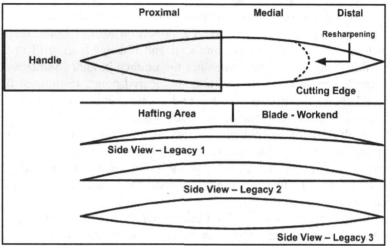

Figure 1-14 – Various Parts of a Bipoint (Bipoint Morphology Model) with Suggested Profiles

One aspect of the bipoint not used as a property here is its indented base bipoint. Bordes (1956, et al.) argues for this property in the Lower Solutrean bipoints. While the dual-pointed bipoint is the predominant form, the indented base and the shouldered bipoint along with cross-face flaking can easily be used as arguments for the Solutrean hypothesis.

As proposed as a Bipoint Morphology Model (BMM), the bipoint class is a linearly (elongated or double pointed[18]) knife with a V-shaped stem (chassis). The **bipoint** is defined as a continuously-made tool in prehistory as follows:

> *The bipoint[19] is a laurel-leaf (foliate) knife form that usually has dual pointed ends, made from high-quality stone, has excurvated lateral margins, and has a thin and D-shaped (blade) cross section and occurs as a unifacially- or bifacially-worked specimen. It has a well-defined long axis and has a bilateral symmetry on the long axis. One end serves as a chassis (handle/stem) and the other as the bit (workend/blade). The basal end can be: pointed, rounded, or clipped (straight). The bipoint's bit tip can range from acute to an obtuse (≈ 20° - 45°) angle and does not have to be exactly pointed. The proximal-distal shape usually has a slight length-wise curve; however, post-Paleoindian bipoints have straight or convex profiles. It usually has a remaining platform or cortex remaining for the chassis end. One lateral margin usually has invasive retouch.*

In referring to Mousterian foliates (bipoints), Dibble and Dibble (1994) comment:

> *Examples of allowable secondary characteristics include basal thinning of the bulb and platform, some bifacial retouch, alternate retouch on opposing edges, concave based, or non-triangular, e.g., ogival, oblong, obtuse, etc., outlines. Any of these features can be present on Mousterian points without affecting their classification.*

The various attributes, forms, elongated shapes, or styles are still classified here as a bipoint (laurel-leaf) class. Their various morphologies are not typeable; however, various bipoint styles as shown – may be a type.

As mentioned, the bipoint is the result of a world-wide culture transmission where its form is a product of ancient social skills, their inherited methods, and becomes a standard knife shape. It is referred to as a technology which is a division of the lithic cutting industry, such as drills, scrapers, etc. Since the size varies,

---

[18] MacNeish (1958) refers to the bipoint as double pointed.

[19] Bipoint technology is a general reference to the way bipoints were made; it can be considered a class in prehistoric lithic implements. They cannot be used as culture markers or time markers.

reference to a bipoint as a micro- and macrotool can only be used cautiously. Also, bipoints are rare in cryptoc cross section; one face is usually flat (Hranicky 2004). It is made off large tabular crystalline materials until late in prehistory. Generally, the Solutreans preferred high-quality stone, such as translucent flints (Bordes 1950 and Alimen 1965).[20] Thus, this stone quality requirement occurs throughout the middle and late paleolithic. Bipoints are generally characterized by several forms of thin, leaf-shaped knives which were shaped by distinctive flat, highly invasive unifacial and bifacial flaking (Tattersall, et al. 1988 and Smith 1964). There are three stages or forms which are the uniface bipoint (Solutrean I), classic laurel-leaf bipoint (Solutrean II), and the narrow willow-leaf and shouldered points (Solutrean III). Were these forms transferred to the New World by Solutreans or other Old World cultures who were making the same tool form? The answer is open to numerous archaeological discussions.

The early bipoint is a blade-made tool which has varying attributes (as defined by the British Museum 1956). Pure uniface bipoints occur as well as specimens that are bifacially reduced in production. As argued, resharpening and retouch often skews the basic bipoint's initial form. As a consequence of manufacture, bipoint technology is presented as neither a completely blade nor biface technology. Biface-made bipoints are common worldwide.

More U.S. specimens are needed to determine lithic preferences and morphologies. While the bipoint dates to Africa 75,000 YBP, the Iberian Solutreans perfected it to what is called a *work-of-art* in lithic technology. This Solutrean technology dates 25,000 to 17,000 YBP and is argued by a few archaeologists as a bipoint legacy for the New World (see Plate 4) and, a formally a theoretically-oriented viewpoint, is now presented as the ancestry to Clovis (Stanford and Bradley 2000, 2002, and 2012 a&b and Hranicky 2017 and 2018).

Plate 4 – Bipoint Legacy for the Western Hemisphere
Hypothesis: The bipoint is the oldest continually made tool in homo sapiens' history. It was invented in South Africa, and this technology spread with humans throughout the world. It is a basic survival tool which functioned as a cutting implement. The technology was brought into the Western Hemisphere prior to Clovis and continued to the metal-age Contact. The principal attribute is outré passé flaking and bold flake scars extending to the point's center.

These two Solutrean laurel-leaf points were discovered in 1874 in France, along with 12 other similar points, by workmen engaged in digging a small canal (Brostrom Cast, Illinois)

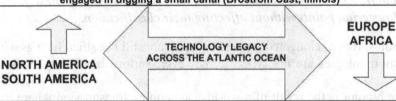

NORTH AMERICA
SOUTH AMERICA

TECHNOLOGY LEGACY
ACROSS THE ATLANTIC OCEAN

EUROPE
AFRICA

---

[20] Solutrean tools have been in the literature since the 1860s; see de Mortillet (1869).

The **Solutrean Hypothesis** builds on similarities between the Solutrean industry and the later Clovis culture / Clovis points of North America, and suggests that people with Solutrean tool-technology crossed the Ice Age Atlantic by moving along the pack ice edge, using survival skills similar to that of modern Eskimo people. The migrants arrived in northeastern North America and served as the donor culture for what eventually developed into Clovis tool-making technology. Archaeologists Dennis Stanford and Bruce Bradley suggest that the Clovis point derived from the points of the Solutrean culture of southern France (19,000 BP) through the Cactus Hill points of Virginia (16,000 years ago) to the Clovis point.[1][2] This would mean that people would have had to move from the Bay of Biscay across the edge of the Atlantic ice sheet to North America. Supporters of this hypothesis believe it would have been feasible using traditional Eskimo techniques still in use today, while others argue that the conditions at the time would not have made such a journey likely.

1. "Stone Age Columbus - Programme Summary". BBC. March 2004, http://www.bbc.co.uk/science/horizon/2002/columbus.shtml. Retrieved 2010-12-10.
2. The North Atlantic ice-edge corridor: a possible Palaeolithic route to the New World. Bruce Bradley and Dennis Stanford. World Archaeology 2004, Vol. 36(4): 459 – 478.
3. Westley, Kieran; Justin Dix "The Solutrean Atlantic Hypothesis: A View from the Ocean" *Journal of the North Atlantic* 2008, 1:85–98.

* * * * * * * * * * * *

French Solutrean Bipoint (After: Sollas 1924).

Note: Resharpened end (right). This property is the major theme of this publication.

And, as furthering the argument, the U.S. Middle Atlantic area has evidence of a Solutrean occupation (Hranicky 2012 and 2018). An excellent bipoint example was found in Rhode Island (Plate 5). This specimen has been cast by the Smithsonian Institution in Washington, DC. This specimen is an inland bipoint and does not appear to have had any maritime association; however, it is a surface find, and we will probably never know its true nature. It is made of a black flint which of this writing has not been sourced. It will become part of the Smithsonian collections. It is exceptionally thin and has a low length/width*thickness (R) factor. It has Solutrean-like flake scars and is the best inland bipoint found in the East.

Plate 5 – Rhode Island Bipoint

Face A drawing shows the excellent flaking on this specimen.

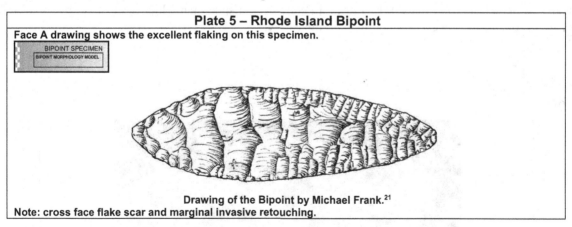

Drawing of the Bipoint by Michael Frank.[21]

Note: cross face flake scar and marginal invasive retouching.

---

[21] Casts of this artifact and the Marion County bipoint can be obtained from www.occpaleo.com.

Face A, Flint, Providence, Rhode Island (L = 168, W = 49, T = 5 mm, R = 17.14, E = 3.43, M = 10YR2/2, g = 78) Small striking platform remains (right). This specimen is exceptionally well made and has numerous Solutrean attributes, which makes it a Legacy 1 bipoint.

Dennis Stanford and Jack Hranicky with the Rhode Island Bipoint.

Bipoints as an Artform

The Clovis and Adena projectile point has some of the best-made qualities of all American points. Many of their high-quality forms are simply called artforms. Another class of lithic artforms is the bipoint. Many of these specimens, namely early forms, exhibit suburb technological flintknapping. The best forms often show no flaking errors; cross-face flake scars; they are extremely thin; made from high-quality stones; and, they are usually made off blades. Figure 1-15 shows a Pennsylvania specimen which was found by Dick Savage in 1991. It has one of the lowest ratio numbers in this study.

Date: Legacy 2.
State: Pointed workend.
Mode: Knife.

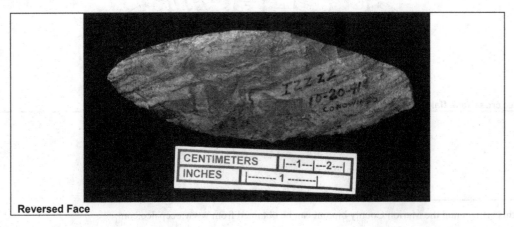

Reversed Face

22

Figure 1-15 – Bipoint Artform, Conowingo Dam Area, Susquehanna River, Maryland/Pennsylvania (L = 108, W = 37, T = 8 mm, E = 2.919, R = 23.351, g = 45)

High-quality bipoints usually show expert micro-resharpening which maintain the implements symmetry. This flaking is always invasive retouch (Figure 1-16). Its resharpening is uniform parallel flaking. Both of these specimens have remnant platforms remaining and were made from high-quality stones, namely Burlington and Coastal Plain cherts.

BIPOINT SPECIMEN
BIPOINT MORPHOLOGY MODEL

Date: Legacy 2.
State: Beveled and pointed.
Mode: Knife.

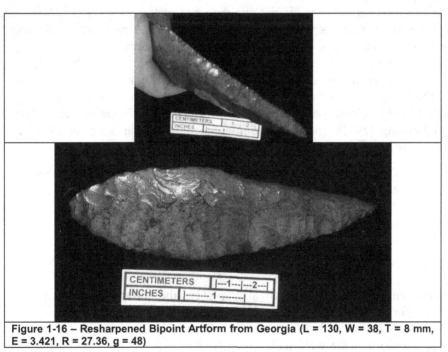

Figure 1-16 – Resharpened Bipoint Artform from Georgia (L = 130, W = 38, T = 8 mm, E = 3.421, R = 27.36, g = 48)

This specimen was made by the knapper using colorful stone. It is well made and was probably a ceremonial implement (Figure 1-17). It was found along the Ohio River in Indiana. It does have henge fractures and invasive marginal retouch. The high ratio number suggests a Holocene era bipoint.

BIPOINT SPECIMEN
BIPOINT MORPHOLOGY MODEL

Date: Legacy 2.
State: Pointed ends.
Mode: Knife.

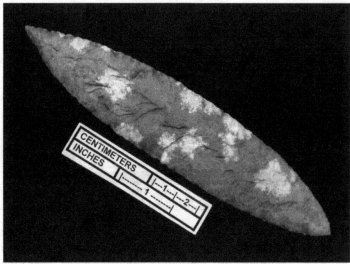

Figure 1-17 – Colorful Southern Indiana Bipoint (L = 156, W = 32, T = 7 mm, E = 4.88, R = 34.13).

Bipoint Metrics

The academic study of American-made bipoints has not been performed in the field archaeologically; thus, basic metric data are not available. The discipline needs to start this study with techniques/methods in Clarke (1968) and follow through to Lycett and Chauhan (2010) and Surovell (2009) as suggested guides for collecting bipoint data in the Americas. For bipoint site data and methods, Ebert (1992) is suggested. The bipoint plays a role in adaptive systems which can be observed in the archaeological record. But most importantly, its continuity across the social landscape is the primary concern.

Without bipoint data, hierarchal and spatial distributions cannot be presently obtained. Once these data are collected, numerous statistical techniques can be performed, such as cluster analyses, Mamm-Whitney U-test, Fourier method, ANOVA, or simply the mathematics of *chaines operatories* (as in Shott 2007).

The methods for this study are essentially the same as in ***Recording Clovis Points*** by Hranicky (2010), typology in Adams and Adams (1991), and quantifying archaeology (as in Shennan 1988). All bipoints in this study were measured for length (ζ L), width (ζ W), and thickness (ζ T).

Ratio = Length/Thickness x Width Ratio - tool measurement by dividing the length by the width and multiplying this number by the width. Ratio is expressed as:

L/T*W

Whereas:
      L = length
      T = thickness
      W = width.

These measurements can be plotted as a metrical graph, but the current sample is too small for valid results (see Collins 1999, for the technique used on blades.). As an example, the Cinmar bipoint (Virginia) has a ratio of 20.88:1 which makes it the best made specimen that has been found in the eastern U.S. Generally, a 20:1 to 35:1 ratio indicate well-made bipoints. And, the Marion County bipoint has an R of 23.35 to 1. The R factor is assumed to represent the bipoint maker's intentions and skills to produce a traditional bipoint.

For comparison, the average Clovis LWT ratio is 12.92 based on a random sample of 333 Virginia Clovis points (Hranicky 2005, 2008, and 2010). If spatial dimensions are significant, then why is the Solutrean bipoint closer to this Virginia Clovis ratio? This R number is equivalent to all Clovis technology. The answer is still not available in American archaeology for *the where* did Clovis come from? Where the bipoint came from is also not available, but as argued, the East Coast is the port-of-entry for the bipoint. This, of course, leaves questions for the West Coast.

A major bipont attribute is the elongated shape which can be calculated as a ratio (ζ E). The ratio presents the length (ζ L) divided by (ζ W). Most major bipoints in this publication have the E factor, or could be equated with tool efficiency[22]. The major problem with this ratio is it does not allow for resharpening of the implements from its initially-made form. The greater the E number (>2), the more elongated the specimen. The E factor may correspond to time era; more data and dates are needed. Numbers over 5.00 are rare. When available, the bipoint's Munsell scale was measured. The bipoint measurements and metrics are:

- Physical Overall Measurements
  - Length
  - Width
  - Thickness
- Ratio
  - Length/Width*Thickness
- Blade
  - Length/Width
- Weight
  - Grams
- Color
  - Munsell scale.

Again, bipoint rejuvenation is the process of resharpening the bit which was essentially a continuous method by which the shape of the original bipoint is altered in a generally stepwise fashion (as in Iovita 2010); it represents the life cycle of the bipoint.

Another eastern artifact class is presented which are called *mega bifaces*. This is a V-stemmed large knife that was studied and is presented generally as having a LWT ratio greater than 50.00:1. They are illustrated in the Mega Biface paragraph. When available, bipoint weight is presented in grams (g). All data were recorded at approximately 75°F.

Bipoint Standards

Standards in the publication are based on Hranicky (2013). Approaches to analyzing bipoints has only been attempted in this publication. Ratios are:

> **Ratio** - mathematical relationship among tool measurements. It is a number that measures a relationship between attributes of a tool. The ratio number is a percentage of the relationship between two or more values. It is calculated by dividing one number by a base and then multiplying the results another value. Ideally, the base should always equal 100; however, this number is never achieved.

Furthermore, each bipoint has an indicator (ζ R) which is its L/W*T ratio or bipoint/blade index. The lower the R number is: 1) reflection of size and 2) reflection of quality, or 3) both. The lower R suggests an optimal efficiency of the bipoint (as in Surovell 2009). The ratio is generally indicative of isometric size, especially length, but it does indicate quality in manufacture.

The following Pleistocene blade tool is used as the standard in this publication for comparative purposes (Figure 1-18). It produced this high ratio:

R = 59.29

---

[22] **Efficiency** - how well a tool works in a social setting for its intended purpose(s). Its value was subjective (usage-tradition) in the prehistoric world; and, objective (stone-metrics) in the archaeological world. However, neither is addressed all that frequently in the literature (see Jeske 1992).

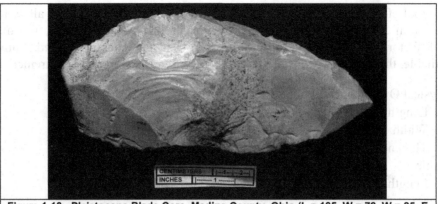

Figure 1-18 - Pleistocene Blade Core, Medina County, Ohio (L = 185, W = 78, W = 25, E = 2.37, R =59.29, g = 461)

Bipoint Ratio Scale

The scale for ratios indicates:

- **1-10 not found**
- **11-20 rare, but high quality, Legacy 1[23] [24]**
- **21-30 well made, probably Legacy 2 bipont (usually blade technology)**
- **31-40 normally constructed, average bipoint, Legacy 3 (usually biface technology)**
- **41 and up – poor quality bipoint.**

Bipoint Size

The bipoint in American prehistory ranges from 500+ to 25 mm (Figure 1-19 a&b). The larger bipoints are argued here as occurring during the Pleistocene which is based on usage in their environmental settings. Large game animals require large knives (torque) for butchering; whereas, smaller implements were used on animals, such as deer, rabbits, etc. The following bipoints are classified as mega-knives. However, later large bipoints were well-made and served as ceremonial implements. For a further discussion, see Section 11.

Flint Bipoint from Todd County, Kentucky (L = 198, W = 58, T = 13 mm, E = 3.41, R = 44.40). It probably is an un-notched Turkeytail point. Note: its cross-face flake scar.

| BIPOINT SPECIMEN |
| BIPOINT MORPHOLOGY MODEL |

Date: Legacy 3.
State: Pointed ends.
Mode: Knife.

---

[23] The Cimar bipoint is **R = 20.88.**
[24] Blackwater Draw (title page) bipoint has a **Rato = 10.22.**

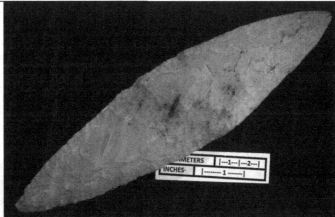

Flint Bipoint from Franklin County, Missouri (L = 211, W = 49, T = 7 mm, E = 4.31, R = 30.14, g = 99)
(Source: Back to Earth)
Note: specimen has completed marginal invasive retouching and has a small platform remaining.
Figure 1-19a – Mega Well-Made Bipoints

Coastal Plain Chert, Bull Island, South Carolina (L = 197, W = 58, T = 14 mm, E = 3.40, R = 47.55, g = 198)

Coastal Plain Chert, Bull Island, South Carolina (L = 242, W = 57, T = 13 mm, E = 4.25, R = 55.19, g = 240)
Note: High Ratio.
Figure 1-19b – Poorly Made Large Bipoints (Heavily Patinated)
Note: These specimens were found together, bottom specimen was broken, and finder glued it back together.

As shown throughout this publication, bipoints were brought into North America by the first migrants and the class continued to, and even after, Contact. Size is a factor in dating them; however, with resharpening and lack of excavated contexts, dates remain allusive. Figure 1-20a shows one of the largest bipoints in this study collection[25]. It dates to the Spiro Mounds era of Oklahoma. Figure 19b shows a comparative collection.

[26]Spiro Mounds (34 LF 40) is a major Northern Caddoan Mississippian archaeological site located in present-day Eastern Oklahoma. The 80-acre site lies near the Arkansas River in Fort Coffee, seven miles north of the town of Spiro. Between the 9th and 12th centuries AD, the local indigenous people created a powerful religious and political center, culturally linked to the Mississippian Ideological Interaction Sphere (MIIS). Spiro was a major western outpost of Mississippian culture, which dominated the Mississippi Valley and its tributaries for centuries. Spiro Mounds is under the protection of the Oklahoma Historical Society and is listed on the National Register of Historic Places. There were three principal producers of Woodland era high-quality bipoints, namely the Mississippian, Hopewell, and Adena cultures.

---

[25] Bipoint and data supplied to the author by Larry Garvin in Ohio.

[26] Wikipedia en.wikipedia.org/wiki/Spiro_Mounds.

This well-made percussion, bifacially-flaked bipoint was made from Peoria chert and was found in LeFore County, Oklahoma. It was found near the Spiro Mounds which date 400 to 800 AD. This large specimen does not show any usage and was probably a ceremonial implement. It has a flat distal-to-proximal end shape. Its material was probably quarried as it has a small remnant platform (right) remaining. Flake scars are pronounced, but this is owing to the quality of the specimen. Date may still be open due to its numerous oxidation spots.

Figure 1-20a – Spiro Mounds Area Bipoint
(L =234, W = 86, T = 12 mm, E = 2.72, R = 32.65, g = 399)
Note: High Ratio which suggests a late Holocene era bipoint.

Comparative Example:

Figure 1-20b - One of the largest Hopewell biface caches (7232 pieces) ever found (Moorehead 1910, page 51), *Stone Age in North America*, Houghton Miffin, Boston, MA.

The term Adena cache blade is common among collectors and some archaeologists. Figure 1-21 shows a classic example, but one that is bipoined. It is from a collection dating to the 1920s. It was percussion flaked and has small cortex patches.

Figure 1-21 – Flint Specimen from Crittendon County, Kentucky (L = 185, W = 100, W = 12 mm, E = 1.85, R = 22.200, g = 337)

Bipoint Cortex

A basic principal for most blade tools is: they almost always have a small patch of cortex remaining on the implement, as perhaps a signature of the knapper. This is especially true for early bipoints. Figure 1-22 shows a large flint bipoint with remaining cortex. For the Late Woodland era bipoints, the practice disappears, mainly because they are biface-produced implements.

> BIPOINT SPECIMEN
> BIPOINT MORPHOLOGY MODEL

Date: Legacy 1.
State: Pointed end with cortex platform.
Low Ratio = 24.81
Mode: Knife.

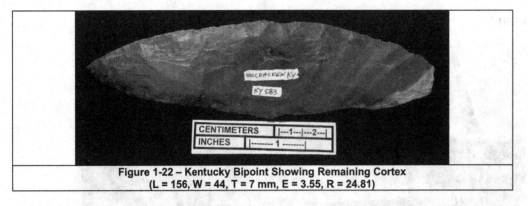

Figure 1-22 – Kentucky Bipoint Showing Remaining Cortex
(L = 156, W = 44, T = 7 mm, E = 3.55, R = 24.81)

Lithic Technology Continuum

There are just so many ways to make stone tools! Over a million years ago, or so, humans discovered stone toolmaking and made what could be called advances in technology as well as other social practices, such as the economics of environmental exploitation. The study of human history has been largely based on the material evidence left by them and physical body parts. Basically, this stone technology started with large hand axes which progressed into retouched bladettes, endscrapers, and modified bifaces. This technology spread throughout the world and eventually into the Americas. It is referenced here as a lithic technology continuum that dates to 2.5 million years to the metal age. It is considered as normative theory of culture and is presented as general methodological paradigm. Additionally, taxonomy for bipoints is treated here as a constant across the entire spectrum of this class of technology. There are, of course, specific chronicles of prehistory based on recording and classifying cultural materials based on specific usage of selected parts (modes) of the continuum.

A technology lithic continuum in human prehistory is only one of specialized knowledge bases in the human experiences. Other continuums are present, such as social, religious, artforms, or economic, which each have their knowledge base. Each continuum is a straight line (unilinear gradualism) of information or a corpus of human memory. For example, the use of red ocher is practiced worldwide and probably dates 200+ k years in prehistory.

Deviation off the continuum is social noise or practices that are usually short term. For example, the use of fluted points is short-term in American prehistory, but knowledge of how to make this high-quality stone tool is not. This deviation is what archaeologists get concerned about, namely artifacts, which causes numerous problems in analysis and interpretation of human history. For example, bifaces are the same product of lithic technology, regardless of where they are found. True, there may be regional deviations, but a biface is a biface – or a flaked rock. All of which, the bipoint (knife) is the oldest continually made tool in human history.

Bipoint Technology: A Continuum or a Tradition

Bryan (1965) refers to a specific technology as a tradition when:

> ▶ Any manufacturing technique which extends through space and time is known as a technological tradition.

Bryan was using Movius (1953) for revealing the necessity of using the concept of technological tradition rather than the concept of an archaeological culture as archaeologists do in the Old World. The best example in the U.S. is the *Clovis culture*.

While he was referring to tradition, his definition can be modified for usage in referring to a specific tool form in the technological continuum, as such:

> ▶ A technological continuum can be defined as the spatial-temporal expression of a group of material objects composed of several definable features, including manufacture, material, traits, heritage, and attributes that are reflected in its construction through time.

As presented here, the bipoint was consistently made over time and from Europe, spread throughout the human social world to Africa and Asia, and subsequently to the Western Hemisphere. Thus, it is treated as a lithic technological continuum or a unilinear process. Once coast-landed in the Western Hemisphere, the bipoint technology took several thousands of years to move inland, namely as a band butchering tool for hunting and gatherering.

Identifying Bipoints

Figure 1-23 shows the basic design for the bipoint (laurel leaf) knife. The implement usually has varying:
- Blade method manufacturing, sometimes with platform remaining
- Blade widths, including ovate forms and straight margins
- Ratio, length is usually three times the width
- Lengths, from 50 to 250 mm
- Basal configurations, such as pointed, rounded, clipped
- Bit (workend) configurations, such as pointed or rounded
- Stones, for the East primarily rhyolite and slate; for the West, the primary material is obsidian and jasper
- Resharpened workends from symmetrical to off-center
- Manufacturing qualities, from poor-to-high quality
- Lateral margins have symmetry from the long axis
- Sharp cutting margins with micro-flaked retouching
- Striking platform is the chassis end
- Cross-face flake scars
- State is a straight end, rounded end, or pointed end.

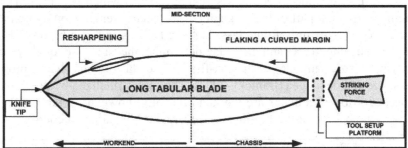

Figure1-23 – Theoretical Bipoint/V-Shaped Stemmed Knife Manufacturing Process.

Figure 1-24 shows a Virginia specimen that can be considered as an ideal specimen with all attributes discussed here except cross-face flaking. Material, patination, and striking platform[27] suggest it has considerable antiquity.

BIPOINT SPECIMEN
BIPOINT MORPHOLOGY MODEL

Date: Legacy 1.
State: Pointed end and straight base.
Mode: Knife.

---

[27] Legacy 1 and 2 bipoints often have reminant platform remaining on the proximal (bulb) end.

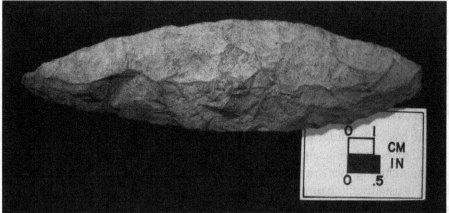

Figure 1-24 - Classic Rhyolite Bipoint, Mecklenburg County, Virginia (L = 149, W = 40, T = 13 mm, E = 3.725, R = 48.42, M = 5YR7/1, g = 68). Note the striking platform remnant (right).

As discussed, classic (or Pleistocene) bipoints are made off a large tabular blade as is the case with this specimen. It is a well-made bipoint and definitely has Solutrean attributes, but it is not proven to be dateable to that era. It is suggested as a primary legacy artifact which would date it to the Pleistocene or at least, non-Clovis era. The state is a pointed end bipoint which copies the classic Solutrean. Bipoints are also made by biface reduction techniques in the Holocene; for the U.S., there does not appear to be a preference in prehistory other than the Pleistocene-Holocene time division.

Basic U.S. Bipoint Manufacture

Figure 1-25 shows the bipoint's basic manufacturing process of obtaining a preform piece for knapping. A few bipoints have a slight-to-pronounced length-wise curve to them which was caused when the blade was removed from the boulder. A small part of the original cortex usually remains on a bipoint's tip or external[28] face; it could be considered a signature of the class. Is it the hafting end of a bipoint? Bipoint wear pattern studies are needed. The striking force and material determine the size and quality of the blade. Early Paleolithic specimens were soft-hammer percussion-flaked into the bipoint shape; probably over 25% of working the blade is suggested debitage (Hranicky 2007). They were finalized by pressure flaking. Published experimentation is needed. Most specimens are worked bifacially; however, produced as uniface specimens occur. Thickness is the principal property of bipoints. See Bipoint Mechanics section.

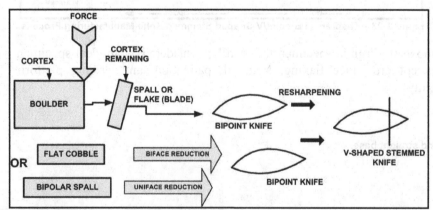

Figure 1-25 – Boulder and Blade/Flaking Removal Model. However, the principal manufacturing method was off a large spall or flake.

The blade-made bipoint is often difficult to discern because facial flaking which destroys evidence of the blade technology. Figure 1-26 shows a blade bipoint which still has one smooth face. The specimen has a small platform remaining and the smooth face have the bulb scar. It was made from a light-colored yellow jasper. It has invasive lateral margin retouching. This type of bipointmaking is assuming to be early or what

---

[28] Bipoint has two faces: internal from the parent rock and external as the outside face.

is called here Legacy 1 technology. This type of bipoint production is not found in the Holocene era; thus, it is classified as a Pleistocene specimen.

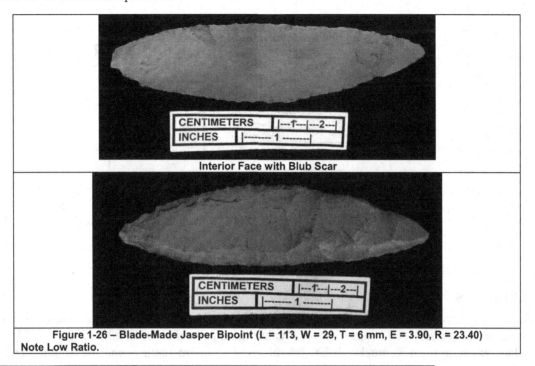

Interior Face with Blub Scar

Figure 1-26 – Blade-Made Jasper Bipoint (L = 113, W = 29, T = 6 mm, E = 3.90, R = 23.40)
Note Low Ratio.

Hypothesis: Bipoints during the Pleistocene were blade-made products. Once Clovis came in with its biface technology, bipoints form that point in time were then made using biface reduction methods. However, in both eras, the bipoint morphology was a standard form with an Old World legacy dating to 75,000 YBP.

Further as mentioned, bipoint technology is the name of a tool class; not the name of a form. True, it has basically two pointed ends, but other properties apply, such as width, length, and thickness, especially the proximal and distal end shapes. Material varies depending on geography and probably time period. Resharpening methods depend on bipoint's chronology with distal-to-proximal end (DP) (length-wise bit reduction) invasive sharpening for early bipoints; whereas, lateral margin's sharpening is common for the later prehistoric specimens. The DP reduction is common on European Solutrean specimens. Reduction is a curation process (Shott 2007). No actual dates are suggested. Montet-White (1973) describes a Solutrean technique of a spall-like triangular method which was finalized into a bipoint. All of which, there were numerous ways to produce a bipoint, but the blade reduction method seems to be the common procedure used in prehistory. For more information on Solutrean bipoint manufacturing, see Aubry, et al. (2003) and Soressi and Dibble (2003). The early Solutrean era bipoints were made off a large blade (Smith 1972). The high-quality Solutrean bipoints were made in the Solutrean 3 archaeological era.

Bipoints exceeding 200 mm were produced by bifacial reduction rather than making them off a large blade/flake (Bradley 2008). There are Solutrean bipoints in France at approximately 400 mm in length. Once the thinned state specimen was initially shaped, then pressure flaking was used to create parallel flake scars.

Bipoint Shape

The generalized BMM bipoint shape has three morphological features:
- Bit (workend)
- Sides (chassis)
- Base (haft end).

33

Table 1-3 shows the common types for each feature (synetic attributes). These various shapes often form bipoint morphologies that have point names in the literature (Hranicky 2011). They can be traced back to the artifact's initializing state.

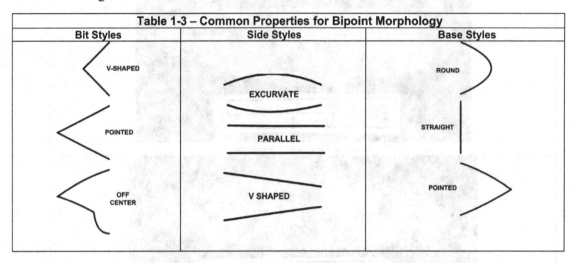

Table 1-3 – Common Properties for Bipoint Morphology		
Bit Styles	**Side Styles**	**Base Styles**
V-SHAPED	EXCURVATE	ROUND
POINTED	PARALLEL	STRAIGHT
OFF CENTER	V SHAPED	POINTED

Blade Bipoints

The bipoint is generally flaked on both faces; however, blade (uniface) forms do occur. The question is: Are they true bifaces? The basic shape comes into analyzing them as in the above table. Figure 1-27 shows an excellent blade example from Kentucky. It has lateral invasive micro-flaking, and the rounded end has the bub scar. It measures: L = 122, W = 25, T = 10 mm.

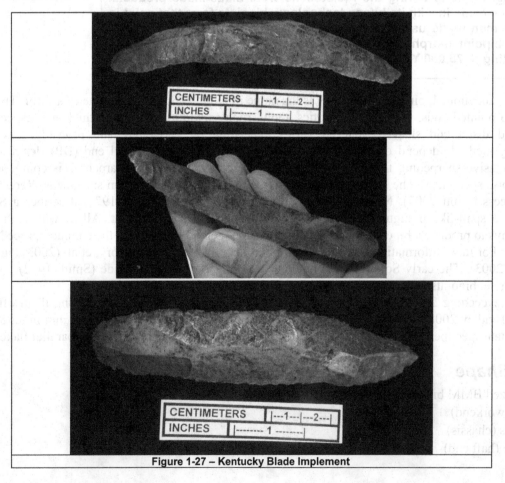

Figure 1-27 – Kentucky Blade Implement

Another example of a blade bipoint is shown in Figure 1-28. It was found at Goreville, Johnson County, Illinois. It is made from a white chert. It has minor microflaking, and the bulb scar remains on it.

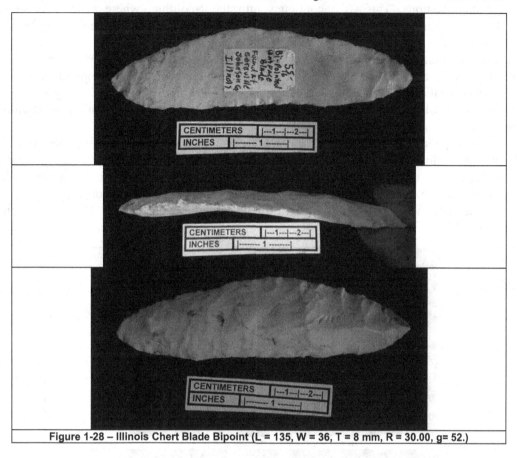

Figure 1-28 – Illinois Chert Blade Bipoint (L = 135, W = 36, T = 8 mm, R = 30.00, g= 52.)

Diagonal Bipoint

An unusual bipoint was found at the Arkfeld[29] site in Clarke County, Virginia (Figure 1-29). It is bipointed, but the tips are at a 45 degree angle, which is opposite each other. This form has not been reported. It has a very high bipoint physical ratio.

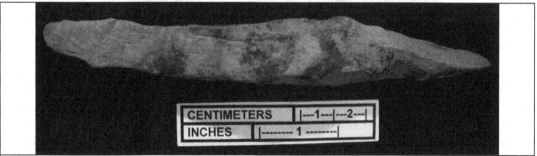

Figure 1-29 – Slender Limestone Bipoint from Mound M (L = 151, W = 20, T = 18 mm, E = 7.55, R = 135.9)

Uniface Bipoints

Also known, uniface bipoints occur back to Auriganacian inventories of eastern and western Europe. They occur in both pointed bases and round bases. This bipoint form argues for the blade-made bipoint. Based on the Kostenki tools of Austria, this form predates the shouldered form (Grigor'ev 1993). Further, he defines

---

[29] A Pleistocene site in Frederick County, Virginia.

parallel-sided blades with distal and proximal pointed ends. This archaeological culture is known as the Kostenki-Avdeevo in the Ukraine and dates 26 to 12 k YBP. It represents the wide-spread use of the bipoint technology and its variations. This style continues into the Neolithic, where smaller versions occur. Importantly, the blade is an early hominid knife; one that is used throughout the Upper Paleolithic – which was transferred to the New World.

Does the blade bipoint occur in the New World prior to Clovis? Yes, but it is difficult to prove (as in Hranicky 2004). They were made with a pointed bit; once the bit was expended, the bipoint form is no longer present and its identification in archaeology is incorrect, which is understandable. Purdy (2008) shows a uniface that could be classified as a bipoint. It was found at the Container Corporation site and quite possibly dates prior to Clovis.

Figure 1-30 shows both sides of a uniface bipoint. It has a semi-round base and a used workend. It is very heavily patinated which may have been its environment, but compared to other paleospecimens in the Suwannee County, Florida this specimen dates prior to Clovis. Of course, patination is a poor indicator of age (Hranicky 1992). The suggestion here: the uniface bipoint occurs in the U.S. Southeast.

The term uniface bipoint is used here to mean a bipoint without facial flaking. Or simply, a pure blade bipoint. See Section 12.

Figure 1-30 – Ocala Chert, Uniface Bipoint, Suwannee County, Florida (L = 94, W = 27, T = 10 mm, E = 3.481, R = 34.81, g = 25)

Figure 1-31 shows a blade-made knife from northern Florida. The material is not from Florida. Since it is a collector-found specimen, it has to remain as interesting. As a guess-estimate, it could be Mesoamerican.

Figure 1-31 – A Florida Blade Specimen with an Interesting Morphology. It is classified here as a Heavily Sharpened Bipoint. (No Measurements.) The bit is the right part of the specimen; note its invasive marginal flaking. The V-shaped part was the hafting (chassis) part of the artifact; however, it may have been simply a hand-held tool.

Pure Blade Bipoints

Old World bipoints are also made from a core blade and pressure flaked into the bipoint form (Figure 1-32). For the Old World, these specimens probably date to the pre-Neolithic and start representing a smaller bipoint. However, as blade-backed bipoints, they do occur in the early Solutrean period. The American variety could be the aforementioned specimen.

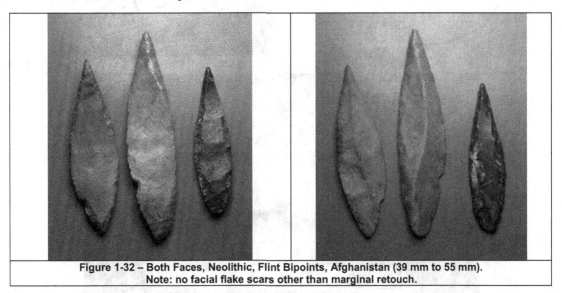

Figure 1-32 – Both Faces, Neolithic, Flint Bipoints, Afghanistan (39 mm to 55 mm).
Note: no facial flake scars other than marginal retouch.

Transverse Bipoint

Hranicky (2004 and 2007) argued for Solutrean (or older) tools to have been imported into the Middle Atlantic area. See Virginia section below. One tool which is a bipoint was found in Virginia's Potomac River valley in January 1928. Its manufacture is unlike any bipoint found in the eastern U.S. It was made using an Old World flaking technique called transversal stone knapping (Hranicky 2018 and Vertes 1954). Figure 1-33 shows two different ways to remove a blade from a core. The blade was then flaked into a bipoint. Figure 1-34 shows a bipoint that was made using the transverse method and its axis. Fortunately for archaeology, the knapper left the striking platform on the bipoint; otherwise, it could not have been identified by this method. The chert stone used in this bipoint is not found in the Potomac River valley.

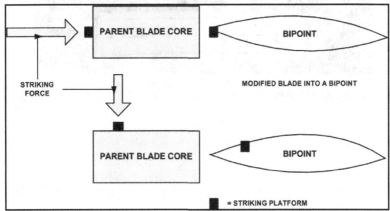

Figure 1-33– Two Methods of Blade Removal from a Core. This specimen was the lower drawing.

37

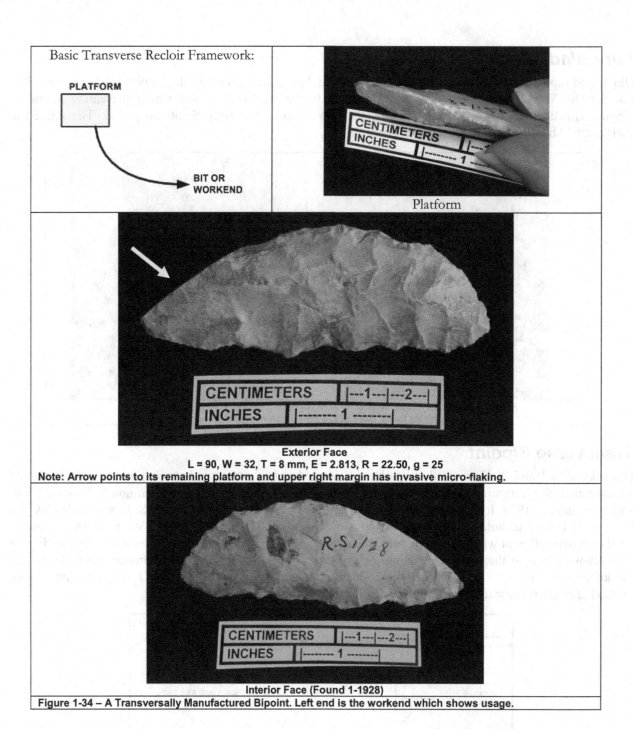

Basic Transverse Recloir Framework:

PLATFORM

BIT OR
WORKEND

Platform

Exterior Face
L = 90, W = 32, T = 8 mm, E = 2.813, R = 22.50, g = 25
Note: Arrow points to its remaining platform and upper right margin has invasive micro-flaking.

Interior Face (Found 1-1928)
Figure 1-34 – A Transversally Manufactured Bipoint. Left end is the workend which shows usage.

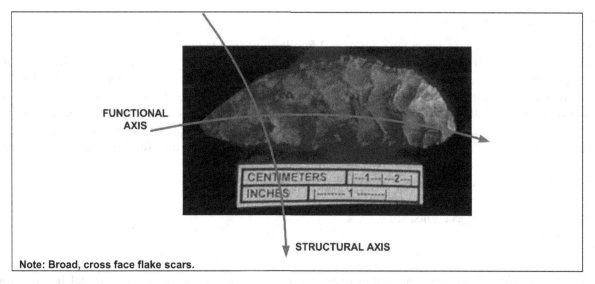

FUNCTIONAL AXIS

STRUCTURAL AXIS

Note: Broad, cross face flake scars.

This specimen has marginal invasive microflaking (both faces), small patch of cortex remaining, and has moderate patination. The platform measures: L = 32, W = 7 mm. The platform length probably offsets it being a true bipoint. Since both ends of the specimen are pointed, it is classified as a bipoint. Based on these properties, its:

- Transversa manufacture, and
- Bipoint morphology, and

this specimen is among the oldest implements found in the Middle Atlantic area of the U.S. It easily pre-dates Cactus Hill by thousands of years.

Lithic Tool Organization

The bipoint does not exist in a vacuum; it exists as a product of a social organization which includes curation and environmental exploitation (as in Binford 1980, Blades 2003, Clarkson 2002, Weedman 2002, and Nelson 1991). Most bipoints show resharpening[30] which confuses classification and identification, especially curation. In this respect, Andrefsky (2005) comments:

> *Central to this concept is the manner in which lithic tools are designed, retouched, resharpened, recycled, and discarded within foraging life and land-use practices…use life of a tool may be defined as simply the service life of tool, which may or may not be reflected in tool resharpening and reduction characteristics.*

In its initial manufacture, the bipoint[31] is simply a dual pointed implement that through usage was resharpened by three basic methods:

- Lateral bit end reduction
- Marginal side bit end reduction
- Off-center and center-lateral manufacturing (discussed below).

These three techniques are present on the majority of recovered bipoints found in the U.S. and are discussed as properties/attributes in the BMM. They represent a specific social organization in prehistory in the U.S. Time depth remains to be established by radiometric and OSL dating. However, these forms can be argued as legacy methods of rejuvenating the tool.

The coastal vs. inland technology is not automatically the same, if only by material. Numerous adaptive mechanisms are different depending on the bipoint's environment, such as weather, resources, games, usage, and social conditions and society make up. The basic aspect of their technology is lithic materials.

---

[30] Resharpening is a subtractive process of a tool's usage.

[31] These factors are the basis of the Bipoint Morphology Model (BMM) presented in this volume.

All Tools – All Dates

As well known, humans have made tools for over 2.5 million years. One of the first to publish on Paleolithic tools was Mercati (1717). Subsequently, archaeologists have classified them into hundreds of classes, industries, types, and numerous categories that, usually, vary from archaeologist to archaeologist. There is usually an agreement for classification, in many cases, which is based on scientific dates. However, as Joffre Coe (1970s) told the author many years ago – all lithic technology is one long continuum, which is divided by archaeologists; a major premise in this publication. These classifications in many cases are often subjective, and these tool classes do not necessarily reflect their true nature in the societies that originated them. As suggested, all lithic tools can be divided into three/four categories:

- Cobble tools, such as axes, celt, etc.
- Blade tools, such as knives, scrapers, etc.
- Biface tools, such as points, knives, etc.

with,

- Blade[32] tools, such as gravers, shavers, etc.

While simplistic, these categories often overlapped technological functions and societal usage. From these bases, there is a lithic panoply of implements. Most tools were multifunctional. The various structures often reflected the social ideologies that dictated design, and simply *how to use the tool*. All tools are viewed as a simple triploid (with blades and bipoints) in lithic technology; it is easy to argue that all lithic tools reflect a legacy that was passed to generations and neighbors for millions of years. Within this human toolset is, of course, the bipoint and problem proving a technological legacy.

Other than the Cinmar's 22,000-year date (Stanford 2011 and Stanford and Bradley 2012) and the Marion County bipoint's 16,000-year date (Hranicky 2012), eastern bipoints have not been dated. Dates on Florida specimens are discussed below. Their form (state) and date (legacy) should follow basic divisions of:

- **Primary** initial entry forms (Pleistocene era to Before Clovis, proto-Paleoindian). It is referred here as Legacy 1 bipoint. The state of a primary bipoint is pointed ends.
- **Secondary** legacy forms after entry (Holocene era to Contact, post-Paleoindian). It is referred here as Legacy 2 bipoint. The state can vary from pointed to round ends.
- **Tertiary** legacy forms which are late small bipoint knives. It is referred here as Legacy 3 bipoint. The state category has all three forms (see Table 1-4).

Table 1-4 – Legacy Bipoint Ranking	
(Original Old World Bipoint)[33]	LEGACY BIPOINT – Original Old World bipoint found in the New World.
Primary	LEGACY 1 BIPOINT – New World bipoint made by Old World people.
Secondary	LEGACY 2 BIPOINT – Made by people who have no direct relations to the Old World.
Tertiary	LEGACY 3 BIPOINT – Made after many, many generations of New World manufacture.

Legacy Requirements

The basic attributes for the bipoint are argued that they come from bipoints technology from the Old World. The American version changes with time; but, these changes are minor. Nonetheless, they can be observed and classified by using the concept of a bipoint legacy. Table 1-5 lists the requirements for each legacy level.

The major morphological (stylistic) difference between Legacy 2 and Legacy 3 bipoints is their cross-section profile. Makers of Legacy 3 bipoints began to have biconvex cross section; however, the quality and craftsmanship remains on most late bipoints.

---

[32] Once a blade or bipoit is flaked on both faces, it is a biface technology.

[33] As of this writing, only two bipoints made of Old World stone have been found: One in Virginia (shown below) and one in Florida (not shown, being published).

Table 1-5 – Legacy Requirements	
Legacy 1	Bipoint with edge-to-edge flake scars and bold flake scars that extend into the middle of the bipoint. It has short parallel flake scars. Specimen usually is less than 6 mm in thickness. The V-shaped bit is common. Specimens are usually over 150 mm in length. Legacy 1 bipoints often have a base-tip slight curve. These specimens often have remnant platforms and minor surface remaining patches of cortex remaining.
Legacy 2	Bipoint has off-set bits. It is usually over 6 mm in thickness. Flake scars are random and not as pronounced. Lateral margins usually have fine retouch.
Legacy 3	Bipoint is usually made from flint/chert. Flake scars are small and random. Round bases occur. Well-made specimens occur, such as Adena and Mississippian bipoints. Small bipoints are common. These bipoints are often biface-produced.

Legacy Bipoint Stones

As shown in this publication, jasper appears to be the preferred stone for bipoints. This is county-wide which may suggest Europe. There is not enough sites and bipoint studies to calculate styles, usage, and stone preferences. Tool stones are basically a form of lithic determinism in prehistory. But there are consequences, namely practically of working the preferred stone and its availably. Archaeology can only evaluate their conditions by being able to count the numbers in stone usage – remains - distributions.

U.S. Bipoint Timelines

As mentioned, the timeline for U.S. bipoints remains to be established. Figure 1-35 shows a proposed diachronic pattern that is based on the Bipoint Legacy Model which is based on the above definitions. As a reminder: Golson (1977) reminds us ***prehistoric cultures can change greatly over long spans while their lithic industries change little***. Furthermore, there was a major migration event on both U.S. coasts, and the bipoint was a standard tool used in these migrations. The various legacy properties:

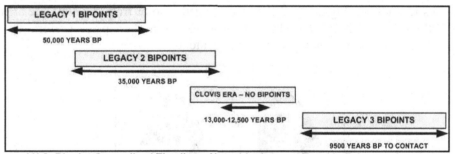

Figure 1-35 – Proposed U.S. Bipoint Generalized Timelines. Note: bipoints are found in Folsom paleo-contexts.

Bipoint U.S. Areas

Based on this study, bipoint areas where specific physical shapes occur. For the present, these large areas are suggested, but not defined (Figure 1-36). These areas are:

- Area #1 – Atlantic coast which has a Solutrean legacy
- Area #2 – Atlantic coast which has an Aterian-African legacy
- Area #3 – Central U.S. which has an El Jobo South American legacy
- Area #4 – Mexico which has a central Mexico (Lerma?) legacy
- Area #5 – Post-Mammoth, but large game hunting in the Southwest which is a Folsom legacy
- Area # 6 – Pacific coast which has an Asian legacy.

At present, no legacies are assigned to the various bipoint areas other than the coastal areas of the Pacific and Atlantic oceans. Interior-found land specimens are assumed to occupy the Holocene era.

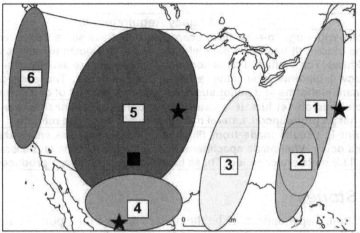

Figure 1-36 – Major Early Bipoint Areas in the U.S. Time and occupation varies, but the bipoint legacy remains for before Clovis to Contact. Note: at Contact, the bipoint is found all over the U.S. The stars represent locations where the bipoint has been found with mammoth kill sites. The box represents Folsom large-game hunting that has associated bipoints.

Clovis and the Bipoint

Presently, there are no confirmed associations of Clovis lanceolates and bipoints. The argument by some archaeologists (Bradley and Stanford 2004 and 2012) that Solutrean bipoints lead to Clovis technology which is (not) present in the archaeological record, such as Boldurian and Cotter (1999), Bonnichsen and Turnmire (1991), Waters, Pevny, and Carlson (2011), Meltzer (1993 and 2009), Collins (1999), Hranicky (2007), or Odell (2009) . For bipoints, Gramly (2009) reports a *near-by knoll* association that may open-the-door as a possible association, but this is not adequate proof of Clovis and a bipoint interaction of technologies. Possibly, Clovis sites have mis-classified expended bipoints, but the bipoint (laurel-leaf) is still missing from Clovis technology. Figure 1-37 shows a utilized bipoint from the Vail site area. The Vail site dates 10,300-11,120 YBP (Gramly 2009). The elongated form could be a paleo-preform for a Clovis point. All said, the laurel-leaf bipoint does not occur in Clovis-contexts.

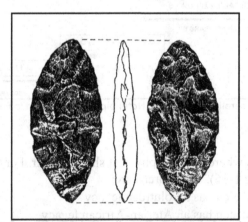

Figure 1-37 – Bipoint Drawing, Vail Site Area, Maine. It is heavily patinated, made from felsite and has a maximum thickness of 9.6 mm. (Gramly 1982)

Ovate knives occur in pure Clovis technology, but the true bipoint has not been reported in Clovis. As a possible cross-over to Clovis-like/age technology, the Paleoindian Crowfield site in Ontario has produced elongated points; some are fluted (Deller and Ellis 1992 and 2011). They can be considered as a bipoint state initially; however, this bipoint assessment may be controversial for some archaeologists. Figure 1-38 shows an example of the basic Crowfield form. This form is often fluted only on one face. Otherwise, bipoints generally escape Clovis.

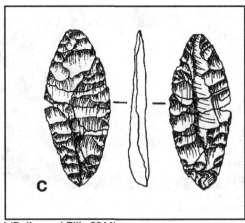

Figure 1-38 – Both Faces of a Crowfield (Deller and Ellis 2011)

For the West, bipoints are found with an Agate Basin type (Roberts (1951). The type has a general date of 10,000 YBP and was named by Roberts (Hranicky 2011). This example may indicate a western pick-up (or continuing) of the bipoint technology in the West. As noted in this publication, the western bipoint also pre-dates Clovis by 1000s of years. Probably, the closest that the bipoint is found in association with Clovis is the Sandia point that was found initially in the Sandia Cave excavation in New Mexico (as in Hibben 1941 and Hibben and Bryan 1941). This site has its controversy in archaeology.

Bipoints and Folsom Points

The major archaeological question: Does Folsom come out of Clovis? No, Folsom has more Old World tool qualities with blade technology than has within Clovis's manufacturing methods. This question is not answered here (see Hranicky 2017). This technology probably represents a large-scale population migration – after Clovis' demise. However, the Folsom bipoint was initiated on the U.S. Plains area.

The bipoint, or ultrathin bifaces, does occur in Folsom assemblages from Texas to the Dakotas (Hoffman 2003). Some archaeologists suggest that it is a preform for the Midland point types; however, this is far from being proved. This bipoint association has been proven in Folsom excavated contexts (Clark and Collins 2002, and Hester 1972). Hoffman (2003) provides two Texas bipoints; their age and association are open. However, they demonstrate pointed-end bipoints and two styles (Figure 1-39).

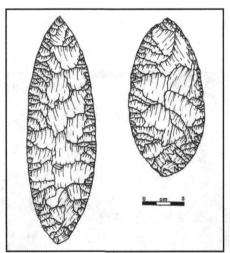

Figure 1-39 – Texas Bipoints with a Probable Folsom Age (From Hoffman 2003). Note the ovate from on the right specimen.

Figure 1-40 shows the thinnest bipoint in this study. Unfortunately, it is not a complete bipoint; however, the excavated part allows reconstruction of its original bipoint shape. This bipoint was found with a mammoth (as in Hester 1972). Note that this specimen is only 3.5 mm thin. This specimen has the lowest (estimated) R and E values in this study.

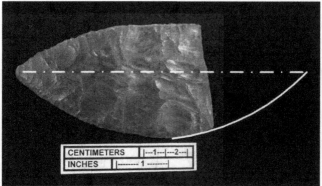

Figure 1-40– Flint, Blackwater Draw, Roosevelt County, New Mexico, L = 107 broken, est. 175.5, W = 49, T = 3.5 mm, est. R = 5.59, est. E = 1.54 Note: the bipoint's original length was estimated.

Figure 1-41 shows three Blackwater-related bipoints. These bipoints are post-Clovis in age and indicative of Folsom ultra-thin flaking. Materials at Blackwater Draw vary and were brought to the site area from great distances. These specimens indicate the high-quality of Folsom bipointmaking. Figure 1-42 shows an excellent bipoint from New Mexico. It has the lowest physical ratio in this study.

Figure 1-41 – Examples of Blackwater Draw Bipoints. Right bipoint: missing base which was probably pointed.

BIPOINT SPECIMEN
BIPOINT MORPHOLOGY MODEL

Date: Legacy 2.
State: Pointed ends.
Mode: Knife.

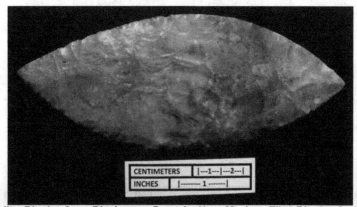

Figure 1-42 – A High-Quality Bipoint from Blackwater Draw in New Mexico. Flint Bipoint from Blackwater Draw Site in Roosevelt County, New Mexico (L = 161, W = 63, T = 4 mm, E = 2.555, R = 10.22, g = 91). Note: its width to thickness numbers.

Expended Bipoints

As illustrated throughout this publication, the expended bipoint causes problems in identification and classification...of bipoints. The expended bipoint has two major attributes:
- Pointed sharpened workends
- Pointed V-shaped stems (chassis) with obtuse workend.[34]

Figure 1-43 shows the major bipont expended forms; however, this only shows a sample of expended forms. The expended bipoint depends on prehistoric usage and the condition this user considered as the end of the bipoint usage. For resharpened bipoints, see Section 6.

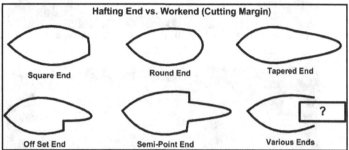

Figure 1-43 – Examples of Expended Bipoints or V-shaped Stemmed Knives.

As presented, all manufacturing methods above can vary in shape and when the knife is used in prehistory. The final bipoint (discard) most likely does not resemble its original bipont form. Figure 1-44 shows a bipoint example with an expended workend. Few archaeologists would classify it as a bipoint but, as discussed, bipoint attributes vary from specimen to specimen. A close-up of the cutting edge is shown. Specimen was probably hand-held and, as such, lateral margins could also have been used as a cutting edge; however, the distal end is the principal cutting edge. This specimen still had a usable cutting margin remaining.

Figure 1-44 – Chert Bipoint, Alachua County, Florida (L = 89, W = 33, T = 7 mm, E = 2.696, R = 18.87). The specimen was resharpened over/over again until its owner thought it was no longer useful.

KNIFE BLADE, SOLUTREAN, Middle to Late Paleolithic - Middle to Late Paleolithic Phase, 40,000B.P. – 15,000 B.P. – Germany, Found along the Danube River Valley Drainage Basin. Length is 2-11/16" or 69mm.

Comparative example: A flint specimen for Culpeper County, Virginia has the same bit/stem configuration (Figure 1-45). The bit is still sharp. The flint is not native to the county or surrounding area; most likely, it is a Kentucky flint. As suggested, some of the flintknapper's stones were obtained at great distances. The other specimen was found on the Thunderbird site in Warren County, Virginia. Both are similar expended bipoints.

---

[34] Once a bipoint was resharpened, which destroys its bipoint morphology, most archaeologists will no longer call it a bipoint; thus, the term V-shaped stemmed knife.

Culpeper County Jasper, Virginia (L = 108, W = 40, T = 13 mm, R = 35.10, E = 2.7, g = 57). Note: bit is still sharp (right end).

Figure 1-45– Expended Bipoints

Warren County Jasper, Virginia (L = 107, W = 38, T = 9 mm).

Figure 1-46 shows two expended bipoints with different stems (right). Also, they show different bit reductions, all of which provides the numerous problems in classifying and identifying bipoints. Bits on both specimens show different resharpening techniques. In the East, these forms are often called Morrow Mountains points after Coe (1964). See Appendix E.

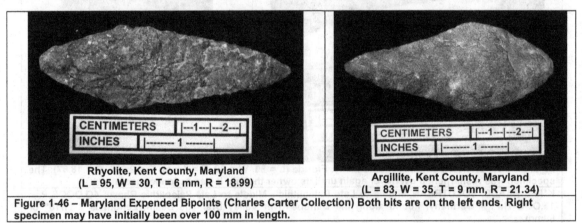

Rhyolite, Kent County, Maryland
(L = 95, W = 30, T = 6 mm, R = 18.99)

Argillite, Kent County, Maryland
(L = 83, W = 35, T = 9 mm, R = 21.34)

Figure 1-46 – Maryland Expended Bipoints (Charles Carter Collection) Both bits are on the left ends. Right specimen may have initially been over 100 mm in length.

As discussed, bipoint reduction due to usage and subsequent resharpening occurred all over North America. Figure 1-47 shows a specimen from Mexico which illustrates a major resharpening and an expended bipoint. Most archaeologists would call it a *stemmed point*.

46

Figure 1-47 – Obsidian, Aztec, Valley of Mexico (L = 49, W = 36, T = 8 mm, E = 1.361, R = 10.88) (Collected by Lorenz Borenstine in the 1950s). It is a resharpened and expended bipoint.

A Bipoint Bit Theory

As argued herein, the bipoint bit was resharpened until expended. This caused numerous bit shapes, many of which caused the bipoint to be un-classifiable by some archaeologists. Figure 1-48 shows a thin bipoint with as unusual bit form, one most archaeologists would call a stemmed point. Its R factor argues it is a Legacy 2 bipoint. However, it has other properties which suggest the cutting bit form. The V-shaped part's margins are not sharpened. The rounded "knob" part has microflaking and is still sharp today. The two notches are also sharp with microflaking – too sharp for hafting. They would be ideal for cutting sinew or hides. Why sharpen these areas if it is going to be hafted? Additionally, it was made from colorful, high-quality chert and maintained the usual bipoint symmetry. Thus, it is classified here as a bipoint with a very-well shaped workend – for cutting.

Figure 1-48 – Monterey Chert, Tulare Lake, California
(L = 141, W = 40, T =6 mm, E = 3.525, R = 21.15)

Note: Plate 6 and low ratio.

Furthermore, the V-shaped stemmed implement has its origins in the Pleistocene. Figure 1-49 shows a weathered limestone tool from the Fawcett Gap site in Frederick County, Virginia. This site is a Pleistocene occupation which was there for the mining of high-quality limestone. It dates to the same era as the Cinmar bipoint (shown herein); the site is similar to the Arkfeld site in Frederick County (Hranicky 2016).

Overall, these V-shaped implement have a bipoint form of technology and are related to the development of Pleistocene implements. With the bipoint's lengthy ancestral legacy, its cutting function led to numerous technological forms.

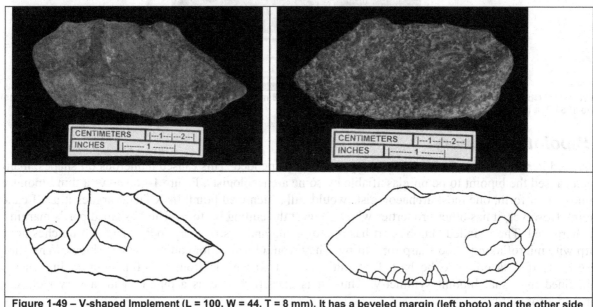

Figure 1-49 – V-shaped Implement (L = 100, W = 44, T = 8 mm). It has a beveled margin (left photo) and the other side has invasive marginal retouching. It was found by Jason Buckman.

Probably the oldest V-shaped implement is one that was found on the Arkfeld site in Frederick/Clarke counties (Hranicky 2015). It has a slight curve to the artifact's shape and is heavily weathered. It is blade-made from limestone (Figure 1-50). It is assumed to have been made initially as a bipoint. It was flaked only on one face; it does have a small remaining platform, but no marginal microflaking. The sharp workend is shown on the left end.

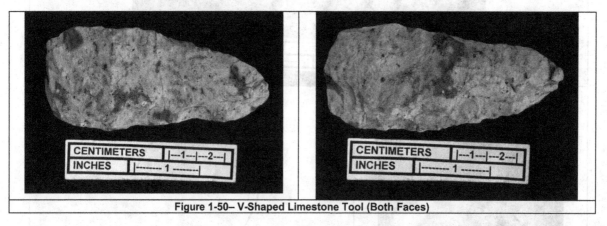

Figure 1-50– V-Shaped Limestone Tool (Both Faces)

The above two specimens argue that the V-shaped form may have been a single style that is out of the bipoint class. Or, half a bipoint was intentional. Unfortunately, they are surface finds and have no associated contexts.

Example Bipoint Model

As the basic bipoint model, Plate 6 illustrates a specimen from North Carolina in banded rhyolite. A Woodland artifact was selected because of the excessive patination of rhyolite in earlier specimens. This specimen has light patination and was associated with pottery. This specimen represents the basic model for bipoint technology. Plate 7 illustrates various resharpened bipoints.

It was examined microscopically to determine usage and wear patterns. Number 6 in the figure shows the suggested basic design of a V-shaped stemmed knife, i.e., bit, and chassis. Numbers 1 and 2 show the bit's striations and edge sharpness. Rhyolite is a self-generative material which re-sharpens itself while cutting. The bit has straight grooves which appear to be filled with an oxidized material, such as organic remains. Numbers 3 and 4 show stem properties, no striations, and a rounded edge. The edge is smooth which is probably due to hafting conditions. Number 5 shows a sample of the uniform surface patination. Once the blade was re-sharpened down to the hafting area, the knife was discarded and a new one was made.

Wear pattern analysis in this study is based on Grace (1989), Keeley (1980), Bonnichsen (1977), Walker, et al. (2004), Kay (1996 and 2003), and Semenov (1964). Again, examine bipoints under the microscope for wear striations.

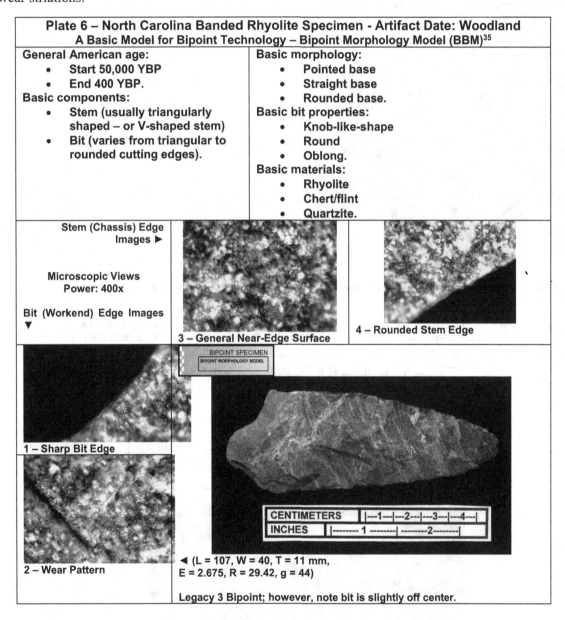

Plate 6 – North Carolina Banded Rhyolite Specimen - Artifact Date: Woodland
A Basic Model for Bipoint Technology – Bipoint Morphology Model (BBM)[35]

General American age:
- Start 50,000 YBP
- End 400 YBP.

Basic components:
- Stem (usually triangularly shaped – or V-shaped stem)
- Bit (varies from triangular to rounded cutting edges).

Basic morphology:
- Pointed base
- Straight base
- Rounded base.

Basic bit properties:
- Knob-like-shape
- Round
- Oblong.

Basic materials:
- Rhyolite
- Chert/flint
- Quartzite.

Stem (Chassis) Edge Images ▶

Microscopic Views Power: 400x

Bit (Workend) Edge Images ▼

3 – General Near-Edge Surface

4 – Rounded Stem Edge

1 – Sharp Bit Edge

2 – Wear Pattern

BIPOINT SPECIMEN
BIPOINT MORPHOLOGY MODEL

CENTIMETERS |---1---|---2---|---3---|---4---|
INCHES |-------- 1 --------|-------- 2 --------|

◀ (L = 107, W = 40, T = 11 mm, E = 2.675, R = 29.42, g = 44)

Legacy 3 Bipoint; however, note bit is slightly off center.

---

[35] This specimen would be classified as a stemmed projectile point by most archaeologists.

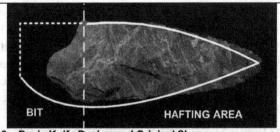

BIT   HAFTING AREA

6 – Basic Knife Design and Original Shape

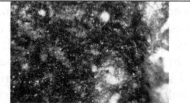

5 – General Surface Patination (200x)

1 – Shows bit edge as being sharp with legacy resharpening
2 – Shows parallel bit striations
3 – Shows stem general edge condition (no straight lines)
4 – Shows stem edge (rounded edges)
5 – Shows general surface patination (400x)
6 – Shows the generalized (dotted line) bit's initial formation. Bit's initial shape can never be determined once it is resharpened.

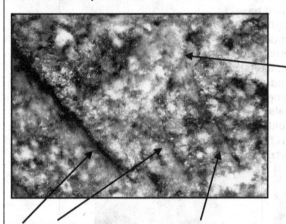

Straight striations (left groove is deep). Arrows show straight wear-caused lines. Analysis procedures are based on Grace (1989).

Knife: Upper part of bit is the cutting margin. It may have been hafted up to the bit assembly. Entire bit assembly shows straight wear lines. Stem edges are rounded and do not show striations (wear patterns).

Plate 7 – Various U.S. Resharpened Bipoints

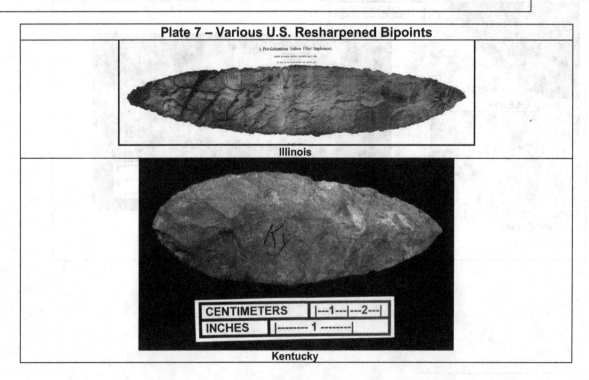

Illinois

| CENTIMETERS | |---1---|---2---| |
| INCHES | |-------- 1 --------| |

Kentucky

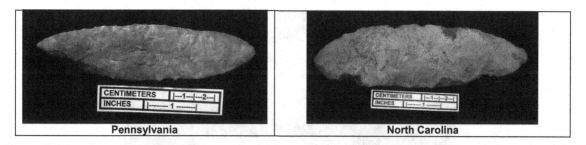

| Pennsylvania | North Carolina |

Bipoint – V-Stemmed Knife – or a General Tool

Again, the major topic of the book is the bipoint in the Western Hemisphere, but major problems occur in archaeology in properly identifying and classifying this tool. And, just what is a bipoint remains archaeologically undefined. While there are numerous knife forms in prehistory; however, one class of tools is found throughout hominid history, namely, as mentioned – the bipoint. It is a cutting implement that served humanity as a basic survival tool and practically every society had a form of it. Figure 1-51 shows an example of a knife; obviously a V-shaped stemmed tool but, as will be described, is it a projectile point? Most archaeologists would classify it as a point that functioned as a knife. Wear patterns present the chassis (blade) and bit (stem) as shown in the bipoint model. As argued, the expended bipoint is the most mis-classified prehistoric implement in the world. There are two manufacturing methods for bipoints: 1) blade[36]/flake forms and 2) biface forms. The biface forms are late in prehistory. For bipoint basics, see Bipoint Mechanics section and Plate 6 above.

Figure 1-51 – Quartzite Knife, Mecklenburg County, Virginia. (L = 148, W = 54.5, T = 9 mm, E = 2.715, R = 24.44, g = 70) Note: in this case, specimen has a stem? (right), but sharp stem side margins. It is well made suggesting an early Legacy 3 bipoint. This bipoint was not used extensively. Of course, most archaeologists would call it a stemmed point.

Figure 1-52 shows the same manufacturing; however, the striking platform is present which confuses it as a large stemmed point. Its bulb scar is still present. It is a bipoint as both side margins next to the so-called stem are sharp. It has evidence of large circular flakes being removed on both sides of the so-called stem. These removal flakes caused shape edges; they are called here a classic resharpening method. These specimens illustrate the difficulty in identifying it as a bipoint. Once again, in the East, these forms are often called Morrow Mountains points after Coe (1964). See Appendix E.

---

[36] The term **blade** is used to mean any flat stone piece that was struck off a parent rock, namely a core, and was subsequently made into a tool. Also confusingly, it means the cutting part of a tool.

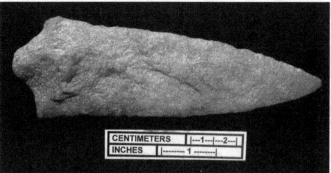

Figure 1-52 – Quartzite Bipoint from an unknown County in North Carolina (L = 148, W = 46, W = 9 mm, E = 3.217, R = 28.95, g = 72). It has a flat end-to-end profile and is well made. It is a Legacy 3 bipoint. This specimen was probably not used. Bit margins show heat treatment. Both sides of the workend (left) are sharp or what is called classic bit resharpening.

Figure 1-53 shows examples where bits are usually called the stem; again, a confusion that is frequently mis-classified in archaeology. They both have sharpened bits which have a legacy resharpening flake. This specimen would be classified as an eastern Morrow Mountain point by most archaeologists.

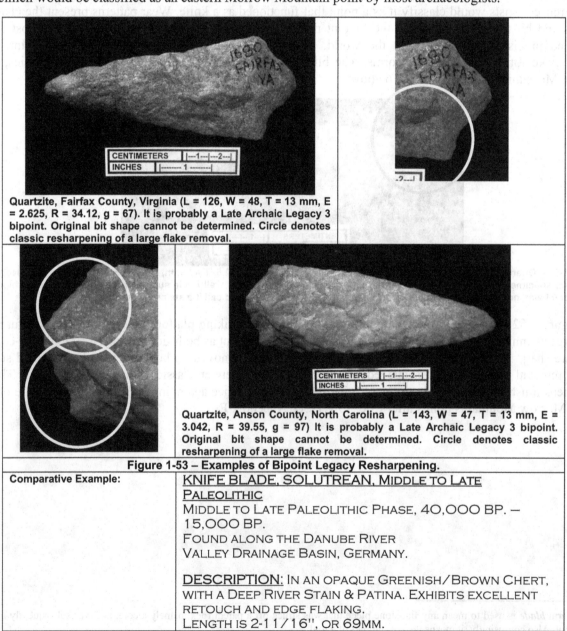

Quartzite, Fairfax County, Virginia (L = 126, W = 48, T = 13 mm, E = 2.625, R = 34.12, g = 67). It is probably a Late Archaic Legacy 3 bipoint. Original bit shape cannot be determined. Circle denotes classic resharpening of a large flake removal.

Quartzite, Anson County, North Carolina (L = 143, W = 47, T = 13 mm, E = 3.042, R = 39.55, g = 97) It is probably a Late Archaic Legacy 3 bipoint. Original bit shape cannot be determined. Circle denotes classic resharpening of a large flake removal.

Figure 1-53 – Examples of Bipoint Legacy Resharpening.	
Comparative Example:	KNIFE BLADE, SOLUTREAN, MIDDLE TO LATE PALEOLITHIC MIDDLE TO LATE PALEOLITHIC PHASE, 40,000 BP. – 15,000 BP. FOUND ALONG THE DANUBE RIVER VALLEY DRAINAGE BASIN, GERMANY. DESCRIPTION: IN AN OPAQUE GREENISH/BROWN CHERT, WITH A DEEP RIVER STAIN & PATINA. EXHIBITS EXCELLENT RETOUCH AND EDGE FLAKING. LENGTH IS 2-11/16", OR 69MM.

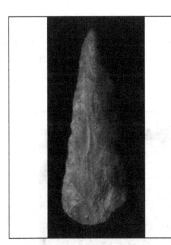

NOTE: THE ROUNDED BIT WHICH WAS RESHARPENED. IT OFFERS A PARALLEL TO AMERICAN BIPOINTS.

Diamond-Shaped Bipoints

The Diamond-shaped bipoint is a heavily expended bipoint that has dual workends (bits). It was initially called the Chesapeake diamond projectile point by Hranicky and Painter (1988). Figure 1-54 shows an example from Pennsylvania. It is suggested as a dual bladed knife.

Date: Legacy 3.
State: Pointed ends.
Mode: Knife.

Figure 1-54– Flint, Hanover County, Pennsylvania (L = 79, W = 57, T = 12 mm, E = 1.385, R = 16.63). Note: low E factor.

Comparative example: The diamond-shaped knife occurs all over the U.S. (Figure 1-55). It is often beveled and called a Harvey knife. It is probably an expended bipoint; however, this assessment is impossible to determine. This specimen suggests a large-flake reduction method.

Figure 1-55 – Flint, Lake County, Oregon (L= 72, W = 32, T = 9 mm, E = 2.250, R = 20.25, g = 21) Note its striking platform (right). Note: crystal pocket.

Figure 1-56 shows small, hand-held, expended knives which illustrate the problem with classifying all knives. Obviously, they are not the same as the above knife, but they share many attributes, namely a cutting function. Again, once the tool was expended in prehistory and discarded, modern archaeology has major problems in even classifying them as *knives*. However, their attributes fit the BMM, namely dual pointed ends.

Figure 1-56 – Expended Knives from Virginia: Bipoints? They have dual workends.

Comparative example: The Solutreans probably have over a 1000 different tool types (archaeologically speaking) which presents a technological coincidence. Figure 1-57 shows a probable legacy for expended bipoints.

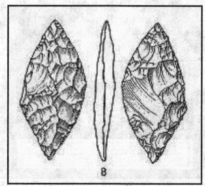

Figure 1-57 – Solutrean Diamond-shaped Expended Bipoints (after Smith 1962).

Needle Bipoints

The needle bipoint is a long, very narrow specimen. Its length is 10 times its width which does not exceed 15 mm. The lateral margin on this bipoint may be the result of extensive edge resharpening, but most needle bipoints were manufactured that way. Figure 1-58 shows an example.

Date: Legacy 3.
State: Pointed ends.
Mode: Knife.

Figure 1-58 – Flint, Western Kentucky (L = 160 mm) (Photograph by Larry Garvin)

Ovate Bipoints

The ovate or elliptical shape is considered here as a bipoint because it has dual pointed ends. And, the ovate form may have a considerable antiquity which suggests it had origins in Africa. However, ovate forms occur on the west coast (Cressman 1960) and Mexico (MacNeish 1958). It has an Asian form at the Verkhne-Troitskaya site in the Sakha Republic (Mochanov and Fedoseeva 1969). Thus, the ovate form is universal; however, not all groups were using this form. Also, the ovate bipoint may simply be a matter of efficiency: wider margins permitted a longer life cycle for the tool. In other words, the ovate bipoint has better economics in the social unit which translates into transport efficiency.

The difference between an ovate biface and an ovate bipoint is thickness. The ovate biface is thick which allows for further reduction. The surfaces on an ovate biface show more random flaking than the bipoint.

The earliest date for an ovate bipoint was obtained at Gypsum Cave, Nevada. The radiocarbon is 8505 +/- 340 BC (uncalibrated) (Harrington 1933).

Figures 1-59a and b show two classic ovate examples. An African specimen is shown (Figure 1-60) and others are presented elsewhere in this publication. These bipoints probably reflect an early bipoint introduction into the U.S. The ovate form does occur in Europe, also. Derev'anko, et al. (1998) reports the long, narrow ovate bipoint in Siberia.

> There is no answer as to "why" for this style bipoint. Do they represent special usage or social class? Do they represent a distinct Old World legacy? They have a wide-spread distribution. They are generally well made and from high-quality stones and considered here as rare. They have an early entry date into North America.

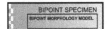

Legacy: 2
Pointed ends.
R factor.

Figure 1-59a– A Kentucky Example of an Ovate Bipoint (L = 124, W = 53, T = 8 mm, E = 2.339, R = 18.71, g = 74). Right tip has a small remnant of the striking platform, has remaining cortex, and the reverse side has a remnant of the bold scar. It was made off a large flake and dates to the Pleistocene era.

Legacy: 2
Pointed ends.
R factor.

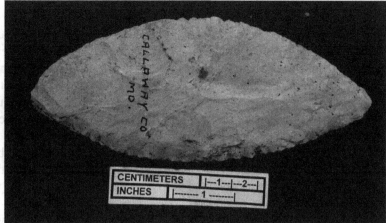

Figure 1-59b – Burlington Chert, Callaway, Missouri (L = 138, W = 59, T = 8 mm, E = 2.338. R = 18.71, g = 73) This Pleistocene specimen has invasive marginal microflaking and shows surface oxidation. Platform area was removed. There are no flaking errors, such a henge fractures. (Mitchel Lewis/Ken Partain/Jake Vahle Collection-owners). Its low ratio factor classifies it as a Legacy 2 bipoint.

Comparative example: This specimen is from Africa and dates to the Upper Paleolithic (Figure 1-60). It has a classic ovate shape and is suggestive also of an African legacy for ovate bipoints.

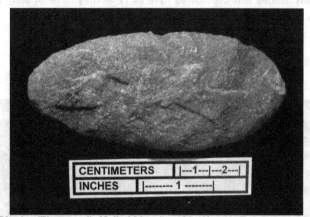

Figure 1-60 – Quartzite, Ovate Bipoint (Elongated), Mali, Africa (L = 98, W = 42, T = 8 mm, E = 2.333, R = 18.66). Note striking platform on the left end; bulb scar is present on the reverse side. Specimen can be considered a preform. This specimen has a low LWT factor.

Another comparative example: It is an ovate bipoint from the Mousterian of France (Figure 1-61). However, the archaeologist may have mis-dated (classified) the specimen.

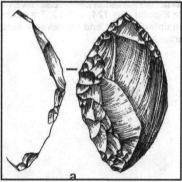

Figure 1-61 Mousterian Bipoint at Saint-Cesaire, France

Figures 1-62 and 1-63 show western U.S. examples of this bipoint style.

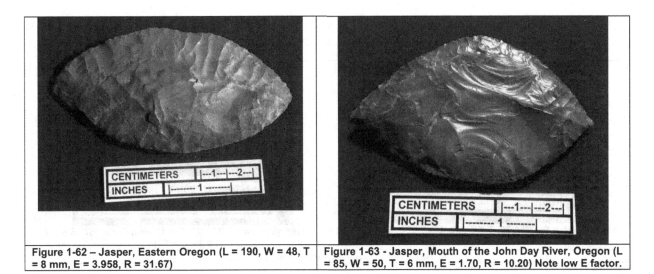

| Figure 1-62 – Jasper, Eastern Oregon (L = 190, W = 48, T = 8 mm, E = 3.958, R = 31.67) | Figure 1-63 - Jasper, Mouth of the John Day River, Oregon (L = 85, W = 50, T = 6 mm, E = 1.70, R = 10.20) Note low E factor. |

The ovate bipoint is probably a hand-held knife and generally does not exceed the hand in size. Figure 1-64 shows an unusual specimen that is relatively thick, suggesting a heavy duty function or purpose. It has edge sharpening along all margins and the striking platform is usually present. The ovate form presents an acceptance problem for bipoint technology by most archaeologists. It is classified here as an ovate state classification.

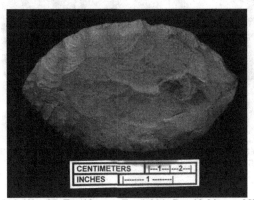

Figure 1-64 – Flint, Pennsylvania (L = 108, W = 65, T = 10 mm, E = 1.661, R = 16.61, g = 92) Note its retouched lateral margins. It probably dates to the U.S. Woodland Period as suggested by its low E factor.

Another comparative example: Figure 1-65 shows a poorly-made ovate bipoint from North Carolina. Its flaking qualities (poor) are similar to the above specimen from Florida. It has right sharpening point, perhaps they are spoke shaves. It suggests a short-term tool. By analogy, they date to the Paleoindian era. Most archaeologists would refer to these specimens as *simply* a biface, or at least – a knife.

Figure 1-65 – Rhyolite Bipoint, Halifax County, North Carolina (L = 108, W = 63, T = 16 mm, E = 1.714, R = 27.42). Perhaps by material, it dates to the Archaic Period in the U.S. Low E factor applies to the Archaic era?

Figure 1-66 shows two small ovate specimens that reflect widespread usage of this form. The ovate form ranges from small to large bipoints. The following are Legacy 3 bipoints.

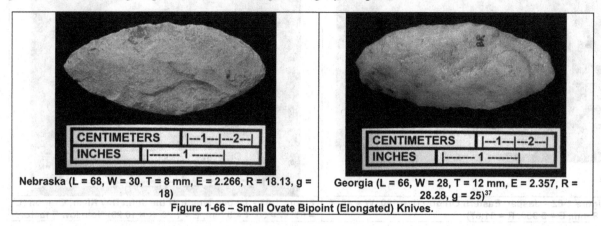

Nebraska (L = 68, W = 30, T = 8 mm, E = 2.266, R = 18.13, g = 18)

Georgia (L = 66, W = 28, T = 12 mm, E = 2.357, R = 28.28, g = 25)[37]

Figure 1-66 – Small Ovate Bipoint (Elongated) Knives.

Comparative examples: These elongated chert specimens are from Florida (Figure 1-67). Florida's bipoints reflect the regular bipoint morphology, but some specimens indicate a different shape and possible usage/function. These small bipoints are late in prehistory.

Figure 1-67 – Chert, Biface Bipoints, Madison County, Florida (Left: L = 83, W = 31, T = 13 mm, E = 2.677, R = 34.80, g = 32 and right: L = 79, W = 30, T = 11 mm, E = 2.633, R = 28.96, g = 23).

Adena Beavertails

Archaeologists are so-often interested in projectile points that one major point type is frequently mis-classified. This is the Adena projectile point from the Ohio River valley. This type is frequently identified as such throughout the East, including Florida. It is frequently called a beavertailed Adena, which is a resharpened bipoint (Figure 1-68). It is so established in the literature that there will never be a correction. Of course, they are resharpened bipoints. The cache blades are probably preforms from which a bipoint could have been made. The pure bipoint does occur in both Adena and Hopewell cultures.

Adena-Florida Point

(Justice 1987)

---

[37] These small oblong specimens occur in Solutrean (Stanford 2012).

Figure 1-68– Adena Beavertail Examples

Adena Blade

Adena Blade - reference to a large, very thin point that has a rounded base. It is probably a preform or trade item. Also, known as a cache blade. They are thin and well made. Basically, they are not bipoints, but they have rounded bases as do many bipoints.

Lithic Tool Organization

All lithic tools, including the bipoint, do not exist in a vacuum; they exist as a product of a social organization which includes curation, maintenance, and environmental exploitation usage (as in Binford 1980, Blades 2003, Clarkson 2002, Weedman 2002, and Nelson 1991). Most bipoints show resharpening[38] which confuses classification and identification, especially archaeological curation. In this respect, Andrefsky (2005) comments:

> *Central to this concept is the manner in which lithic tools are designed, retouched, resharpened, recycled, and discarded within foraging life and land-use practices…use life of a tool may be defined as simply the service life of tool, which may or may not be reflected in tool resharpening and reduction characteristics.*

Repeating, in its initial manufacture, the bipoint[39] is simply a dual pointed implement that through usage was resharpened by three basic methods:

- Lateral bit end reduction
- Marginal side bit end reduction
- Off-center and center-lateral manufacturing (discussed below).

These three techniques are present on the majority of recovered bipoints found in the U.S. and are discussed as properties/attributes in the BMM. They represent a specific social organization in prehistory in the U.S. Time depth remains to be established by radiometric, Raman Laser technique, and OSL dates. However, these forms can be argued as legacy methods of rejuvenating the tool.

The coastal vs. inland technology is not automatically the same, if only by material. Numerous adaptive mechanisms are different depending on the bipoint's environment, such as weather, resources, games, and social conditions and general make up. As of this writing, all middle U.S. bipoints date post-Clovis and are Legacy 3 bipoints.

---

[38] Resharpening is a subtractive process of a tool's usage.

[39] These factors are the basis of the Bipoint Morphology Model (BMM) presented in this volume.

Section 2 – Resharpened Bipoints

This section provides an overview of the methods that were used to resharpen bipoints. A model for Legacy resharpened bits is proposed. Country-wide examples of bit resharpening are illustrated.

There is no evidence that the bipoint was universal or used by all prehistoric societies in the U.S.; however, it is found in every state. Thus, this factor contributes to the difficulty in dating a bipoint. And, once a bipoint was resharpened, this dating is compounded to a degree of impossibility. There is evidence observed in this study to suggest that some bipoints were manufactured with a V-shaped bit initially.

The bipoint is a product of manufacture, maintenance, and usage events. Change of any of these factors (variables) affects the bipoint's lifecycle (Surovell 2009). Of course, these translate to tool efficiency which is probably evident on expended bipoints, namely wear patterns and remaining residues. Figure 2-1 shows an excellent example of bipoint high-quality-skilled resharpening.

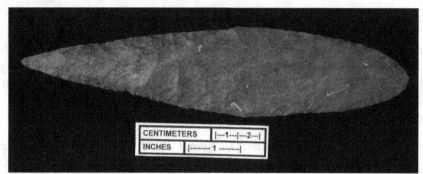

Figure 2-1 - Flint Knife, Chattanooga, Tennessee (L = 198, W = 44, T = 8 mm, R = 36.00). It has edge-to-edge flake scars. V-shaped blade has lateral edge resharpening. Right: chassis beginning with the end of micro-flaking of each lateral margin.

This specimen argues lateral usage and resharpening. With this aspect, the functional axis point is somewhere on both lateral margin. Also, resharpening suggest the length of the hafting area (chassis). All of which, 50% of a bipoint was its workend; the remaining was the handle.

The bipoint was a cutting implement and, like most lithic tools, the cutting edge became dull with usage and was resharpened (chaines operatoire approach[40]). This process, curation, changed the bipoint's initial morphology until it no longer resembles a bipoint; thus, most archaeologists fail to recognize it as a bipoint. At this stage of the life cycle, it is often called a V-shaped stemmed knife, but it is a product of the reduction process. Naturally, resharpening modifies the bipoint's original state (classification). This is one major problem in presenting bipoint technology to the archaeological community; most refuse to accept a modified resharpened form as part of bipoint technology.[41] Obviously, Early Americans used the basic tool. For most archaeologists, any tool that has a remnant use life can be measured (as in Brantingham 2010).

As with Paleoindian point studies, Flenniken and Raymond (1986) argue:

> *...resharpening has the potential to alter projectile point blade shape in such a way that blade shape no longer distinguishes it as a type.*

This problem was analyzed by Buchannan and Collard (2010) with their studies of Clovis, Folsom, and Plainview points from which they concluded that after resharpening, 35% of the points were often mis-classified. The mis-classification of bipoints is probably a much higher percentage.

Numerous specimens are illustrated in this publication which reflects various stages of resharpening. Again, once the bipoint's tip has been removed, the basic argument among archaeologists is that the knife is no longer a bipoint. Figure 2-2 shows this condition. The resharpening of the bipoint is a stage in its life cycle. The bipoint's life cycle depends on material, usage, and cutting target which varies by culture and users (Hranicky 2007). As such, once resharpening reaches mid-point, it was probably an expended bipoint.

---

[40] Reference to tools, waste material, and archaeological context – spatial analysis. It is basically the acquisition, production, intensity, use, and discard of tools (Leroi-Gourhan and Brezillion 1972). Concept is rarely used in the U.S.
[41] The V-shaped stemmed knife is common on most post-Clovis archaeological sites.

As mentioned numerous times, this stage creates numerous problems for most archaeological analyses and interpretations.

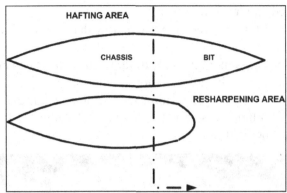

Figure 2-2 – Drawing of the Resharpening Morphology. Is the resharpened form still a bipoint? The resharpened bit determines the legacy of the bipoint.

The location of resharpening a margin of a bipoint depends on two technical factors: location on the bipoint and a functional-time of the bipoint's service in the social unit. Based on generalized methods in Bordes (1947, et al.), the location of a retouched edge is:

- Distal/Proximal (workend) or both ends (ζ Length) – possible Legacy 1 bipoints.
- Lateral margins (single and both) (ζ Width) – possible Legacy 2 bipoints.
- Bifacially or unifacially flaked (ζ Thickness) - possible Legacy 3 bipoints.
- Continuous or partial (abrupt) flaking – All legacy bipoints.

By studying modifications to the basic bipoint form, analysis should determine that the specimen was resharpened (or not), which surface area was modified, and the types of resharpening.

Bipoint Resharpening

Resharpening easily dates to the beginnings of the bipoint era in human history. Once the bipoint was used and resharpened, its original morphology (ζ **L, W, T**) was changed, and the subsequent shape depended entirely on the user. The V-shaped stem was usually maintained, but the symmetry of the bit varied. Figure 2-3 shows a sample of Solutrean bipoints from France. With variations in the bipoint shape and resharpening occurring worldwide, the basic bipoint is difficult to classify unless the generalized bipoint form is used. These bipoints illustrate this principle. Resharpening indicates function and usage; once it can no longer be resharpened, it was considered by the user to be an expended tool and was discarded. The process is directly relatable to the bipoint's initially manufactured length (ζ L).

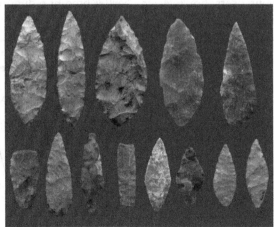

Figure 2-3 – Flint, France, Solutrean Bipoints Reflecting Different Morphologies and Resharpenings.

61

Bipoint Resharpening Stages

Unless ceremonial, all bipoints were resharpened due to usage. The following stages are suggested:

- Stage one: a resharpened bipoint were the tip remains.
- Stage two: a resharpened bipoint were the pointed tip has been removed, but the general bipoint shape remains.
- Stage three: a resharpened bipoint where 75% of its original shape can be observed.
- Stage four: resharening where only half of its form remains.
- Stage five: resharpening was no longer perform and the bipoint was expended.

An example of a Legacy Two bipoint is shown in Figure 2-4. Only the tip has been used; 75% of the bipoint remains. Former bit is to the right.

Figure 2-4 – Bottom: Rhyolite specimen from Burlington, New Jersey. Note its reharpened (right) end which is still sharp (L = 113, W = 34, T9 mm). This specimen is a uniface bipoint; it has no facial flake scars.

Legacy Reshapening

The study of American bipoint resharpening has identified specific methods that have a considerable antiquity. The bit and resharpening method has a leverage that allows the user more tensile strength in a cutting edge; however, this may vary regionally. This bit form is usually V-shaped; however, rounded forms do occur.

This type of reharpening is called here legacy resharpening, and the method dates to the Solutrean age. For the Middle Atlantic area, the legacy of Old World bipoints continues into the Woodland era, especially the eastern coastal plain. Resharpening does not reflect bipoint function or the economics of un-resharpened implements. It is an allometric process that changes the bipoint's shape.

Resharpening starts within months of the bipoint's initialization. The original pointed bit is reduced to a new cutting bit which varied among users; however, the earlier bipoint reduction retained their Old World bit form until expended. Figure 2-5 shows several bit styles by legacy.

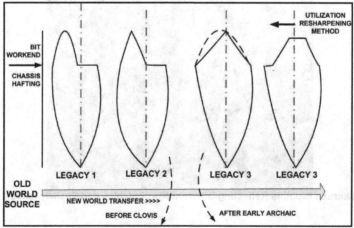

Figure 2-5 – Various Resharpening Legacy Stages for Bipoints.

Figure 2-6 shows Legacy 3 resharpened specimens. The bits vary; however, there is an across county shape of the stem. While bits are remnants, the stem (chassis) style classifies these specimens as BMM bipoints with resharpening. Again, most archaeologists fail to recognize them as bipoints. These specimens are assumed to be expended bipoint forms and were discards.

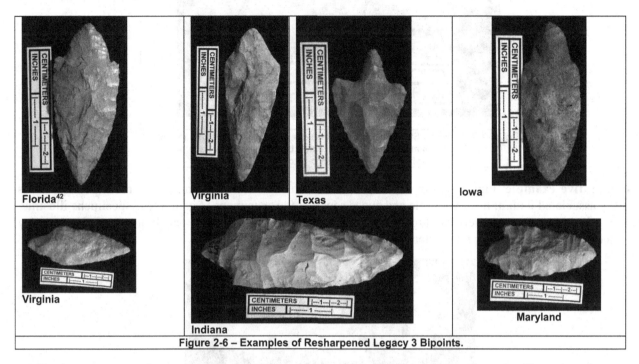

Florida[42] Virginia Texas Iowa

Virginia Indiana Maryland

Figure 2-6 – Examples of Resharpened Legacy 3 Bipoints.

Furthermore, specimens in Figure 2-7 would be classified as stemmed projectile points by most archaeologists; however, if examined closely (microscopically), they show that the area generally called the stem is sharp, and they were used as a chisel, scraper, etc. The supposed blade was the hafted part of the tool. Far too many similar tools are *quickly* classified as projectile points[43] by archaeologists; for example, Rick (1996) attempts to divide points in Peru into stylistic types. He failed to establish resharpening methodologies in his prehistoric sample. The original state cannot be determined, but most likely it was a pointed end bipoint.

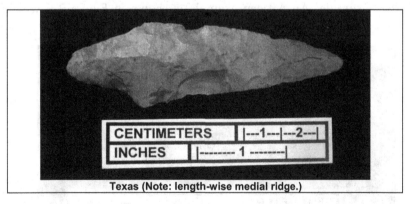

Texas (Note: length-wise medial ridge.)

---

[42] Point is often called an Adena beavertail point.

[43] The term *projectile point* is the biggest mis-nomer in American archaeology. Few were ever thrown. The term **hafted biface** should be used.

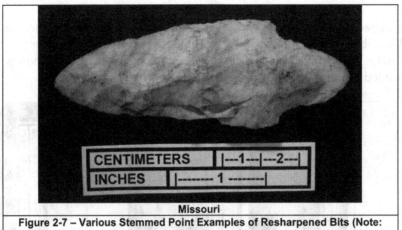

Missouri

Figure 2-7 – Various Stemmed Point Examples of Resharpened Bits (Note: Triangular stems are a basic structure and both specimens have bit resharpening with micro-retouching.)

Comparative example: Figure 2-8 shows a specimen from Alabama with similar bit resharpening. It has pottery associated with it; however, time and space separate the specimens. Again, these specimens illustrate that the bipoint was manufactured throughout U.S. prehistory, and it was a pan-Indian tool. Note: many archaeologists would classify it as a stemmed projectile point.[44]

Figure 2-8 – Jasper, resharpened with lateral edge usage. Top left bit is sharp. It is from Eufaula, Barbour County, Alabama (L = 83, W = 27, T = 8 mm, R = 24.59).

Additional Comparative Example: An African example is shown in Figure 2-9 which has comparative resharpening. It could easily be lost in the Southeastern U.S.

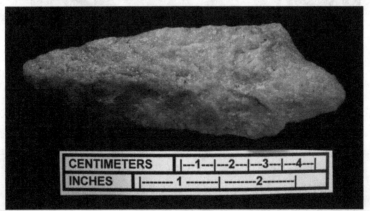

Figure 2-9 – Quartzite, Niger River, Nigeria, Africa (L = 115, W = 34, T = 12 mm). Right end shows bit resharpening.

---

[44] In archaeology, most so-called projectile points are not flyable on a spear shaft. They are knives.

Resharpening Standards

The resharpened bipoint has no standards for users in prehistory; each user decided the best for his skill (ability), his intended function, type of stones, and general conditions for the day it was resharpened. As discussed in this book, there is a classic (legacy) form of bit modification; however, through time, bipoints become smaller and resharpening is not as obvious or standard (Figure 2-10).

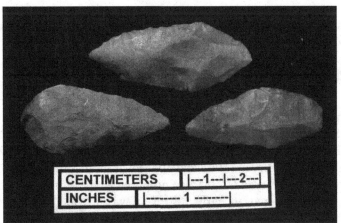

Figure 2-10 – Resharpened Bipoints from Central Texas.

Comparative example: Figure 2-11 shows a comparative specimen that was not used extensively. It has a remnant striking platform, but the specimen is thick and poorly made. These small knives are often called projectile points. All of which can be answered by microscopic analyses.

Figure 2-11 – Lightly Resharpened Rhyolite Bipoint from Central Pennsylvania. Left: chassis or stem, right: slightly round bit which is sharp. Worn flake scars seem to indicate a considerable antiquity for the specimen – maybe its preservation environment.

Section 3 - Bipoints and Prehistory

> The bipoint is the most frequently mis-classified artifact in American archaeology. This is due to the fact that few archaeologists accept its antiquity which is greater than Clovis. This section presents an overview of the bipoint's place in North American prehistory.

While projectile points "are" mainstream American archaeology, the bipoint overrides them in all of North American prehistory. As a consequence and presented here, they are the dominant lithic tool form in prehistory as they have twice the antiquity that points have.

Early American Archaeology

For most of American archaeological history, the Bering Strait was the a priori reasoning of most archaeologists. And, for many, it is still the starting place to look for early Americans. Holmes (1918), Sollas (1924), Roberts (1937), Sellards (1917), Figgins (1927), Gildey and Loomis (1926), Howard (1930), and Cook (1926) addressed the antiquity of mankind in the Americas; thus, the New World topic is not a new one. For the Pacific northwest coast, Bryan (1965 and 1968) was among the first to discuss bipoints, or as he called it … the willow-leaf bipoints. Bryan (1978) also proposed a circum-Pacific model for bipoints.

Magoffin and Davis (1929) offered an early review of world-wide archaeology in which they were probably the first to publish the Folsom[45] point find after its initial publication. Also, they provide an argument for very early entry time for the First Americans.[46] They comment:

> *Florida has been the happy hunting ground chosen by a number of scientists bent on unearthing America's past. Sellards, a Florida geologist, Lommis of Amherst, Gidley of the Smithsonian, and others have dug into Florida soil and found arrowpoints and human bones buried in a layer of earth which contained the bones of mammoths and mastodons. These giants of the elephant family have been extinct since the Ice Age, it is generally believed. If men shot darts into these creatures, it implies that those men were living at least 20,000 years ago (1929:200).*

The mammoths and mastodons were hunted worldwide until their probable extinction by Nature's climate change. Far too many mega-animals became extinct at the same time as to blame humans (Lister and Bahn 2007).

Over the last 50 years, more archaeologists began to suggest that various aspects of early Americans' lithic toolkit suggested Europe as the source and that these tools were a legacy that was transferred into the New World via various transoceanic voyages…a long time ago. Even with this shift, archaeologists are evenly divided on whether humans were in the Americas before/after 15,000 YBP (Wheat 2012).

Over the last 50 years, more archaeologists began to suggest that various aspects of early Americans' lithic toolkit suggested Europe as the source and that these tools were a legacy that was transferred into the New World via various transoceanic voyages…a long time ago. Even with this shift, archaeologists are evenly divided on whether humans were in the Americas before/after 15,000 YBP (Wheat 2012).

Harrington (1933) was among the first to suggest that the Europeans, namely the Magdalenians, crossed the Atlantic via Iceland to Canada. However, Huntington's (1919) *wind-bridge* across the Atlantic was a *course* that would lead many American archaeologists to look for *new trails* for the first Americans. Munro (1912:Plate VI) was the first to publish and argue that the bipoint was Solutrean.

Archaeology has been restricted to the physical evidence, via stone tools, to explain the history of humans. Like most sciences or humanities, a classification scheme was needed to organize the social objects into a logical progression, none of which ever satisfied all archaeologists. On a world-wide perspective, too many ancient tools are similar. To overcome the problem, archaeologists began to subdivide various toolkits into classification based on micro-attributes by regions, when, in fact, technology is pan-human with cores, blades, denticulates, scrapers, burins, perforators, wedges, spokeshaves, choppers, hammerstones, etc., and bipoints occurring nearly everywhere over the last 100,000 years. Naturally, there are various regional tools

---

[45] The association of a flaked tool with extinct mammals date to the 1880s (Russell 1885).

[46] Magoffin and Davis' (1929) publication was the first to refer to the *First Americans*.

that have *a technological coincidence*, but when analyzed correctly, it is simply a legacy toolkit. The American projectile point is unique in World prehistory, which has caused more problems rather than solution in archaeology.

The discipline is full of papers arguing diffusion and independent inventions of stone toolmaking. And, perhaps there are specific tools that are not found elsewhere, but the major problem is the failure of archaeologists to recognize the mechanics and functions of all tools, especially those placed in special categories by archaeologists (Barton 1990). Case in *point* is the mess caused by typologists for the American projectile point…no point type can exist prior to the lanceolate Clovis point?

The problem with classification is not recent, as McGuire (1896) comments:

> *The various ancient remains of man throughout the world have been so divided and subdivided by archaeologists as to present great difficulties when we attempt to study them chronologically. Is there sufficient evidence to sustain any such mechanical difference among the races of the world? By the majority it is contended there is an abundance of such evidence; the writer (McGuire) contends the contrary.*

A lithic technology continuum is a time-depended transition of human's knowledge of toolmaking. Archaeologists often used the term *terminal* to refer to the ending of various archaeological cultures. Of course various technologies disappear; best case example is Clovis. However, except for the Clovis point, Clovis toolmaking techniques continue into the so-called Archaic Period. Change is simply a gradualism in technology. It is a modification, discontinuance, or addition of attributes to a specific tool industry. And, change can be short-term (several generations) or long-term (last for millennia). For a further discussion of this philosophy and approach, see Straus (2011), Clark (2011), or Bar-Yosef and Kuhn (1999) for other opinions or tool dininations in Hranicky (2004). All of which indicate the discovery of prehistoric America is not a recent topic. Finally, Short (1882) comments:

> *May not the beginning be pushed even farther back, and the ancient history of America receive the attention of the historiographer? …the fact that the evidence is of preponderating character that the American continent received its population from the old world.*

Magoffin and Davis (1929) offered an early review of world-wide archaeology in which they were probably the first to publish the Folsom[47] point find after its initial publication. Also, they provide an argument for a *very* early entry time for the First Americans.[48] They comment:

> *Florida has been the happy hunting ground chosen by a number of scientists bent on unearthing America's past. Sellards, a Florida geologist, Lommis of Amherst, Gidley of the Smithsonian, and others have dug into Florida soil and found arrowpoints and human bones buried in a layer of earth which contained the bones of mammoths and mastodons. These giants of the elephant family have been extinct since the Ice Age, it is generally believed. If men shot darts into these creatures, it implies that those men were living at least 20,000 years ago (1929:200).*

Dates for Early Sites

The number of Before Clovis sites is increasing, and they often have outside Clovis era radiocarbon dates. Sites, such as Meadowcroft (PA), Topper (SC), Cactus Hill[49] (VA), Saltville (VA), Wilson-Leonard Rockshelter (TX), Boaz (WV), Cooperton (OK), Grundel (MO), Hot Springs (SD), Le Sena (NE), Miami (MO), Old Crow (Yukon), Petronila Creek (TX), Pendejo Cave (NM), Burham (OK), Hebior (WI), DeLong (NV), Buttermilk Creek Complex (TX), Saskatoon (Sask.), Sloth Hole (FL), El Jobo (Mex.)[50], have one factor working for their validity – Paleoamerican site numbers are increasing. Perhaps one, two, or even 10

---

[47] The association in archaeology of a flaked tool with extinct mammals dating to the 1880s (Russell 1885).
[48] Magoffin and Davis' (1929) publication was the first to refer to the **First Americans**.
[49] Cactus Hill may not be pre-Clovis; the Cactus Hill point occurs with Clovis (Hranicky 2010).
[50] El Jobo points are suggested here as occurring in the eastern middle area of the U.S. The suggested date is approximately 14-16,000 YBP.

sites may be false, 15 or more – the statistical probability starts pointing towards the reality of a Before-Clovis occupation in the U.S. These are not recent observations (see Wright (1892), Krieger (1957), Jennings (1989), MacNeish (1976), Bryan (1965)), just to name several proponents of *Early Man)* in the U.S.

Most archaeological textbooks start American prehistory with Clovis people, their lifeways, and their technology. Even then, most authors readily admit that they do not know where Clovis came from, and the literature is full of erroneous dates for Clovis. With Clovis being the prima facie argument for starting U.S. prehistory, they have one major problem – an argument for a uni- or multi-populations that existed prior to 13,000 YBP. Once again, *everything* has to go through Clovis? No. Multiple world-wide populations made numerous migrations to the U.S.; some survived, others did not survive. In order to present the bipoints into American prehistory, a *new* prehistory must be re-written to account for all the old sites and dates that archaeologists have acquired during the last decade. The archaeological periods covered are shown in Figure 3-1 (Hranicky 2011) which shows a suggested bipoint legacy for the Americas. Somewhere…there is an Old World (Legacy) bipoint waiting to be found in the Americas.

BEFORE CLOVIS (PRE-PROJECTILE POINT)	PALEOINDIAN (SIMPSON, CUMBERLAND) PERIOD	ARCHAIC (DESERT) PERIOD	WOODLAND (MISSISSIPPIAN, PUEBLOAN, ETC PERIOD
50,000+ YBP>>>	PALEOINDIAN ERA		<<<400 YBP
LEGACY AND LEGACY 1 BIPOINTS	LEGACY 1 AND 2 BIPOINTS		LEGACY 3 BIPOINTS

Figure 3-1 – Archaeological Timeframe for Bipoints in North America. Note a pure legacy bipoint would be one that is found in the New World that is made from Old World material.

U.S. Early Chronology

The chronology for the eastern U.S. has a human occupation of at least 50 k YBP, but its acceptance varies among archaeologists. As with most theatrical viewpoints based on limited data, especially dates, the prehistoric scene suggests possibilities, not probabilities. Table 3-1 presents a framework that allows the inclusion of bipoint technology into the North American continent.

These sites and dates are reflecting a trend in archaeology that starts presenting a picture of American prehistory that confirms transatlantic migrations. If these eastern dates represent early European/African occupations, then the failed colonization hypothesis is the only answer. Failed colonization argues that these populations were on the Atlantic seaboard, but died out before establishing a genetic human linage. The Pacific coast has an Asiatic orientation which remains to be investigated and reported. Genetic evidence supports the western source for early populations.

Table 3-1 – Various Early Sites and Dates.				
Site	Location	Date	Source	Comment
Topper	South Carolina	50 k YBP	Goodyear (2005)	Deep artifacts, blades
Cinmar Bipoint	Virginia	25 k YBP	Lowery (2008)	C-14 date
Meadowcroft	Pennsylvania	16 k YBP	Adovasio, et al. (1975)	C-14 date
Miles Point	Maryland	16 k YBP	Lowery (2009)	OSL date
Jefferson Island	Maryland	13+ k YBP	Lowery, et al. 2010)	Paleosol date
Arkfeld	Virginia	25,000+ YBP	Hranicky (2016)	Limestone tools
Cactus Hill[51]	Virginia	16 k RCY	McAvoy (1997)	C-14 date
Saltville	Virginia	14.5 k YBP	McDonald (2000)	C-14 dates
Higgins	Virginia	None	Hranicky and Higgins (2018)	Shallow site, Pleistocene tools
Phil Sratton	Kentucky	14.500-	McNutt, et al.	OSL loess date

---

[51] For an overview of the Cactus Hill and Saltville sites in Virginia, see Hranicky (2010).

(Cumberland)		15,000 k YBP	(2010), Gramly 2012)	
Page-Ladson	Florida	12.6 k YBP	Dunbar, et al. (1988)	C-14, bone engraving
Container Corporation	Florida	26-28 k YBP	Purdy (1981)	Thermoluminescence date
Channel Islands	California	14 k YBP	Hill (2011)	C-14, boat needed [52]
Millard Creek	Canada	17 k YBP	Rutherford, et al. (1981)	
Paisley Cave	Oregon	14 k YBP	Jenkins (2011)	DNA/C-14
On Your Knees Cave	Alaska	13.6 k YBP	U.S. Forest Service Website (2012)	Bipoint
Hot Springs	South Dakota	21-26 k YBP	Agenbroad (1989)	Altered bones
Pendejo Cave	New Mexico	30 k YBP	MacNeish and Libby (2003)	Flake tools
Friedkin (Buttermilk Creek)	Texas	13.2-15.5 k BYP	Waters, et al. (2011) and Waters (2012)	OSL date; flake tools
Little Salt Spring	Florida	13-14 k YBP	Zarikian, et al, (2005)	Underwater sample
Vero	Florida	Pleistocene	Sellards (1916)	Fossil human skull
Gault[53]	Texas	14.500 YBP	Collins (2012)	OSL on a floor
Tule Springs	Nevada	23-28 k YBP	Harrington and Simpson (1961)	C-14 date with megafauna
Marion County Bipoint	Florida	16,400 YBP	Hranicky (2012)	Raman laser date
Old Crow	Yukon, Canada	36-27,000 YBP	Adovaso and Pedler (2016)	Biface and bones
U.S. Megafauna Kill Sites				
Cooperton	Oklahoma	15-19,000 YBP	Anderson (1984)	Modified bone
Burnham	Oklahoma	34,000 YBP	Wyckoff, et al. (2004)	Modified bone
Skeleton Evidence (Discounted ? But not Forgotten)				
Del Mar	California	48,000 YBP (+/- 25%)	Bada, et al. (1974)	Amino Acid technique
Midland	Texas	10,000+ YBP	Wendorf, et al. (1955)	Disputed analysis

Scientifically but not conclusively, there are over a dozen megafauna kill sites that date 20,000 to 30,000 YBP in the U.S. For example, the Cooperton mammoth kill in Oklahoma (15-19,000 YBP), Burnham Site in Oklahoma (34,000 YBP), Miami mastodon kill site (34,000 YBP), Grundel mastodon kill in Missouri (25,100 YBP), Ground Sloth kill near a Cleveland Wetland in Ohio (13,000 YBP), Old Crow in the Yukon (25,000 YBP), China Lake in California (14,000 YBP), and the Frye site in Illinois (35,000 BP) are examples which have suggestive human presence (Holen 2012). The human evidence of at least a 50,000-year occupation in the Americas is beginning to become an acceptable philosophy in American archaeology. Table 3-2 shows a sample of early American skeletons.

---

[52] See Pacific coastal seacraft in Des Lauries (2005).
[53] Thanks to Michael Collins, the Gault paleosite now belongs to the Archaeological Conservancy. Current excavation will be completed.

Table 3-2 – Sample of Early American Skeletons	
Mummy in Spirit Cave, Nevada	10,550 TO 10,750 YBP
Arch Lake Woman (Eastern New Mexico)	11,640 TO 11,260 YBP
Kennewick Man (Colorado River, Oregon)	9,415 TO 9,490 YBP
Horn Shelter #2 Skeleton, (Brazos River, Texas)	11,000 YBP

Reference: Owsley, Douglas W. and Sally M. Walker (2012) *Their Skeletons Speak*. Carolrhoda Books, Minneapolis, MN

Early U.S. Bipoint Reporting

In early U. S. archaeology, reports containing bipoints were relatively common, especially for the western states. Examples of reports are: Ellsworth Falls, Maine (Byers 1956), Farmington, California (Tregange 1952), Humbolt Valley, Utah (Campbell 1936), Lake Chapala, Baja California (Arnold 1957), Manix Lake, California (Simpson 1960, Natalkuz Lake, British Columbia (Bordon 1952, Russell Cave, Alabama (Griffin 1974), San Dieguito – Playa, California (Rogers 1929), Wikiup Damsite No. 1, Washington (Cressman 1937), Sandia Cave, New Mexico (Hibben 1941), Odell Lake, Oregon (Cressman 1948), Goldendale, Washington (Warren, et al. 1963), Manis Mastodon, Washington, and Indian Wells, Washington (Butler 1961). These selected sites demonstrate the universality of the bipoint through time and space.

For another recent example, On Your Knees Cave produced an early date for Alaska and … a bipoint (Figure 3-2). This specimen's location is the furthest north on land of a U.S. bipoint. This bipoint technology's origins are suggested as Asia. See West (1969) for examples and data.

Figure 3-2 – Bipoint from On Your Knees Cave in Alaska (U.S. Forest Service).

> There were non-Clovis human populations occupying the Atlantic and Pacific coastal plains during the pre-Paleoindian era (50,000 to 13,000 YBP). They were basically littoral and neritic maritime people who lived on the then exposed continental shelf. Inland expeditions were common for additional resources.

Early Eastern U.S. Historical Framework

The prehistory of the Atlantic seaboard is complicated and, at best, sketchy. Few Pleistocene dates occur, but those that exist are beginning to suggest a human occupation of 50,000 or more years. This is not a continuous occupation, but a time period that reflects multiple entrances into the eastern U.S. During this time period, most of the Old World tool technology(s) was transferred into the Americas – as a lithic technology continuum. The major problem is identifying these tools archaeologically. Next problem is establishing the chronology(s) for these tools. Figure 3-3 proposes Atlantic/Pacific coast chronologies that are based on artifact discoveries and scientific dates.

> **As a special insert**, around 30k YBP, the bipoint as one tool class was well established in Europe, Asia, and Africa. However, its ancestry probably dates to 100 k YBP in Europe. Once ocean voyages occurred, the social and technological attributes of humans were transferred around the world which includes the New World. Presently, there are four principal sources for lithic microtool technology into the eastern Americas, which are:

- Solutreans (France/Spain)
- Magdalenians (France/Spain)
- Aterians (North Africa)
- Lupembans and Sangoans (Central Africa).

A little known culture in world-wide archaeology is the Lupembans of Central Africa, dating to 30 k YBP. This culture has modern human attributes, such as art, red ocher usage, blades, microtools, etc., but most importantly, high-quality bipoints and similar bifacially-flaked lanceolates (McBrearty 1988 and Braham 2007). It occupied most of central Africa, including the western coast. Assuming they made transatlantic crossings to South America, could they have walked (sailed) from the southern continental shelf, into the southeastern U.S.; thus, another possibility for the source of bipoint technology in the Western Hemisphere. This culture is argued as one possible source for lithic technology in the Americas, especially South America.

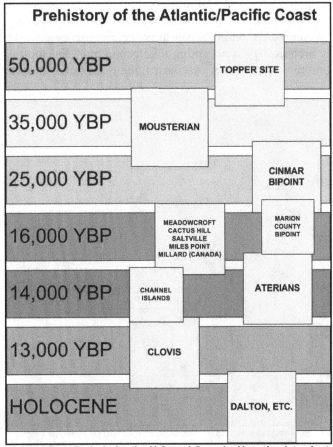

Figure 3-3 – Suggested Chronological Time Periods for the U.S. and Canada. Note the date cluster at 16,000 YBP. For the Atlantic side of the Western Hemisphere, a 50,000 year date is argued for both North and South America.

"In my own view (Shutler 1983:11), probably most significant advancement in the Paleoindian field is that we can now place the minimum time for the first occupation of North America at 20,000 years ago, with some probability of this event having occurred 30,000 years ago, and the possibility that it occurred as long ago as 50,000 years.[54]"

As noted in the above figure, the Topper burin compares favorably with the Mousterian-age burins in Europe; however, what are the attributes needed for this analogy. Of course, one tool does not make a culture complex, but in any archaeological research, there must be a *first artifact*...theories follow in the literature.

---

[54] At the American Anthropological Association meeting held in San Diego, California, Noverber 18-22, 1970, Richard Shutler organized a symposium titled ***Early Man in North America, New Developments: 1960-1970***. Basically, this symposium started the Early Man studies in the U.S.

This site does have a 50K years date. For another example, Peyrony, et al. 1930) set up this classification, and Movius and Judson (1956) provide numerous French burin examples. With backed blades and other tool types, the Clovis toolkit has numerous Old World similar lithic implements as discussed elsewhere in this publication. The burin is often called a flake perforator in U. S. archaeology.

First U.S. Ports of Entry

While the Pleistocene Beringia is the land bridge into North America for most of archaeology, the U.S. ocean coasts are argued here as the principal entry points for early immigration. These ports of entry are:
- Pacific coast – the northwestern area and Alaska (circa. 45,000 YBP)
- Atlantic coast – the middle and southeastern areas (circa. 50,000 YBP).

Basically, the Pacific and Atlantic coasts were ports-of-entry. Their physical remains are largely continental shelf-based (Figure 3-4). Regardless of entry times, any site(s) before Clovis are referred to as PaleoAmerican.

With eastern dates starting at 25-50,000 YBP and western dates going back to 17,000 (probably 25+k) YBP (discussed and referenced herein), a migration theory into the New World as a single event is a non-question in archaeology. In other words, bipoints appear on both coasts prior to 15,000 YBP; what seems to be the problem in American archaeology is accepting this technology? Far too many archaeologists are still projectile point-orientated and missed the *boat*. As shown, there are three sources for blademaking in North America:
- Western Europe
- Eastern Asia
- Northern Africa.

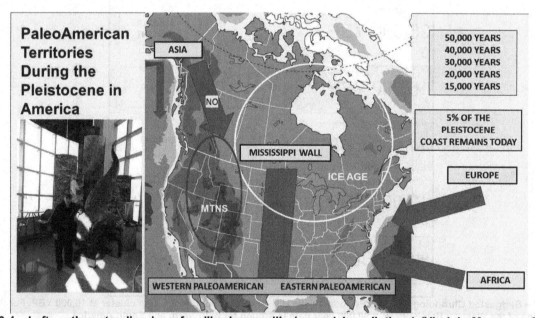

Figure 3-4 - Left: author standing by a fossilized crocodile (crocodylus niloticus) (Virginia Museum of Natural History). Right: map showing a generalized U.S. with its glacial overlay dating 15 to 50,000 years ago. The U.S. is divided by the Mississippian river system – the Mississippi Water Wall (Background Map: United States Geological Survey).

East and West PaleoAmerica

The PaleoAmerican era is now in American archaeology as any time before Clovis. Also, few archaeologists now question the before Younger Dryas geological era human occupation of the Americas. With early radiocarbon dates being found all over North America, the basic question becomes what physical evidence did the early people leave behind? Naturally, the first concern is the lithics as these are best preserved in the "ground." Next comes sites where these lithic clusters which are not assumed to be archaeological sites. All of which leaves the professional community presenting a multitude of mis-classified, subjective opinions, and somewhere in between – reality of what actually happened at some time and place.

Probably the biggest error in analyzing the PaleoAmerican era is using Holocene concepts, methods, and procedures and applying them to Pleistocene archaeology sites and materials. The Holocene is composed of biface and core; whereas, the Pleistocene is mainly blade and core technology. Agreeing on some overlap, these technologies are totally different; thus, analytical methodologies and interpretation must be different, especially when these tools are found in different environments. Behavior in both cases are survival activities-based resource management and exploitations. There is one overlying proposition: lithic technology is one long continuum starting a long time ago in Africa and somehow was carried into the New World. In other words, technology followed hominids who at various times modified it to meet their perceived social needs. Naturally, archaeologists call these modifications types, classes, industries, and so forth. These are placed in time periods, hopefully based on radiocarbon dates which generate historic chronologies. But the question remains: whose chronologies?

With this in mind, can we assume a long-term continuation of lithic technology that is based on Old World ancestry? Surely, no one believes stone tools were invented in the New World, only that they change over time and place. Other than the blade and biface, this publication does not attempt to define them in social contexts, only to say they were here in the Pleistocene.

Most archaeologists argue that the Bering Strait was the "origin" route of humans into the New World via genetics. But, given the PaleoAmerican time period, namely 25+ to 13,000 YBP, were there physiographical barriers? How did humans make it into the eastern part of the U.S.? When viewing the following map starting backwards around 15,000 YBP, the northern part of the continent was covered with glaciation, namely few living creatures. Also, western mountains had mountain glaciers restricting eastern travel (based on Butzer 1971). These emigrants were restricted to along the Pacific coast (Chatters, et al. 2012 and Dixon 1999) As dates indicate, they made it to Monte Verde in South America. Once to the American Southwest, did they turn East? Could they have made it to the eastern part of the U.S. No, they would have had to cross the Mississippi River which was probably five-ten-or even fifteen miles wide and had numerous swamps, marshes, and bayous. An ecological assessment depends on the definition of this river and where a river stops becoming a river and becomes an estuary or a gulf or an inland sea. One creature occupied the region which was the alligator who often grew to 30 feet in length. Try rowing across their environment. Few know that this creature can travel 30 miles per hour and can jump the length of its tail. Avoiding them might be difficult to say the least. The assumption here is the Mississippi River was a liquid wall in many areas nearly 50 miles wide.

Then where did the easterners come from? The answer is Europe and probably Africa (Stanford and Bradly 2012, Tankersley 2002: Hranicky 2013). Naturally, lithic technology accompanied them. It is a simple case of archaeologists finding this evidence and analyzing it. The major problem is few archaeologists are trained in Old World technology and would-be identifiers go unnoticed. We can assume that their tools, travel patterns, and hunting methods were the same as their "home" continents.

These migrational patterns argue that the PaleoAmerican occupation of the U.S. has to be divided into East and West. This hypothesis would present archaeology now with an European-oriented toolset and an Asian-sourced toolset. However, both would be based on blade and core toolmaking methodologies for their respective origins.

Pacific Occupation Area

The U.S. northwest coast has been considered as the entry area for bipoints (Bryan 1968). He called these bipoints a technological tradition which he considered as dating before Clovis. The principal bipoint is the Cascade type (Butler 1961). These bipoints are part of MacNeish's (1959) Cordilleran Tradition which is rarely used today in archaeology. Bryan (1965 and 1978) suggested that the bipoint (willow-leaf-varieties) tradition as analogous with the fluted point tradition…only earlier. The Pacific Northwest, including the area from California to Alaska, is considered a member of the Circum-Pacific coastal land masses (Bryan 1978).

Cascade Point

Hranicky (2010) argued that the Cascade point dates to the before Clovis era. However, using it as a bipoint type name (trans-Cascadian) should be discontinued. The bipoint has been dated on the Pacific coast to at least 17,000 YBP.

One cascade bipoint has its physical human remains; it was found in the Kennewick Man (Owsley and Jantz 2018). It was embedded in the man's hip. The bipoint measures: L = 53.0, W = 20.3, T = 6.7 mm which is serrated and has a biconvex cross section.[55] The specimen is made of a fine grain material possibly basalt. According to Stanford (2018 in: Owsley and Jantz 2018):

> *The limited views provided by the scans gave a general estimate of the projectile's shape and size, and showed that the point had partially serrated edges. These serrations, along with the general shape of the point, led to the conclusion that it was an early type known locally as Cascade. Cascade points were used by groups, including members of the Old Cordilleran Tradition (OCT), from roughly 10,000–5,000 years ago who lived throughout the Northwest Coast region and Cascade Mountain Range from Alaska southward into the northern Great Basin and California. There are three sub-varieties of Cascade projectile points termed Cascade A (dated to 8,000–4,000 RC yr. BP), Cascade B (8,500–6,500 RC yr. BP), and Cascade C (8,000–4,000 RC yr. BP).*

Another bipoint was found at DkSf-2, 7.5 m asl, 0.4 km from mouth of Millard Creek, 3.2 km south of Courtenay, Comox District, Vancouver Island, British Columbia. It has tentatively been dated at 16910 ± 270 (uncorrected). Capes (1964) and Rutherford, Wittenberg, and Wilmeth (1981) contend that the site is contaminated by coal and the date is invalid. The Gwaii Haanas site in British Columbia contains a bipoint which could date 9300 YBP (Magne 2004).

California's Cross Creek site has a possible bipoint date of 11,000 YBP (Jones, et al. 2002). However, this specimen probably dates late in prehistory. The Channel Island off California's coast has bipoints which date 14,000 YBP (Hill 2011).

Figures 3-5 and 3-6 show a California specimen which is typical on the West Coast. This is another example of coastal travel on the Pacific side of North America which has its early entry location(s). The boat has not been recovered archaeologically for before Clovis times (Smith 2011). But it is needed; an example of the boat migration was found via artifacts on the Channel Island off California's coast (Hill 2011). The California coast has remained relatively stable from prehistoric times (Broughton 1999); thus, archaeological maritime studies are still possible (as in Torben, et al. 2001). However, there is an extensive continental shelf which has 1000s of sites.

Figure 3-5 - Cascade Point (Perino 1985)

---

[55] Because of its being serrated, Stanford suggests the point is a Haskett type. Also, both ends are broken; thus, the point's type remains to be determined. If it is this type, the point's date is not accurate.

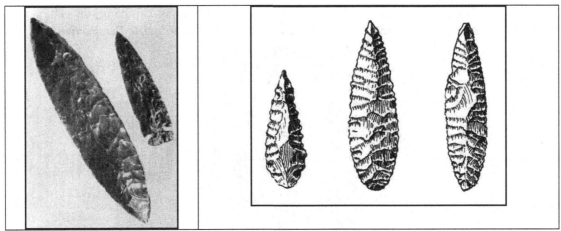

Figure 3-6 – Various Cascade Bipoints

Lerma Point

Lerma lanceolate point was named by Richard S. MacNeish and described by Dee Ann Suhm, Alex D. Krieger, and Edward B. Jelks in 1954 (Figure 3-7). It is an ovoid-shaped lanceolate point. Type dates from 10,000 to 8500 BP and is found all over the southern U.S. Turner and Hester (1985) suggest: ... bipointed outline, usually thin on one end.

Figure 3-7 - Lerma Point
Date: 10,000 BP (Hranicky 2018).

Note: Resharpening, drawing by Floyd Painter.

Alaska's Paleo-Doorways

Most of the Yukon's interior remained ice-free during most LCM ice advances during the Late Pleistocene. Thus, the doorway to the American Plains was unlocked for early immigrants from Asia. While dates for this occupation vary, Harrington, et al. (1975) argues a 27,000 YBP date, which again places humans in the Americas at an early date. Based on various authors, the date assigned here to Alaska is 45,000 BP (based on Pitulko, Pavlova, and Nikolskiy 2015). While the Old Crow site has numerous archaeological opinions, it is the principal site for the Beringia gateway.

The human association with mammoths and other megafauna was confirmed at Locality 80 at the Old Crow site. A flesher was found with a mammoth; thus, adequate clothing is suggested for these immigrants who probably had been living in the area for thousands of years (see Irving and Harrington 1973).

The bipoint has been reported in Alaska (Giddings 1963). It was found with projectile points, but the date has not been established for it. MacNeish (1963) argues the bipoint before lanceolate points in the Yukon.

Walking from Alaska along the Pacific coast to Washington state was difficult, if not impossible because of the steep coast line. Boat travel or inland travel was needed for this coastal area.

U.S. Pacific Coast Continental Shelf

While the eastern continental shelf is the focus because of the Cinmar bipoint, the Pacific coast also has an extensive continental shelf which contains human occupational materials. For the present, only the above water-level islands have been investigated. Figure 3-8 shows the area from Washington to California for principal (as possible) cultural resources. Circum-Pacific migrations were as common as those on the East

Coast. And, they probably date to 50,000 YBP. For an overview of bipoints on the northwest Pacific coast, see Bryan (1965), read his (1978) *Early Man in America From a Circum-Pacific Perspective*.

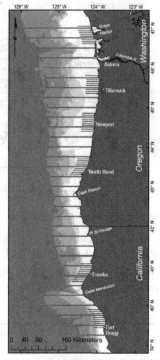

Figure 3-8 – Pacific Coast Continental Shelf (USGS Map) – Washington, Oregon, and California.

U.S. Atlantic Occupation Area

The American Atlantic coastal plain has produced numerous submerged bipoints. Comparative specimens from the rest of the U.S. are included.[56] There is evidence that the bipointmakers' occupation occurred at least 24,000 YBP on the continental shelf off the coast of Virginia (Stanford 2011 and Stanford and Bradley 2012). This publication suggests 35,000 years for the eastern bipoint, as discussed below. However, the early bipoint technology is found along the entire Atlantic coast. Figure 3-9 shows the area under discussion. One major problem is that the actual habitation area is now under sea-water which, of course, inhibits archaeological investigations. Bipoints are found on the piedmont; but their frequency is lower than the coastal area. Inland resource exploitation should be assumed for a coastal occupation; thus, their presence is expected. For an example, Virginia's Cinmar bipoint was made from banded rhyolite from South Mountain in Pennsylvania (Stanford 2011). This material suggests that once the Europeans/Africans made landfall and tools were becoming expended, they started exploring inland in search of preferred stones.

---

[56] Early Before Clovis dates also occur on the Pacific coast.

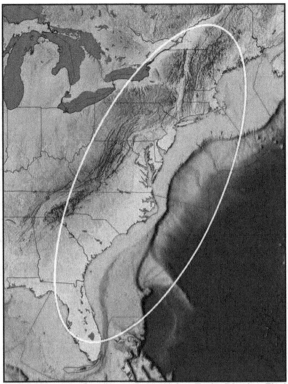

Figure 3-9 – U.S. Atlantic Coast Plain Showing Continental Shelf for Early Bipoint Finds (Map: United States Geological Survey).

Sea-level varied with climate during the Pleistocene. The water level along coasts has several factors. It starts from land and shore, epicontinental sea-level, and finally sea level of the ocean. Below the water is the shore, continental shelf, end of the shelf, and ocean basin. All these factors affect archaeological research and interpretation, including locating sites. The shelf, then and now, was subject to constant tidal and wave actions which caused erosions which erased numerous sites. Finding what is left is almost impossible in archaeology; however, accidental discoveries are found. The shelf, of course, is the occupation area in prehistory. As such, the sea is an ever ending condition of storms, ground-swell and depilation of the shelf, is always changing. The surface of the ocean is like an ever-moving horizontal scraper which ceaselessly cuts, gnaws, and erodes the shelf. With all said, early cultural artifacts still survive.

The Atlantic coastal area has numerous complete bipoints which have Solutrean bipoint attributes, such as blade manufacturing, diagonal- or parallel-flaked scars, excurvate blade edges, thinness (<10 mm), flat ventral faces, curved interior length shapes, striking platform remnant, clipped-base (straight), and edge-to-edge flaking (Hranicky 2003 and 2011). The average American BMM bipoint has most, but not all, of these attributes. There are numerous world-wide varieties for bipoints; shape varies, but the dual, V-shaped, pointed ends persist and are referred to in the literature as Solutrean; thus, it's popular identification and name. These early bipoints have a high frequency in the Middle Atlantic area but, as suggested, they are found from Maine to Florida. However, most bipoints escape both a date and culture origin.

Migration along the North Atlantic Ice

The northern migration route as proposed by Bradley and Stanford (2004 and 2012) is an extension of Iberian high sea fishing. Because of the change in paleogeography due to glacial isostasies, the routes and actual landing location will probably never be known; fortunately, there are Mesolithic sites that are preserved in Europe. The U.S. coast-lines have undergone long-term submergence and accumulation of marine sediments and eradications. For both continents, coastal areas have suffered extensive modification over time.

The ancient technology that coastal people used is basically the same as the pre-metal Eskimos. By sailing along the ice frozen north, they had water and could kill sea mammals for food and replacement clothing and making necessary boat repairs with skins. One of the better ethnographic sources for the life of

Eskimos is the story told by Frank Andrew (Miisaq) published by the Anchorage Museum Association under Frank's (2008) name. It provides the daily life of the Yup'ik Eskimo in the Yukon-Kuskokwin delta, Alaska (Birket-Smith 1947).

U.S. Middle Atlantic Maritime Occupation

At present, the U. S. Middle Atlantic area appears to be the principal occupation by people that made cross-Atlantic migrations starting around 50 k YBP. This landing was a coastal adaptation in the New World by coastal Old World people who practiced a specific maritime lifestyle. By examining this practice in the Old World, a New World pattern can be determined. Or, what was the Pleistocene biography for the newly acquired environment; survival is assumed based on their homeland coastal adaptation.

Moss (2011) provides the Pacific coastal occupations model for consideration. Early U.S. occupation is first on the coast from which people move inland to exploit natural resources. What was the adaptive mechanism(s) for these two biographies? Table 3-3 provides an overview. Other Eskimo maritime studies are Bandi (1969), Dumond (1975), Cassell (1988), Collins (1947), and Yesner (1981).

One of the early Eskimo studies with excellent ethnography is Magoffin and Davis (1929: 283-298). In addition to numerous cultural attributes, they describe and illustrate living conditions, namely a whale bone house structure. The architecture of the dwelling is related to the animal oil lamp which is warming, cooking, drying clothes and other social functions. However, its most important function is melting ice for drinking water.

Table 3-3 - Lateral Maritime Atlantic Coast Occupation		
Culture Pattern	Technology	Type
Coastal Fishing/General Foraging Band Organization	Sea Craft Pick up Stone for Tools Organic Tools	Seagoing Boats Bipoints/knives Pointed Implements Tools for Fishing
Inland Hunting/Gathering Band Organization Regional Bands	River Craft Quarry Stone for Tools	Specialized Tools River Boats Tools for Hunting

Plate 8 shows an ethnographic example.

Plate 8 – Camp for Greenland Eskimos

V277203 Eskimos WITH SUMMER TENTS, GREENLAND
(Viewgraph from: Keystone View Company, probably the 1920s)

Greenland Eskimos - 1920s

This is one of the most northerly points where human beings live. It is of course, midsummer. Grass and flowers are found in these low hills in July. That tent is made of sealskins sewed together by the women with needle of bone and sinews of the narwhal for thread. The winter dwelling (igloo) would be a snow house with very thick walls. Those tent poles are considered great treasures, for nothing in the shape of lumber can be had except as the sea may leave a bit of driftwood or the crew of some exploring vessel may bestow a bit of timber as a gift. Evidently these people have friends who come from civilized regions. Notice the clothes proudly worn by that most important man! The women do not often wear petticoats, but are usually arrayed almost exactly like the men. The trousers and shirts are of sealskin with the fur inside. The shirts are often made of deerskin. In order to keep such skins from drying hard and unmanageable these women chew and suck them all over the inside, removing all the adherent fiber and leaving them soft and pliable.

That youngster at the left wore not a scarp of clothing of any sort until he was two years old, but was fitted snugly into a furry pocket inside the back of his mother's shirt, between her shoulders.

Ducks' eggs are favorite summer luxuries here in the way of food. Walrus meat and the blubber of seals and whales (raw) are the main diet for cold weather.

Those yellowish and white dogs are indispensable members of the family; they draw the master's sledge in winter and haul heavy carcasses of seal and walrus home for food. One meal in two days keeps them in condition.

Comparative West Coast example:

A family of Weiser Shoshone Indians.
Oregon Historical Society photo

Atlantic Coast Artifact Examples

From this publication's perspective, looting activities, such as artifact mining going on weekly in Atlantic costal states and river/ocean relic diving[57] was wide-spread in Florida, all of which are overwhelming archaeological investigations and prevent scientific data recovery from sites. Archaeology is losing valuable prehistoric data, resources, and sites. Unfortunately for Before-Clovis studies, some of these nonarchaeological activities involve early inhabitants of the Southeast and, with little prehistoric archaeological fieldwork being performed, namely site excavations in Virginia and Florida, we are losing ground to relic collectors affinity for looting.

The archaeology profession as a whole seems unwilling to take on its site loss/destruction problem and, furthermore, many archaeologists are not convinced that a Before-Clovis occupation existed anyway. Regardless of the circumstances surrounding the recovery of the prehistoric artifacts, Figure 3-10 shows two blade artifacts that provide a dual technology that is the basis for this publication. Both are in flint and found in close underwater association in the Santa Fe River in Northern Florida. Noteworthy, this is not archaeology; the inference is based on the author's (nonparticipative) assessment of the circumstances among Florida collectors. Both tool types (and industry) can be replicated in Virginia and are argued as having an Aterian legacy (Hranicky 2007). If the legacy and/or importation of a technology are confirmed, then the tools must be Before-Clovis artifacts.

Figure 3-10 – Left: a Limande, Blade Implement, Right: Tanged, Blade Implement (Northern Florida). Ventral face on both specimens is flat. They argue for a cross-Atlantic contact.

---

[57] Diving for artifacts in Florida waters without a state permit is now illegal in the state.

Regardless of whether they are bipoints or not, the earlier specimen has lateral marginal wear patterns with microflaking. Certainly, some archaeologists would argue that they are simply bifaces knives or preforms that were going to be flaked into an established tool type. However, the older specimen does have a *work history*.

There are still archaeologists, if they read this far, who do not accept cross-ocean contacts. Africa has a Before Clovis technology and afterwards involvement in Florida. Far too many tools have U.S. and African counterparts...again arguing that people made it across the Atlantic numerous times in prehistory. The only question that remains is when. Figure 3-11 shows another tool comparison between New and Old World implements. This tool is found in Clovis toolkits. The tool was first named a racloir by de Perthes (1847), who dated them to the Mousterian era.

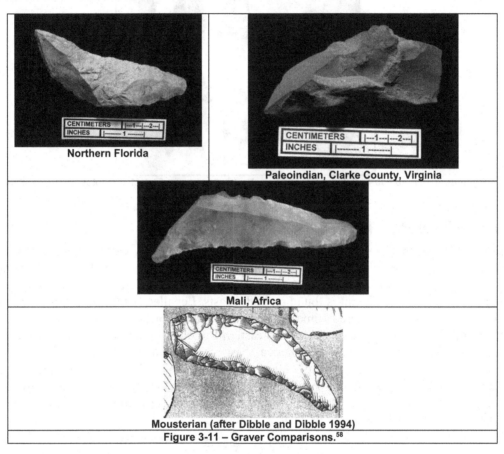

Northern Florida

Paleoindian, Clarke County, Virginia

Mali, Africa

Mousterian (after Dibble and Dibble 1994)

Figure 3-11 – Graver Comparisons.[58]

Bipoints on the U.S. Pacific Coast

The Pacific coast has been practically from day-one in American archaeology the focus for the First Americans emigrants. Numerous dates have considerable antiquity for Before Clovis; thus, the only suggestion is both American coasts were ports-of-entry for these people who would become the American Indians. The Pacific coast is simply another entry point for Old World lithic technology via Asia.

The west coast has the Cascade point type which dates by archaeologists from paleo-times to 5000 YBP (Hranicky 2011). However, sites are being dated to Before Clovis times, such as the Manis site (Gustafson 1979) in Washington state. Otherwise, Figure 3-12 shows a sample of bipoints from five western sites. They are suggested that their legacy is Asia; thus, these specimens argue the world-wide distribution for the bipoint. Unless, one is willing to accept (east-to-west) rapid cross-U.S. diffusion. Pitulko, et al. (2004) and Mochanov and Tedoseeva (1969) suggest 25,000 YBP for humans in the Siberia.

These bipoints have a variety of morphologies; none of which suggest a basic form other than two pointed ends. Bryan (1968) argues that the bipoint is a product of circum-Pacific migrations.

---

[58] Note: See On Your Knees Cave artifacts shown above.

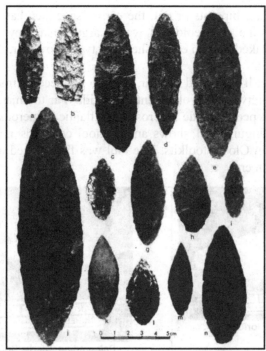

Figure 3-12 – Bipoints dating 10,000 to 8,000 YBP, Milliken, Namu, Lochnore, Five Mile Rapids, and Bear Cove Sites. (From Calson 1983).

South American Bipoints

South America, like North America, has two avenues for approaches by early immigrants: the Pacific and Atlantic oceans. The continent also had extensive continental shelves during the Ice Age. The entry dates for both sides is probably around 50,000 YBP, which is based on the Pedra Furada site, Lapa cave, and the Toca rockshelter in Brazil. And, the bipoint is found on both coasts. Levallee (1995) offers an excellent prehistory of South America. As argued numerous times by the author, the shortest Pleistocene trip across Atlantic to the Western Hemisphere is from western Africa to eastern Brazil. With double sails, the trip can be made in approximately 10 days. And, as with North America, there was two-way traffic on the high seas.

Bryan (1983) was an early proponent of early dates in South America. This publication uses his definition/drawing of an El Jobo bipoint (Figure 3-13). Another site having bipoints dating around 7000 YBP is Telermachay, Junin, Peru. The ovate form occurs in the Toldense complex (Lavallee 1995). Recently, Dillehay (2017) advocates a 14,000-year prehistory in Peru.

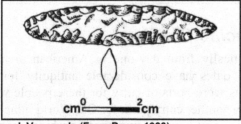

Figure 3-13 – El Jobo Bipoint, Rio Pedregal, Venezuela (From Bryan 1983).

African Routes for the Bipoints

The shortest distance across the Atlantic is from West Africa to East Brazil. Depending on seasonal winds, the trip can be as short as one week; this assumes the dual sail. Once in South America, the immigrants could walk to North America via the continental shelf. Around 30,000 YBP, African lithic technology is well-developed, including the bipoint (Phillipson 2005). With new prehistoric interpretations based on the African bipoint, does this dispute the Solutrean northern trans-Atlantic migrations? The Solutrean argument has always had a time gap problem. Also, multi-migrations vs. one-time migrations are a major consideration for worldwide occupations. See bipoints in Figure 3-14 for Mali, Africa.

Bifacially-Flaked Ovate Bipoint (L =103, W = 34, T = 12 mm, R = 36.35, g = 48)

Blade-made, Round Base Bipoint (L = 92, W = 35, T = 10 mm, R = 26.28, g = 33)

Elongated Bipoint (L = 110, W = 49, T = 13 mm, R = 29.18)

Figure 3-14 – Quartzite Bipoints from Mali, Africa

Note: rounded bases.

Comparative example: The ovate bipoint form is found with bipoints and has a world-wide distribution (author's opinion). Figure 3-15 shows an example from France.

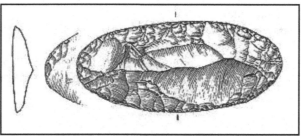

Figure 3-15 – Ovate Bipoint (Elongated Tool) from France (after Miller 1962) Note rounded base.

The distance from Africa to South America is approximately 1300 miles during the late Pleistocene. The above map is based on USGS data. Shaded area indicated a shelf extending up to 200 miles from the continents. A north Atlantic route has a considerable shelf and is generally the preferred route in archaeology. The southern route could represent two-way traffic for early humans. Of course, this implies that Old World populations knew of the New World 50,000+ years ago, but this is considered speculative by most archaeologists. The key to this migration is the bipoint.

Section 4 - North American Bipoint Specimens

This section provides bipoints from all over the U.S., Canada, and Mexico with presumably varying time periods. This section shows varying workmanship, size, materials, and resharpening. Several bipoints have Old World comparisons.

After presenting a world-wide history of the bipoint, samples from North America are presented to show the range of variation for the basic bipoint morphology. Dates for most of these specimens are suggested as late in prehistory, as they do not have solid radiometric chronologies or site contexts. During these times, the bipoint was a relativity common knife. The basic premise is the bipoint was manufactured throughout American prehistory and is found all over the U.S., Canada, and Mexico.

Without metric dates, the source and various times of the bipoint technology remain controversial within archaeology. As noted in a following section, the expended form is rarely reported and illustrated in American archaeology. However, these bipoints represent a lithic technological legacy from the Old World which was first transferred into the U.S. probably 50-20,000 YBP.

The following bipoints represent the state (classification) form (BMM - morphology) of bipoint in the U.S. They are synethic types which are only one tool property in the Indians' toolkit. The lithic bipoint functions as a knife and is found with drills, scrapers, shaves, perforators, projectile points, etc.

A Bipoint Morphology Model (BMM) was argued which includes basic attributes, morphology, and physical properties (antholitic structure). And, classic bipoints are marked with this symbol. The symbol implies a prehistoric legacy to the Old World.

BIPOINT SPECIMEN
BIPOINT MORPHOLOGY MODEL

4-1 Timelines for Late Bipoints

While most classic bipoints occur in the early stages of American prehistory, the Archaic, and Woodland eras in the East have small pointed implements which are still classified as bipoints. For an example, see Plate 9. These specimens are often crudely flaked and are seldom over 50 mm in length. They are bifacially made. However, high-quality bipoints do occur in the Adena, Mississippian, and Hopewell cultures, namely all the mound building people in the East. The basic timeline for bipoints is:

- Blade-made bipoints (Pleistocene)
- Biface-made bipoints (Holocene).

The reason the plate was shown was to illustrate that 80-90% of all bipoints are found in their expended (prehistoric throw-away) form. As a problem and as mentioned, archaeologists rarely recognize the expended form as being a bipoint (Figure 4-1).

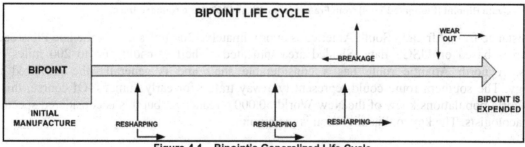

Figure 4-1 – Bipoint's Generalized Life Cycle

Plate 9 – Late Biface Bipoint Forms

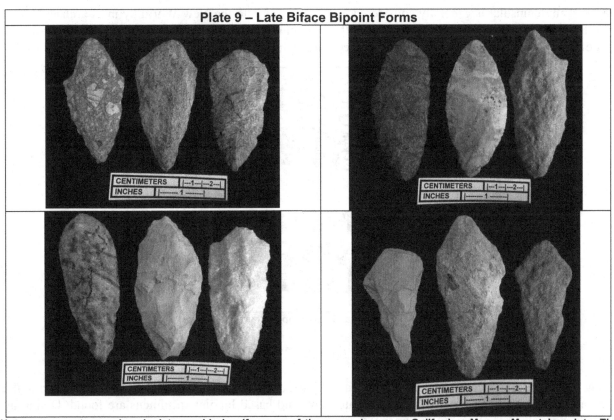

Note: many eastern archaeologists would classify some of these specimens as Guilford or Morrow Mountain points. They easily classify as used bipoint tools.

4-2 Alaska Bipoint Specimen

The Alaskan peninsular is generally considered as the gateway into the New World by most archaeologists. Regardless of the viewpoint, Alaska does have the bipoint (as in Giddings 1963). Figure 4-2-1 shows both faces of an Alaskan bipoint. Of course, the source(s) and entry date(s) remain an archaeological question(s).

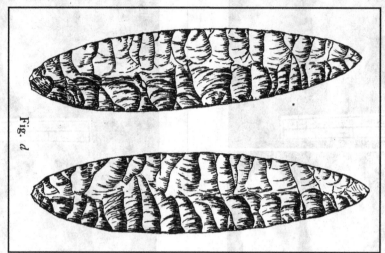

Fig. d

Figure 4-2-1 – Drawing of an Alaska Bipoint (after: Giddings 1963)

4-3 Florida Bipoint Specimens

Florida has an extensive continental shelf and was an ideal environment for people occupying the area in the paleo-era. Today, most of the shelf is under water, but land-based bipoint specimens are found. Diving by relic collectors also has produced specimens.[59]

Florida appears to have some of the oldest tools on the Atlantic coast. A summary of the dating method is presented in Appendix B. Also, see Early Florida Bipoints section.

Florida has an ovate form which is often classified a *simply* as biface or an ovate knife. They are presented here as Before-Clovis bipoints. Figure 4-3-1 shows a form which could have been a bipoint preform. The pointed bit could be the last stage of manufacture. The specimen does present a problem: it is an elongated, semi-pointed shape, and how far off a classic bipoint shape is the researcher willing to accept as being a bipoint; however, it is classified here in the bipoint class. This elongated biface has been reported on numerous paleosites; for one example, Shott (1993) reports them on the Leavitt site in Michigan.

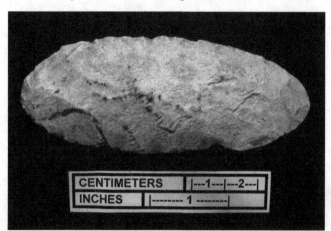

CENTIMETERS |---1---|---2---|
INCHES |-------- 1 --------|

Figure 4-3-1 – Ocala Chert Bipoint, Alachua County, Florida (L = 104, W = 41, T = 9 mm, R = 22.82, E = 2.54, g = 47). Note: this specimen could be a paleo-preform for Clovis; however, lateral retouched margins suggest an elongated knife.

---

[59] Florida law now prohibits diving for artifacts in Florida waters which still occurs; it only prevents getting actual provenances and contextual materials; numerous sites are still available to archaeology.

The small bipoint is relatively common in northern Florida and southern Georgia. Almost exclusively Ocala chert, Coastal Plain chert does occur. The small bipoint around 50 mm is considered here as a late bipoint. Figure 4-3-2 shows an example which has a moderated length-wise curve. The back side has light flaking, and the bulb scar is present. It may have been heat treated. It is not a classic bipoint.

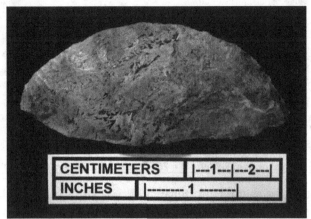

Figure 4-3-2 – Chert, Suwannee County, Florida (L = 77, W = 34, T = 8 mm, R = 18.11, E = 2.26, g = 23). Note straight lateral margin.

Comparative example: Shott (1993) reports a similar form at the Leavitt paleosite in Michigan. He calls this lunate form a Malkin uniface.

Cross-face flaking (outré passé) occurred on American bipoints, but the frequency is low. Figure 4-3-3 shows a bipoint from northern Florida that is made from Ocala chert. While originally having a probable bipoint form, it has a worn bit which makes it a possible expended knife. The author estimates by marginal curves that the original length was approximately 250 mm. It has a flat profile (proximal-to-distal ends) and is extremely thin for its size. It has a LWT ratio at 26.5:1. It has several cross-flake scars suggesting, along with heavy patination, that it dates to the early (pre-) Paleoindian era (primary legacy). It is unusually large which is suggested here as a knife for mega-game. When initially manufactured, it was one of the largest on the East Coast.

Date: Legacy 2.
State: Round end.
Mode: Knife.

L = 145, W = 41, T = 7.5 mm

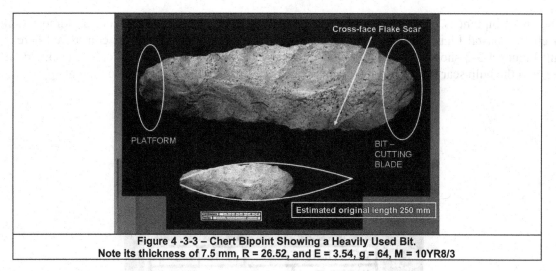

Figure 4 -3-3 – Chert Bipoint Showing a Heavily Used Bit.
Note its thickness of 7.5 mm, R = 26.52, and E = 3.54, g = 64, M = 10YR8/3

While the bit is worn, it still is sharp. Unfortunately, it is a surface find and has no associated cultural materials. As mentioned, bipoint technology is the initial form of the implement and is the manufacturing technique used to make the implement. It has the bipoint form (BMM) properties and, as shown, the original manufacture outline resembles a bipoint.

Figure 4-3-4 shows a Florida specimen that is made from Coastal Plain chert which is rare in early Florida bipoints. It has bold flake scars, good symmetry, and a well-defined medial ridge. Although flaked over, the bulb scar is present indicating a large flake/blade for its initial manufacturing. Also, it has heavy patination on both faces; of course, most archaeologists would simply classify it as a biface. The semi-round base is considered as one form of the bipoint technology. However, it is possibly a simple biface paleo-preform. It is a state bipoint form.

Date: Legacy 2/3.
State: Round base with pointed tip.
Mode: Knife.

Figure 4-3-4 – Bipoint, River-stained, Coastal Plain Chert, Suwannee River Near Live Oak, Florida (L = 113, W = 39, T = 12 mm, R = 4.76, E = 2.90, g = 61, M = 10YR4/6) (Kevin Dowdy Collection). Note: it can be classified as an elongated biface.

The following specimen (Figure 4-3-5) is from Florida which is made from Ocala chert. It has edge retouch and exhibits usage. It was produced by the bifacial cobble/spall reduction method which made it with a biconvex cross section. It is probably a reject by the knapper although one bit margin shows wear.

Figure 4-3-5 – Bipoint, Ocala Chert, Hernando County, Florida (L = 97, W = 40, T = 13 mm, R = 31.52, E = 2.43, g = 59).

Comparative example: Montet-White (1973) discusses Solutrean preforms. The method she describes involves a spall-like piece which was flaked into a bipoint. Figure 4-3-6 shows a Solutrean preform drawing. It has a striking platform (P) remaining and has a flat face, indicating a blade-sourced preform. At present, the bipoint preform has not been published.

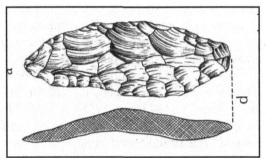

Figure 4-3-6 – Solutrean Preform from Le Maplas, France. Note: microflaking on lower left margin.

This specimen was made from Coastal Plain chert (Figure 4-3-7). It is well made and has a rounded bit

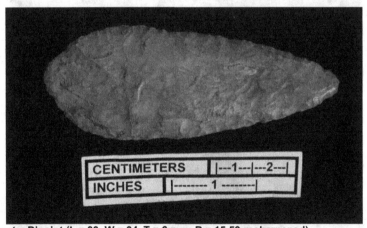

Figure 4-3-7 – Alachua County, Bipoint (L = 88, W = 34, T = 6 mm, R = 15.53-resharpened).

This small specimen was bifacially produced in northern Florida (Figure 4-3-8).

Figure 4-3-8 – Coastal Plain Chert, Biface, 68, Northern Florida (Lx = W = 34, T = 12 mm)

4-4 South Carolina Bipoint Specimens

As presented, the Topper site in South Carolina supports an early eastern date of 50,000 YBP (Goodyear 2005) on the Atlantic coast. The presence of bipoints should be common in South Carolina, but the sample is limited, presently. The cause may be the lack of desired primary stage lithic materials.

Figure 4-4-1 shows a long narrow bipoint which has numerous outré passé flake scars. It has cortex and striking platform remaining which classifies it as a large blade-made bipoint. The patination is heavy on the chert (Hranicky 1992). It possibly represents a primary legacy bipoint for the Southeast. However, it strongly resembles the Agate Basin type as in Roberts (1943 and 1951) or Nebo Hill as Shippee (1948) which are later age point types. The bit is elongated suggesting a secondary stage (post-Clovis) bipoint form. Without context, the date cannot be determined. The straight base is acceptable as a bipoint form. Note remaining cortex on platform.

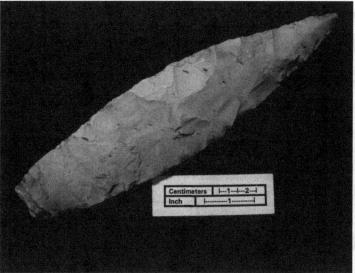

Figure 4-4-1 – Ocala Chert Specimen from Kershaw County, South Carolina (L = 175, W = 42, T = 12 mm, R = 49.99, E = 4.17, g = 80). Note: wide striking platform with remaining cortex (lower left).

Comparative example: Figure 4-4-2 shows a similar specimen which has the same bit shape. It was made using the blade method and has fine flaking. This specimen also has remnant cortex remaining which indicates the hafting end. Again, the straight base and the remaining cortex on platform.

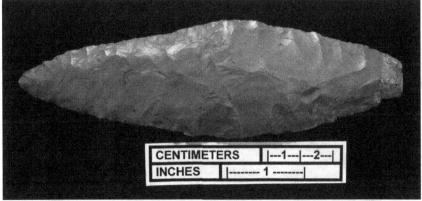

Figure 4-4-2 – Chert, Tennessee (L = 129, W = 39, T = 10 mm, R = 33.08, E = 3.31, M = YR6/2, g = 47).

Figure 4-4-3 shows a specimen from the Big Pine Tree site in South Carolina. It is well made with edge-to-edge micro-flaking. It has a round base which is acceptable as a bipoint form. Flake scars are thin and wide.

BiPOINT SPECIMEN
BIPOINT MORPHOLOGY MODEL

Date: Legacy 3.
State: Round end.
Mode: Knife.

Figure 4-4-3 – Red Modeled Chert, South Carolina (no measurements). It is classified as an elongated bipoint. It has marginal retouch. It also could be classified as an elongated biface.

This specimen was made out of a black flint (Figure 4-4-4). It was found on the Combahee River. It has crystals in the stone.

Figure 4-4-4 – Bipoint (L = 127, W = 35, T = 10 mm, E = 3.628, R = 36.29).

4-5 Georgia Bipoint Specimens

Early Georgia specimens available for any study are rare. The following cache shows the bipoint during the Mississippian era. The Mississippian bipoints show trails and shape of large bipoints, such as those in Neolithic Denmark (as in Callahan and Apel 2011). They also occur in Mesoamerica. The common lithic material is Ocala chert rather than Coastal Plain chert. Figure 4-5-1 shows an ovate, but elongated, well-made Georgia specimen. It is suggested as a prior to Clovis bipoint. It has remaining cortex and has a flat profile.

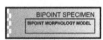

Date: Legacy 1.
State: Pointed ends.
Mode: Knife.

Figure 4-5-1 – Chert, Burke County, Georgia (L= 126, W = 55, T = 12 mm, E = 2.29, R = 27.49) (Jim Hill Collection).

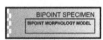

Date: Legacy 2.
State: Pointed ends.
Mode: Knife.

Figure 4-5-2 show a coastal bipoint off the Flint River, Dougherty County, Georgia. Its flake scars were measured with an average scar depth of .001 inch. The resharpening on the lateral margin has a bevel to it with parallel scars. It is an extremely well made specimen from Coastal Plain chert.

Resharpened area and flake scar measurements.

Figure 4-5-2 – Coastal Plain Chert, Flint River, Dougherty County, Georgia. (L = 129, W = 38, T = 10 mm, R = 33.95-resharpened)

Columbia Cache of Georgia

In 1995 in Columbia County, Georgia, a building contractor was digging a foundation for a house; he discovered 11 well-made large flint bipoints. Two were broken, and all were found within a two-square meter area approximately at a depth of one meter. The cache was split between two collectors. Six specimens were available for study that are shown in Figure 4-5-3. This part of the cache shows no evidence of usage. This quality of bipoints is common during the late eastern Woodland era.

The cache dates to the Mississippian era. These specimens (cache) have all the basic Solutrean attributes and have BMM properties. These bipoints are assumed to be ceremonial; as a similar *laurel leaf* was found in Mound E at Moundville, Alabama (Knight 2010) and Smith and Moore (1999) report a Woodland bipoint at the Hooper site in the Cumberland River valley.

The Columbia cache is a high quality set of bipoints that provides a basic identification for ideal bipoint morphology. Structure should be obvious in these implements – they are cutting tools. Function is not obvious, but as will be discussed, their functional usage was intended to be a specific knife for butchering large animals. And most likely, the cache was intended as a ceremonial function. When the cache is viewed synchronically and diachronically with other bipoints found throughout eastern prehistory, a technological continuum has been argued. Most importantly, this cache presents four different bipoint styles and exhibits the following attributes:

- Paper-thin edge-to-edge flaking
- Edge-to-medial axis flaking
- Medial ridge alignment from distal to proximal ends
- Beveling
- Spokeshave
- Multicolor flints (cryptocrystalline)
- V-shape bits and stems
- Perfect margin symmetry
- Length-wide curve
- D-shaped cross section
- L/W*T ratio greater than 25 to 1.

Each bipoint is made from multicolored cryptocrystalline flint. The assumption is one flintknapper, but since each bipoint shows a different set of attributes, this assessment remains speculative. Two bipoints have a length-wise curve to them. The overall morphology and quality suggest one highly skilled flintknapper. They were probably traded into Georgia.

BIPOINT SPECIMEN
BIPOINT MORPHOLOGY MODEL

Date: Legacy 3.
State: Pointed ends.
Mode: Knife.

Columbia Cache of Georgia

CENTIMETERS |---1---|---2---|
INCHES ||-------- 1 --------|

Blade #1 (Both Faces)

CENTIMETERS |---1---|---2---|
INCHES ||-------- 1 --------|

CENTIMETERS |---1---|---2---|
INCHES ||-------- 1 --------|

Blade #2 (Both Faces)

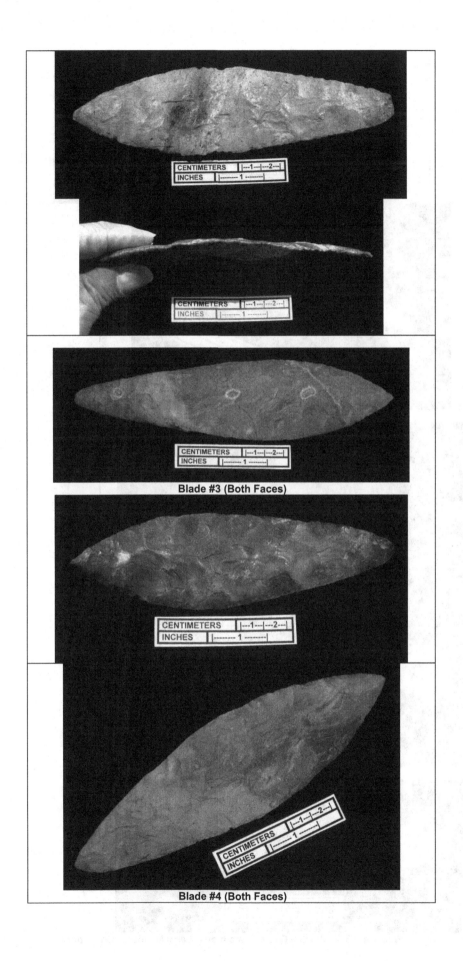

Blade #3 (Both Faces)

Blade #4 (Both Faces)

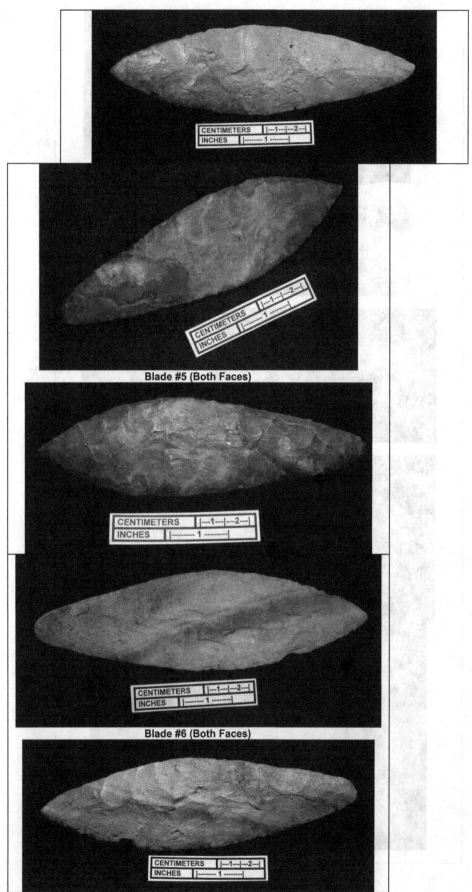

Blade #5 (Both Faces)

Blade #6 (Both Faces)

Figure 4-5-3– Columbia Cache Specimens (Larry Meadows Collection).

The cache's basic metrics are presented in Table 4-5-1. All blades share approximate LWT ratios (average 29.13 to 1), but each has different physical properties. The other five cache blades need to be recorded before performing comparative statistics. However, the sample offers generalized data for large Mississippian bipoints. As blades, they have several similar type names, such as Lerma, unnotched Folsom, Haskett, Adena, Agate Basin, Cascade, Stanfield, Nebo Hill, Nodena, Plano, or Thonotosassa, but there are enough morphological differences among these types and the cache to argue for the basic, standalone bipoint typology(s). The bipoint's LWT ratio is usually greater than 25 to 1 which is the highest among all the point/knife varieties and is the separating criteria for bipoint classification.

Table 4-5-1 - Columbia County, Georgia Cache Metrics *						
Number	Description	Material	Color	Length	Width	Thickness
1	Round base, blade, beveled	Flint	Brown	124.0	53.0	12.0 R = 28.08
2	Straight base, blade	Flint	Tan/dark brown	127.0	52.0	8.0 R = 19.54
3	Narrow base, blade	Flint	Light brown, dark yellow	164.0	47.0	7.0 R = 27.34
4	Bipoint, blade	Flint	Light brown, mixed dark brown	184.0	53.0	10.0 R = 34.72
5	?, blade	Flint	Dark brown	?	48.0	10.0 R = ?
6	Semi-round base, blade, spokeshave	Flint	Dark yellow w/ brown streaks	183.0	53.0	10.0 R = 34.53
Averages				156.4	51.0	9.5

* Five specimens from the cache were not available for study.

Cache blade #6 has one attribute that is reported on Solutrean bipoints, namely, the laurel leaf (bipoint) found at the Le Ruth site in France. Both of these blades contain a spokeshave. Other points/knives have blade spokeshaves, for example, Morrow Mountain points occasionally have this notch, but it may have been a hafting device as opposed to a shaver. Also, Clovis points occasionally have the blade notch; for example, Virginia's McCary Survey point number 22 has a blade notch (McCary 1947). The spokeshave for the before-Archaic era is suggested.

The Columbia bipoint structure occurs elsewhere in the Southeast but, as argued, blade exhaustion makes them difficult to identify. Additionally, unused, pristine examples have not been reported in a dateable archaeological context. In the *ole days* of artifact field collecting before the 1970s, these large specimens were found occasionally and occur in old collections. Today, most fields no longer have any large artifacts, which further skews their interpretation. Since most bipoints are reported from surface *finds*, there is no site-established typology for the bipoint (Hranicky 2007a). And, most collectors still look for *arrowheads* in fields and pass by/over real (important cultural data) artifact information. As such, the Columbia cache is a rare find but, as an isolated find, it provides comparative data for examining other bipoint technology. There is no date for the cache.

4-6 North Carolina Bipoint Specimens

North Carolina bipoints are generally made from shale, flint, slate, or rhyolite. Figure 4-6-1 shows a bipoint that is not well made except from its colorful flint. While a North Carolina find, its material is suggestive of being from outside the state. It is extremely thin and has minor resharpening. It cannot be assigned a date estimate and the bit/stem components are difficult to differentiate. It has marginal invasive retouching.

Date: Legacy 3.
State: Semi-Round end.
Mode: Knife.

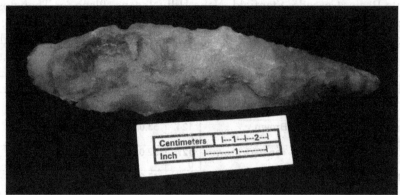

Figure 4-6-1 – Flint, Warren County, North Carolina (L = 140, W = 36, T = 9, R = 34.99, E = 3.89) (Cliff Jackson Collection).

Figures 4-6-2 (a&b) show a Johnson County specimen that was made from a large flake/blade. The striking platform has been removed, and it has an ovate shape. It has minor hinges.

Date: Legacy 2.
State: Round end.
Mode: Knife.

Figure 4-6-2a – Side A, Slate, Johnson County, North Carolina (L = 119, W = 50, T = 8 mm, R = 19.04, E = 2.38). This is an exceptionally well made bipoint.

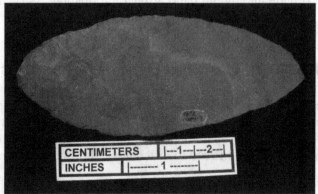

Figure 4-6-2b – Side B, Slate, Flat Site.

Figure 4-6-3 shows a rhyolite bipoint that has an obvious V-shaped bit. The edges of the bit are sharp, but the pointed end is dull/worn. It is not well made. Since it is made from rhyolite, it is assumed to date to the middle Archaic era, but this is speculative.

Date: Legacy 3.
State: Pointed ends.
Mode: Knife.

Figure 4-6-3 – Rhyolite, Warren County, North Carolina (L = 165, W = 49, T = 15 mm, R = 50.51, E = 3.37).

Comparative example: Figure 4-6-4 shows a Virginia specimen with a pronounced bit. It is not well made and is unusually thick. Since it is made from quartzite, it is assumed to date to the late Archaic era, but this is speculative.

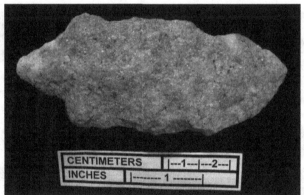

Figure 4-6-4 – Quartzite, Sussex County, Virginia (L = 105, W = 47, T = 16 mm, R = 35.74, E = 2.23).

Figure 4-6-5 shows a bipoint that has minor usage; however, the bit is becoming V-shaped (left in photograph) and is slightly off-center. The chassis has a somewhat pointed end. It is well patinated.

Date: Legacy 1.
State: Pointed ends.
Mode: Knife.

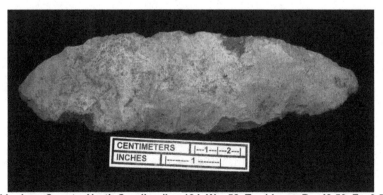

Figure 4-6-5 – Slate, Rockingham County, North Carolina (L = 184, W = 52, T = 14 mm, R = 49.53, E = 3.54).

The bipoint has numerous flaking techniques through history; however, the Middle Atlantic area has crudely soft hammer-flaked bipoints. Figure 4-6-6 shows a long narrow slate specimen.

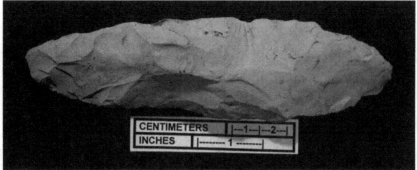

Figure 4-6-6 – Slate, Bipoint, Mt Olive, North Carolina (L = 147, W = 39, T = 14 mm, R = 52.77, E = 3.77, g = 86).

Figure 4-6-7 shows a crudely made specimen that was probably a discard and never used. It is unusually thick and has numerous hinges. The workend is difficult to define, but it appears to be a semi-rounded bit (left). It probably can be classified as a bipoint preform which was discarded after this stage of manufacturing.

BIPOINT SPECIMEN
BIPOINT MORPHOLOGY MODEL

Date: Legacy 3.
State: Semi-Round ends.
Mode: Knife.

Figure 4-6-7 – Slate, Halifax County, North Carolina (L= 189, W = 53, T = 18 mm, R = 64.18, E = 3.57).

Figure 4-6-8 shows a narrow bipoint that when the curved margins are projected, it probably exceeded 200 mm in length. It has the classic Solutrean legacy form. However, it is poorly made as evidenced by numerous stacked hinges on a lateral margin. Bit is the right end in the photograph; it has polishing from usage. This style is often called a Guilford projectile point (as in Coe 1964).

BIPOINT SPECIMEN
BIPOINT MORPHOLOGY MODEL

Date: Legacy 2.
State: Pointed ends.
Mode: Knife.

Figure 4-6-8 – Rhyolite, Stanly County, North Carolina (L = 111, W = 29, T = 10 mm, R = 38.27, E = 3.83).

Figure 4-6-9 shows primary and secondary legacy bipoints; however, they may be classified as tertiary legacy forms. As such, they are not classified. The right specimen is shown as a Guilford in Coe (1964) which mixes the definition of the Guilford type. Most of the tertiary stage bipoints tend to become smaller as they move up the history scale.

Rhyolite
(L = 84, W = 30, T = 9 mm, R = 25.20, E = 2.80, g = 24)

Quartzite (L = 92, W = 27, T = 13 mm, R = 44.29, E = 3.41, g = 31)

Figure 4-6-9 – Bipoints from Randolph County, North Carolina and Mecklenburg County, Virginia.

Comparative example: Coe (1964:40) shows Figure 4-6-10 as a Guilford point which dates to the Middle Archaic Period. This style is often not referred to as a bipoint, but it is a small knife in archaeology. The form is a rounded base bipoint.

Figure 4-6-10 – Guilford Point as defined by Coe (1964) (Approximately L = 63, W = 27 mm).

This specimen is from western North Carolina (Figure 4-6-11). It has remaining cortex, resharpened bit, and a twist from the distal-proximal ends.

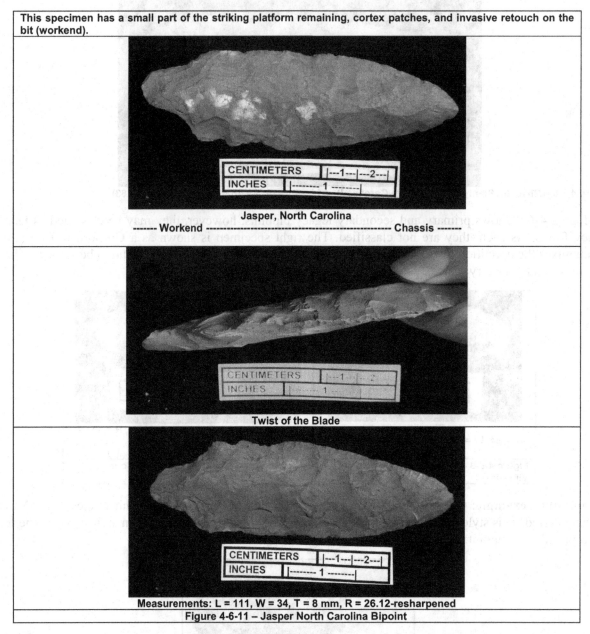

This specimen has a small part of the striking platform remaining, cortex patches, and invasive retouch on the bit (workend).

CENTIMETERS |---1---|---2---|
INCHES |-------- 1 --------|

Jasper, North Carolina

------- Workend -- Chassis -------

CENTIMETERS |---1---|---2---|
INCHES |-------- 1 --------|

Twist of the Blade

CENTIMETERS |---1---|---2---|
INCHES |-------- 1 --------|

Measurements: L = 111, W = 34, T = 8 mm, R = 26.12-resharpened

Figure 4-6-11 – Jasper North Carolina Bipoint

This specimen is a thick jasper bipoint from western North Carolina (Figure 4-6-12). It has a sharp bit (right). It has excellent marginal symmetry and uniform flaking. It is probably a Woodland implement.

CENTIMETERS |---1---|---2---|
INCHES |-------- 1 --------|

Figure 4-6-12 – Bipoint (L = 152, W = 41, T = 12 mm, R = 44.49).

This specimen is made from the same stone as the above bipoint. It was found in Montgomery County (Figure 4-6-13). It is a poorly made bipoint.

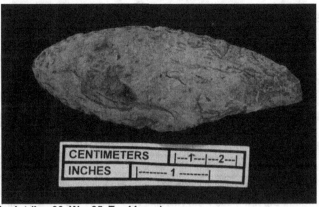

Figure4-6-13) – Resharpened Bipoint (L = 90. W = 35, T = 11 mm).

4-7 Virginia Bipoint Specimens

Virginia has several Legacy 1 and 2 specimens. Numerous inland specimens suggest an early prior to Clovis occupation of Old World people. The majority of Virginia's bipoints are made from slate or rhyolite; few were observed out of flint. See Early Virginia Bipoint Section 7.

Figure 4-7-1 shows a Virginia specimen discussed previously. It is well made and has its striking platform remaining (right). It has bold Solutrean-like flake scars.

BIPOINT SPECIMEN
BIPOINT MORPHOLOGY MODEL

Date: Legacy 1.
State: Pointed and straight ends.
Mode: Knife.

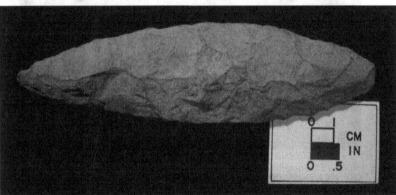

Figure 4-7-1 - Classic Rhyolite Bipoint, Mecklenburg County, Virginia (L = 149, W = 40, T = 13 mm, R = 48.42, E = 3.73, g = 78).

Figure 4-7-2 shows such a specimen (Hranicky 2011). It has light (lateral side bit end) resharpening which maintains the V-shaped bit. It was discussed previously. It shows parallel edge scars.

BIPOINT SPECIMEN
BIPOINT MORPHOLOGY MODEL

Date: Legacy 1.
State: Round and pointed ends.
Mode: Knife.

Figure 4-7-2 – Semi-Expended Virginia Bipoint Made from Rhyolite (L = 111, W = 34, T = 11 mm, R = 35.91, E = 3.26, g = 43). It has edge notches between the blade and chassis.

Figures 4-7-3 and 4-7-4 show specimens that are surface finds and cannot be associated with sites. They are representative of typical Virginia bipoint form and materials. They are inland specimens, probably represent the post-paleo era, and do not show any extensive usage. No dates can be assigned to them other than classifying them as secondary legacy bipoints.

BIPOINT SPECIMEN
BIPOINT MORPHOLOGY MODEL

Dates: Legacy 2.
State: Round and pointed ends.
Mode: Knife.

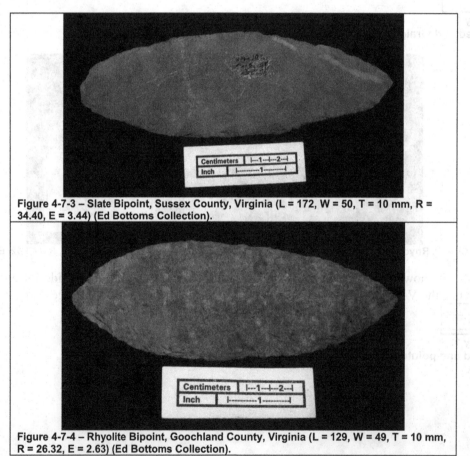

Figure 4-7-3 – Slate Bipoint, Sussex County, Virginia (L = 172, W = 50, T = 10 mm, R = 34.40, E = 3.44) (Ed Bottoms Collection).

Figure 4-7-4 – Rhyolite Bipoint, Goochland County, Virginia (L = 129, W = 49, T = 10 mm, R = 26.32, E = 2.63) (Ed Bottoms Collection).

While Solutrean-like bipoints are a major focus in Virginia, Figure 4-7-5 shows problems most archaeologists have in classifying bipoints, especially the expended forms. This specimen has no evidence of usage and was made using blade technology. It is not the classic bipoint; it illustrates the difficulty in classifying this class of tools. A basic attribute for the bipoint is its striking platform which is present (arrow - right end). The straight base occurs on approximately 10% of bipoint specimens. This form is difficult to argue as a bipoint.

Figure 4-7-5 - Slate Bipoint from Halifax County, Virginia, Arrow shows striking platform remnant. (L = 139, W = 41, T = 13 mm, R = 44.07, E = 3.39, g = 88). Tip (left) was broken in prehistory.

Figure 4-7-6 shows a quartz specimen which has a rounded base. This form is argued as a round-base bipoint. Once again, it would be classified as a Guilford (as in Coe 1964 and Hranicky 2011). The quartz material probably excludes it from being a Guilford point.

BiPOINT SPECIMEN
BIPOINT MORPHOLOGY MODEL

Date: Legacy 3.
State: Round end.
Mode: Knife.

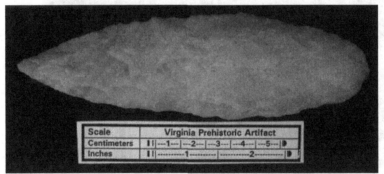

Figure 4-7-6 - Quartz, Halifax County, Virginia (L = 135, W = 41, T = 12 mm, R = 39.51, E = 3.29). It was probably made from a large flake; it has a large flat area and medial ridge is off center.

Figure 4-7-7 shows a quartzite bipoint. Due to the material, it is thicker than most Virginia bipoint specimens. The material may suggest a Late Archaic timeline.

BiPOINT SPECIMEN
BIPOINT MORPHOLOGY MODEL

Date: Legacy 3.
State: Pointed end.
Mode: Knife.

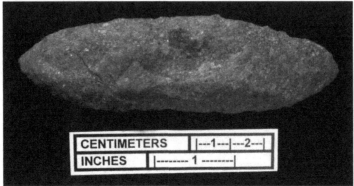

Figure 4-7-7 – Quartzite, Sussex County, Virginia (L = 116, W = 29, T = 12 mm, R = 48.00, E = 4.00, g = 45).

A classic banded rhyolite bipoint is shown in Figure 4-7-8. It was struck off a blade core as it has an end-to-end curve. Also, it has a sharp rounded bit. It has one of the lowest E ratios in this study.

Figure 4-7-8 – Banded Rhyolite, Southampton County, Virginia (L= 92, W = 47, T = 11, R = 21.53, E = 1.96, g = 50). Note: round bit (left).

Figure 4-7-9 shows another rhyolite bipoint. It is poorly made with numerous flake hinges; however, while it is included, it is questionable as a bipoint. It has a wide striking platform. This style specimen is often classified as a Guilford projectile point (as in Coe 1964 and Hranicky 2011). It is classified only as a knife.

Figure 4-7-9 – Slatty Rhyolite, Halifax County, Virginia (L = 132, W = 36, T = 11 mm, R = 40.33, E = 3.67, g 53). It is classified here as a knife only.

14th Street Bipoint – This jasper bipoint was found in 1864 during the construction of the 14th Street bridge between Washington, DC and Virginia (Figure 4-7-10). It was turned over to the newly-formed Smithsonian Institution in Washington, DC. It was used on the SAA's 2018 program for the annual meeting in Washington, DC. It probably dates to the Pleistocene era.

Figure 4-7-10 - 14ᵗʰ Street Bridge Bipoint

More lithic sourcing is needed for the following artifact which indicates that it could match a French Solutrean's source for flint (Figure 4-7-11). Other U.S. bipoints should be found that are made from French flints. In the site report, Howard MacCord remarks (Buchanan and Owen 1981:146):

Of particular interest in the feature (#4) was the finding of two halves of a restoreably laurel leaf blade made from a honey colored (French) flint. This blade is identical to those typical of the Solutrean culture of around 20,000 BC in France and Spain. The blade is 10.54 cm long and 3.35 cm wide with a thickness of 7.5 mm. Its outer surface is patinated with a thick white layer of corrosion products. It had been broken before burial, since two small wedge shaped slivers of the stone are missing, and the two larger pieces were physically separated about 2 feet when found.

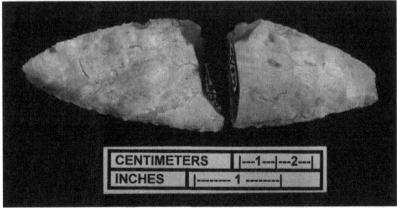

Figure 4-7-11 - Bipoint from the Browning Farm Site, Charles City County, Virginia with recent breakage. The bipoint patination surfaces indicate one face was up during its prehistoric era buried environment or laying on the ground.

The MacCord Bipoint

Howard MacCord (1967) found a resharpened bipoint in the area (44WR5) that was to become the Thunderbird complex (Figure 4-7-12). It was made off a blade with bifacial flaking. It is the one of the longest blade-made implements found to date in Virginia. Judging by its morphology, it dates to the Pleistocene era. It is presently lost; new photograph to be supplied when archaeology finds it…again.

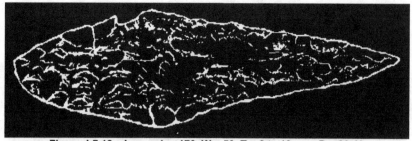

Figure 4-7-12 - Jasper, L = 170, W = 50, T = 6 to 10 mm, R = 20.40

This jasper bipoint was found in Southwest Virginia (anonymous) by a collector in the 1990s (Figure 4-7-13). It is an extremely well-made knife. It has about 3 mm of the striking platform remaining. The knapper told us it was made off a blade. Its best property is cross face flaking. However, one face has major henge fractures. It has microflaked retouching which is of the Pleistocene technique. And, one face has a small area of cortex remaining. It measures: L = 130, W = 35, T = 5, R = 18.51 mm. Of course, its age cannot be determined, but its physical properties argue the PaleoAmerican era.

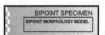

Date: Legacy 2.
State: Pointed ends.
Mode: Knife.

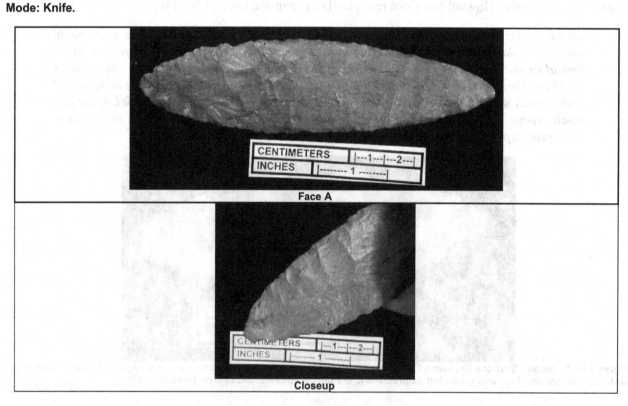

108

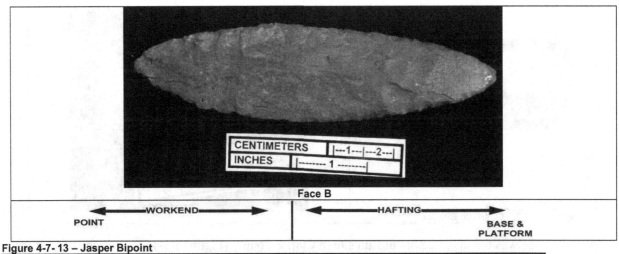

Face B

←——————WORKEND——————→   ←——————HAFTING——————→

POINT   BASE &
                                                         PLATFORM

Figure 4-7- 13 – Jasper Bipoint

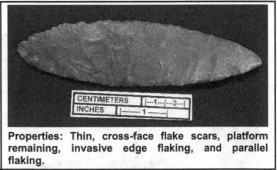

Southwestern Virginia

Jasper, L = 131, W = 34, T = 6, mm, R = 23.12

Properties: Thin, cross-face flake scars, platform remaining, invasive edge flaking, and parallel flaking.

The following bipoint was found on Gwynns Island, Mathews County (Figure 4-7-14).

Figure 4-7-14 - The finder was Mr. Sadler, a waterman, who was deep-water dredging for scallops. Area where found was about 6 miles out from the Haven Bar Buoy near the Southern end of Gwynns Island, Mathews County. The specimen is made from rhyolite.

This heavily re-sharpened specimen was found in Caroline County (Figure 4-7-15). It is made out of quartzite and measures: L = 145, W = 45, T = 10 mm. It was bifacially made by percussion flaking and probably dates to the late Archaic. It was found by Agnes Skinner and is on display in the collections at the Port Royal Museum of American History, Port Royal, Virginia.

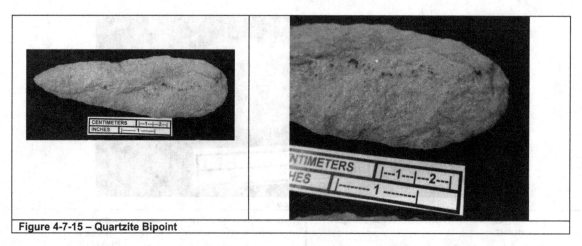

Figure 4-7-15 – Quartzite Bipoint

This specimen was found on the Spout Run site in Clarke County (Figure 4-7-16). It has the bipoint form but was made off a quarry spall.

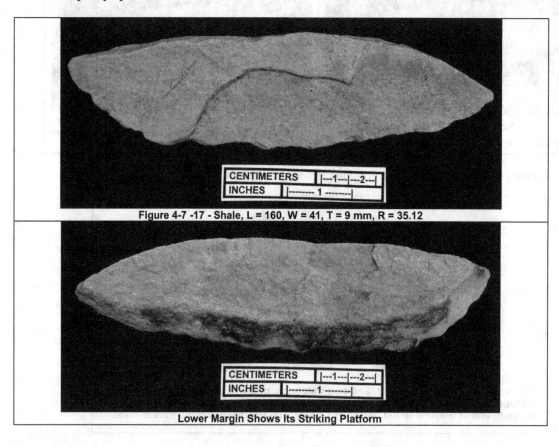

Figure 4-7 -17 - Shale, L = 160, W = 41, T = 9 mm, R = 35.12

Lower Margin Shows Its Striking Platform

110

Arkfeld Site Bipoints

The Arkfeld Site (44FK731) is located on the Opequon Creek which separates Frederick and Clarke Counties in northern Virginia. It is part of a large prehistoric complex named here, called the Opequon Complex, which has occupation areas that are buried 7+ feet below the current pasture level. The primary lithic material is limestone which was quarried near the site, and minor usage of shale and argillite. Presently, the site has been estimated as a complex at 10 acres.

Most importantly, the bipoint (foliate or laurel-leaf) is present (see Figure x). There are numerous bipointed implements in the surface (creek-collected) specimens. The major industry appears to be dual pointed implements (Figures 4-7-18 a&b). They were resharpened by grinding new edges(?). The bipoint form has considerable antiquity and is found worldwide; naturally, it was brought into the Americas (Hranicky 2012a and 2013a). Presently, all recovered bipoints are made from shale or limestone and are made from quarry flaked pieces. The bipoint is considered here as the primary formal tool at the site.

#1 Shale: L = 185, W = 72, T = 16 mm

CENTIMETERS |---1---|---2---|
INCHES |------- 1 -------|

Figure 4-7-18a – Large Bipoint Examples

CENTIMETERS |---1---|---2---|
INCHES |------- 1 -------|

 # 2 Shale: L = 193, W = 48, T = 8 mm, R = 32.17

CENTIMETERS |---1---|---2---|
INCHES |------- 1 -------|

#3 Shale: L = 183, W = 60, T = 14 mm, R = 42.70. Note: rounded bit.

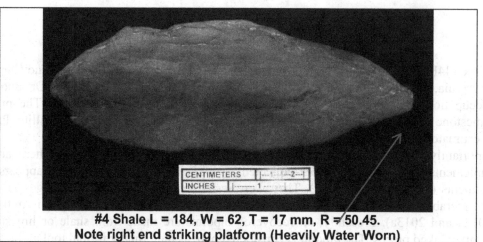

#4 Shale L = 184, W = 62, T = 17 mm, R = 50.45.
Note right end striking platform (Heavily Water Worn)

Figure 4-17-18b – Bipoint Examples
Bipoint (?)

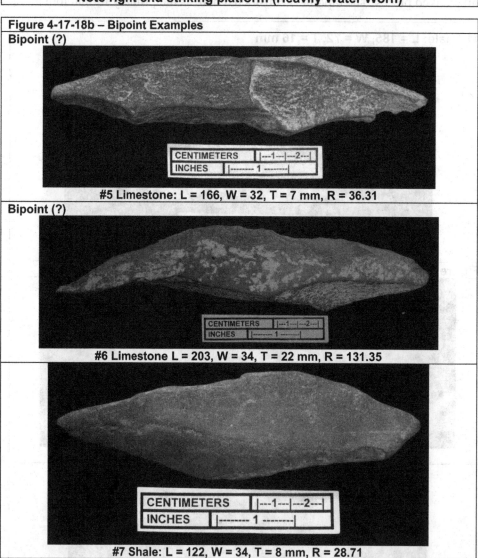

#5 Limestone: L = 166, W = 32, T = 7 mm, R = 36.31

Bipoint (?)

#6 Limestone L = 203, W = 34, T = 22 mm, R = 131.35

#7 Shale: L = 122, W = 34, T = 8 mm, R = 28.71

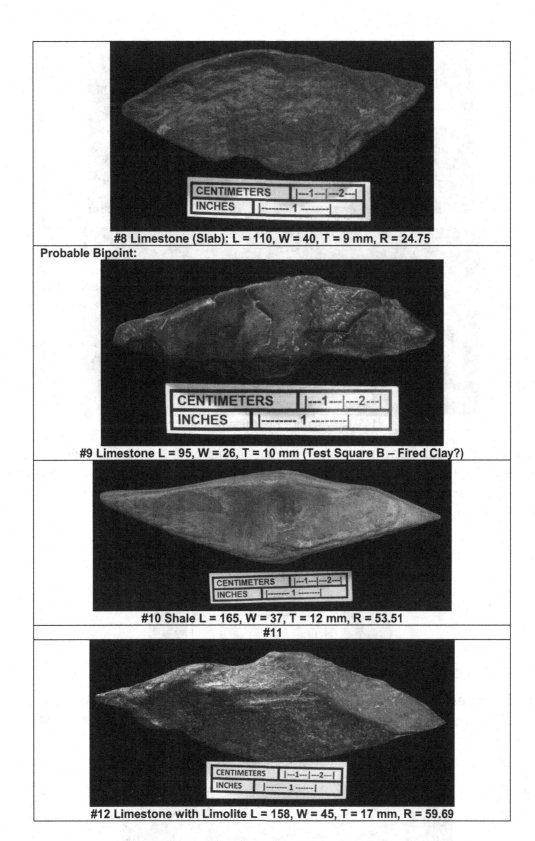

#8 Limestone (Slab): L = 110, W = 40, T = 9 mm, R = 24.75

Probable Bipoint:

#9 Limestone L = 95, W = 26, T = 10 mm (Test Square B – Fired Clay?)

#10 Shale L = 165, W = 37, T = 12 mm, R = 53.51

#11

#12 Limestone with Limolite L = 158, W = 45, T = 17 mm, R = 59.69

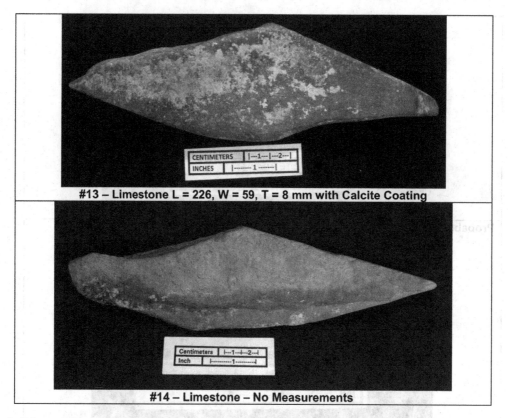

#13 – Limestone L = 226, W = 59, T = 8 mm with Calcite Coating

#14 – Limestone – No Measurements

External Shouldered Bipoint:
A variety in the bipoint class is a bipoint with an external side protrusion (Figure 4-7-19). Numerous tools have this protrusion which may be a form of shouldering.

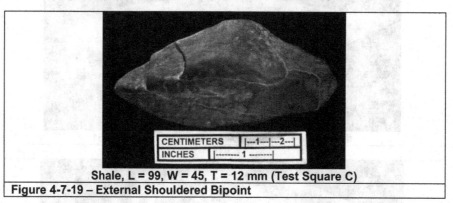

Shale, L = 99, W = 45, T = 12 mm (Test Square C)

Figure 4-7-19 – External Shouldered Bipoint

Internal Shouldered Bipoint:
The form of an internal shouldered bipoint is highly suggestive of Old World origins (Figure 4-7-20). As mentioned, the shouldered form in tool design is common at Arkfeld.

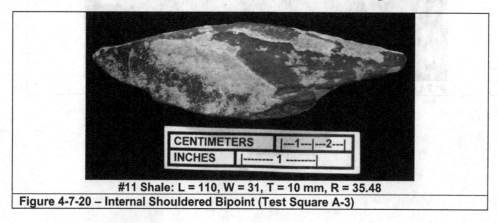

#11 Shale: L = 110, W = 31, T = 10 mm, R = 35.48

Figure 4-7-20 – Internal Shouldered Bipoint (Test Square A-3)

V-Shaped Stem Knife

There are implements that were made as V-shaped knives. Figure 4-7-21 shows a high-quality jasper specimen from Warren County. It has alternating beveled margins which were finely flaked. Since it was a surface find, there is no way presently to date the specimen. The straight base(?) is unusual; it is flaked which makes it sharp. The specimen is well-made and thin; it has minor henge fractures. See Maryland specimens below.

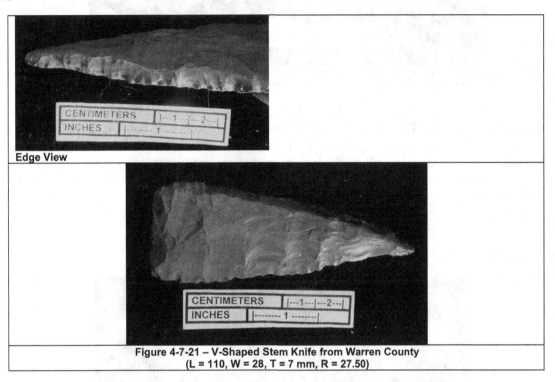

Figure 4-7-21 – V-Shaped Stem Knife from Warren County
(L = 110, W = 28, T = 7 mm, R = 27.50)

4-8 Maryland Bipoint Specimens

Numerous ovate bipoints made from jasper are found in Maryland. These specimens are called un-notched Turkeytail points by professional and amateur archaeologists, which they are not. These bipoints are attributed to the Adena in Maryland.

Maryland has the potential for Before Clovis bipoints. The state occupies the northern side of the Chesapeake Bay which is argued here as being a fresh-water glacier run-off during the Paleoindian era. The eastern shore of Maryland has the highest number of paleosites in the East (Lowery and Stanford 2012).

Figures 4-8-1 and 4-8-2 show bipoint specimens for the eastern shore of Maryland. While their stones do occur in cobble form in eastern Maryland, their size suggests out-crop prehistoric sourcing for the material. Actual travel to quarry areas remains to be proven but is not unexpected. They have Solutrean forms, but do not necessarily date to that age. The following specimen has weak remaining flake scars; it is a very old specimen. It probably represents an early bipoint manufacture in the East. Rather than a blade-made specimen, it shows the classic Solutrean biface reduction flaking method (as defined by Bradley 2008). It is one of the largest bipoints found on the East Coast.

BIPOINT SPECIMEN
BIPOINT MORPHOLOGY MODEL

Date: Legacy 2.
State: Pointed ends.
Mode: Knife.

Figure 4-8-1 – Flint Bipoint from Dorchester County, Maryland (Terry Crannell Collection) (L = 165, W = 47, T = 10 mm, R = 35.10, E = 3.51) Note stem breakage is modern. Specimen is a Legacy 3 bipoint and is exceptionally well made.

The quartzite specimen is a bipoint which was found in a field containing Clovis materials; however, a clear relationship is unproven (Figure 4-8-2 top). It has a tip-to-base curve, but it is crudely made. It has minor lateral bit resharpening suggesting a primary legacy date. The other specimen is flint (Figure 4-32 bottom), has outré passé flaking, is well made, which suggest the early date, but not an original Solutrean bipoint. These specimens show range and variation, and suggested generalized timeframes. Specimens are probably early, namely (pre-) Paleoindian era bipoints.

Dates: Legacy 1.
State: Pointed ends.
Mode: Knife.

Quartzite, Dorchester County, Maryland (Thomas Phillips Collection)
(L = 185, W = 55, T = 15 mm, R = 50.45, E = 3.63)

Flint, Dorchester County Historical Society
(L = 176, W = 58, T = 15 mm, R = 45.51, E = 3.03)
Figure 4-8-2 - Bipoints from the Eastern Shore of Maryland.

As mentioned, the classification of bipoints in archaeology is difficult because most specimens have been used with various modified bits. However, the V-shaped stem is a key for their identification (Figure 4-8-3). One other factor, most bipoints are thin because of their blade manufacture. Would archaeologists be tempted to classify the bit (left) as the stem; perhaps they may be correct? This specimen offers this question:

if not a bipoint, then why do so many points have no edge-wear on the supposed blade? The specimen is heavily patinated for quartzite. It has the Iberian curve to its stem.

Figure 4-8-3 – Quartzite Bipoint, Eastern Shore, Maryland (L = 140, W = 38, T = 11 mm, R = 40.52, E = 3.68) Left shows bit resharpening.

This specimen shows extensive resharpening (Figure 4-8-4). It was made bifacially.

Figure 4-8-4 – Resharpened Argillite Bipoint from Dorchester County (L = 77, W = 35, T = 11 mm).

Comparative example: This bit formation is not common in the eastern U.S. Its function remains to be studied. All the specimens (N=6) that have been observed were made from quartz. The quartz is a Type 2 which is brittle. Figure 4-8-5 shows another example.

Figure 4-8-5 – Brittle Quartz, South Carolina (L = 59, W = 32, T = 12 mm, R = 22.12, E = 1.84, g = 19).

Figure 4-8-6 is indicative of small Maryland bipoints. They are usually well made and from high quality stones. As mentioned, size is probably a functional condition and probably can be equated to time; however, in these respects, bipoints remain problematic artifacts. The expended form is common in the Woodland era, but identification and classification are again a problem in archaeology. The legacy bipoint is still assumed here. The size/shape of the Maryland bipoint compares favorably to European artifacts. Of course, these are not related other than by legacy.

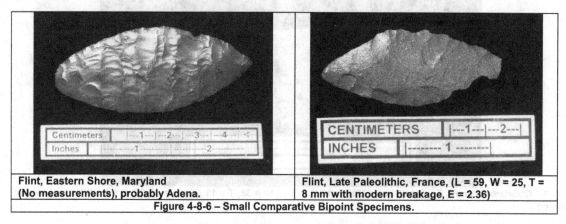

| Flint, Eastern Shore, Maryland (No measurements), probably Adena. | Flint, Late Paleolithic, France, (L = 59, W = 25, T = 8 mm with modern breakage, E = 2.36) |

Figure 4-8-6 – Small Comparative Bipoint Specimens.

Figure 4-8-7 shows resharpened specimen with a sharp bit. It is made from rhyolite and reflects an eastern shore form. The material was probably obtained from the piedmont area of Maryland.

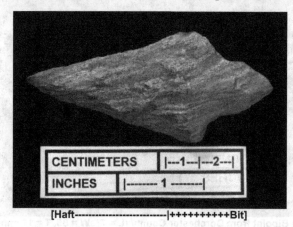

[Haft-------------------------|++++++++++Bit]

Figure 4-8-7 - Rhyolite, Dorchester County, Maryland (L = 81, W = 35, T = 8 mm, R = 18.51, E = 2.31). Bit is on the right end and is acute.

Comparative example: A bipoint with a similar bit is shown in Figure 4-8-8. This bit form is found all over the U.S.; it is poorly identified in the archaeological literature. As shown previously, this form of bit resharpening dates to the Solutrean age. This specimen dates to late prehistory.

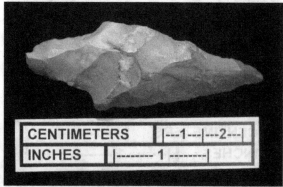

Figure 4-8-8 – Chert, Louisiana (L = 64, W = 23, T = 6 mm, R = 16.69, E = 2.78). Bit is on the left end and has fine retouch.

One interesting specimen in Maryland is a bipoint made from copper. While this specimen may be or may not be considered in the bipoint continuum, it at least reflects the basic form (Figure 4-8-9). Notching: is it on the stem or bit?

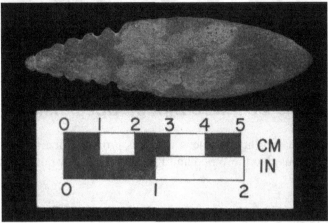

Figure 4-8-9 - Adena Copper Point, Talbot County, Maryland (L = 82, W =27, T = 4 mm, R = 12.14, E = 3.03).

Parson's Island, Maryland – on-going research by the Smithsonian Institution. Publication is forthcoming (Figure 4-8-10). Age: 17,133 +/- 88 14C years or 20,525 +/- 341 cal years BP (Smithsonian, Washington, DC).

Figure 4-8-10.

Smithsonian, Washington, DC

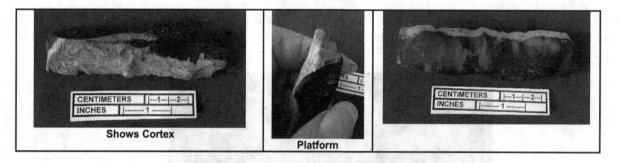

Shows Cortex

Platform

4-9 Delaware Bipoint Specimen

Delaware is under-represented in bipoint specimens which is probably due to under reporting. Figure 4-9-1 shows a bipoint that can be attributed to the Woodland Period. It probably dates to the Adena era.

BIPOINT SPECIMEN
BIPOINT MORPHOLOGY MODEL

Date: Legacy 3.
State: Pointed ends.
Mode: Knife.

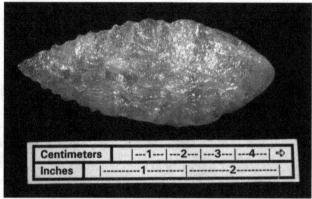

Figure 4-9-1 - Quartz, Oak Grove, Delaware (L = 75, W = 31, T = 8 mm, R = 19.35, E = 2.42) (Brian Richardson Collection).

4-10 Rhode Island Bipoint Specimens

This flint specimen from Rhode Island shows bipoint in this area; this bipoint is often called a Boats Blade (Dincauze 1968) by collectors and archaeologists. It has a specific form of bit resharpening which is basically a V-shaped bit reduction method (Figure 4-10-1). This specimen is well made, extremely thin, and shows excellent flaking. Note its low ratio number.

BIPOINT SPECIMEN
BIPOINT MORPHOLOGY MODEL

Date: Legacy 2.
State: Pointed ends.
Mode: Knife.

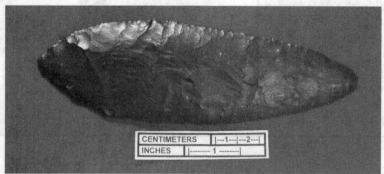

Figure 4-10-1 – Face B, Flint, Providence, Rhode Island (L = 168, W = 49, T = 5 mm, R = 17.14, E = 3.43, M = 10YR2/2, g = 78) Small striking platform remains (right). This specimen is exceptionally well made. Drawing by Michael Frank.

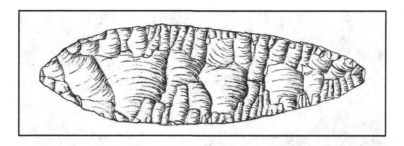

4-11 New Jersey Bipoint Specimens

New Jersey has a rich prehistoric occupation because of its coastal location; however, modernization has reduced its potential for bipoints on sites. There are few bipoints in private collections. For the present, rhyolite appears to be the principal lithic material (Figure 4-11-1). This specimen is heavily patinated.

BIPOINT SPECIMEN
BIPOINT MORPHOLOGY MODEL

Date: Legacy 2.
State: Pointed ends.
Mode: Knife.

Figure 4-11-1 – Rhyolite, New Jersey Coastal Area (L = 105, W = 38, T = 14 mm, R = 38.68, E = 2.76, g = 56).

This New Jersey specimen was found in Salem County, New Jersey. The most interesting property about it is: it is not made from any stone found in New Jersey. Or at least, this was expressed by numerous people at the show. It was also on display at the Eastern States Archaeological Federation's 2017 Annual Meeting in New London, Connecticut. Again, at the 2018 Middle Atlantic Archaeological Conference, most observers suggested it was possibly made from Normanskill flint from the Hudson River valley. As there were numerous opinions on the stone, nothing was conclusive by the author. It needs to be chemically sourced.

The New Jersey bipoint (Figures 4-11-2, 4-11-3, and 4-11-4) has this description: It is a blade-produced dual pointed implement that has one flat unflaked face, a remaining small platform, invasive marginal retouch, and four large flake scars that reached the medial axis. The tip-to-tip profile is flat and has a consistent thickness. It measures: L = 112, W = 36, T = 6 mm, R = 18.67. The surface has spotty, but heavily patinated areas which suggest a lengthy ancestry – before Clovis, or, what is commonly called pre-Clovis – or, namely, its low ratio number.

BIPOINT SPECIMEN
BIPOINT MORPHOLOGY MODEL

Date: Legacy 2.
State: Pointed ends.
Mode: Knife.

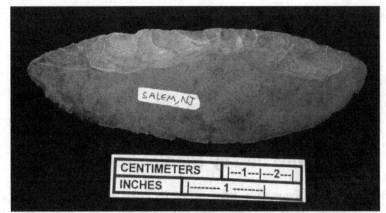

Figure 4-11-2 - Dorsal Face

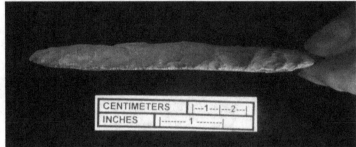

Distal-to-Proximal Side View

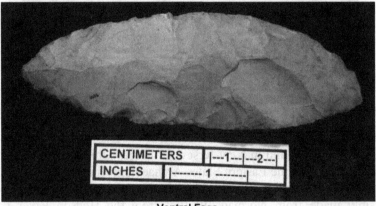

Ventral Face

The platform end (base) is considered here as the chassis (hafting area). The workend starts at mid-point with minor evidence of an indention for the top part of the haft, which was probably wood or bone. However, it could have been a hand-held tool. The work end shows resharpening which resulted in leaving a curved opposite margin. The basal end has small areas of cortex. And, it can be classified as a well-made prehistoric artifact. Figure 5 shows drawings of the flake scars.

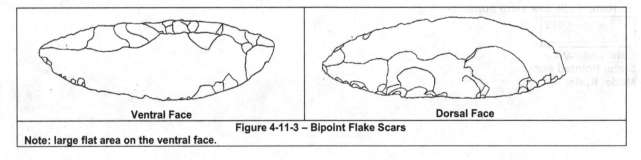

Ventral Face

Dorsal Face

Figure 4-11-3 – Bipoint Flake Scars

Note: large flat area on the ventral face.

Flake scars are thin and wide. One margin has uniform, invasive flaking. This specimen compares favorably with the Virginia specimens shown below. For the Atlantic coastal area, high-quality early bipoints are found (Hranicky 2012). Figure 4-11-4 shows a close-up of flaking of the New Jersey artifact.

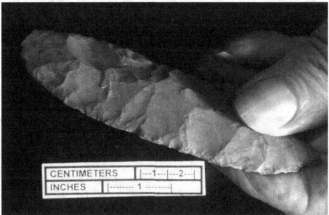

Figure 4-11-4 – Flaking on the New Jersey Specimen

As a surface find any stratigraphic or geologic associations are lost, e.g. context origins to an excavated site. However, its find location can be inferred to derive from the Lower Delaware Valley, yet its earliest origins may relate to a former Atlantic coastal plain.

4-12 New York Bipoint Specimen

This specimen was found near Albany in New York (Figure 4-12-1). It is an unusually thick bipoint which suggests it was made late in prehistory. Flake scars are broad. It has the remains of a medial axes suggesting blade production. The lateral margins are sharp but have no microflaking.

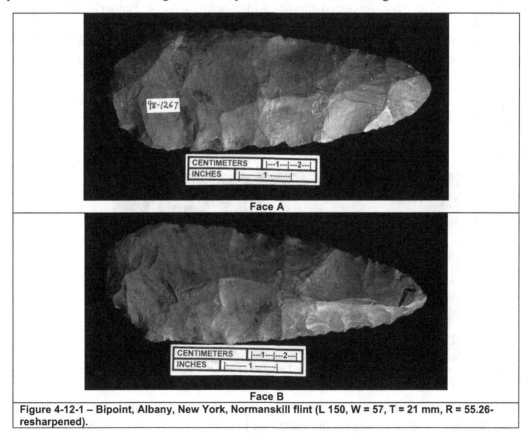

Face A

Face B

Figure 4-12-1 – Bipoint, Albany, New York, Normanskill flint (L 150, W = 57, T = 21 mm, R = 55.26-resharpened).

4-13 Connecticut Bipoint Specimen

The Northeast as an area has reported few bipoints. Figure 4-13-1 shows a narrow specimen that probably dates after the Clovis era. The narrow style may be related to the Lerma point type, but this is too far from the type's source (Mexico) and their homeland (Hranicky 2011). Regardless, it has a rounded base and has basic BMM properties.

BIPOINT SPECIMEN
BIPOINT MORPHOLOGY MODEL

Date: Legacy 1/2.
State: Round and pointed ends.
Mode: Knife.

Figure 4-13-1 – Rhyolite or Hornfels Bipoint, Found in Windham County, Connecticut (L = 111, W = 32, T = 8 mm, R = 27.75, E = 3.47, g = 41). (Northeast corner of Connecticut, which borders Massachusetts and Rhode Island).

4-14 Pennsylvania Bipoint Specimens

Figure 4-14-1 shows a typical blade-produced bipoint which was found in Pennsylvania. The quartzite material suggests that the artifact was made numerous generations from the original entry of the Solutreans; however, this material occurs in the European specimens. It is relatively thick and probably dates to the Woodland era; otherwise, definitely a tertiary legacy artifact. The Northeastern coastline is so heavily modified by urbanization that archaeology will probably never know the extent of the bipoint distribution in that area.

BIPOINT SPECIMEN
BIPOINT MORPHOLOGY MODEL

Date: Legacy 3.
State: Straight and pointed ends.
Mode: Knife.

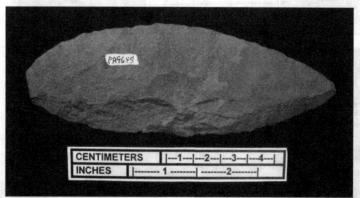

Figure 4-14-1 – A Quartzite Inland Pennsylvania Bipoint. Note: Left end shows the striking platform remnant (L = 126, W = 43, T = 15 mm, R = 43.95, E = 2.93, g = 71).

The primary lithic material is rhyolite; however again, the study sample is small. The later bipoints tend to be smaller and narrower (Figure 4-14-2). This specimen is probably a Ft. Ancient bipoint (as in Griffin

1943 and 1966). The flaking quality is poor on this specimen, and its date is purely subjective. It has numerous hinge fractures.

Date: Legacy 3.
State: Pointed ends.
Mode: Knife.

Figure 4-14-2 – Rhyolite, Lancaster County, Pennsylvania (L = 147, W = 38, T = 9 mm, R = 34.81, E = 3.87, g = 51).

Figure 4-14-3 presents evidence of long-distance bipoint materials. It was found in the 1950s in Clinton County, Pennsylvania. It is made from Ohio Flint Ridge chert which indicates long-range sourcing or origin. It was manufactured using the blade removal method as it has a tip-to-tip curve. The remnant bulb scar is present, but it was lightly flaked over the scar. The specimen shows lateral-end resharpening which is worn smooth. This process argues for the non-pointed end (right) is the bit. The workend tip is no longer acute and has minor polish.

Date: Legacy 3.
State: Pointed ends.
Mode: Knife.

Figure 4-14-3 – Chert, Clinton County (Great Islands), Pennsylvania (L = 118, W = 28, T = 8 mm, R = 33.71, E = 4.21, g = 32). Note resharpening and use-polish is on the right end; left end is the hafting area.

Figure 4-14-4 shows a comparative example for Pennsylvania, which is also a large knife. It suggests hafting notches and has a V-shaped stem. The bit is sharp with lateral retouching flake scars. While rhyolite is a poor indicator of weathered age, there are few flake scars showing on the specimen, except deep scars. Its size suggests a heavy duty function. Its basic shape is an ovate morphology.

Figure 4-14-4 – V-stemmed Knife from Pennsylvania
(L = 156, W = 73, T = 12 mm, R = 25.64, E = 2.14).

While many archaeologists view the mega biface (see Mega Bifaces paragraph) as simply a preform that would be further knapped into a smaller tool, knife, projectile point, scraper, etc., Figure 4-14-5 shows a percussion-flaked bipoint before it became a used knife. While it is certainly not a normal style, it has several features:

- Striking platform remaining on the hafting (?) end
- V-shaped stem
- Irregular bit (workend)
- Distal-to-proximal bipoint bit reduction
- Enlarged workend or reduced handle
- Overall bipoint shape
- Heavy weathering
- Biface reduction flaking method.

Unfortunately, the specimen is a *surface find* in eastern Pennsylvania, but it is argued here as a key to understanding the bipoint class in eastern archaeology. It has an overall bipoint shape, even though the lateral margins have been modified. Its striking platform is still present; and, it argues the continuity of the bipoint method down through prehistory. Unfortunately, there is no way to determine its date, but the suggestion is the Woodland era. It may be a Contact-influenced knife. Note: a similar stemmed specimen is shown in the Ohio section.

126

Figure 4-14-5 – Rhyolite Bipoint, Pennsylvania (L = 185, W = 58, T = 15 mm, R = 47.84, E = 3.20). Note obvious chassis area.

Figure 4-14-6 shows a bipoint from Northumberlnd County, Pennsylvania. It has cross-face flaking and bold, paper thin scars. These bipoints are associated with the Crowfield points in the Northeast (Deller and Ellis 2011). Most of these specimens have a full-face flute on one face; this specimen is not fluted. It has a low ratio number suggesting legacy.

BIPOINT SPECIMEN
BIPOINT MORPHOLOGY MODEL

Date: Legacy 2.
State: Pointed ends.
Mode: Knife.

Figure 4-14-6 – Jasper Bipoint, Northumberland County, Pennsylvania. (L = 117, W = 45, T = 7 mm, R = 18.20)

Flake Scars

This specimen was found along the Susquehanna River near Harrisburg (Figure 4-14-7). It has well defined flake scars and shows minor usage. Stone has faint layering. The upper left margin has light retouching. It has a low ratio number suggesting a legacy.

BIPOINT SPECIMEN
BIPOINT MORPHOLOGY MODEL

Date: Legacy 2.

127

State: Pointed ends.
Mode: Knife.

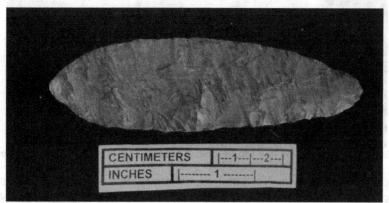

Figure 4-14-7 – Rhyolite Bipoint (L = 103, W = 31, T = 6 mm, R = 19.95).

This specimen (Figure 4-14-8) was found with the above bipoint. They were made from the same Susquehanna rhyolite. It has a low ratio number suggesting a legacy.

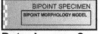

Date: Legacy 2.
State: Pointed ends.
Mode: Knife.

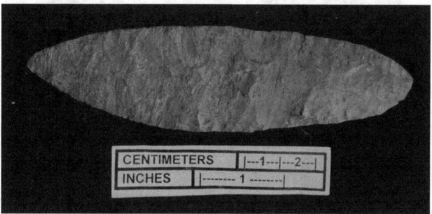

Figure 4-14-8 – Susquehanna Bipoint (L = 114, W = 31, T = 6 mm, R = 22.06).

4-15 West Virginia Bipoint Specimens

Most West Virginia bipoints are reflective of the Ohio River Valley and probably date to the Ft. Ancient era. Figure 4-15-1, shown previously, is an example. As with most expended V-stemmed knives, it is impossible to determine the original form of the implement; thus, the flaking/manufacturing method cannot be determined. Most archaeologists would classify this specimen as a Morrow Mountain projectile point, but bit wear patterns suggest differently.

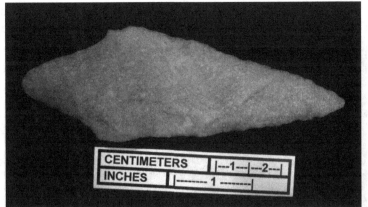

Figure 4-15-1 – Quartzite, Hampshire County, West Virginia. Note its bit is sharp (left end) with wear polish. (L = 117, W = 40, T = 8.5 mm, R = 24.86, E = 2.93, g = 32). This specimen is exceptionally well made.

This specimen was made out of black flint (Figure 4-15-2). It probably is an Adena or Hopewell bipoint. It was found in Monroe County. It has small patches of cortex remaining.

Figure 4-15-2 – Bipoint (108, W = 42, T = 12 mm).

This specimen was found near Charleston (Figure 4-15-3). Its flint is unknown to the author, which suggests that the specimens were transported along the Ohio valley. It is not well made and has oxidation stains suggesting some antiquity.

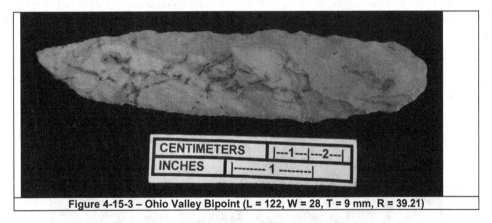

Figure 4-15-3 – Ohio Valley Bipoint (L = 122, W = 28, T = 9 mm, R = 39.21)

4-16 Ohio Bipoint Specimens

While somewhat removed from the Atlantic ocean possible bipoint source, bipoints are numerous in the Ohio valley, especially those that date to the Woodland (Adena to Ft. Ancient). Ohio occupation probably dates 13 k YBP as argued by the Crossing Site and the butchering of the Burning Tree mastodon butchering site (in Dancey 1994). There are no bipoints associated with these sites.

An unusual bipoint was found on the Wabash River in Ohio (Figure 4-16-1). It has a pronounced blade which has micro-edge flaking. The striking platform is present. The E ratio is the highest in the study sample.

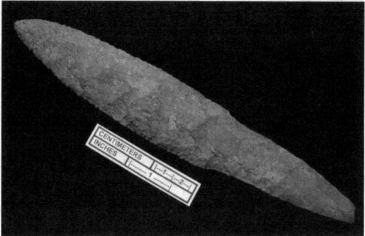

Figure 4-16-1 – Flint, Ohio (L = 227, W = 37, T = 14 mm, R = 85.89, E = 5.97). Bit is the lower part in the photograph. (Terry Burdette Collection).

Comparative resharpening example: The bit on this French specimen shows similar lateral resharpening (Figure 4-16-2). It was made off a blade from a blade core (livres-de-beurre). It is approximately 175 mm in length. As discussed, bit resharpening varies through space and time. There is no inferred date on this specimen.

Once again, lithic technology is a continuum which includes a knowledge base for toolmaking. These and numerous comparative specimens in this publication argue this philosophy.

Figure 4-16-2 – Flint, Pressigny Le Grand, France (after Evans 1867).

Ohio has numerous classic bipoints that have been recovered and occur in private collections; additionally, few have been excavated and reported. Figure 4-16-3 shows a surface-find bipoint made from Flint Ridge stone.

BIPOINT SPECIMEN
BIPOINT MORPHOLOGY MODEL

Date: Legacy 3.
State: Pointed ends.
Mode: Knife.

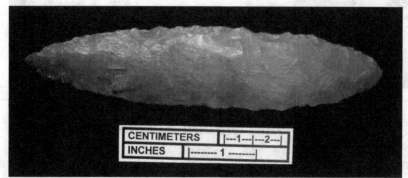

Figure 4-16-3 – Flint, Ohio River, Ohio (L = 137, W = 31, T = 13 mm, R = 57.45, E = 4.42, g = 61).

This specimen is a typical hand-held bipoint (Figure 4-16-4). It has a pronounced platform. It is made from the same stone as the above bipoint.

Figure 4-16-4 – Ohio Bipoint (L = 117, W = 29, T = 11 mm, R = 44.40).

Figure 4-16-5 shows a specimen that was found in a creek in Delaware County, Ohio. It has marginal invasive micro-flaking. It is a thin, flat piece. It has a low ratio number suggesting a legacy.

BIPOINT SPECIMEN
BIPOINT MORPHOLOGY MODEL

Date: Legacy 2.
State: Pointed/round ends.
Mode: Knife.

Figure 4-16-5 – Flint, Delaware County in a creek, Ohio (L = 139, W = 52, T = 10 mm, R = 26.73).

Figure 4-16-6 shows a bipoint that was made off a thick flake. It has edge-to-edge flake scars and a semi-round base. There is minor bit edge flaking which produces sharp margins.

BIPOINT SPECIMEN
BIPOINT MORPHOLOGY MODEL

Date: Legacy 3.
State: Round and pointed end.
Mode: Knife.

Figure 4-16-6 – Flint, Ohio (L = 120. W = 36, T = 12 mm, R = 39.99, E = 3.33, g = 47).

Figure 4-16-7 shows a well-made bipoint that has edge-to-edge flaking. It is exceptionally thin. This specimen was extremely large when initially manufactured.

BIPOINT SPECIMEN
BIPOINT MORPHOLOGY MODEL

Date: Legacy 3.
State: Pointed ends.
Mode: Knife.

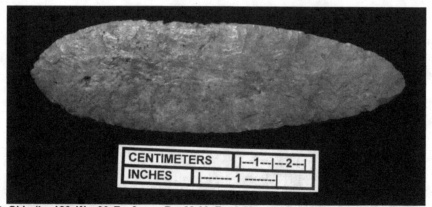

Figure 4-16-7 – Flint, Ohio (L= 126, W = 36, T = 8 mm, R = 28.00, E = 3.50, g = 44). This is an exceptionally well made specimen.

Figure 4-16-8 shows a heavily weathered bipoint that has a small remnant striking platform remaining. The platform indicates the chassis as the bit end has usage (straight edge).

BIPOINT SPECIMEN
BIPOINT MORPHOLOGY MODEL

Date: Legacy 3.
State: Pointed ends.
Mode: Knife.

Figure 4-16-8 – Chert, Ohio L = 111, W = 34, T = 10 mm, R = 32.65, E = 3.26, g = 36). Note: chassis (left) and bit (right) ends.

Cache bipoint find by Warren Moorhead, Siciota County, Ohio (Figure 4-16-9).

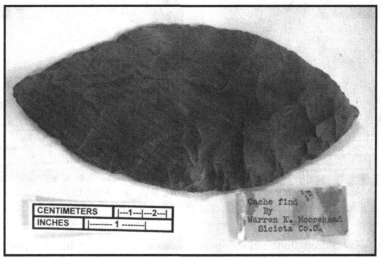

Figure 4-16-9 – Cache Blade

The Turkey-tail point is essentially a notched bipoint. Its manufacture is the same – off a large, predominantly flint flake/blade. It is thin, has a flat length-wise profile, and has excellent symmetry. Figure 4-16-10 shows one in production; it was not completed. Notching was a mistake on this specimen.

> BIPOINT SPECIMEN
> BIPOINT MORPHOLOGY MODEL

Date: Legacy 3.
State: Semi-Round and pointed ends.
Mode: Knife.

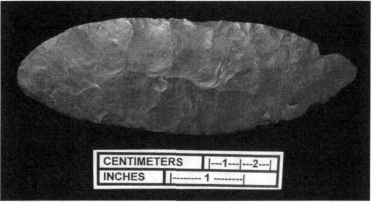

Figure 4-16-10 – Flint, Ohio (L = 124, W = 40, T = 8 mm, R = 24.80, E = 3.10, g = 42). Specimen is well made.

Figure 4-16-11 shows a typical ovate specimen; however, narrow specimens usually occur. While discussed, the ovate bipoint remains to be classified in American prehistory. The elongation ratio is usually below 3:1. There is probably a time consequence for the ovate bipoint.

Comparative example: Figure 4-16-12 shows a similar specimen from Indiana and Ohio which illustrates the Ohio valley form.

| Figure 4-16-11 – Flint, Huron County, Ohio (L = 93, W = 43, T = 8 mm, R = 17.30, E = 2.16, g = 37). | Figure 4-16-12 – Flint, Ovate Bipoint, Indiana (L = 77, W = 36, T = 7 mm, R = 14.97, E = 2.14, g = 22). |

This specimen is a two-colored stone made bipoint (Figure 4-16-13). It has a nicely shaped cutting bit. It was found in Adams County. It was called a Harahay knife.

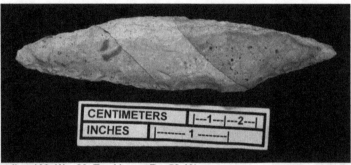

Figure 4-16-13 – Ohio Bipoint (L = 109, W = 23, T = 11 mm, R = 52.13).

The following specimen is also from Ohio (Figure 4-16-14). It is made from Ohio flint and probably has Adena/Hopewell properties. It has a low ratio number suggesting a legacy.

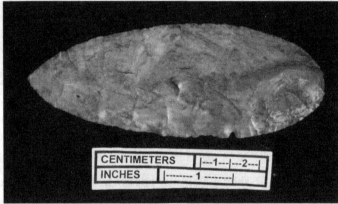

Figure 4-16-14 – Flint Bipoint from Cosnection, Ohio (L = 107, W = 42, T = 7 mm, R = 17.83).

4-17 Tennessee Bipoint Specimens

Tennessee does not appear to have had large bipoints although it may be a sampling problem. Figure 4-17-1 shows a well-made specimen. A bipoint was found at the Flint Creek Rockshelter in Tennessee. It probably is associated with Le Croy projectile points (Cambron and Waters 1959).

BIPOINT SPECIMEN
BIPOINT MORPHOLOGY MODEL

Date: Legacy 3.

134

State: Pointed ends.
Mode: Knife.

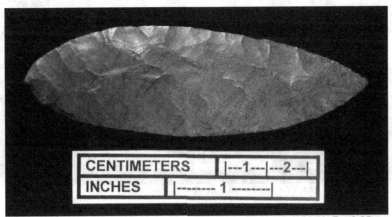

Figure 4-17-1 – Flint, Chattanooga County, Tennessee (L = 91, W = 28, T = 8 mm, R = 26.00, E = 3.25, g = 22). Specimen was not placed into service.

One of the largest bipoints found in Tennessee is shown in Figure 4-17-2. It is well-made and was resharpened several times (Gramly 1992). It has cross-face flaking and probably dates to the Woodland era.

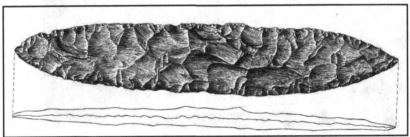

Figure 4-17-2 – Dover chert, Bipoint, Cross Creek Site, Tennessee (L = 253, W = 45, T = n/a mm) (John McKendry Collection, drawing from Gramly 1992).

This specimen is probably an Adena point from Choathna (?). It was made from Dover flint (Figure 4-17-3). It has a low ratio number suggesting a legacy.

Figure 4-17-3 Adena Bipoint (L = 114, W = 32, T = 8 mm, R = 28.50).

This specimen was found in Tennessee. It does not show usage as both pointed ends are sharp. It is well made from Dover flint.

Date: Legacy 2.
State: Pointed ends.
Mode: Knife.

Figure 4-17-4 – Tennessee Bipoint (L = 144, W = 42, T = 10 mm, R = 34.29).

This specimen is from Sommer County. It is made from jasper. It has a thick cross section with a slightly resharpened bit. It probably dates to the Holocene era.

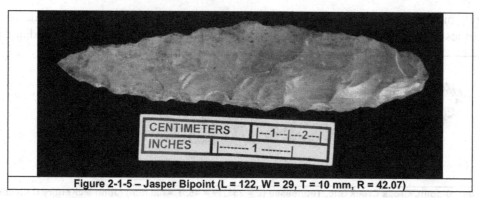

Figure 2-1-5 – Jasper Bipoint (L = 122, W = 29, T = 10 mm, R = 42.07)

This well-made specimen was found in Morefield, Montgomery County (Figure 2-17-6). It is made from flint and probably was never used. Top margin has fine retouching.

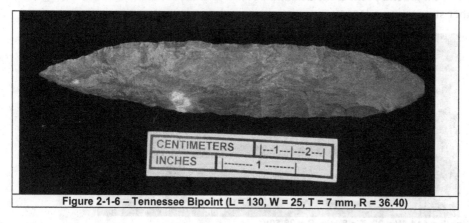

Figure 2-1-6 – Tennessee Bipoint (L = 130, W = 25, T = 7 mm, R = 36.40)

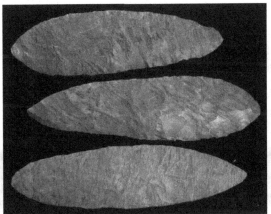

Adena-Dover Flint Cache of Bipoints,
Chatham County, Tennessee
(Source: Back to Earth)

The **Duck River Cache** was the archaeological discovery of 46 Native American artifacts by a worker on a farm in Western Tennessee in 1894. It has been called "perhaps the most spectacular single collection of prehistoric Native American art ever discovered in the eastern United States" and included "two human statues representing the community's ancestral founding couple" and "nearly four dozen ceremonial stone knives, daggers, swords, maces, and other striking examples of prehistoric stonework". It has 11 bipoints of which one is the longest ever found.

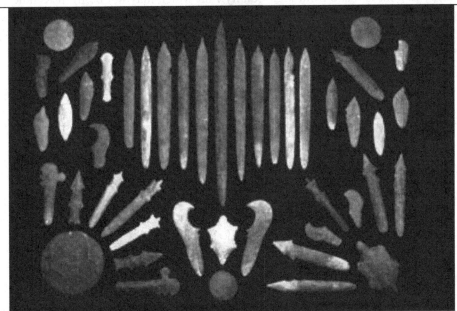

Duck River Cache

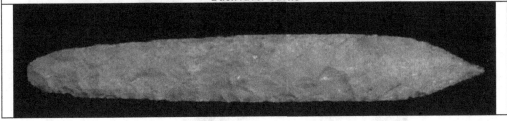

137

4-18 Kentucky Bipoint Specimens

Kentucky has a long history of bipoint usage, primarily Adena, Hopewell, and Ft. Ancient. Figure 4-18-1 shows a basic well-mode bipoint. It is a classic ovate bipoint.

BIPOINT SPECIMEN
BIPOINT MORPHOLOGY MODEL

Date: Legacy 3.
State: Pointed ends.
Mode: Knife.

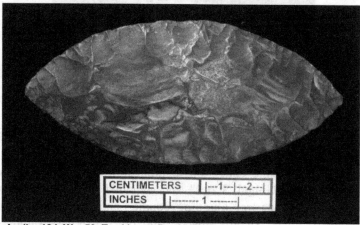

Figure 4-18-1 – Flint, Kentucky (L= 124, W = 53, T = 11 mm, R = 25.73, E = 2.34, g = 74).

The following Kentucky bipoint is made from high-quality flint which may not be from Kentucky; thus, distant travel is suggested (Figure 4-18-2). It has large areas of heavy patination and marginal edge microflaking.

BIPOINT SPECIMEN
BIPOINT MORPHOLOGY MODEL

Date: Legacy 2.
State: Pointed ends.
Mode: Knife.

Figure 4-18-2 – Kentucky Flint Specimen (L = 146, W = 43, T = 10 mm, R = 33.95)

Figure 4-18-3 shows a well-made flint specimen. It has light parallel edge trimming suggesting it was not hafted or used.

BIPOINT SPECIMEN
BIPOINT MORPHOLOGY MODEL

Date: Legacy 3.
State: Pointed ends.
Mode: Knife.

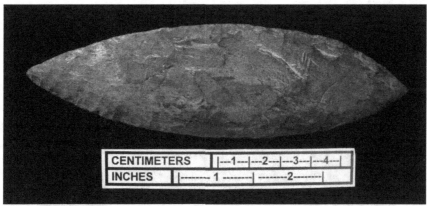

Figure 4-18-3– Flint, Kentucky (L = 136, W = 38, T = 13 mm, R = 46.52, E = 3.58, g = 64).

A specimen was located that had a beveled edge on opposite faces of the blade (Figure 4-18-4). It suggests the hafting as described in the basic style. Also, the material suggests a late Woodland date. The notched midwestern turkeytail point is a bipoint with notched alterations. While not always dateable, the earlier specimens provide various procedures of how they were resharpened; however, it was basically a blade-length reduction method. A small notch sometimes separates the two bipoint parts. As a suggestion, once the practice of making bipoints from flint began, they can be classified archaeologically as Woodland in the East. Also, resharpening tends to be lateral on the bit's edge which is the case with this specimen.

BIPOINT SPECIMEN
BIPOINT MORPHOLOGY MODEL

Date: Legacy 3.
State: Round ends.
Mode: Knife.

Figure 4-18-4 – Flint with Beveling, Kentucky (L = 96, W = 27, T = 7 mm, R = 24.88, E = 3.56).

Figure 4-18-5 shows a bipoint that was made off a large flat flake. It has an enlarged bit (left) and the medial ridge remains. It has pronounced bit sharpening flake micro-scars.

BIPOINT SPECIMEN
BIPOINT MORPHOLOGY MODEL

Date: Legacy 3.
State: Round ends.
Mode: Knife.

Figure 4-18-5 – Flint, Kentucky (L= 99, W = 35, T = 9 mm, R = 25.45, E = 2.83, g = 34) Specimen has heavy patination and is an early Legacy 3 bipoint. Bit is on the left end.

Figure 4-18-6 shows a classic bipoint. It is well made and has a small striking platform remaining. One face has a slight medial ridge. It was probably hand-held as it has retouch on both lateral margins.

BIPOINT SPECIMEN
BIPOINT MORPHOLOGY MODEL

Date: Legacy 3.
State: Pointed ends.
Mode: Knife.

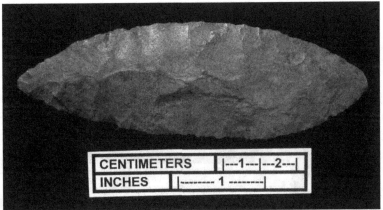

Figure 4-18-6 – Flint, Kentucky (L = 110, W = 34, T = 10 mm, R = 32.35, E = 3.24, g = 34) Specimen has heavy patination and is an early Legacy 3 bipoint. Bit is on the right end.

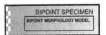

Date: Legacy 3.
State: Pointed ends.
Mode: Cache Blade.

Figure 4-18-7 shows a cache bipoint from Kentucky. The bipoint shape suggests a religious factor for the Adena culture in the Ohio River valley. Caches of bipoints are numerous and some contain of 300 items.

Figure 4-18-7 – Flint, Bipointed Cache "Blade," Crittonden County, Kentucky. (L = 188. W = 104, T = 14 mm, R = 25.31).

This ovoid bipoint has outstanding flake scars (Figure 4-18-8). It was found at Norwich, Kentucky. It is well made and has a low ratio number.

Figure 4-18-8 – Kentucky Bipoint (L = 89, W = 42, T = 8 mm, R = 16.95).

This large specimen was often classified as a stemmed point. The bit (right) is sharp with microflaking. The specimen is a biface that was percussion flaked (Figure 4-18-9).

Figure 4-18-9 – Large Central Kentucky Bipoint (L = 182, W = 43, T = 11 mm, R = 46.56).

4-19 Missouri Bipoint Specimens

Figure 4-19-1 shows a Missouri bipoint which has the basic model attributes. It has wide excurvate lateral margins and shows two pointed ends.

BIPOINT SPECIMEN
BIPOINT MORPHOLOGY MODEL

Date: Legacy 3.
State: Pointed ends.
Mode: Knife.

Figure 4-19-2 - Burlington Chert, Fort Ancient, Missouri. (L = 141, W = 55, T = 7.5 mm, R = 19.22, E = 2.56, g = 76). This specimen is one of the best bipoints in the study.

Figure 4-19-3 shows an example that has had its bit resharpened numerous times. It retained its symmetry and is well made. The length-wise profile is flat.

Date: Legacy 3.
State: Semi-Round and pointed ends.
Mode: Knife.

Figure 4-19-3 – Burlington Chert, Missouri (L = 96, W = 43, T = 7 mm, R = 15.62, E = 2.23, g = 37).

Figure 4-19-4 shows a specimen with wide lateral margins and a chipped base. Flake scars are bold, and the specimen is thin.

Date: Legacy 3.
State: Straight and pointed ends.
Mode: Knife.

Figure 4-19-4 - Pike County, Missouri (L = 163, W = 58, T = 10 mm, R = 28.10, E = 2.81). Right: straight remnant of a striking platform.

Figure 4-19-5 shows a large bipoint with heavy patination.

Date: Legacy 2.
State: Pointed ends.
Mode: Knife.

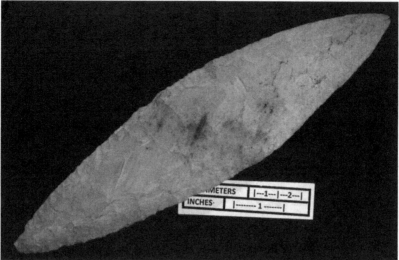

Figure 4-19-5 - Flint Bipoint from Franklin County, Missouri (L = 211, W = 49, T = 7 mm, R = 30.14) (Source: Back to Earth). Note: marginal invasive retouch.

4-20 Iowa Bipoint Specimen

In the French Town Mounds of Clayton County, Iowa, a cache of hornstone bipoints were found; they average 150 mm in length (Theler and Boszhardt (2003). Bipoints are common in late prehistoric mounds. Iowa represents the Plains area of the U.S. While broken or missing the pointed end, the following bipoint is well made and has a slightly flared workend (Figure 4-20-1). It has a beveled tip-end on one margin. The base is thin and was probably straight.

BIPOINT SPECIMEN
BIPOINT MORPHOLOGY MODEL

Date: Legacy 3.
State: Pointed end and base?
Mode: Knife.

Figure 4-20-1 – Chert, Appanoose County, Iowa (L = 81, W = 28, T = 8 mm, R = 23.14, E = 2.89, g = 21).

2-21 Illinois Bipoint Specimens

Figure 4-21-1 shows a narrow bipoint that has the striking platform remaining. This specimen is suggestive of the El Hobo bipoint in South America. These specimens are often called a spike point. The long narrow bipoint needs more study as it may reflect an ancient bipoint form. The bipoint form is called here a needle bipoint.

Date: Legacy 3.
State: Pointed ends, needle bipoint.
Mode: Knife.

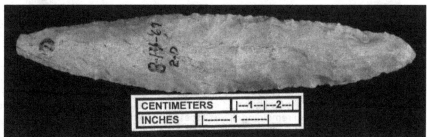

Figure 4-21-1 - Found in 1967 in Illinois, chert (L = 167, W = 30, T = 12 mm, R = 66.79, E = 5.57, g = 63). Clearly made from a blade as platform remains, D-cross section, and pronounced medial ridge. Note striking platform (left).

Figure 4-21-2 shows a classic ovate bipoint from Illinois. It has a semi-ovate form and is well made. The striking platform remains. Also, margins have retouch usage. It probably dates to the Adena era. This bipoint form is common in the Ohio valley. Resharpened expended forms are rarely reported.

Date: Legacy 3.
State: Pointed ends, ovate form.
Mode: Knife.

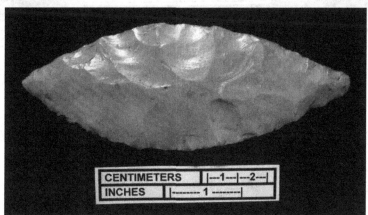

Figure 4-21-2 – Chert, Greene County, Illinois (L= 117, W = 44, T = 9 mm, R = 23.93, E = 2.66, g = 48). Note: the striking platform (right).

The following specimens are representative of the bipoint continuum in the U.S. As argued, the basal end can be pointed, straight-like, or semi-round (Figures 4-21-3 and 4-20-4). The top specimen is heavily patinated and has cross-face flaking.

Dates: Legacy 3.
States: Round and pointed end.
Modes: Knife.

145

Chert, Illinois (L = 169, W = 46, T = 14 mm, R = 51.43, E = 3.67) Note parallel edge-to-edge flaking and platform remaining. It has cross-face flake scars.

Figure 4-21-3– Large Knife Sharing the Bipoint Legacy

Chert, Illinois (L = 163, W = 50, T = 13 mm, R = 42.38, E = 3.26). Note it is also common in the Southwest as the Lake Mojave knife. It has cross-face flake scars.

Figure 4-21-4 – Rounded Base Bipoints.

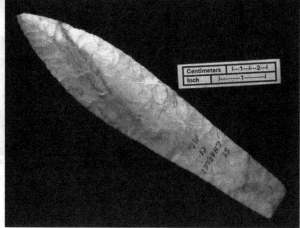

Morse Knives

Figure 4-21-5

Morse [Knife] Type - named by Gregory Perino in 1969 for a site in Illinois. It is a long, thin unnotched knife with a constricting stem (Figure 2-21-5). Forms are found from 150 to 350 mm (6 to 14 inches). Type dates around 3000 BP and is found in areas around the Great Lakes.
Flintknapping: superior quality.
Major attribute: long stem.
Type validity: traditional.
Type frequency in area: low as in rare.
Similar to: Lake Mohave.

Dates: Legacy 2.
States: Pointed ends.
Modes: Knife.
This well-made specimen is from Cook County, Illinois (Figure 4-21-6). It was classified as an Adena blade, but it is a bipoint. It has a remaining small platform and has invasive lateral retouching. There are few black crystals in the stone's matrix. It has a low ratio number.

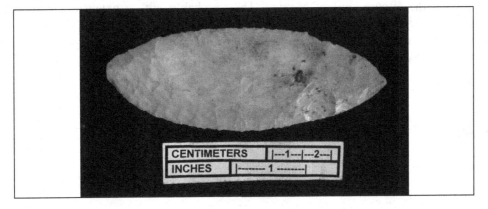

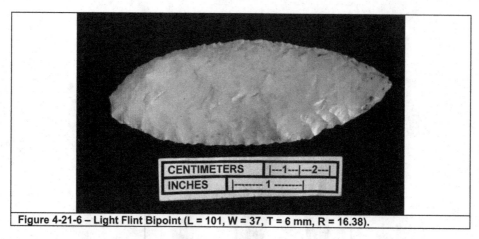

Figure 4-21-6 – Light Flint Bipoint (L = 101, W = 37, T = 6 mm, R = 16.38).

This bipoint is reportedly from Illinois (Figure 4-21-7). It is made from chert and has an even symmetry to its form. It has a uniform convex cross section and is relatively thick. Flaking suggests it is a Pleistocene bipoint. One end has slight usage with invasive retouching.

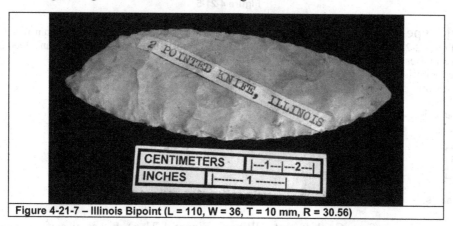

Figure 4-21-7 – Illinois Bipoint (L = 110, W = 36, T = 10 mm, R = 30.56)

4-22 Mississippi Bipoint Specimen

Bipoints occur around the circum-Gulf of Mexico. They probably are an extension of the early Florida bipoints, but again, there are no dates. Figure 4-22-1 shows a coastal Mississippi specimen. It was made using blade technology as noted in the pronounced medial ridge and D-shaped cross section. There is a very small remnant of the striking platform on the left end; therefore, the right margin is the suggested bit (workend).

BIPOINT SPECIMEN
BIPOINT MORPHOLOGY MODEL

Date: Legacy 3.
State: Pointed ends.
Mode: Knife.

Figure 4-22-1 – Chert, Lake Arbuckle, Tunica, Mississippi (L = 135, W = 32, T = 16 mm, R = 67.50, E = 4.22, g = 61).

4-23 California Bipoint Specimen

Figure 4-23-1 shows a California specimen which is typical on the West Coast. This is another example of coastal travel is the Pacific side of North America has its early entry location(s). The boat has not been recovered archaeologically for Before Clovis times in the U.S. (Smith 2011). But, an example of the boat needed for migration for the Americas was among artifacts found on the Channel Island off California's coast (Hill 2011). The California coast has remained relatively stable from prehistoric times (Broughton 1999); thus, archaeological maritime studies are still possible.

BIPOINT SPECIMEN
BIPOINT MORPHOLOGY MODEL

Date: Legacy 2.
State: Round and pointed ends.
Mode: Knife.

Figure 4-23-1 – Red Franciscan Jasper, California Coastal Area (L = 89, W = 28, T = 10 mm, R = 31.78, E = 3.18, g = 26).

Figure 4-23-2 shows an obsidian bipoint from California. Specimen has a low ratio number.

BIPOINT SPECIMEN
BIPOINT MORPHOLOGY MODEL

Date: Legacy 2.
State: Pointed ends.
Mode: Knife.

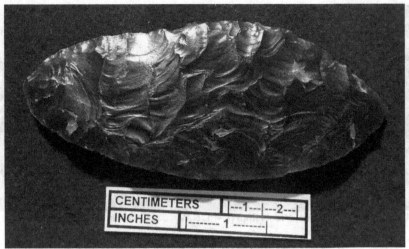

Figure 4-23-2 – Obsidian, Modoc County, California (L = 117, W = 47, T = 7 mm, R = 17.43)

4-24 Nebraska Bipoint Specimen

Westfall (2011) reports a turkey-tail notched bipoint found on the South Platte River made of Niobrara flint. The tri-state area is poorly reported. Figure 4-24-1 shows a Nebraska specimen.

BIPOINT SPECIMEN
BIPOINT MORPHOLOGY MODEL

Date: Legacy 2.
State: Semi-round and pointed ends.
Mode: Knife.

Figure 4-24-1 – Chert, Nebraska (L = 69, W = 31, T = 8 mm, R = 17.80, E = 2.22, g = 17).

4-26 North Dakota Bipoints

Huckell and Kilby (2009) report two bipoints from North Dakota which they classify as being of Clovis age because of the bipoints' flaking quality. No Clovis points were found with the bipoints. No photograph was available.

4-27 Colorado Bipoint Specimens

Obsidian is indicative of western bipoints. Along with quartz, obsidian has one of the naturally sharpest edges in Nature. Quartz is not common for bipoints in the East; however, obsidian was common for bipoints in the West. Figure 4-27-1 shows a specimen for the western Plains. Bipoints were probably initiated in Rocky Mountain area in obsidian; bipoints have a high frequency in this stone. Figure 4-27-2 shows a Blackwater Draw-like bipoint.

150

Date: Legacy 3.
State: Pointed ends.
Mode: Knife.

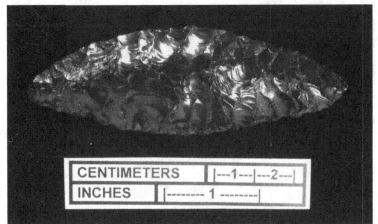

Figure 4-27-1 – Obsidian, Fremont County, Colorado (L = 87, W = 28, T = 12 mm, R = 37.28, E = 3.11, g = 21). It has parallel flake scars.

Date: Legacy 2.
State: Pointed ends.
Mode: Knife.

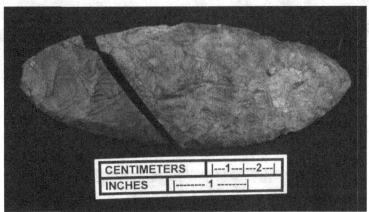

Figure 4-27-2 – Bipoint, Volcanic Turf, Steward Cattle Guard, Colorado, L = 103, W = 41, T = 5 mm, R = 12.56, E = 2.51).

4-28 Oregon Bipoint Specimens

The western U.S. has bipoints, and they are principally made from obsidian. The Cascade type is controversial in that some archaeologists consider it to have a (pre-) Clovis date (Hranicky 2010); however, this remains to be proven. Figures 4-28-1 and 2-28-2 show two obsidian bipoints from Oregon. While controversial, the Cascade point may date 17,000 YBP (Capes 1964 and Rutherford 1981).

BIPOINT SPECIMEN
BIPOINT MORPHOLOGY MODEL

Date: Legacy 2.
State: Pointed ends.
Mode: Knife.

Figure 4-28-1 – Obsidian, Oregon (L = 140, W = 49, T = 6 mm, R = 17.14, E = 2.86, g = 53). This bipoint is exceptionally well made.

Date: Legacy 2.
State: Pointed ends.
Mode: Knife.

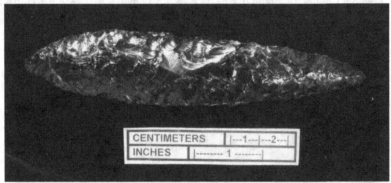

Figure 4-28-2 – Obsidian, Oregon (L = 142, W = 29, T = 10 mm, R = 50.71, E = 4.90, g = 40).

Figure 4-28-3 shows two additional Oregon specimens that have a semi-ovate form. They have heavy patination and show average flaking. Usage has produced dull lateral margins which suggest that they are expended knives.

Figure 4-28-3 – Obsidian, Both are from Harney County, Oregon (Left: L = 91, W = 38, T = 11 mm, R = 22.63, E = 2.51, g = 37 and Right: L = 88, W = 35, T = 9 mm, R = 22.63, E = 2.51, g = 30).

The following may or may not be classified as a bipoint (Figure 4-28-4). It is poorly made.

Figure 4-28-4 - Klamath Basin Bipoint (no measurements)

The following specimen is heavily patinated only on one face (Figure 4-28-4). It is made from the common stone in Oregon.

Figure 4-28-4 - Obsidian, Fort Rock, Lake County, Oregon (L = 182, W = 60, T = 12 mm, R – 36.40)

This specimen shows heavily resharpening (Figure 4-28-5). Jasper is the second most common stone in the state. Also, specimen has a low resharpened ratio number.

BIPOINT SPECIMEN
BIPOINT MORPHOLOGY MODEL

Date: Legacy 3.
State: Pointed ends.
Mode: Knife.

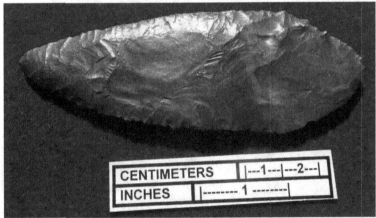

Figure 4-28-5 – Jasper, Lake County, Oregon (L = 102, W = 35, T = 5 mm, R = 14.57)

Figure 4-28-6 shows a bipoint with a twist to its length-wise shape.

Figure 4-28 6 – Jasper, The Dallas, Wasco County, Oregon (L = 124. W = 49, T = 5 mm)

This specimen has a twist from end-to-end which does occur throughout bipoints (Figure 4-28-7). It is also beveled. Also, specimen has a low resharpened ratio number.

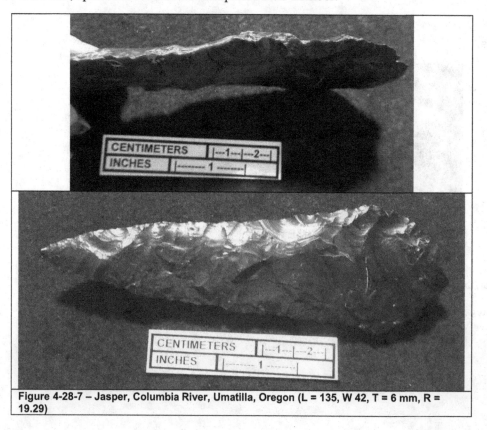

Figure 4-28-7 – Jasper, Columbia River, Umatilla, Oregon (L = 135, W 42, T = 6 mm, R = 19.29)

4-29 Nevada Bipoint Specimen

As discussed, the secret for analyzing the bipoint (V-shaped stemmed) knife is its bit resharpening. Figure 4-29-1 shows how the bit-style was maintained throughout prehistory. Are these specimens a technological coincidence? No. The Nevada specimen has the classic V-shaped Solutrean bit (workend). It is not culturally related in time or space, but it is an excellent example of a bipoint legacy. One of the earliest V-shaped stemmed resharpened bipoints (obsidian) was discovered by Russell (1885) at Lake Lahontan or Walker Valley (McGee 1889) in Nevada. It was associated with extinct mammals and dates to the Pleistocene.

Another example is a Great Basin obsidian cache, known as the McNine cache that dates to the terminal Pleistocene (Amick 2004). It contained six Parman points, but the important part is the cache contained bipoint. These bipoints are referred to as preforms (Amick 2004); however, these bipoints are probably associative knives. They have a classic bit resharpening, which suggests that some bipoints were manufactured this way initially.

BIPOINT SPECIMEN
BIPOINT MORPHOLOGY MODEL

Date: Legacy 2.
State: Pointed ends.
Mode: Knife.

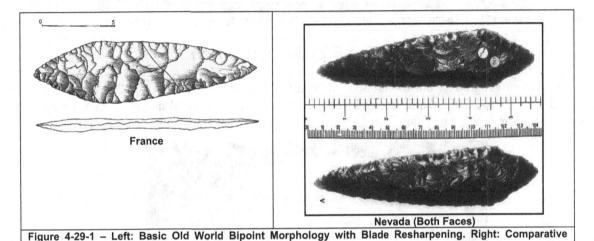

France

Nevada (Both Faces)

Figure 4-29-1 – Left: Basic Old World Bipoint Morphology with Blade Resharpening. Right: Comparative obsidian example from Nevada. Note: These bipoints are not related in time, space, or culture; however, they share a common technology legacy.

This specimen has an unusual morphology, but it does have pointed ends (Figure 4-29-2). The specimen for its size has a low ratio number.

CENTIMETERS
INCHES

Figure 4-29-2 – Black Rock Desert, Nevada (L = 180, W = 72, T -= 11 mm, R = 27.50)

This specimen has fine marginal retouching (Figure 4-29-3). It has a low ratio number.

Date: Legacy 3.
State: Pointed ends.
Mode: Knife.

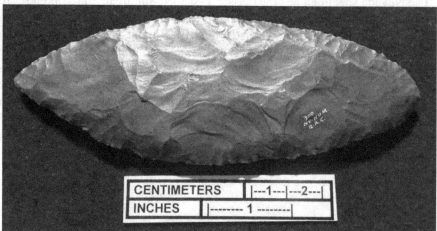

Figure 4-29-3 – Olive Green Chert, Quinn River Crossing, Nevada (L = 126, W = 45, T = 7 mm, R = 19.60)

4-30 Texas Bipoint Specimen

Texas covers a large geography, but the number of reported bipoints is less than smaller states. However, Figure 4-30-1 shows a specimen that is not well made, is thick, and has several major stacked hinges. It has edge flaking; however, it could be a failed preform.

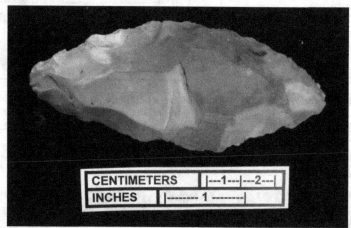

Figure 4-30-1 – Chert, Canyon Lake, Texas (L = 104, W = 38, T = 14 mm, R = 38.31, E = 2.74, g = 50).

Texas probably has the earliest western bipoints. This specimen is well-made and has large remaining areas on both faces of cortex (Figure 4-30-2). This specimen probably dates to the Pleistocene era. For its size, it has a low ratio number.

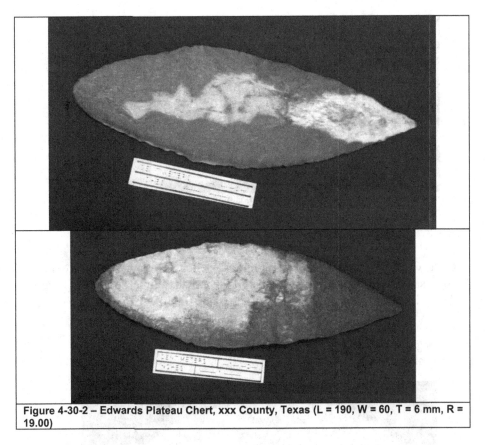

Figure 4-30-2 – Edwards Plateau Chert, xxx County, Texas (L = 190, W = 60, T = 6 mm, R = 19.00)

4-31 Alabama Bipoint Specimens

One of the first publications to identify bipoints from Alabama was Cambron and Hulse (1964). They attributed the bipoint to the Lerma projectile point type. They present data on 20 specimens as maximum of: L =104, W = 23, W = 10 mm (Figure 4-31-1).

Figure 4-31-1 – Bipoint Drawing from Cambron and Hulse (1975) (L = 110, W = 28, T = 9 mm, R = 35.36).

Cambron and Hulse (1975) also describe a round base bipoint. This presents a minor problem in identifying bipoints in Alabama to the Great Lakes area. Does it represent a new (or earlier) elongated knife form? This aspect of bipoints certainly needs more study. However, it is suggested as an El Hobo point from South America (Hranicky 2011). Gramly (2012) also notes this possibility in Alabama. The round-based bipoint is discussed elsewhere in this publication. See Mexico and South American Bipoints section.

Figure 4-31-2 shows narrow bipoint from Alabama made from a reddish flint which may have been heat treated. It has fine marginal retouch. Heat treating seems to be a minor practice for making bipoints.

BIPOINT SPECIMEN
BIPOINT MORPHOLOGY MODEL

Date: Legacy 3.
State: Pointed ends.
Mode: Knife.

Figure 4-30-2 – Flint, Central Alabama (L = 114, W = 32, T = 10 mm, R = 35.62, E = 3.56, g = 34).

4-32 Indiana Bipoint Specimens

Indiana has Ohio River valley influences on its bipoints, such as Hopewell and Adena. The following specimen has the bipoint state from which the maker could have made numerous tools (Figure 4-32-1). Most archaeologists would classify it as a simple biface or a trade blade. It shows no evidence of being used.

Date: Legacy 3.
State: Pointed end, semi-pointed end.
Mode: Knife.

Figure 4-30-1 – Flint, Ovate Bipoint State, Indiana (L = 139, W = 68, T = 24 mm, R = 49.05, g = 155).

Figure 4-30-2 shows a well-made bipoint.

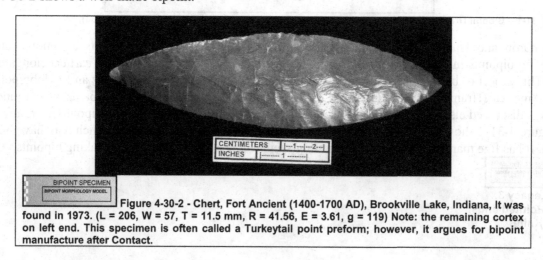

Figure 4-30-2 - Chert, Fort Ancient (1400-1700 AD), Brookville Lake, Indiana, It was found in 1973. (L = 206, W = 57, T = 11.5 mm, R = 41.56, E = 3.61, g = 119) Note: the remaining cortex on left end. This specimen is often called a Turkeytail point preform; however, it argues for bipoint manufacture after Contact.

158

Figure 4-30-3 shows an unusually shaped bipoint.

Figure 4-30-3 – Chert, Biface, Northern Alabama (L = 70, W = 30, T = 13 mm, R = 30.33)

4-33 New Mexico Bipoint Specimens

Based on Sandia Cave, the bipoint is present; admittedly a shouldered form. The site has had controversy (Haynes 1986 and Thompson, et al. 2008) and its original date of 14,000 YBP is not generally acceptable in archaeology (Hester 1960). However, the Sandia point has been found elsewhere (Hranicky 2010); its date is not a major concern here. Figure 4-33-1 shows excavated specimens from the cave site (Hibben 1941) with Charles McNutt's effort to re-locate the Sandia points. Hranicky (2010) argues for 14,000-year date for the type; however, there were fluting attempts on some of the Sandia points.

Figure 4-33-1 – Picture from the Smithsonian Report Volume 99, Number 23.

Sandia Cave Specimen (Photograph by Charles McNutt).

BIPOINT SPECIMEN
BIPOINT MORPHOLOGY MODEL

Date: Legacy 2.
State: Pointed ends.
Mode: Knife.

Figure 4-33-2 - Flint Bipoint from Blackwater Draw Site in Roosevelt County, New Mexico (L = 161, W = 63, T = 4 mm). Note: marginal invasive retouch.

Figures 4-33-3 and 4-33-4 show specimens from the Blackwater Draw site area. They are ultra-thin specimens were typical of the Folsom pointmakers. The quartzite specimen is only one millimeter thicker. They have the lowest R factor in this study.

BIPOINT SPECIMEN
BIPOINT MORPHOLOGY MODEL

Date: Legacy 3.
State: Pointed ends.
Mode: Knife.

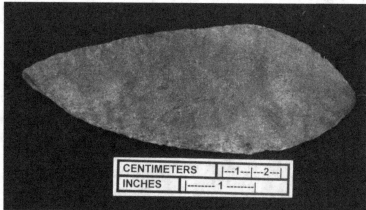

Figure 4-33-3 – Bipoint, Mitchell Locality of Blackwater Draw, Quartzite L = 127, W = 49, T = 7 mm, R = 18.14, E = 2.59).

BIPOINT SPECIMEN
BIPOINT MORPHOLOGY MODEL

Date: Legacy 3.
State: Pointed ends, broken.
Mode: Knife.

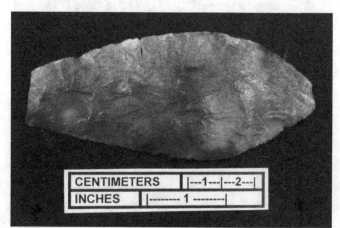

Figure 4-33-4 - Bipoint, Franks Site, Blackwater Draw, Alabate Flint, L = 96, W = 42, T = 5 mm, R = 11.43, E = 2.29).

4-34 Wisconsin Bipoint Specimen

A 300 mm bipoint made from Hixton silicified sandstone was reported from Jackson County, Wisconsin. It was associated with the Silver Mound complex (Theler and Boszhardt (2003). Figure 4-34-1 shows a well-made Wisconsin bipoint with a semi-rounded base. It is thin and has excellent flaking patterns.

BIPOINT SPECIMEN
BIPOINT MORPHOLOGY MODEL

Date: Legacy 3.
State: Pointed ends.
Mode: Knife.

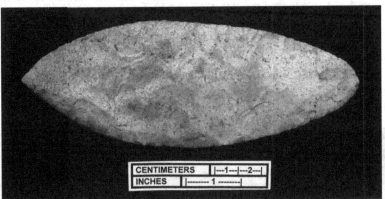

Figure 4-34-1 – Chert, Dodge County, Wisconsin (L = 158, W = 55, T = 11 mm, R = 31.59, E = 2.87, g = 99).

4-35 Arkansas Bipoint Specimen

This well-made specimen is from Hot Springs, Arkansas (Figure 4-35-1). Data and point supplied by Waslace Guslar.

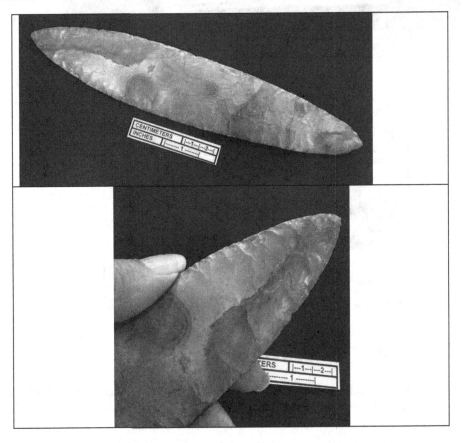

161

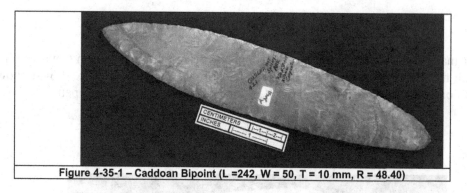

Figure 4-35-1 – Caddoan Bipoint (L =242, W = 50, T = 10 mm, R = 48.40)

4-36 Idaho Bipoint Specimen

Idaho specimens are rare due to its high altitude and general archaeological investigations. This specimen was found on War Eagle Mountain, Elmore County (Figure 4-36-1). It is made from a fine-grade white flint. It has lateral margin invasive retouch. As with many blade bipoints, it has a low ratio number.

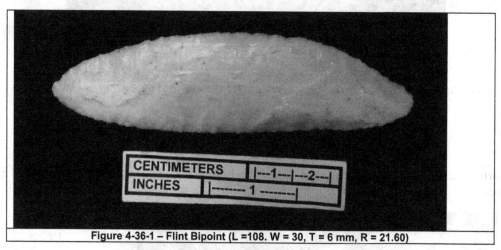

Figure 4-36-1 – Flint Bipoint (L =108. W = 30, T = 6 mm, R = 21.60)

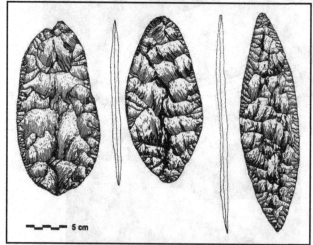

Figure 4-36-2 – Drawing of Turkeytail Preforms from Idaho (After: Pavesic 1985)

4-37 Canada Bipoint Specimen

Figure 4-37-1 shows a Canadian specimen which has crystals that have eroded out over its prehistoric years. The rounded base tends to be typical in the Great Lakes area. Also, the northern specimens tend to be wider than southern bipoints. A Florida specimen with crystals is shown below. Three specimens in this study have crystal pockets.

Bipoints occur on Canada's west coast and from Florida (Hranicky 2012) to Labrador (Fitzhugh (1972) on the Atlantic coast.

> BIPOINT SPECIMEN
> BIPOINT MORPHOLOGY MODEL

Date: Legacy 3.
State: Semi-round and pointed ends.
Mode: Knife.

Figure 4-37-1 – Chert, Oxford County, Ontario, Canada, (L = 149, W = 61, T = 12 mm, R = 29.31, E = 2.44, g = 108). Note crystal pocket.

New Brunswick Bipoint

This Canadian specimen was found with a hafted knife (Figure 4-37-2). The base of the knife appears to be irregular; it was probably a bipoint initially. It was made from basalt and measures: L = 113, W = 43, T = 5 mm. Knife has an overall length of 167 mm. Both specimens have light invasive edge retouch.

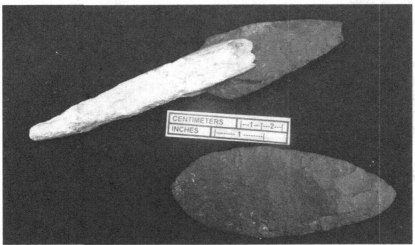

Figure 4-37-2 – New Brunswick Basalt Bipoint and Knife

4-38 Mexico Bipoint Specimens

Known as the Colima bipoint dagger, it is a heavily patinated and mineralized semi- translucent gem agate mottled with chalcedony. This specimen was one of a cache of 10 blades collected in the Valley of Mexico in the Tenochtitlan area of Mexico in 1928 (Figure 4-38-1). For Mesoamerican lithic technology, see Hirth (2003) which discusses the tabular piece of obsidian to produce a bipoint (Pastrana and Hirth 2003: 197).

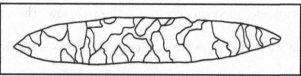

Figure 4-38-1 – Bipoint Drawing of a Mexican Bipoint (L = 176 mm).

Figure 4-38-2 shows a notched bipoint. It probably served as an attachment for a wand/staff. It is well made, thin, and has parallel flake scars along all lateral margins.

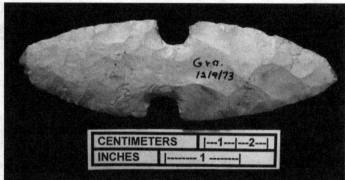

Figure 4-38-2 – Chert, Mezcaia, Guerro, Mexico (L = 112, W = 33, T = 17 mm, R = 57.70, E = 3.39, g = 31, M = 10YR8/2).

Furthermore, the Aztec and Maya cultures made high quality bipoints. For a classic paper on the bipoint and other tool manufacture, see Shafer and Hester (1983). A bipoint is described from Mexico City in Mahan (1955) who reports a mammoth association with a bipoint (secondary reference).

Figure 4-38-3 shows a bipoint that was reported in MacNeish (1958). It has possible El Hobo attributes. The bit has the classic V-shaped resharpening.

BIPOINT SPECIMEN
BIPOINT MORPHOLOGY MODEL

Date: Legacy 2.
State: Round and pointed ends.
Mode: Knife.

Figure 4-38-3 – Flint, Bipoint, Tamaulipas, Mexico (no measurements).

Baja California Bipoints

Baja California is an extension of the Southwest. Lauriers (2010) reports several elongated knives at the PAIC-44 site of which two are bipoints (Figure 4-38-4). Lauriers classifies them as San Dieguito phase tools. The lithic material is white quartz; no dimensions are given. They are from Isla Cedros which has demonstrated the need for watercraft (for watercraft, see Lauriers 2005).

164

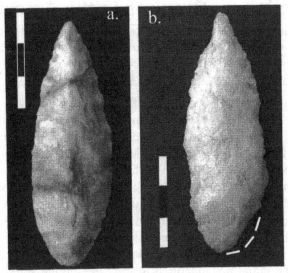

Figure 4-38-4 – Two Bipoints from PAIC-44 Site, Baja California, Mexico.

Section 5 - Bipoints in the Americas

> This section provides a history of bipoints in the U.S. It introduces the probability that the Solutreans were present on the Atlantic coast. African and Asian cultures are also discussed as possible sources for early people into the U.S. A suggested bipoint history is argued and a lithic continuum for stone technology with a bipoint chronology is discussed.

The bipoint, laurel leaf, or V-shaped stemmed knife is found worldwide and is a technology that is as old as humanity dating back to 75,000 YBP (Mourre, Villa, and Henshilwood 2010). Does its invention by humans represent an innate ability to create a cutting implement that becomes a standard for the entire history of humanity? Perhaps, but it is the best known knife in the Old World, namely the Solutrean bipoint, and this style knife continues through African-to-European prehistoric cultures which subsequently was carried into the New World. As a tool class, it has a long history and becomes common for most world-wide prehistoric cultures. The European bipoints usually show better quality specimens, but, none-the-less, most prehistoric cultures were producing and using them. Whenever Old World people(s) made transocean[60] migrations to the Americas (Bradley and Stanford 2004 and Stanford and Bradley 2012 a&b), they brought the bipoint with them and, when heavily resharpened, it can only be classified as a V-shaped stem, when it was a foliate or laurel-leaf knife. However, the initial manufactured form is the bipoint state which has various shapes. Or, what is called the Bipoint Morphology Model (BMM). Bipoint specimens representing the entire spectrum of Atlantic coast prehistory are presented below.

From the Virginia perspective, Miller (1962) was among the first to understand and demonstrate an Old World connection to the New World for lithic technology. He referenced Old World as opposed to Asian sources and comments:

> *Various Virginia forms appear to display certain typological analogies to some of the Old World types, but these cannot be judged to be synchronous because there is a putative age difference. This conjecture is based on a series of geological and cultural chronologies. However, whenever absolute chronologies, based upon controlled conditions, are once established, it is surmised that the presumed older Old World artifacts will be found to be much younger and the New World specimens to be much older, with a meeting and possible overlaps of the two chronologies. It is inconceivable to the writer (Miller) that Early Man in the Old World took a couple of hundred thousand years to develop and overspread Eurasia and Africa and only twenty or more thousand years to completely people the New World, and to set up various complicated linguistic families and ideologies with varying degrees of cultural advancement in such a short time span.*

Bipoints in American Archaeological History

In 1882, John Short published *The North Americans of Antiquity* in which he discussed and illustrated a large bipoint which would become known as a *stone sword* (Short 1882: 61). The most famous artifact is known as the Duck River sword in Tennessee. His early works show various forms of bipoints (resharpened). Charles Abbot's *Primitive Industry* was the first book to contain an eastern coastal bipoint which was found in New Jersey (Abbot 1881:81).

Thus, the bipoint in American archaeology has been known for nearly 130 years (Munro 1912, Kidder 1932, Short 1882, Abbot 1881, Moorehead 1900, and Wilson 1899). Along with the discovery of Clovis and Folsom, the bipoint was published in the West at about the same time (Roberts 1951); however, his focus was mainly on lanceolates, not bipoints. In this paper, Roberts notes: *the culture may be older than Clovis*. Another early publication with bipoints was Kidder's (1932) *The Artifacts of the Pecos*. Most of these archaeologists did not focus on the bipoint, but focused on what would become American projectile point typology.

The oldest bipoint photograph is an obsidian bipoint found in 1869 at Maripose County, California which is in Holmes (1899). Moorehead (1900) published the largest bipoint found in the U.S. (Figure 5-1). His

---

[60] In: A Very Long Way to Eat Rhino, Zorich (2018) reports the homo erectus made it to the Philippines 700,000 year ago. The idea of ocean travel is beginning to have some antiquity to it.

publication shows numerous bipoints, including resharpened specimens. Most importantly, he published the first bipoint cache found and reported in the U.S. (1900:23). This cache contained 95 flint bipoints. It was found by E. C. Mitchell in Michigan.

Figure 5-1 – Bipoint, Flint, Union County, Illinois Found by H. M. Whelpley of St. Louis, Missouri (L = 22, W = 4, T = 1 inches).

From 100 Texas specimens, Wheat (1953:222) was one of the first to type the bipoint. He called it a leaf-shaped knife which he notes: *These range widely in space and time, and consequently are of little value for tracing areal and temporal relationships*. He states that this artifact shape varies from symmetric to asymmetric; and bases are from convex to round. He does not classify bits (workends). Bryan (1965) was another early archaeologist to study bipoints of which he called them a *willow leaf* bipoint tradition in western U.S. states. He identified small bipoints which he called a Lozenge-shaped point tradition. His large leaf-shaped point tradition included North and South America. He argued a circum-Pacific origin for bipoints, which included Eurasia.

Additionally, the northwestern area of the U.S. has late bipoints which suggest it was a common knife in the ceramic age of prehistory (Shiner 1961). Also, bipoints are found as far north as Labrador (Fitzhugh 1972). For the Dakotas, Smith and Grange (1958) report bipoints, including the ovate form. This bipoint was common all over the U.S.; only the chronology needs to be defined archaeologically.

For the collector community, the earliest publication was Brown (1942) which shows bipoints for the entire U.S. prehistoric geography and era. These early writers referred to bipoints as leaf-shaped knives and usually did not have site or provenance contexts (Figure 5-2).

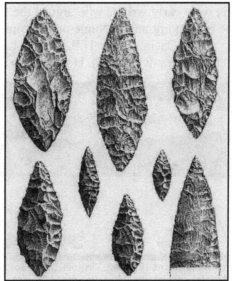

Figure 5-2 – Basic European Solutrean Bipoints (After Munro 1912). The top center drawing shows the Iberian curve. The bottom curve is straighter (less curved) than the top curve edge.

Figure 5-3 presents an early set of drawings for classic Solutrean bipoints by Osborn (1922). He calls them – *typical Solutrean implements of war and chase*. These bipoints are *points en feuille de laurier* or laurel-leaf points. This drawing demonstrates knowledge of the Solutreans in the middle 1800s.

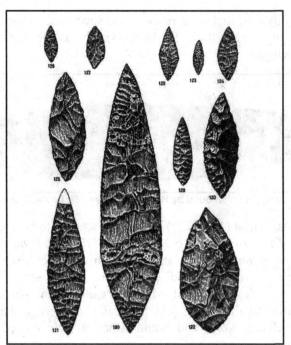

Figure 5-3 – Bipoints Drawing in Osborn (1922). Drawing based on de Mortillet (1869). Note the state (classification) is pointed end bipoints.

Holmes (1903) made an interesting observation on a bipoint at Afton Spring in (then) Indian Territory of Oklahoma. This bipoint was found in somewhat of a non-professional archaeological investigation. The excavation involved removing bones from Mammoths and other smaller animals. The bipoint association is totally impossible to determine; however, the investigation is interesting to say the least about it. There were numerous point types in his site collection.

Archaeologically, the leaf (foliate) or laurel-leaf classification is often used to describe bipoints. McCowan (1939) and Jelinek (1971) were early writers who argued the Clovis and the European Solutrean connection; others followed with the bipoint argument. Numerous bipoint forms occur in the literature, such as Lerma (Figure 5-4), Excelsior, Agate Basin, Nebo Hill, Boats, Lake Mohave, Lind Coulee, Bliss, Angostura, Cascade, and other point types (Hranicky 2010). Do these types share the bipoint legacy? Yes!

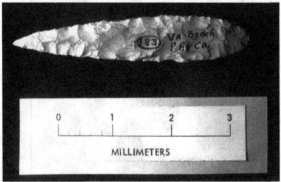

Figure 5-4 – A Probable Slate Lerma Form, Princes Anne (Suffolk), Virginia. It has Solutrean attributes, especially if the left part is the hafting part; bit would match other bipoint specimens. It is a well-made bipoint.

As a bipoint source and around 50,000 YBP, the bipoint as one tool class was well established in Europe (Phillipson 2005, Gamble 1999, and Clark 1970). From this beginning, the bipoint spread throughout the Old World eventually to the Americas. Three principal sources are suggested for lithic technology into the eastern Americas, which are:

- Solutreans (France/Spain) (Bradley and Stanford 2004 and 2012 a&b)
- Aterians (North Africa) (Hranicky 2007 and Miller 1962)
- Lupembans (Central Africa) (Phillipson 2005, possible U.S. migrations).

With these possible Old World areas, the pure bipoint source remains to be proven as the primary focus for early Americas. The bipoint survived in the U.S. but the *from/where/when* remains a controversy in American archaeology. As such, the bipoint chronology and morphology remains speculative by many archaeologists. As a consequence, the Solutrean name for the class has become frequent in the literature; thus, the generalized name is used by many archaeologists. Solutrean attributes are found in other Old World prehistoric cultures, but numerous specific properties in the American population suggest a Solutrean occupation. Presently, this publication suggests Iberia as one of the American sources for the bipoint; however, its legacy for post-Pleistocene populations in the U.S., especially the Southeast, remains to be established and dated. See Early Virginia and Florida Bipoint sections.

From the Virginia perspective, Miller (1962) was among the first to understand and demonstrate an Old World connection to the New World for lithic technology. He referenced Old World as opposed to Asian sources and comments:

> *Various Virginia forms appear to display certain typological analogies to some of the Old World types, but these cannot be judged to be synchronous because there is a putative age difference. This conjecture is based on a series of geological and cultural chronologies. However, whenever absolute chronologies, based upon controlled conditions, are once established, it is surmised that the presumed older Old World artifacts will be found to be much younger and the New World specimens to be much older, with a meeting and possible overlaps of the two chronologies. It is inconceivable to the writer (Miller) that Early Man in the Old World took a couple of hundred thousand years to develop and overspread Eurasia and Africa and only twenty or more thousand years to completely people the New World, and to set up various complicated linguistic families and ideologies with varying degrees of cultural advancement in such a short time span.*

A Lithic Technology History

Figure 5-5 shows a technological history or continuum model for all lithic tools. As mentioned, lithic technology starts with the Oldovai Gorge in Africa (Leakey 1935) and followed hominids throughout the world. For Europe, the ending of the continuum is found in the Neolithic Danish daggers (Callahan and Apel 2011). While local variations occur, the overall classes and industries are found everywhere. Thus, when analyzing stone tools, data and artifacts are collected from a site that is analyzed as a particular local dataset which was based on the knowledge base from a larger culture area. The analysis then involves intrasite comparisons. All artifacts have a specific time and place within a particular culture that exists at that time and place. The knife, drill, spearhead, arrowhead, celt and other tools are found throughout the prehistoric world which can be called a universal toolkit of mankind. The prehistoric knowledge how to make and use tools and their effects on culture in a social setting is the New Archaeology. Old forms of archaeological typing for local tool varieties have passed with the 20th century ways of recording and interpreting artifacts.

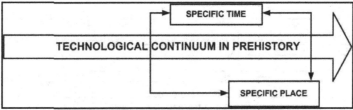

Figure 5-5 – A Technological Continuum Model Showing Continuum at a Time and Place.

For the U.S. Southeast, the bipoint complicates archaeology. This tool and its numerous tool forms are found that do not fit the eastern simple Coe (1964) axiom of Dalton-Hardaway-Palmer-Kirk chronology. Points, such as the Suwannee, Cumberland, Simpson (Page-Ladson), Angelico, St Charles, Haw River, and others, cover the landscape and, for the moment, escape archaeological excavated contexts and dates. Recently, a bipoint was found in association with Suwannee and Simpson points in Florida (Austin 2006). While this specimen does have a semi-round base, it fits in the bipoint tradition for the lower eastern U.S.

The bipoint technology is argued as a justified technology proposition for the connection to Old World stone technology dating 50,000 (or plus) YBP.

Bradley and Stanford (2004 and 2012 a&b) provide a parallel between Solutrean and Clovis technologies. Their basic argument is the present of over-shot flaking. Figure 5-6 illustrates the technological similarities. However, the **bipoint** is a basic tool in the Solutrean culture – Why is it **not** found in Clovis technology and sites? Maybe, see an exception in Howard (1935:plate xxix). Is bipoint technology a *run around* Clovis?

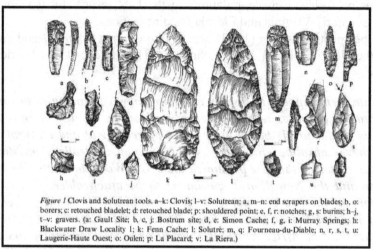

Figure 1 Clovis and Solutrean tools. a–k: Clovis; l–v: Solutrean; a, m–n: end scrapers on blades; b, o: borers; c: retouched bladelet; d: retouched blade; p: shouldered point; e, f, r: notches; g, s: burins; h–j, t–v: gravers. (a: Gault Site; b, c, j: Bostrum site; d, e: Simon Cache; f, g, i: Murray Springs; h: Blackwater Draw Locality 1; k: Fenn Cache; l: Solutré; m, q: Fourneau-du-Diable; n, r, s, t, u: Laugerie-Haute Ouest; o: Oulen; p: La Placard; v: La Riera.)

Figure 5-6 – Solutrean vs. Clovis Lithic Tools (From: Bradley and Stanford 2004).

American Bipoint Age/Chronology

The widespread usage of the bipoint suggests it was an established technology that was transported into the eastern and western New World and, most importantly, was a sustained technology throughout American prehistory. Technology transfer involves an initial movement into a new land as a knowledge base, maintenance of the technology knowledge, and then the technology becomes a legacy from the home land that continues the original ways of manufacture and usage. Of course, change processes among prehistoric users are factors. The cross-over time for the bipoint from primary to secondary stages probably will never be determined for the U.S. Figure 5-7 illustrates this technological continuum. Over time, the original implement (design) is modified, but basic properties are still maintained – a legacy implement which is defined in the BMM.

Perhaps, most likely, when a bipoint is found in the U.S. that was made in the Old World, it will be called the *legacy* bipoint. Presently, no such bipoint has been found, only ancestral forms. All subsequent U.S. made bipoints are various legacy (stages) bipoints. At present, the earliest legacy bipoint dates to the Pleistocene.

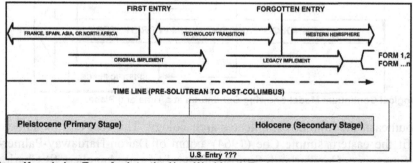

Figure 5-7 – Technology Knowledge Transfer into the New World – A Technological Continuum. The importing of tools into America reflects a technological continuum.

As expressed elsewhere in archaeology, the major argument against the Solutreans into the eastern U.S. is the time of European Solutreans vs. the time of the first cultures in the U.S., namely Clovis. Trying to establish the bipoint in the Paleoindian Period is open for research as it does occur with Clovis assemblages.

This topic is not addressed here, but it is a factor for the Solutrean-Clovis connection arguments. Florida's geography (extensive shelf) offers early landfall areas for searching for European and African immigrants (Brown 1994 and Hranicky 2004). There are bipoints in Florida, but their dates remain speculative. Chronologically for the Solutrean's bipoints in the U.S., archaeology has to account for at least 4000 years prior to Clovis times. Other immigrants possibly arrived and probably have varying occupation times. The principal secondary possible immigrants are the Aterians (Hranicky 2007).

Comparative examples: As an Aterian example, a recent find on the North Carolina/Virginia border is shown in Figure 5-8 and compared to Aterian points. Note: the Aterian had the bipoint in their toolkits.

Figure 5-8 – Aterian and North Carolina/Virginia Comparison Specimens.

McBurney (1960), Tixier (1961), Clark (1970), and Higgs and Coles (1969) were among the first to illustrate the Aterian tanged tool. Figure 5-9 provides a sample of Clark's illustration. Note the presence of tanged and bipoint tools – all on a blade framework.

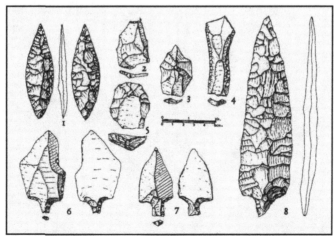

Figure 5-9 – Aterian Tanged Tools of North Africa (After: Clark 1970). Note resharpened bit on right specimen).

171

Figure 5-10 shows another example of tanged African points which are associated with the bipoint.

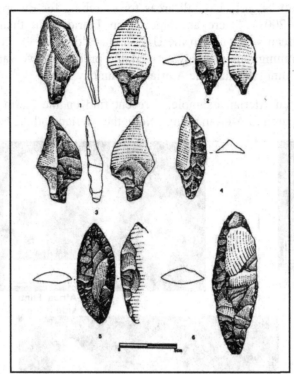

Figure 5-10 – Aterian Artifacts from Edeyen of Murzuq, Africa (After Cremaschi 1998)

As a side note for the above illustrations, the bipoint occurs in Mousterian, Solutrean, Magdalenian, and Aterian toolkits. This form has been argued as a trademark for these cultures; this tool form is found in the New World, especially South America. There, it is called the El Jobo point which is a long, narrow bipoint. These bipoints complicate the bipoint's origin as solely Old World. They suggest a south-to-north continental migration – even if the morphology is based on *shaky grounds*. Most importantly, the El Jobo points have a South American legacy (Gramly 2012 and Hranicky 2011). And further complicating this focus, the bipoint is found on the upper Pacific Coast with dates of 14,000 YBP or older. This bipoint is called the Cascade type and is associated with the skeleton of *Kennewick Man*. The bipoint technology is not *going to be easy* to analyze in Western Hemisphere archaeology. Genetically, some archaeologists argue a European origin for this skeleton, once a person. See previous text.

Section 6 - Old World Bipoints

This section provides an overview of Old World bifaces and bipoint manufacture. It discusses bipoint origins. The Mousterians, Solutreans, and Aterians are presented with dates and suggested bipoint usage. The Mousterians are credited here with the bipoint invention and distribution.

Bipoint Origins

One question that is often asked pertaining to bipoint class technology is: what relationship(s) is there for the various forms and culture found around the world that use this technology? The technology was learned (discovered) early in hominid history; this technology has *wings* and is not culture dependent. It spread throughout the world. For example, once blademaking was learned, most cultures in Europe and Africa were practicing this technology within thousands of years. The same is true for the earlier biface making. There are regional bipoint variations, but the technological class remained essentially the same everywhere.

Clark (1967) was among the first to argue that the manufacture of large blades occurred in the middle Acheulian era. This era led to Levallois-like technology (Tryon, et al. 2005). This allowed the first bipoint to start being made...in Europe (Figure 6-1)? But, the technology originated in Africa; the discovery (or invention) remains controversial. Did bipoint technology come out of the Archeulian Levallois technology? This specimen was made off a large blade/spall; its striking platform remains. It has a superficial form which could be called a bipoint – legacy?

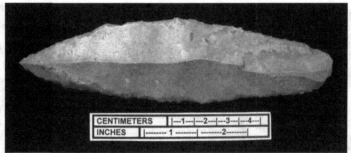

Figure 6-1 – Example of the Earliest Bipoint Technology. It is from the Ater/El Beyed Acheulian area of Northwest Africa (L = 157, W = 40, T = 12 mm, R = 47.10, g = 72). Note: the platform remnant on the right basal end.

Some of the Levallois blades had a raised medial axis that was produced on the blade core by previous blades which increased its tensile strength. Dating earlier than 200 k years, the method allowed the striking of large blades off the large boulder and cores which were percussion flaked into large knives. This method produced a striking platform (and bulb scar) which is usually found on the knife throughout prehistory (Van Peer (1992), Gamble (1999), de Heinzelin de Braucourt (1962), and Dibble and Bar-Yosef (1995)). The *tool logic* implies the early discovery of the curved, cutting edge which was incorporated into knives throughout prehistory. Lateral marginal retouching and resharpening (chipping) was hard-stone or soft-antler flaked. The angle between the blade and the chassis area on the following specimen is obvious.

There are no radiometric dates for these specimens/sites in these figures, but when comparing the form to other known sites, it is highly suggestive of this antiquity. This large blademarking technique was transferred into the New World as evidenced in some Paleoindian toolkits. Bipoint studies need to argue that the original bipoint form occurred as a large blade technology.

Figure 6-2 shows an interim blade/bipoint from the Solutrean in France. The shouldered bipoint is a basic characteristic of Solutrean technology (Bordes 1956). Upon examination, the striking platform is obvious. The medial aris (axis) is present on the bit. The basic outline of both knives suggests a historical legacy which starts in the upper Paleolithic Africa and ends in the prehistory of the U.S. Of course, this legacy argument has many viewpoints by readers. Semenov (1964) suggests that the Solutrean shouldering made the tool a hand-held implement.

Figure 6-2 - Pointe à Crane Upper Solutrean, ca. 16,000 BP (LMA 4.6.138) (Logan Museum of Art, Beloit College). Note: shoulder.

Figure 6-3 shows an African Aurignacian specimen which suggests a bipoint blade-like specimen. The long flute (previous flake scar) has a considerable antiquity on this type of tool. It has a small striking platform remaining. This curve is called the Iberian curve here by the author after specimens that were first observed in Europe. It was made from flint blade. It probably initially had a pointed perforator (upper left) which now shows heavy wear. For a discussion of the blade-tool manufacture, see Bordes (1956) and Chazan (2001). This tool curve is referred to here as the Iberian curve.

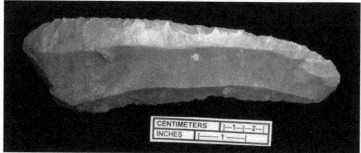

Figure 6-3 – Flint Blade from Mauritania, Africa (L = 176, W = 49, T = 14 mm, R = 50.28, g = 125). Note the curve for holding the tool.

Comparative example: The following specimen was found on the Paleoindian site known as the Thunderbird (44WC3) in Warren County, Virginia (Figure 6-4). While the Virginia specimen lacks the center channel, it has the curve that is called the Iberian curve in this publication. Both specimens were struck off a blade core. The workends are similar. Both have upper marginal retouch. They simply illustrate a continuum in toolmaking. The R factor is approximately the same.

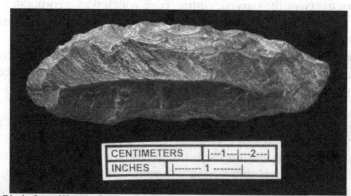

Figure 6-4 – Rhyolite Paleo-Blade from Warren County, Virginia (L = 115, W = 34, T = 18 mm, R = 60.88, g = 71).

Bipoint Firsts

Present archaeological thinking has the bipoint's beginning in Europe, namely the Solutrean bipoint. The Levallois and leaf point technologies were first developed in the area of central and eastern Europe

(Kozlowski 2003). Leaf points[61] were recovered on Bryvar Hill at Korolevo (Gladilin and Sitlivyi 1990). However, without an in depth presentation, the Micoquians probably developed the leaf point at 180 k YBP (Zakharikov 1999). This places the leaf-shaped point in Mousterian context in Europe and the Near East. However, they are a *long way* from the classic bipoint technology. It does not answer the *who/first* for the bipoint. However, as noted below in this publication, classic Solutrean-like bipoints occur in South Africa at 75 k YBP. Even Britain has been argued as an early source for the bipoint (Garrod 1926). Also, for Asia, the bipoint appears to have been used in the middle Paleolithic Aurignacian (Otte 2004).

In Europe, archaeologists classify the basic pointed implement as a variety of classifications, each defined differently, as in de Heinzelin de Braucourt's typology (1962). He defines the *foliace* as having over 12 different forms.

The Mousterian Factor

The Mousterians produced bipoints which are the oldest in Europe (Sorcessi and Dibbie 2003). Some of the earliest Mousterian bipoint publications are in Osborn (1922), Mellars (1969), Hoerens (1903), Binford and Binford (2009), and Sollas (1924); also, they illustrate bone barbed harpoons, which compares to today's Eskimos. The basic Mousterian bipoint classification is suggested as in Bordes and Bourgon (1951). The brutish physiology of Neanderthals (Mousterians) was probably introduced by Henry Field of the Field Museum of Natural History in the full-scale displays in their Ernest R. Graham Hall (Farrington and Field 1929). Later *viewpoints* were presented (Figure 6-5).

Figure 6-5 – 1930s Photograph of a Display from the Chicago Natural History Museum – Formerly the Field Museum of Natural History.

Early Mousterian lithic technology was a continuation of basically early biface flaking methods. Large flakes were struck off boulder outcrops or field/stream cobbles. It usually has a bulb scar remaining. It was hard hammering process which did not produce well-made tools, but essentially *tons* of flakes. Figure 6-6 shows a large flake reduction failure.

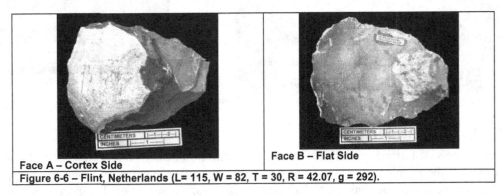

Face A – Cortex Side
Face B – Flat Side
Figure 6-6 – Flint, Netherlands (L= 115, W = 82, T = 30, R = 42.07, g = 292).

---

[61] The term *leaf point* is used because European archaeologists used the term differently than U.S. archaeologists; otherwise, bipoint is used. European archaeologists generally refer to them as *points*.

Early bipoints are not true laurel-leaf bipoints that become common in later ages (Figure 6-7). They tend to have a round-end state. They were first found in Korolevo (Kozlowshi 2003), which are dated between 220 and 280 k YBP. They appear to have been invented independently, although some archaeologists suggest Acheulian sources or at least from the Levallois technology (Allsworth-Jones 1986, Gamble 1999, and Hibble and Monet-White 1988). For the most part, the Mousterians occupy the late Eem and early Wurm glacial eras and disappear around 35,000 YBP. They hunted large and small game, such as from the reindeer to the mammoth. They were in Asia by 45 k YBP (Kuzmin 2004); thus, the bipoint had a world-wide distribution by 40 k BYP. The direction from Europe to Asia is interesting in that the Czech Republic (41-31 YBP) does not have the bipoint (Svoboda and Bar-Yosef 2003).

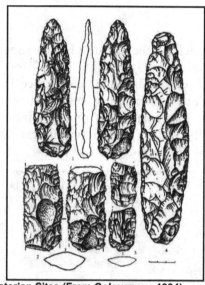

Figure 6-7 – Elongated Bipoints from Mousterian Sites (From Golovanova 1994).

Figure 6-8 shows an early Mousterian knife that is beginning to show the bipoint form. It probably dates around 50-100 k YBP and was found outside Paris, France. It is this form that suggests Europe is the first *home-land* for the bipoint or elongated knife. The author readily admits he does not know the true(first) bipoint home-land, but this area is suggested. As mentioned, the bipoint comes out of the Levallois technology and was first a uniface bipoint. This specimen has a spoke shave (lower), unifacially flaked, and a well-worn end (right) which is retouched to a beveled edge. The bulb scar is present. Note its high LWT ratio (R).

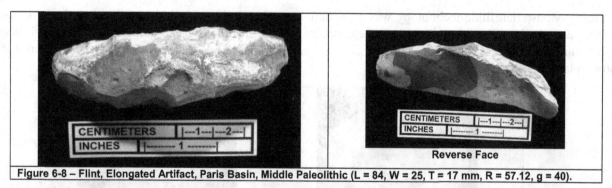

Figure 6-8 – Flint, Elongated Artifact, Paris Basin, Middle Paleolithic (L = 84, W = 25, T = 17 mm, R = 57.12, g = 40).

The Case of Neanderthalensis

The Neanderthals of Europe are often classified by anthropologists as a separate *race* of hominids. And, the popular view of the people is that they were a *primitive-lot* living in caves and roaming Europe during the Ice Age. Popular medias, such as National Geographic, offer sensational reports on the so-called last Neanderthal (Hall 2008). This article argues that they existed from 200 to 28 k YBP. And, as a note, the European plain was not ice free until the later Pleistocene (Eriksen and Bratlund 2002).

Neanderthals were as human as anyone, but classify is what anthropologists (and archaeologists) do! Evolution, like technology, is a continuum, but… For technology, the Middle Paleolithic is often called a transition and extinction (interbreeding) for the people living at that time period. A time period of 5,000 to 10,000 years is suggested for the separation of Neanderthals and modern humans for eastern Europe (Adams 2009).

Somewhere, someone invented the bipoint. The *who* will probably never be resolved, and neither will the where nor when. As discussed in this publication, southern Africa is the home for the bipoint's invention; however, a lone cave in Hungary, called Szeleta, may counter this argument. It has a date range from 42,960 +/-860 to 11,761 +/-62. Another close cave has a date range of 27,933 +/- 224 back to 33,101 +/- 512 which both have leaf-shaped points (Figure 6-9). The two bipoints shown would simply be classified as bifaces…but probably knives by most archaeologists. Regardless, they reflect a bipoint's chronology in Europe. The round base is often simply called a biface by most archaeologists.

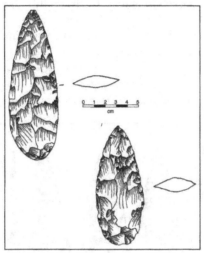

Figure 6-9 – Rounded Base Bipoints from Istallosko Cave (From: Vertes 1955).

The Neanderthal practiced the Mousterian technology at a site called La Roche a Pierrot near Stint-Cesaire, France. The average site date is 40,000 YBP (Leveque, Backer, and Guilbaud 1993). It supplements Saint-Casaire's inventory and both define the Neanderthal of France. One artifact found at both is the foliate point with a retouched base. In addition to the bipoint, this foliate is common and diagnostic in the Mousterian toolkit (Figure 6-10). This retouched foliate may lead to the lanceolate form on later prehistoric Europe which was transferred to the New World? This tool form occurs on the U.S. southern coastal plain; most archaeologists do not accept and/or recognized it (Hranicky 2018).

Figure 6-10 – Foliate Points from Saint-Cesaire, France.

The Solutrean Factor

The Solutreans of France and Spain are a relatively short-lived culture of 4000 years (Smith !972 and Straus and Clark 1986). Its earliest date is at Les Eyzies which dates 21-22,000 YBP (Movius 1960). They borrowed the laurel-leaf implement and probably perfected it around 17,000 YBP; thus, they can be the people who perfected it and transported it to other areas, some suggest the New World. As argued, the

Solutreans did not invent the bipoint, and where they came from is unknown. Montet-White (1973) found shouldered and bipoint in abundance at Le Malpas rockshelter. The remarkable homogeneity of assemblages from Fourneau du Diable, Laugerie Haute, or Les Jamblanes exemplifies the skill associated with the manufacture of Solutrean implements. The use of invasive retouch may be a diagnostic attribute for their bipoints. However, the principal state for Solutrean is the pointed end form. The semi-round base found elsewhere is probably not related to Solutrean bipoint technology.

Sollas (1924) was the first to suggest that French bipoints have counterparts in the Americas, namely Argentina, California, and Mexico. He comments:

> *The industry may have survived the people, as it certainly survived the Paleolithic epoch, reappearing in the flint weapons of Neolithic Europe and spreading in ever widening circles till it found its way in later times over the greater part of the world* (1924:506).

While Sollas (1924) suggests Africa as the source of the Solutreans, he has a drawing of Solutrean tools identified as being from Cantabria and Catalonia. He further suggests the modified bipoint which resembles the Clovis lanceolate point (Figure 6-11). Note the resharpened bipoint (right) and the indented-base bipoint drawing. This indented base along with channels (like fluting) on blades is highly suggestive of Clovis technology. The problem, of course, is transferring this technology to the New World. If one considers a technological continuum philosophy, there is **NO** problem; it is a normative technology process occurring throughout prehistory. It becomes simply a *when* problem; high-sea crafts are assumed.

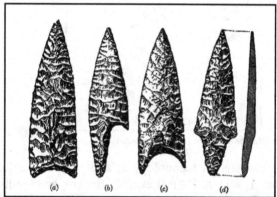

Figure 6-11 – Solutrean Points: (a) Laurel leaf point with concave base; (b) Notched point of Galliean type; (c) and (d) of Calalonian type (after Sollas 1924). All these morphologies show up in the U.S., naturally in the PaleoAmerican era.

The Middle Atlantic coast has received attention as a possible occupation area for the Solutreans in the Before-Clovis time period (Hranicky 2007). While the continental shelf appears to be the obvious occupation area, unless they moved inland for exploiting additional natural resources, archaeology can only find a small picture of the occupation, namely the bipoint. However, like all cultures using this technology, there are numerous other tools used for daily activities, such as burins, scrapers, etc. Assuming the presence of Solutreans on the east coast, there should be numerous tool classes that can be specifically attributed to them. A New World Solutrean toolkit has not been defined; thus, archaeologists do not know what to *hunt* archaeologically. Figure 6-12 shows a sample of French Solutrean tools. One problem persists, is this core area exclusively Solutrean for first Americans?

> **Solutrean Technique** - pressure flaking on the edge of a flint rough-out not just to remove tiny flakes and alter the angle of the point and shape of the blade, but also to take off large and relatively thin flakes from across the surface (Semenov 1964). It increased the plastic possibilities of knapping. While initially an Old World technique, it was transferred to Early Americans and used by them as legacy tools. However, Solutrean terminology is rarely used in American archaeology, but with pre-Clovis sites, this technique is being re-examined.

Based on *true* for the U.S. immigration for the Solutreans, a Landfall Model is argued on the following:
1) Favorable southeastern U.S. environment vs. glacially-dominated Spain/France environments
2) Ocean crossings were commonplace in the Pleistocene

3) North Carolina-Virginia above-water continental shelf provided an ideal landing and habitation area
4) The *then* Chesapeake River provided a constant supply of fresh water and inland resources
5) Inland Solutrean-like artifacts (blade industry) are found supporting the migration and landfall
6) Initially adaptive strategies were the same as those in their homeland
7) Source for Old World microtool legacies.

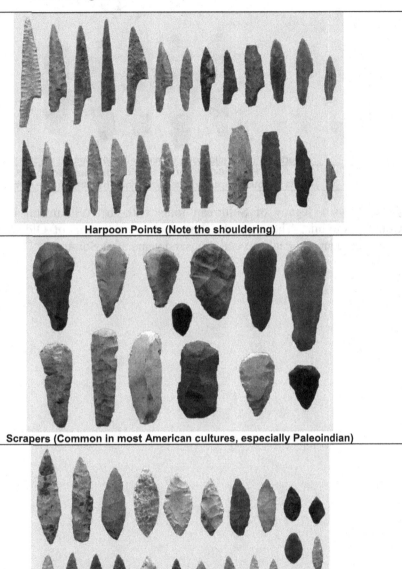

Harpoon Points (Note the shouldering)

Scrapers (Common in most American cultures, especially Paleoindian)

Bipoints (Common in most American cultures)
Note: over 25+ different styles with pointed ends.

Perforators (Similar form common in most American paleocultures)
Figure 6-12 – Part of the French Solutrean Toolkit.
Note various shapes and usage conditions (British Museum, London).

Figure 6-13 shows a legacy of Solutrean tools with the Williamson Paleoindian (44DN1) site in Dinwiddie County, Virginia. The example shows the continuation of Old World tool forms. Naturally, Williamson is Paleoindian and dates several thousand years after Solutrean.

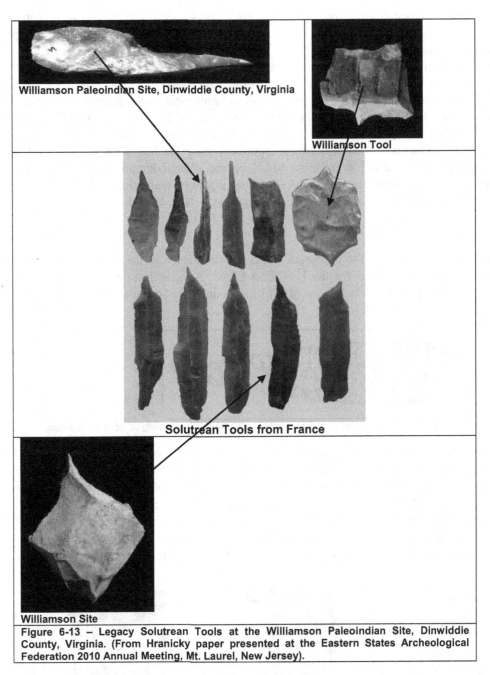

Williamson Paleoindian Site, Dinwiddie County, Virginia

Williamson Tool

Solutrean Tools from France

Williamson Site

Figure 6-13 – Legacy Solutrean Tools at the Williamson Paleoindian Site, Dinwiddie County, Virginia. (From Hranicky paper presented at the Eastern States Archeological Federation 2010 Annual Meeting, Mt. Laurel, New Jersey).

Other than the bipoint, scrapers and perforators are ideal candidates for early Atlantic coast before-Clovis tools. As Solutrean tools are all made off blades and pressure flaked, so these would be assumed to exist on the Atlantic coast. However, these tools would be difficult to discern for Virginia Paleoindian toolkits as having an Old World legacy. The Solutrean scraper does not have a spur which occurs in the Paleoindian era scraper. The needle-nosed perforator is also a possibility. One major condition: where did the Solutreans require Old World flint, or did they adapt to Middle Atlantic area stones?

Solutrean and Transatlantic Migrations

Without a lengthy discussion, but a reminder, the Solutrean hypothesis (or theory for many archaeologists) is a reality for Before Clovis in eastern North America. McCowan (1939) was the first to start the Solutrean migration theories, hypotheses, propositions, or other forms of scientific logic that followed. Also, many American archaeologists were familiar with Robert Munro's (1912) work that provided comparative examples that added the *romance* to the Solutrean connection to the New World. However, the Solutrean factor does not become a major archaeological topic until the late 1990s. As a scientific note, Solutrean immigration into the U.S. does not necessarily mean the remaining people into early times; it can simply mean the remainder of their lithic technology.

Arguably, there are no eastern land-based U.S. dates, artifacts, or sites to establish Solutrean stone toolmaking firmly in the eastern U.S. Of course, the *classic* time gap (6000 + years) has been argued repeatedly in archaeology for Solutrean and Clovis. While various technological methodologies do appear to be similar, other Old World areas have the same technology as the Solutreans. Dates of 25,000 BP for trans-Atlantic lithic technology transfers are not unrealistic (Hranicky 2011). This author agrees with the sea-faring Atlantic crossings, not with the voyagers' homeland being reportedly only for Iberia (as in: Stanford and Bradley 2002 and 2004 a&b). The time depth problem for Solutrean, Magdalenian, and Aterian trans-Atlantic New World voyages is not a major one. Or perhaps, it does not exist technologically. With all that said, Old World technology, like wings of information, made its way to the New World.

Indented-Base Bipoint

Stanford and Bradley (2012 a&b) argue that the lanceolate form has its origins in the Solutreans of Iberia. This lithic form/technology is argued by them for the U.S. East Coast. And, their examples justified their argument for Solutrean; it is not without merit. Bordes (1956) has a drawing for an indented base bipoint (Figure 6-14) which can be used as an example.

Figure 6-14 – Solutrean Indented Base Bipoint from Spain (after Bordes 1956). Note: basal thinning or concaved shape.

Hranicky (2011) argues for a small lanceolate point on the Middle Atlantic coastal plain (Figure 6-15). Stanford and Bradley (2012a) make the same argument for small lanceolates in the East. While they may be the Fox Creek projectile point type (Woodland), their environment suggests otherwise, namely they are heavily patinated. As noted, chronology based on patination is a poor indicator of age (Hranicky 1992). Lowery (2008) calls this lanceolate the jasper Miles type. These specimens are only place holders at 16,000 YBP; they do not answer the Clovis origin problem. Many archaeologists would classify the U.S. specimens as *poor* Clovis examples. These small triangles occur on South America's Atlantic coast (see Roosevelt, et al. 2002).

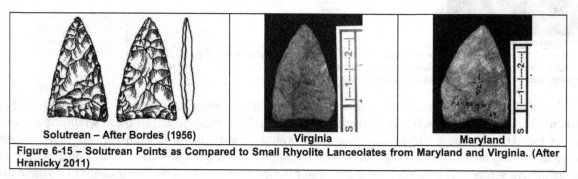

Solutrean – After Bordes (1956)   Virginia   Maryland

Figure 6-15 – Solutrean Points as Compared to Small Rhyolite Lanceolates from Maryland and Virginia. (After Hranicky 2011)

The African Factor

An alternative to the Solutrean factor is the African source for bipoints. Their state is both round- and pointed-base forms. The Middle Atlantic area is argued here as the Solutrean occupation; however, the Southeastern U.S. has bipoints that suggest that they do not have a true Solutrean legacy…probably African (Figure 6-16). The major difference between them is Solutrean bipoints are longer and narrower; and, the African bipoints tend to replicate Solutrean forms but have an ovate form. Africa, depending on the authority, has Solutrean in North Africa (Otte 2002). As a note: large Egyptian bipoints are restricted to the Early Bronze Age (Rosen 1997). Figure 4-17 shows another specimen.

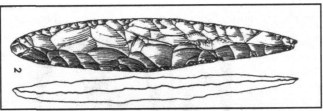

Figure 6-16 – Middle Paleolithic Bipoint from Africa (After: Bordes 1956).

Figure 6-17 - This Aterian specimen is a 2 15/16" African Paleolithic to Neolithic, bi-pointed, Leaf blade Artifact. This artifact is estimated to be 5,000 - 1,000 years old.

The following bipoint is from Niger, Africa. The ventral face is flaked; however, the dorsal face is not flaked. It shows the smooth blade production (Figure 6-18). This specimen demonistrates the world-wide distribution of the bipoint.

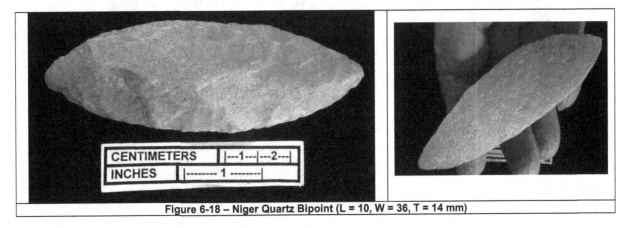

Figure 6-18 – Niger Quartz Bipoint (L = 10, W = 36, T = 14 mm)

Aterian Tool Legacy

The Aterian tanged tool represents a technology transfer from Africa to the American Middle and Southeastern states (Hranicky 2007). Once the technology arrives in the Southeast, it basically becomes an American version of Old World technology. Figure 6-19 shows a probable technological continuum. Unless there is continuous maintenance of the African form, such as multiple cross-Atlantic migrations, any tool technology undergoes change, modification, or numerous factors that create different structures of the former tool class. However, the primitives of the tool's construct continue. Archaeology should trace technology legacies, if only for sources of the technology and the people who made the tools.

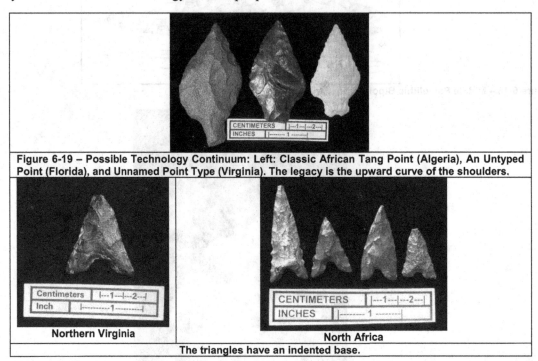

Figure 6-19 – Possible Technology Continuum: Left: Classic African Tang Point (Algeria), An Untyped Point (Florida), and Unnamed Point Type (Virginia). The legacy is the upward curve of the shoulders.

Northern Virginia

North Africa

The triangles have an indented base.

North Africa has lanceolate/triangle points that places the Aterians in the quest for the origins of Clovis. Numerous small paleopoints occur in the Middle Atlantic area. While this is outside the discussion for the bipoint's origins, it amplifies the possibility of the numerous European (all) sources for the first population to migrate to the American east coast. Figure 6-20 shows comparative specimens. All specimens have basal grinding. All specimens have shallow basal fluting.

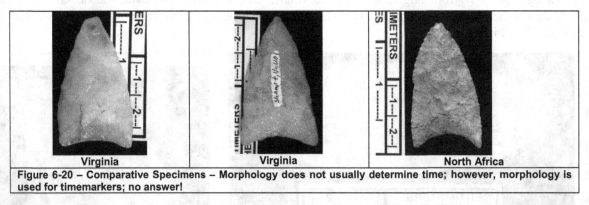

Virginia

Virginia

North Africa

Figure 6-20 – Comparative Specimens – Morphology does not usually determine time; however, morphology is used for timemarkers; no answer!

Figure 6-21 shows Aterian bipoints with resharpening examples; this resharpened bit method occurs throughout the U.S.[62]

---

[62] Most archaeologists would classifiy these resharpened bipoints as stemmed projectile points.

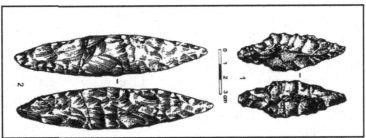

Figure 6-21 – Resharpening from Bipoint to Expended Tool (After Camps 1974).

The Magdalenian Factor

The Magdalenians of Europe cannot be ruled out as a possible source for the peopling of the New World. They were manifested in south-western France from which they get their culture name (Capitan and Peyrony 1928), and probably had origins well before the Solutrean invasion into the area. After the Solutreans, they dominated western Europe. Oakley (1959) suggested: ***The material culture of the Magdalenians resembled that of the Eskimos, possibly because of the adaptation to a partly similar environment.***

This toolmaking industry and artistic tradition of the Upper Paleolithic of Europe followed the Solutreans (Hemington 1980). They represent the culmination of Upper Paleolithic cultural development in Europe. The Magdalenians lived some 17,000 to 11,000 YBP, at a time when reindeer, wild horses, and bison formed large herds; the people appear to have lived a semisettled life surrounded by abundant food. They killed animals with spears, snares, and traps and lived in rockshelters, or substantial dwellings in winter and in tents in summer. Their technology did include the bipoint, and they did have the lanceolate biface. They are ideal candidates for the founding of Clovis. See Ruspoli (1986).

They continued the Solutrean's finely made bipoint and added the bone harpoon which suggests fishing (with the boat?). Their artwork suggests they hunted the mammoth as well as game herds. They overlap with Clovis, and they are a more likely candidate for Clovis technology in the New World; however, they receive little attention in public media and archaeological literatures. The lithic shouldered tool form of the Solutreans is not present in the Magdalenian era. Figure 6-22 shows two examples of Magdalenian tools that are suggestive of Clovis technology – especially the spurred scraper/graver. The lanceolate form has basal thinning, perhaps ancient fluting. The European disappearance of shouldering may argue why it is not found in the New World. Thus, this technology can be the one that is the transfer form to the eastern U.S.

As discussed above, Stanford and Bradley (2012 a&b) argue that the lanceolate biface is present in the Solutrean toolkit. True, it does have an indented base and resembles to 4000-5000 year later Clovis lanceolate form. However, the Magdalenians also had an indented base biface, and their date is comprehensibly the same as Clovis. And, they had backed blades. Figure 6-22 shows a sample.

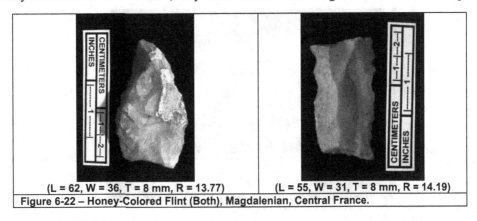

(L = 62, W = 36, T = 8 mm, R = 13.77)   (L = 55, W = 31, T = 8 mm, R = 14.19)
Figure 6-22 – Honey-Colored Flint (Both), Magdalenian, Central France.

Again, Hranicky (2004) argued that the earliest dimension in East Coast toolmaking was blademaking as opposed to biface production. This aspect of lithic technology is present at the 50,000-year old Topper site in South Carolina (Goodyear 2011). For this reason, the bipoint is argued here as essentially a blade technology which predates Clovis. Note: early Topper does not have bifaces nor the bipoint (Goodyear 2011).

As stated by many, once the Levallois blade technology was discovered, it became a major part of most prehistoric toolkits; it was a technology carryover worldwide. Figure 4-23 shows a sample of well-made Magdalenian blades.

Collins (1999) spends hundreds of pages attempting to define a Clovis blade *as some kind of unique creature* in a specific period of prehistory… and passes A+. Like bifaces, the core-produced blade (chapeau de gendarme) is impossible to classify it continuously to a specific culture and a specific chronology. Blademaking does not make Clovis unique; blademaking is a major factor in the whole Paleoindian era. The same proposition is true for the bipoint.

Tranchet blades are somewhat different from Solutrean in that they are long, and slender with little or no retouch. The knapper made few attempts to maintain blade symmetry. They are present in Texas Clovis sites.

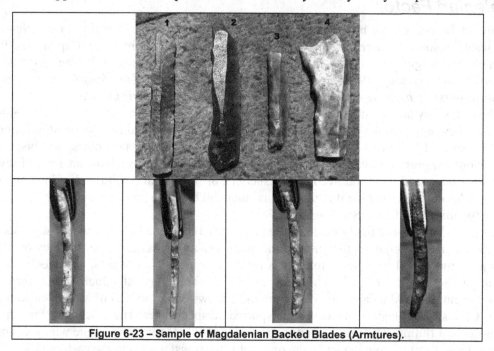

Figure 6-23 – Sample of Magdalenian Backed Blades (Armtures).

Comparative examples: Figure 6-24 shows comparative bladelet examples. The small blade occurs frequently on Hopewell and Adena sites. But as a technological consequence, the following small blades are from the Paleoindian Williamson site in Dinwiddie County, Virginia. Since Williamson is a quarry site, these specimens show little wear but have extensive retouch.

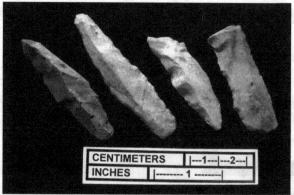

Figure 6-24 – Chalcedony Paleo-Bladelets from the Williamson Site in Virginia.

Figure 6-25 provides another sample of their toolmaking, namely the bipoint. They also have a variety of bit shapes, but each specimen maintains the V-shaped chassis. Other than their archaeological context, they are difficult to determine from Solutrean bipoints.

After the Last Glacial Maximum (LGM), climatic conditions remained cold and open herbaceous environments were dominant during the Dryas I. Around 13,000 YBP, temperatures and humidity increased in western Europe and mark the onset of the Bölling phase in western Europe (Guiot 1987). Does this become a factor in Magdalenian expansion?

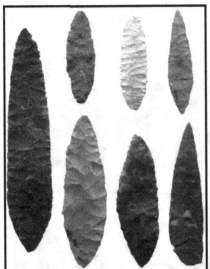

Figure 6-25 – Magdalenian Bipoints from France. Note the maintenance of the Solutrean pointed-base form (after Guiot 1987).

Circum-Pacific Bipoints

The Pacific Ocean occupies a greater area than the Atlantic Ocean; thus, voyages across it presented a greater difficulty for humans crossing it. Most populations migrated around the shore-edges. This migration is referenced as a circum-Pacific area for bipoints and other lithic technologies (Bryan 1978).

With occupation in Japan dating to 132 K YBP (Ikawa-Smith 1978), the coastal Pacific realm has numerous sites yielding Pleistocene dates. The Pacific realm has numerous major sites, such as Diuktai Cave, Ushki, Iwajuku, Sozudal, Mapa, and Choukoutien that offer toolkits that can be found on the American side of the Pacific.

For the Asian bipoint, Diuktai Cave has several specimens dating to approximately 13,000 YBP (Mochanov 1978). Bipoints are also found at the Ushki Lake sites in Siberia (Dikov 1978).

The Asian Factor

As argued, the bipoint is found worldwide. Derrv'anko, et al. (1998) reports long, narrow and ovate bipoints in Siberia's Paleolithic at Selemdzha site in Russia (Figure 6-26). Also, Zakharikov (1999) excavated the Nepreyakhino site in which laurel leaf points were found which date to the final Mousterian at 31k BYP. Grigorieva (1983) reports them as being bifacially worked leafs. The Pacific realm has numerous bipoints (and early dates) that have an origin in Asia. See Bryan (1978). In a popularized report, Parfit (2000) illustrates a bipoint from Dyuktai in Siberia which is argued on the pathway to the Bering Strait. The morphology is principally a semi-pointed form.

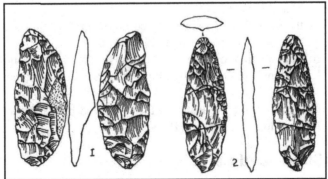

Figure 6-26 – Elongated Bipoints at Selemdzha Site, Russia (After: Derev'anko 1998).

There is a bipoint date at the Ust'-Ul'ma I site in Siberia, Russia as Derv'anko, et al. (1998) reports a date of 19,369 +/- 60 YBP for two bipoints that were excavated (Figure 6-27). With this date, trans-Pacific migration is certainly a real possibility in American archaeology. American archaeologists insist on early populations *walking* into the New World via the ice-free corridor. A Pacific coastal route by boat is suggested here.

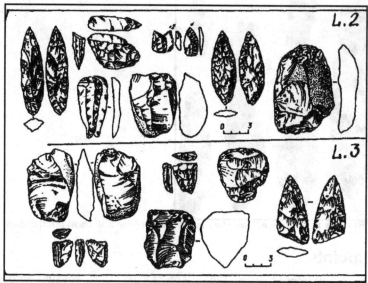

Figure 6-27 – Artifacts Found in Level 2 at Ust'-Ul'ma I, Russia. Note bipoints in Level 2.

Another high-quality bipoint was reported by Kornfeld and Tabarev (2009). This specimen was found in Russia (Figure 6-28). This specimen has outré-passé flaking which equals the quality of Solutrean specimens. The Far East is also a legacy for the American bipoint, namely the U. S. west coast. It offers a parsimonious alternative to the European hypothesis of Stanford and Bradley (2012 a&b).

Figure 6-28 – Bipoint, Osipovka Site, Kavarovsk, Russia (L= 150 mm). From Gerasimov (1928).

Southeastern Asia

Sites in southeastern Asia, such as Indo-China, Borneo, Sumatra, or Java, do not have the bipoint or any elongated implement. This assessment is based on Lower Paleolithic Choukoutienian, Anyathyian, Tampanian, and Patjitanian sites (Movius 1949). The sites reflect an out-of-Africa lithic technology from the Lower Paleolithic (Movius 1949 and Dennell 2009).

China has microlithics with pointed ends. They are common in Manchuria and date to era before the Neolithic. The country generally repeats the phenomenon in Europe.

Tolstoy (1958) reported bipoints in the Lake Baikal and Lena River of northern Asia. Also, Upper Paleolithic sites, such as Verkholenskaia-Gora (Okladnikov 1959); however, small bipoints do not occur until the Khin'skaia period.

For Japan and the Pacific margins, the bipoint was first reported by Chard and Befu (1960). There is a circum-Pacific distribution for the bipoint in Bryan (1978).

Case for Australia (Sunda and Sahul)

The prehistory of Australia dates back to 50-60 k YBP. While blades are present, the bipoint is missing from the toolkit (White and O'Connell 1983, Veth 2011, and Mulvaney 1961). This missing artifact may be due to under reporting. The Australians probably made the western coast of South America. Sites such as Niah Cave and Kow Swamp offer an insight to the circum-Pacific migrations of humans.

Monte Verde is an archaeological site in southern Chile that may be evidence of the sea trip, which basically dates 13,000 YBP (Gibbons 1997). However, for some archaeologists, the date is approximately 33 k YBP (Monte Verde 1 (MV1), Zone C, - ca. 33,000 years). A bipoint-like artifact was found at the site. Dilleyhay (Collins and Dilleyhay 2011) comments: ... *although the stratigraphy is intact, the radiocarbon dates are valid, and the human artefacts are genuine, I hesitate to accept this older level without more evidence and without sites of comparable age elsewhere in the Americas.*

Old World Bipoint Dates

The anthropic origin of bipoint technology is as old as western humanity and is the most consistently-made implement throughout prehistory. One early African date comes from Blombos Cave in South Africa, which has produced archaeological evidence for soft hammer, pressure flaking of stone tools, and suggests homo sapiens sapiens evolved earlier than previously thought (Wadley 2010). With art (engraving), shell beads, and the use of red ocher, the Blombos social/technology includes the refined bipoint (Mourre, Villa, and Henshilwood 2010). Figure 6-29 shows the African bipoint which revolutionizes archaeological theories about early humans and their social/technology, particularly between European and African anthropologists (Barham and Mitchell 2008). It dates to 75 k YBP. It is the first bipoint that meets the requirements for the BMM. Its shape, design, and manufacture are the same as what would become the popular Solutrean bipoint; however, it outdates the Solutreans by 50,000 + years. Its form shows an extremely pointed chassis, more than the classic Solutrean bipoint. Its discovery makes the world-wide proposition for the bipoint a reality. With this date on a bipoint, the concept of technology organization is the world is left with a state of confusion archaeologically.

Figure 6-29 – Bipoint Found in Blombos Cave, South Africa. It dates approximately 75 k YBP.

Another Africa bipoint found at Pinnacle Point (PP13B) dates 71,000 YBP. The site also has seashells, red ocher, blades, and bone tools (Marean 2010). See Figure 6-30. With the presence of bipoints, these early date should indicate problems in archaeological methods and classifications...especially technological chronologies.

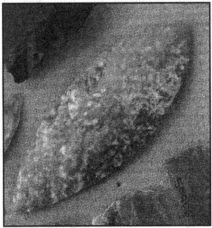

Figure 6-30 – The Pinnacle Point Specimen (Scientific American 2010).

189

Further, these refined bipoints dispute that Europe was the homeland for the bipoint; however, are they simply a movement of technology back into Africa from Europe? Does it argue the homo sapien sapien movement back into Africa? The answer is beyond the scope of this publication. They do redefine dating for this class of artifacts in the Old World. The Blombos specimen is an expended tool that was probably discarded in the cave; the tool's bit has been used extensively. Its pressure flaking technique was not present in northern Africa and southern Europe at this suggested time. The Solutreans are generally credited with inventing pressure flaking and, of course, high-quality bipoint technology. Solutreans are well-known for bipoint overshot flaking which is not present on the Blombos specimen. Other Old World areas have bipoints, but not as well made. Could the basic bipoint morphology have been developed in Africa, and was carried by humans migrating to other parts of the world? The Solutreans continued the African technology to include poor-to-finely-made bipoints. The quality of bipoints varies regardless of where…and through time! The presence of the bipoint cannot be automatically called Solutrean or, for that matter, Aterian or Lupemban cultures in Africa. As argued, the bipoint/V-shaped stemmed technology transcends culture; it is a legacy for cultures found around the world. Even with these dates, the source for the bipoint is still suggested as occurring in the Mousterians of Europe.

As mentioned, the literature suggests that Solutreans were the first to the New World (Bradley and Stanford 2004 and 2012 a&b). But, did Africans cross the Atlantic during the Late Pleistocene? The question is: which continent was the source(s) for the New World populating: Asia, Europe, and/or Africa? All of which suggest poly-migrations. For years, archaeologists have maintained a mono-migration theory into the New World, namely from Asia. Far too many early (30,000+) dates contradict this premise, such as the Topper site (50 k YBP) in South Carolina or the controversial Taima Taima site (30 k YBP) in Venezuela.

Classic Bipoint Forms

Bipoints have numerous structural definitions depending on archaeological perspectives and interpretative viewpoints. The following presents a description based on Figures 6-31 and 6-32 which show Solutrean bipoints that represent the basic morphology. In addition to the above definition, it has edge-to-edge parallel flake scars, no flake hinges, pointed at both ends, obvious workend, thin, and made from flint. Presently, **no** specimen of this quality has been found outside of Europe.

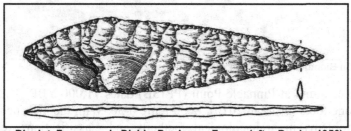

Figure 6-31 – Lower Solutrean Bipoint. Fourneau du Diable, Dordogne, France (after Bordes 1956).

This flintknapping quality does not occur in the Americas until Clovis which is the reported archaeological connection to Solutrean technology. Does it represent the general Solutrean bipoint, especially ones that were transported to the Western Hemisphere? No, even for the Solutreans, there was variation in knapping skill. The flaking quality argument connection to the Americas was started with Fraison and Bradley (1999). The Solutrean argument continues as the principal bipoint source in American archaeology for the eastern U.S. Atlantic coast. The state/shape of this bipointed chassis (V-shaped) constitutes its bipoint legacy.

The large Iberian bipoints, upwards of 400 mm were made off large slab (broken boulder) of flint. They were bifacially flaked by soft-hammer percussion into large bipoints (Bradley 2008). Then, they were pressured flakes into the final form. This manufacturing technique presents the first problem in establishing the New World Solutrean legacy. The eastern U.S. specimens tend to demonstrate a blade technology rather than a bifacial reduction method.

Figure 6-32 - Classic Legacy French Solutrean Bipoint (Permission: British Museum). Volgu, 16,000 BC, Laurel Leaf (Approximately 200 mm in length). Note: the quality of this bipoint is not normal for the Solutreans, but it is often used for New World paleo-flaking qualities. (Trustees 1956).

Large Iberian bipoints were probably ceremonial in that they are seldom used, often occur in caches, and often are coated with red ocher. They may have been trade, status, or tribute items.

While the Solutrean form sets requirements for the bipoint model (BMM) for archaeology, the above highly stylized form is not found on the American coast. Also, this flaking quality is not common in Europe or African continents. These bipoints and associated toolkits vary in composition, especially in expended tool forms. Two attributes can be derived from this specimen: 1) the V-shaped stem and 2) the V-shaped resharpened bit. These two bipoint attributes are found on specimens from Maine to Nevada.

Bipoint Bit Resharpening

Once resharpening occurred on the bipoint's bit (workend), it is virtually impossible to define it as an originally-shaped bipoint. Each end varies but, overall, it has a general bipoint outline. Figure 6-33 shows a large specimen that is suggested as being originally a bipoint. Its state (classification) is a bipoint. Resharpening modified the specimen's morphology until its shape is now considered *simply* a stemmed projectile point; however, upon closer examination it has sharp margins that are not on the *so-called* blade. This resharpened bipoint argument occurs throughout this publication and is found coast-to-coast. The chassis (stem) is almost always unbroken and forms a triangle. It must be a knife as it is certainly not flyable as a spearpoint. See Resharpened Bipoints section.

While not provable here, there are regional methods of bit reshaping; thus, this may imply regional usage and function (see Bipoint Resharpening section.). However, as argued, bit resharpening has a chronological aspect. The basic knife (and cutting) form is assumed. The literature is full of classifications of the bipoint as a *projectile point*; there is **no** evidence that it was ever thrown.

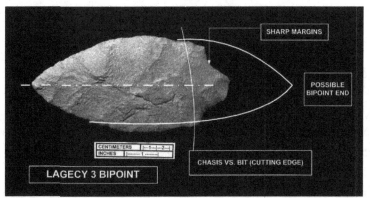

Figure 6-33 – Quartzite Bipoint, Found on Chesterfield-Prince George County line off the Appomattox River in 1966 (L = 159, W = 78, T = 14 mm, R = 28.53). It has sharp (right) margin with bold flake scars (formerly Fred Morgan collection).

Comparative example: This bipoint style has numerous bit reshaping forms. Figure 6-34 shows another example with a similar chassis form. It was made off a large flake by hard hammer flaking. Instead of a pointed-stem-like shape, it has rounded bit which is still sharp. It is also assumed to be a heavy-duty tool.

Figure 6-34 – Coastal Plain Chart, Flint River in Baker County, Georgia (L = 125, W = 62, T = 17 mm, R = 34.27, E = 2.02, g = 121).

At the modified stage by usage and resharpening, it becomes a V-shaped stemmed knife. In prehistory, once the cutting blade was exhausted, it was discarded and becomes archaeologically an expended knife which is relatively common but seldom identified and reported as to its original form. As a suggestion, the expended bipoint was possibly turned around, and re-hafted, thus, doubling the life of the tool. Few pure U.S. bipoints have been found which truly represent the *classic* model; however, Figure 6-35 shows such a specimen (Hranicky 2011). It has light (lateral side bit end) resharpening which maintains the V-shaped bit.

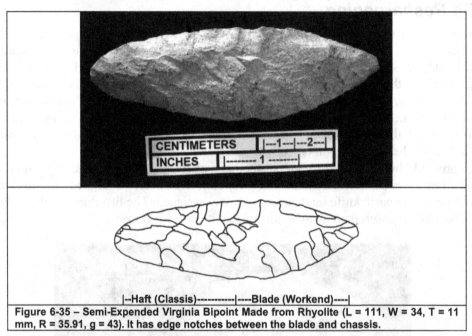

|--Haft (Classis)------------|----Blade (Workend)----|

Figure 6-35 – Semi-Expended Virginia Bipoint Made from Rhyolite (L = 111, W = 34, T = 11 mm, R = 35.91, g = 43). It has edge notches between the blade and chassis.

Figure 6-36 shows some of the various forms of bit resharpening on bipoints. Throughout this publication, bit resharpening is a major topic in classifying bipoints. These bipoints are often called eastern Morrow Mountain projectile points by most eastern archaeologists that is completely false, especially the implied date.

192

Figure 6-36 - Two Bit Examples from North Carolina. These bipoints are often called Morrow Mountain projectile points by most archaeologists. Note differing bits.

The V-shaped bit has the best evidence of being a direct Old World legacy bipoint; however, the associative age remains a factor (see Early Virginia bipoints section). The time period for the actual Old World bipoint into the U.S. will never be known, let alone the primary occupation area. We can only infer that the occupation lasted generations and probably disappeared after several hundred years.

Figure 6-37 shows an Alabama resharpened bipoint. It was made from jasper which is a common stone in the middle eastern U.S. area. While assigned to the bipoint class, it may have enough properties to simply be a V-shaped stemmed knife. Note its large bit (workend).

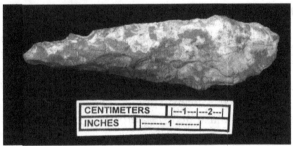

Figure 6-37 – A Central Alabama Resharpened Bipoint (L = 109, W = 29, T = 8 mm).

How extensive was the occupation, specifically in terms of its geography, can be surmised from the distribution of the *true* V-shaped bit? Figure 6-38 suggests that the initial people moved inland to the uplands. There is no date for the specimen. For example, the flintknapper who made Virginia's Cinmar bipoint used rhyolite from the Maria Furnace road rhyolite quarry in Pennsylvania.

This Virginia specimen has had active service but is expended. As discussed previously, the bit is a classic V-shape It has weather flake scars and has the classic V-shaped stem. More importantly, it is made from upland Virginia rhyolite. However, this specimen could be a crudely made late era artifact (Hranicky 2008). Regardless, it is classified as a Legacy 2 bipoint.

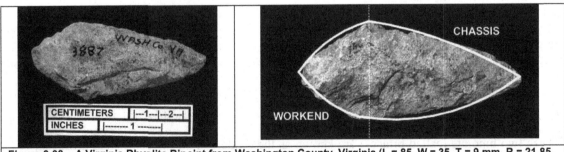

Figure 6-38 – A Virginia Rhyolite Bipoint from Washington County, Virginia (L = 85, W = 35, T = 9 mm, R = 21.85, g = 26) Note left cutting margin can still be seen. It is a Legacy 2 bipoint.

Figure 6-39 again illustrates a time line for most bipoints. This same usage is present on Solutrean bipoints. As argued, the key to bipoint identification of form is the microscope.

Once more, the major mistake in American archaeology is the failure to recognize the resharpened bipoint. The following specimen would be classified as an Adena projectile point by most archaeologists. As discussed, left end (often called the stem) is sharp on all margins and is the bit; whereas, the right haft or chassis (often called the blade) shows no lateral margin wear or striations. Additionally, the chassis shows no polish. And, as discussed, it has the legacy large flake removed on both sides at the junction of the bit and chassis. All said, it is a resharpened bipoint. For an example, this mis-classification often places the Adena culture in areas that they never visited!

Figure 6-39 – Rhyolite, Grayson County, Virginia
(L = 114 W = 44, T = 13 mm, R = 33.68, g = 71) Arrows point to sharp edges.
Note: wear patterns and striations are on the left bit.

Establishing Bipoint in the U.S.

As this publication discusses, establishing the bipoint along the Atlantic coast has been difficult because of its lack of association in archaeological contexts, and most archaeologists are projectile-point oriented (as in Morrow and Gnecco 2006 or Justice 1987) or insistent on the Beringia entry into the Americas (as in: Walker and Driskell 2007 or Meltzer 2009) or proclaim Asian genetics (as in: Olsen 2002 or Wells 2006). Furthermore, the chronology problem has been a major concern which is essentially missing in most archaeological interpretations. And as illustrated, resharpening the bipoint's bit causes it to *look like* a different knife form.

The U.S. continental shelf was the landfall of early Old World sailors making the western lands (Hranicky 2008). It is, of course, under sea-water now, and the water is a barrier for archaeological investigations. Scalloping by fishermen has brought up three bipoint examples. One was found off the coast of Virginia (Lowery 2010) now called the Cinmar bipoint. Two others were brought up off the coast of Maine (Crock, et al. 1993).

The important aspects of the Virginia discovery are:
- Solutrean-like flaking
- A mastodon association
- Continental shelf association with a Pleistocene date (Stanford 2011)
- Travel for rhyolite material
- Large size.

The important aspects of the Maine discovery are:
- Specimens found separately; one specimen has a semi-rounded base, and the other specimen has a pointed base, and
- Made from rhyolite
- Continental shelf association suggesting a Pleistocene time period.

These two bipoints (called bifaces) are known as the Anderson and Green Island artifacts (Crock, et al. 1993). See Figure 6-40.

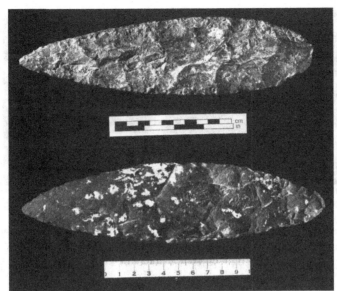

Figure 6-40 – Examples of the Maine Bipoints (based on Crock, et al. 1999). They show two states of bipoints.

The Maine specimens support the above bipoint class definition. Both finds indicate occupation at least to the Paleoindian era or earlier. The Virginia specimen provides attributes for modeling the bipoint.

A specimen was dredged up in the lower Chesapeake Bay around 10 years ago (Figure 6-41). The exact location is unknown, but it does show being underwater for a *few years*. It has an expended bit, and it maintains a V-shaped stem (chassis).

Figure 6-41 – Rhyolite Bipoint from the Chesapeake Bay in Virginia.

A land-based bipoint was found in a 1980 Browning Farm site (44CC8) excavation in Virginia (Buchanan and Owen 1981). The artifact was found in the Epps Island site that dates intermittently from the Early Archaic through to Early Contact. It was found in a trash pit and is not associated with the time period and cultural materials of the historic component. The specimen is now at the Smithsonian Institution in Washington, DC which performed X-ray Fluorescence (XRF) analysis (lithic *fingerprinting*) on the specimen and compared it to French gun flints. There was a near-perfect match suggesting that the bipoint's material originated in France (Stanford 2011). Figure 6-42 shows the artifact. Note its straight-like base and outré passé flaking. Stanford and Bradley (2012a) argue that it was transported to Virginia by the Solutreans.

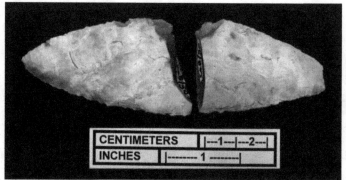

Figure 6-42 – Bipoint from the Browning Farm Site, Charles City County, Virginia with recent breakage. The bipoint patination surfaces indicate one face was up during its prehistoric era buried environment or laying on the ground.

More lithic sourcing is needed as the artifact indicates that it could match a French Solutrean's source for flint. Other U.S. bipoints should be found that are made from French flints. In the site report, Howard MacCord remarks (Buchanan and Owen 1981:146):

> *Of particular interest in the feature (#4) was the finding of two halves of a restoreably laurel leaf blade made from a honey colored (French) flint. This blade is identical to those typical of the Solutrean culture of around 20,000 BC in France and Spain. The blade is 10.54 cm long and 3.35 cm wide with a thickness of 7.5 mm. Its outer surface is patinated with a thick white layer of corrosion products. It had been broken before burial, since two small wedge shaped slivers of the stone are missing, and the two larger pieces were physically separated about 2 feet when found.*

As MacCord pointed out to the author, an early settler could have brought the piece into the U.S., could have been part of a ship's ballast, or picked up by an English soldier serving in France or Belgium. It is tenuous as it probably represents a piece picked up in France and transported by someone planning to make gun flints out of it. These possible questions will never be answered; however, the specimen provides one more data-set of evidence in the increasing inventory of bipoints found on the Atlantic coastal plain. The shape of this bipoint can be used for investigating other eastern bipoints, particularly primary stage and broken and resharpened potential specimens. However, the reader should note that in the 1980s, no one was looking for Solutrean on the U.S. east coast.

A bipoint that is a surface find in Florida has produced a date of 16,400 +/- 325 YBP (Figure 6-43). It compares favorably with French Solutrean small bipoints; it is discussed in the Early Florida Bipoints section. Figure 6-44 shows bipoint testing (see Appendix B for test methods).

Figure 6-43 - Chert, Marion County, Florida (L = 72, W = 37, T = 12 mm, R = 23.35, E = 1.95, M = 5YR8/1, g = 27).

196

Figure 6-44 – Charles McNutt (Memphis State University) running the Raman Laser test on Florida bipoint specimens.

Four of five of the above specimens led to the conclusion that the Europeans made landfall in the Middle Atlantic initially at 22,000+ YBP. Other specimens described below reinforce the conclusion; however, again, there is no genetic evidence to support the eastern U.S. occupation for Europe – only artifacts and the genetic controversy.

Bipoint Patination

Patination is the process of stone tool aging; however, it is a poor indicator of age (Hranicky 1992). With most bipoints being surface finds, patination is the best indicator of age (Figure 6-45). Patination varies by geography, by material, by environment, and by time. These factors are difficult to measure; thus, age determination is precarious. It is interesting the number of eastern Atlantic coastal bipoints made from rhyolite that have heavy patination. Patination is not an indicator of a legacy assignment.

Figure 6-45 – Two Rhyolite Bipoints from Southeastern Virginia Showing Different Patinations. They are early legacy bipoints but are not Solutrean. They are Legacy 3 bipoints, respectively.[63]

---

[63] These specimens would simply be called Morrow Mountain points by many archaeologists.

Section 7 – Early Virginia Bipoints

> This section provides the first bipoints in the U.S. They are classic bipoints that show Old World forms and workmanship. The important aspects of these points are the environment in which they resided in the U.S. The section presents a landfall model.

The bipoint technology reflects time, space, and environmental factors that present a prehistory in Virginia; a history which is so poorly understood by archaeologists in that most archaeologists refuse to accept any argument or hypothesis that it actually existed. Tidewater Virginia land area has better promises, but most of the area is under concrete, buildings, etc. Numerous bipoint, and V-shaped stemmed knives have been found in the Dismal Swamp area in the tidewater of North Carolina and Virginia. Investigation needs a more rigorous approach, such as paleosols in Lowery, et al. (2010) and genetic stratigraphy in Vento, et al. (2008), Losco, Stephens, and Helmke (2010), Markewish, et al. (2009), Johnson (2012), and Alley (2004). Additionally, these references are used and an overview of Virginia's coastal plain paleoenvironment is presented.

Virginia has the antiquity; what are needed are serious, professional investigations and excavations before this tidewater prehistory is completely lost in this area (Hranicky 2004 and 2007). However, first, archaeologists must accept before Clovis human occupation in the Middle Atlantic area and elsewhere.

The Landfall Model is argued for Virginia based on the following:

1) Favorable Southeastern U.S. environment vs. glacially-dominated Spain/France environments

2) Ocean crossings were commonplace in the Pleistocene

3) North Carolina-Virginia above-water continental shelf provided an ideal landing and habitation area

4) Inland Solutrean-like artifacts (blade industry) are found supporting the migration and landfall.

Environmental Factors

From 50,000 years ago, the world-wide environment (geomorphology) presented human beings with conditions that were not normal for their established lifeways. These changes, especially coastal environments, are major factors in population movements (as in Westley and Dix 2006 or Butzer 1971). Most coastal populations relied on the sea for food (Rick and Erlandson 2008); thus, they had basic sailing knowledge … and, the boat.

As a generalized environmental summary for world-wide climates and habitation areas during the Late Pleistocene, several areas had extreme living conditions. For example, Alaska has large sand dunes and barren sand plains that extend across a significant part of Arctic Alaska north of the Brooks Range. Most archaeologists still maintain that humans *walked* into the New World through the so-called land bridge. Humans had the boat and sailed up and down the northern coast and exploited inlands a few miles for food stuffs. A single port of entry for Pleistocene humans will die slowly in archaeology. Holocene migrations were certainly a real way (and time) into the New World, as argued here for the port of Southeastern America. These environmental inferences and the following are based on NOAA data, Bradley (1999), Brown (1978), Denton and Hughes (1981), Lowery, et al. (2010), Lasca and Donahue (1990), Straight (1990), and Saltzman (2002).

Following with another desert environment due to glaciation is the Sahara in Africa. Inland areas were dry; whereas, the coastal areas were damp and cold. It was an environment that was not conducive to comfortable living. During this time period, the southeastern part of the Americas was a greenland with plenty of food and a moderate year-round temperature. As an environmental perspective, the rationale among early humans for New World migrations seems appropriate, especially when they had the means to move from one environment to another.

Virginia's Pleistocene environment during the last 50 k years has varied and one of the archaeological focuses has been on the Younger Dryas mini-ice age. However, the Middle Atlantic coastal area presents an environment that varied from a wet-boreal forest to a cold savannah grassland. The climate varied from warm to cold during (interstadials) the last 50,000 years. The best understood features of the last interstadial age are the paleosol horizons that separate losses or till sheets. At least some tools were found in the Before Clovis Eocene (Lowery, et al. 2010). The Middle-Southeastern U.S. probably had coniferous forests with a subartic climate. The various interstadials had climates similar to the Holocene. The Holocene is probably an interglacial event.

As Redman (1999) stated for more recent population, it was appropriate for early populations:

> *The archaeological record is strewn with the wrecks of communities that obviously had not learned to cope with their environments in a sustainable manner or had found a sustainable path, but veered from it only to face self-destruction.*

Virginia Paleoenvironment for Bipoints

The paleogeography for coastal Virginia is an ecozone that is separated from Delmarva by the river that became the Chesapeake Bay. This area has a complicated geology which may have up 50 feet of soil deposition. The date range is suggested here as dating to 50,000 YBP. As mentioned previously, three climatical shifts occur: 30, 16, and 12 k YBP.

For underwater sites, archaeological sites that occur within and below the preserved ocean facies and within back-barrier deposits have a high potential for being preserved. Virginia's coast has marsh-lagoon-barrier systems that are still available, such as estuary systems of:

- Chesapeake Bay
- Albemarle Sound
- Pamlico Sound.

Virginia's prehistoric soils are known to be products of environmental factors such as climate, vegetation, topographic setting, parent material, and time for formation so that paleosols, or fossil soils, can potentially reveal changing environments of the past (Retallack 2007).

Virginia's coastal plain has a vast area containing wetlands (Doyale 1998). The entire Atlantic coast has more wetlands than any other area in the U. S. These wetlands protect shorelines and are refuge for fish, birds, and mammal species; thus, in prehistory this environment was more attractive than inlands to early populations.

Johnson (2012) reports paleosols dating by OSL to 30 k YBP with quartzite artifacts above this level. The argument here is: this area (Coastal Plain and lower Piedmont) has early human occupations dating 30,000 years and beyond.

Virginia Early Bipoints

Several Virginia bipoints probably exist in this Pleistocene environment from which people survived and left a lithic legacy. But, at present, two Virginia bipoints were found that argue that the European people made landfall on the Middle Atlantic coast approximately 35,000 YBP. These artifacts are:

- Cinmar bipoint
- Norfolk bipoint
- Suffolk bipoint.

The Norfolk Point

The Norfolk bipoint was found in Norfolk in the 1970s (Figure 7-1). It was broken, probably by early farming operations. The bipoint is made from a fine grain, translucent chalcedony. It measures:

- L = x, 71 mm
- W = 37 mm
- T = 8 mm
- R = 15.35
- Wt = 17g.

The Norfolk bipoint was a bipoint based on its similarity to French Solutrean resharpened bipoints. While its material is unusual, it is consistent with the Solutrean usage of fine grain materials (Bradley 2008). It has remnant, bold, thin flake scars which are difficult for this material (Hranicky 2007).

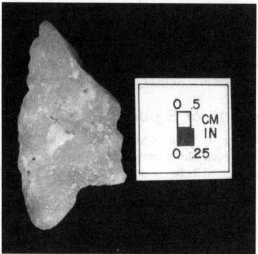

Figure 7-1 – Norfolk Bipoint Found in the 1970s. It is classified here as Solutrean.

It has enough of the stem remaining to estimate its stem length; however, its total original length will never be known. The principal factor here is the bit is part of the lateral margin's curve; it is continuous. The bit is off center which is similar to bipoint usage in Solutrean bipoints (Figure 7-2). The bit is still relatively sharp, and it has the classic flake removal at the juncture of the bit and stem. This area also is still sharp. One part of the lateral margin has the classic curve that is found on numerous Solutrean bipoints. The curved lateral margin has enough of the curve left to establish the bipoint morphology.

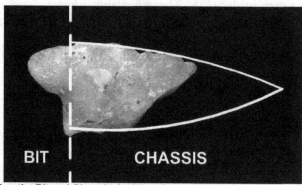

Figure 7-2 Norfolk Bipoint Showing the Bit and Chassis. It shows its bipoint probable form.

Fortunately, the bit end was recovered which can be examined against Solutrean bits (Figure 7-3). Smith (1962) provides drawings of French bipoints that have usage. The off-set bit is obvious. In fact, he illustrates specimens that have resharpening identical to the Norfolk bipoint.

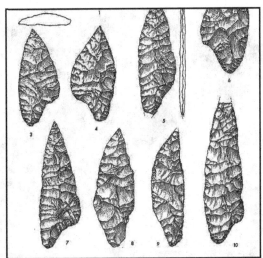

Figure 7-3 – Solutrean Expended Bipoints from France (Smith 1962). Note: continuous lateral marginal curve into the bit.

Actual bipoint photographs by the British Museum in London show bit forms from which the Norfolk bipoint can be measured. Again, these bits are similar to the Norfolk bipoint. Also, this bit usage was used for the Legacy 1 bipoint. Lower right bipoint in the picture is identical to the Norfolk bipoint (Figure 7-4).

Figure 7-4 – Expended French Solutrean Bipoints Showing Various Resharpened Forms.

Comparative examples: Years ago, missionaries working in Village of Fugar, on the Nigar River, Kenya brought back artifacts. Figure 7-5 shows an artifact sample. The quartzite (left) specimen has a legacy bit similar to the Norfolk specimen's bit.

201

Figure 7-5 – Paleolithic Specimens from Kenya, Africa.

The Norfolk bipoint has Solutrean attributes that go beyond probably or chance that an American bipoint could be manufactured to resemble French bipoints. However, it was a surface find which is not an absolute proof in archaeology. Other bipoints have (and will) be found; thus, the story goes on. Its argument is presented with a suggested proof.

The Cinmar Bipoint

The Cinmar bipoint was dredged up in 1970 by Capt. Thurston Shawn from the waters offshore from Hampton, Virginia. It is named after the captain's ship. It came up with a mastodon skull which provided the radiocarbon date of 22,760 +/- 90 RCYBP (UCIAMS-53545). The depth of the find was from 38-40 fathoms (Lowery 2008). It has become the major focus of the Solutrean hypothesis by Dennis Stanford and Bruce Bradley (2012a&b). Stanford and Bradley (2012a) describe the Cinmar bipoint as:

> *It exhibits well-controlled percussion-thinning flaking on both faces. Use wear studies demonstrate that it was a hafted knife, and non-invasive retouch along its distal margins resulted from resharpening dulled edges.*

The rhyolite Cinmar bipoint[64] measures:
- L = 188 mm
- W = 54 mm
- T = 6 mm
- R = 20.88.

The Smithsonian Institution tested the rhyolite and found it was from South Mountain in Pennsylvania. The well-made bipoint has a length-wise slight curve which is the result of its initial manufacture from a large flake or spall. This is suggested by the very small remnant platform at one end. Otherwise, it is flaked bifacially. It has polish from usage and the patination is light due to its water-buried environment. It has several large, bold flake scars; however, none of the scars transverse from edge-to-edge across each face. The cross-section is biconvex which suggests an alternate manufacturing technique of large cobble biface reduction. Edge trim has microflaking scars which finalized its shape and provided a sharp edge. It was probably a hafted implement. It has pointed and semi-round ends (base and tip). Figure 7-6 shows both faces. The Cinmar bipoint is easily a classic Solutrean bipoint which was made from American stone. With its date, rhyolite is suggested as the first choice of the bipoint's maker.

---

[64] The Cinmar artifact has been returned to its owner and is not curated at the Smithsonian.

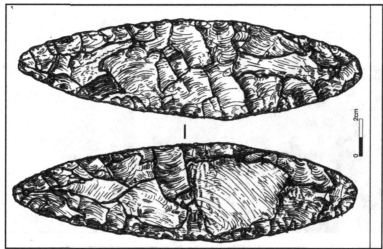

Figure 7-6 – Drawing of both faces of the Cinmar Rhyolite Bipoint. Drawings by Dennis Stanford and Bruce Bradley in preparation for Stanford, et al. (2011), which were enhanced by the author.

The major question: is it Solutrean? Based on flaking qualities and various attributes, the specimen best fits Solutrean bipoint manufacturing. It was found out on the continental shelf, which in its location, argues for a Pleistocene date. The Middle Atlantic area was argued as a Solutrean land fall (Hranicky 2007). Additionally, its LWT ratio is one of the lowest for any bipoint found in the eastern U.S. Basically, the argument here is it is Solutrean.

As a note, there is a possible mammoth-bipoint association at Afton Springs in Oklahoma (Homes 1903), but unfortunately, the excavation was not a desired procedure in archaeology, and the bipoint association cannot be confirmed. Another reported mammoth and a three bipoint association was in found Santa Isabel, Iztapan, Mexico (Aveleyra 1956). The famous Blackwater Draw site has bipoints associated with mammoth bones (Hester 1972).

This artifact "stirred" up American archaeology. The division for "good/bad" is split approximately 50% among American archaeologists.

> **For references:** (Bradley and Stanford, 2004, 2006; Collins et al., 2013; Lowery, 2009; Oppenheimer et al., 2014; Stanford and Bradley 2000, 2002, 2012, 2014; Stanford et al., 2014; Stanford and Stenger, 2014).

> **Against references:** (Boulanger and Eren, 2015; Dulik et al., 2012; Eren et al., 2013, 2014; Eriksson et al., 2012; Goebel et al., 2008; Kashani et al., 2012; Meltzer, 2009; O'Brien et al., 2014, 2014b; O'Rourke and Raff, 2010; Philips, 2014; Raghavan et al., 2014; Raff and Bolnick, 2014; Rasmussen et al., 2014; Straus, 2000; Straus et al., 2005; Westley and Dix, 2008).

The Dismal Swamp of Virginia and North Carolina

The Dismal Swamp covered millions of acres in prehistory. Modern urbanization has reduced the swamp's size greatly (Figure 7-7). It is one of the largest natural refuges for wildlife in the East. It has a long history; even George Washington surveyed the Dismal Swamp in 1763. And, a canal was constructed in 1805. It is one of the largest natural refuges for wildlife in the East. It has suffered numerous fires, namely the 1923 fires and the 2011 fire. It has a thick under-cover which makes access to stop fires difficult. For the geology, see Whitehead (1972). The swamp has to be a golden paradise archaeologically, especially for Pleistocene era studies.

Figure 7-7 - The Great Dismal Swamp National Wildlife Refuge is located in southeastern Virginia and northeastern North Carolina. The refuge consists of over 112,000 acres of forested wetlands. Lake Drummond, at 3,100 acres and the largest natural lake in Virginia, is located in the heart of the swamp.

The swamp has produced numerous bipoints, but they have failed to be recognized archaeologically. While various bipoints are discussed from the swamp, Figure 7-8 shows a crude, but typical, bipoint. It was struck off a core as it has a medial ridge remaining. It is heavily patinated, probably due the swamp's environment.

Figure 7-8 – Rhyolite, Dismal Swamp, Virginia (L = 94, W = 42, T = 14 mm, R = 31.33, E = 2.24, g = 57). The state is a bipoint preform or poorly made knife.

The Suffolk Bipoint

American archaeological orthodoxy, especially those who fail to dissolve the Clovis blockage into the lithic continuum, refuses to accept the 30,000 years as a possible entry date for humans into the Americas. Dates are continually reported that are of the 30-k year range, such as El Cedral of Mexico date 33,300 YBP (Lorenzo and Mirambell 1986), Taima in Venezuela 30-k year date (Ochsinius and Gruhn 1979), Tlapacoya, Mexico at 24,000 years (Lorenzo and Mirambel 1999), or the controversial Pedra Furada at 40,000 YBP, and 32-k year reports such as Guidon (1986). The problem is, of course, suggesting this timeframe for Virginia.

The following rhyolite bipoint is suggested as having a considerable antiquity in Virginia; but like the bipoint in general, Virginia's bipoints do not have solid land-based dates, namely an excavated date association with datable organic materials (Figure 7-9). The Suffolk bipoint was found in the tidewater area of Virginia; thus, its name. Its reported *find location* is near the Dismal Swamp area in Virginia. It is a swamp mostly of cypress forest today. Pirsson and Schuchert (1915/20) provide an analysis of the swamp's formation as a marine marsh and its lagoonal processes on the Atlantic coast line. At present, this bipoint's shape is unique in the Middle Atlantic coastal area; it is a narrow bipoint with an off-set tip with an indented base (Figure 6-9).

The Suffolk bipoint[65] has an ovate shape; however, its main attribute is the notch in the base of the specimen. This notching practice is found on European bipoint specimens in context that are older than Solutrean.

This specimen has heavy patination which removed the flake scars. However, this condition could be the result of water-worn processes and damage. But, most importantly, it has a tip-to-base curve which is present on a few Solutrean specimens. Other Virginia bipoints have this structural curve, namely the Cinmar bipoint. The two specimens in the figure have similar morphologies. However, considering the distance between them, most archaeologists would consider them technological coincidences however interesting they may be. They have D-cross sections, basal notches, and similar blade shapes. The Virginia specimen represents a primary stage of bipoint and manufacture for Virginia and the East. Speculatively, its date has considerable antiquity … 35,000 YBP. Date estimate is based on similar dated forms found in Europe.

As a comparative drawing, Osborn 1922:312 shows a similar bipoint which he attributes to the Solutreans. He classifies it as a laurel leaf.

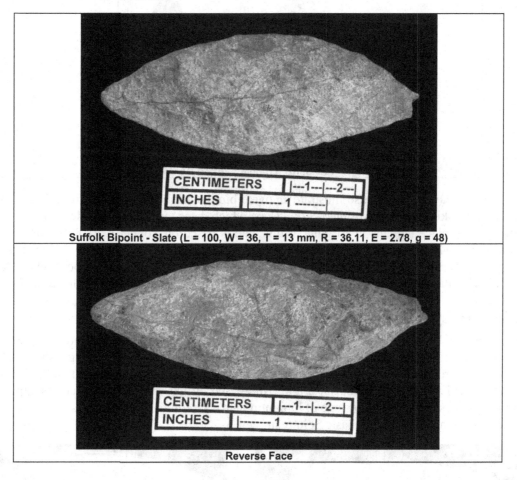

Suffolk Bipoint - Slate (L = 100, W = 36, T = 13 mm, R = 36.11, E = 2.78, g = 48)

Reverse Face

---

[65] Archaeologically, there is always a first artifact in any investigation, for example the first Clovis find.

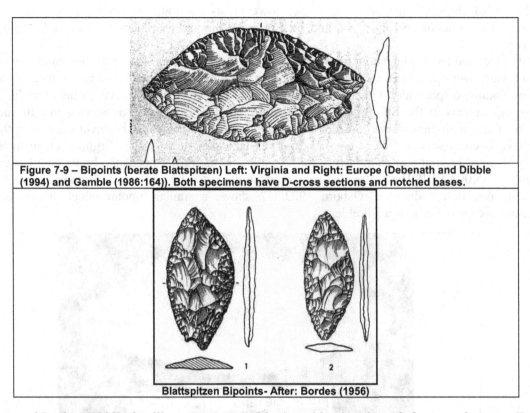

Figure 7-9 – Bipoints (berate Blattspitzen) Left: Virginia and Right: Europe (Debenath and Dibble (1994) and Gamble (1986:164)). Both specimens have D-cross sections and notched bases.

Blattspitzen Bipoints- After: Bordes (1956)

Guslitzer and Pavlov (1993) also illustrate an ovate bipoint with a basal notch from northeastern Europe. It is part of the toolkit known as Kostenki-Streletskaia which dates to the Middle Paleolithic.

Attempting to place humans in Virginia at this date is based on Topper's 50,000 YBP date and current paleosol analyses which presents the possibility of the early Virginia date. Certainly, an excavated, dateable context is needed. But without the *first find*, archaeologists will not look for this possibility. As suspected, the artifact will remain controversial, but a few archaeologists will start looking for this time period.

Virginia Legacy 2 Bipoints

Next, Figure 7-10 shows two Virginia specimens with similar morphologies and sharp bits (workends). Both specimens are heavily patinated with few flake scars remaining. While this suggests an ancient date, it may simply be a product of a harsh environment (Hranicky 1992). Note: one specimen has an off-center bit which is suggested as being of European origin. And based on the distal-to-proximal resharpening method, they probably represent the primary stage of bipoint manufacture in the East. These specimens were made by a biface reduction method which is basic Solutrean.

CENTIMETERS |---1---|---2---|
INCHES |------- 1 -------|

HAFTING AREA

WORKEND

Quarried Rhyolite, Dismal Swamp, Virginia (L = 100, W = 33, T = 12 mm , R = 36.36, E =3.03, g = 38).

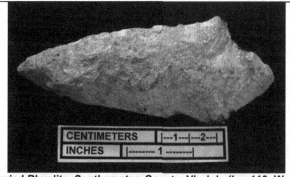

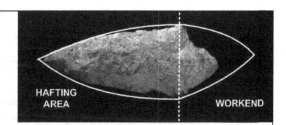

HAFTING AREA   WORKEND

Note: The bit area has a large circular flake removed which produced a sharp cutting edge.

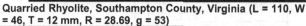

CENTIMETERS |---1---|---2---|
INCHES |-------- 1 -------|

Quarried Rhyolite, Southampton County, Virginia (L = 110, W = 46, T = 12 mm, R = 28.69, g = 53)

Figure 7-10 – Virginia V-shaped Stemmed Knives with Heavily Used (Resharpened) Workends (Bits). Drawings of proposed initial form. Legacy 2 bipoints (Fred Morgan collection).

Bit or workend resharpening started when the original bipoint tip/blade became dull. As the blade was reduced through resharpening, various bit styles were created. The process continued until the blade was expended and the knife was discarded. Coe's (1964) Morrow Mountain shows a few of these variations. Note: Coe's specimens all have the same triangle *blade* form with no usage on the edges, only the point's assumed bases vary in shape. If the Old World assumption is correct, the expended Solutrean bipoints offer examples for resharpening and expended forms that were shown previously.

Pre-Clovis Lithic Tools

In order for American bipoints to have their European and African ancestry, there must be evidence that people were in the eastern U.S. prior to Clovis. Once confirmed, it is a matter of looking for the lithic evidence (Hranicky 2011).

Most prehistoric archaeologists have no working knowledge of: *What constitutes pre-Clovis toolkits.* For the Middle Atlantic area, the Williamson paleosite in Dinwiddie County offers numerous examples of legacy Old World stone tools. As shown in this publication, many of the site's tools can be compared to the classic Solutrean toolkit which, of course, is one of the reasons for the *Solutrean Hypothesis.*[66]. For the Middle Atlantic area, there are four sites with 16,000 YBP dates that argue for human presence in Before-Clovis times (Figure 7-11). They are based on Hranicky (2011).

---

[66] See page xii.

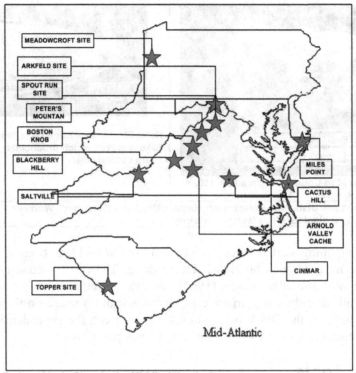

Figure 7-11 – Map Showing Before-Clovis Sites in the Middle Atlantic Area.

The Topper site in South Carolina provides Before-Clovis tools which can be used as a guide for finding other early (or pre-) Paleoindian sites. These tools were produced by blade technology, but flake-made specimens occur (Figure 7-12).

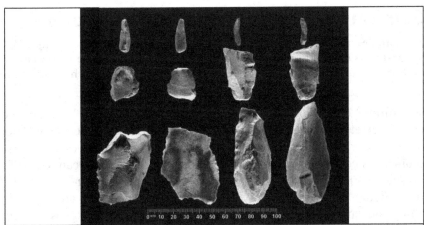

Figure 7-12 – Flake Examples from the Topper Paleosite, Allendale, South Carolina (Credit as SCIAA Photo, Daryl P. Miller Photographer).

The Topper site does not have the classic biface technology and, at present, no bipoints; however, it does start the timeline for the U.S. Atlantic coast. These tools present a starting toolkit for Before Clovis people. They are American blade-produced technology.

Section 8 – Early North Carolina Bipoints

This section provides examples of North Carolina bipoints which are argued as occupying a Before Clovis time period. Material is suggested as basic criteria for early bipoints. An example cache is presented as evidence for this argument. North Carolina has numerous early bipoints; however, those that have been found are surface finds.

There are numerous confirmed early bipoints in North Carolina. They do not have defined archaeological contexts; thus, dates are speculative. However, the Rights cache probably represents the Before Clovis era.

Archaeologically, North Carolina is an extension of Virginia because many of the rivers start in Virginia and end in North Carolina. Its coastal plain probably contains numerous European sites but, of course, they are under water. At present, North Carolina bipoint data suggest that they are generally made from rhyolite or slate. The specimen in Figure 8-1 has a heavily resharpened bit; for most archaeologists, it would be classified as a Morrow Mountain point (after Coe 1964). However, it is a suggested Legacy 2 expended bipoint with an expended bit; it is still sharp today.

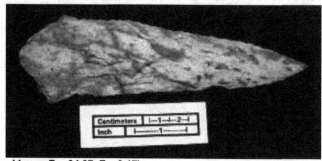

Davis County (L = 130, W = 41, T = 11 mm, R = 34.87, E = 3.17)
Figure 8-1 – North Carolina Rhyolite Bipoint

The Rights Cache, North Carolina

Before Cactus Hill, the basic assumption is that *Early Man* used fine-grain flints and cherts for tools (Hranicky and Painter 1988 and numerous others). Cactus Hill provided the information that fine-grain quartzite was the primary material for tools prior to Clovis (Johnson 1997 and 2012). This stone is called Sussex (Cactus Hill) quartzite, and its usage *somewhat* parallels Old World usage, especially for the European and Aterian toolmakers. The early area of human occupation on the Atlantic Coast had one major *inconvenience* for Before-Clovis people, namely lack of immediately useful local lithic resources. Thus, inland trips for preferred fine-grain stones account for inland sites, such as Cactus Hill (Virginia) and Topper (South Carolina). The author is not suggesting these sites are Solutrean – the suggestion (conclusion) is that these sites have ancient European occupations. When examining these sites in terms of blade-core technology, Old World legacies are implied (as in Hranicky 2005).

When combined with the landfall hypothesis, Cactus Hill is a natural consequence of the coastal occupation. Other Before-Clovis sites are probably in North Carolina waiting to be discovered. The bipoint occurs and expended forms also are present only in surface finds. For example, Figure 8-2 shows a four-point cache found in the 1920s by Douglas Rights. The flake scars have weathered to an indiscernible level so that their identification cannot be determined. They are presented as expended bipoints that date to the Before-Clovis era. Unfortunately, there are few publications showing Solutrean tool usage and wear patterns from which to justify these points as Solutrean. And, these points could have been deposited in a heavily acidic soil that would have removed the flaking surface. Due to their size, material and especially, edge curve, they are assessed as Before Clovis. This cache is, perhaps, the most important discovery in the Middle Atlantic area that has been made - prehistorically speaking. It amplifies the need for professional archaeologists to go to the collectors and examine their collections. In most cases, collectors do not know what they have found let alone report it. This cache has disappeared into the relic world. Large blade tools are assumed to have been used for butchering megafauna.

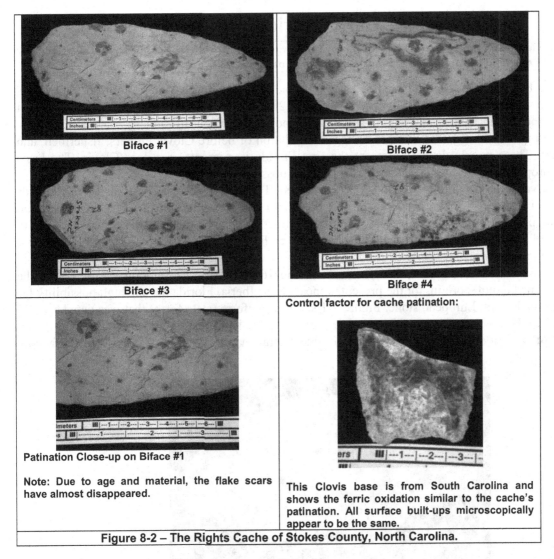

Figure 8-2 – The Rights Cache of Stokes County, North Carolina.

Table 8-1 provides metrics for the Rights Cache implements.

Table 8-1 – The Rights Cache from Stokes County, North Carolina		
Specimen	Measurements	Description
Bipoint #1	L = 164, T = 13, W = 61 mm, R = 34.95	Weathered, stained, rhyolite, thin
Bipoint #2	L = 153, T = 12, W = 66 mm, R = 27.82	Weathered, stained, slate, thin,
Bipoint #3	L = 165, T = 23, W = 64 mm, R = 59.30	Weathered, stained, slate, thick, edge trim
Bipoint #4	L = 147, T = 12, W = 55 mm, R = 32.07	Weathered, stained, slate, thin, edge trim, platform remaining

These specimens are well made and reported in the finder's notes that these pieces were found together. The cache function is assumed; however, an abandoned toolkit seemed likely as the cause for the tool deposit. Notably, Biface #1 is made from a different material, but ferric stains appear on all pieces. This stain is often present on Early Archaic points but, based on author observations, are not present on Middle Archaic slate tools, namely Morrow Mountain bifaces. The overall shape and size are similar, suggesting they may have been communal tools. Hranicky (2008) suggests these tool shapes are knives.

The suggestion is: The Rights Cache dates to the Paleoindian era or earlier. Obviously, most archaeologists will argue that these specimens are Morrow Mountain bifaces (such as Harris 2011). Patination is a poor indicator of age but, excusing the pun, time will tell the story – namely somewhere an excavated context (Hranicky 1992). At least, the 1920s Rights Cache is reported.

Section 9 – Early Florida' Bipoints

This section provides early paleo-bipoints from Florida. The ovate bipoint form is illustrated, and specimens are compared to French Solutrean bipoints. Florida has numerous Before-Clovis dates and sites.

The prehistory of Florida has started archaeologically with paleolance points, namely Simpson, Suwannee, and Clovis points with *which* the first-who varies (Hranicky 2010). The points are defined as having direct megamammal associations (Dunbar and Vojnovski 2007). Bipoints are absent from these lanceolate toolkits. And as such, the bipoint is suggested as representing a population of before Clovis hunters, fishermen, and general gatherers. These people do not represent the first Florida immigrants, nor does Clovis. The basic proposition is Europe; however, as suggested, Africa is also a possibility.

Florida has a vast area containing wetlands (Doyale 1998). The entire Atlantic coast has more wetlands than any other area in the U. S. These wetlands protect shorelines and are refuge for fish, birds, and mammal species; thus, in prehistory this environment was more attractive than inlands to early populations. In prehistory, most of Florida was wetlands; the highest in the U.S. Florida has the best possibility of an artifact being found that is made from Old World stone.

As will be shown, Florida has an old history, one dating 16,000 YBP. The bipoint occurs before the lanceolate point. The bipoint's origin, for the present, appears to be Iberia. Florida has the high possibility for finding a bipoint made from European stone. Figure 8-1 shows a preform (state form) that was dated at 7595 YBP (see Appendix B for method). As a bipointed preform, it could have been intended as a BMM bipoint, or any number of microtools. It has light retouch on one lateral margin. And, it was probably bifacially reduced from a cobble.

Figure 8-1 – Chert Preform, Bipoint, Northern Florida (L = 157, W = 65, T = 21 mm, R = 50.72, E = 2.41).

The following bipoint occurs in a private Florida collection which has a supposed association with a mammoth rib bone which has cut marks (Figure 8-2). It is heavily patinated and has edge retouching.

At another location, two fossil mammoth bones, forearm and rib with cut marks were found on the Page-Ladson site in Florida (Brown 1994). While the following specimens are not scientific archaeology, we need to examine them as possibilities, even in the collector community; however, their associations are anecdotal. Purdy (2008) comments:

> *It is theoretically possible that homo sapiens sapiens was in the Western Hemisphere about 30,000 years age.*

The bipoint dates to the Before Clovis era which is assumed here; its earlier date remains tentative for Florida. This artifact has a nearby mammoth rib bone associated with it (Kurten and Anderson 1980). Tankersley (2002) reports a similar ovate bipoint in the Crook County Clovis cache. A culturally modified mastodon rib was reported in New York which has several dates of which the oldest is 11,390 +/- 80 YBP (Laub 2000). Hemmings, et al. (2004) also reports bone and ivory tools. The presence of bipoints does not exist in Florida Clovis toolkits.

Purdy (2008) also reports a Florida mammoth vertebral spine bone with cut marks. Purdy (2008) also provides an excellent overview of the Paleoindian era in Florida. At the Container Corporation of America site, Purdy (1981 and 2008) got thermoluminescence date of 26-28 k YBP.

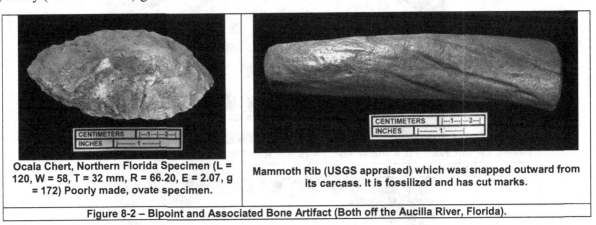

Ocala Chert, Northern Florida Specimen (L = 120, W = 58, T = 32 mm, R = 66.20, E = 2.07, g = 172) Poorly made, ovate specimen.	Mammoth Rib (USGS appraised) which was snapped outward from its carcass. It is fossilized and has cut marks.

Figure 8-2 – Bipoint and Associated Bone Artifact (Both off the Aucilla River, Florida).

Comparative example: Figure 8-3 shows a drawing of a large Solutrean bipoint. It compares favorably with this Florida specimen.

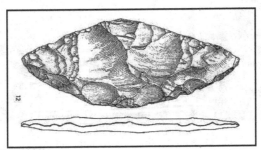

Figure 8-3 – France, Solutrean (After Miller 1962).

Figure 8-4 shows another bipoint, which the specimen's association is assumed to date to the paleo-era.[67] It was not found with paleo materials, but it has a true Solutrean outline. The base angle is the same for these specimens. The bit angles are slightly different, but both specimens have moderate usage on the bits. The French example has a shave (bottom). While not common, it does occur on American specimens; example shown below. It compares favorably with the French specimen that is shown. This Florida specimen typifies the Florida's primary stage and suggests a heavy duty cutting implement.

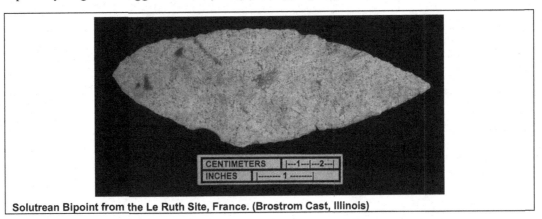

Solutrean Bipoint from the Le Ruth Site, France. (Brostrom Cast, Illinois)

---

[67] For a similar dated specimen, see Apendix A.

Bipoint, Lamont, Florida (L = 162, W = 64, T = 18 mm, R = 45.56, E = 2.53) (Hranicky 2011)

Comparative Bipoints. Note base angles are the same, bits have usage and wear.

Figure 8-4 – Bipoint Preform, Chert, Burke County, Georgia (L= 126, W = 55, T = 12 mm, R = 27.49) (Jim Hill Collection). It is a bipoint; chassis (hafting) on the left, and bit (workend) on the right. Right lateral bit margin has retouching and no longer is pointed.

Figure 8-5 shows Michael Collins (Texas) and Bruce Bradley (England) examining several Florida bipoint specimens used in the publication.

Figure 8-5 – Michael Collins and Bruce Bradley examining several of the author's Florida bipoints at the Society for American Archaeology April 2012 Annual Meeting in Memphis, Tennessee.

Figure 8-6 also shows comparative specimens which share similar morphologies. Flaking patterns suggest the manufacturing technique was the same for both, but the geographic distance between them argues that they are not related. They may share a technological coincidence, but the bipoint morphology is obvious. Both specimens have bold, thin flake scars.

The Florida specimen was dated at Memphis State University at 16,400 +/- 325 by the newly developed Raman Infrared Laser Spectroscopy (R-ILS) as in McNutt, Cherry, and Walley (2010). The reflectance wave length test was performed by McNutt on seven chert Marion County bipoints of which only this specimen yielded the before Clovis date. A Marion County chert Clovis point was used to baseline the sample dates. All materials were made from the same chert and assumed to have been in the same local environment (see Appendix A for method).

Before Clovis, Chert, Marion County, Florida | **Solutrean, Flint, France (British Museum)**

Figure 8-6 – Comparative Bipoint Examples from Florida and France.

Figure 8-7 shows an Ocala chert broken specimen that may have been a large bipoint. It was a tool made with pockets of quartz crystal areas which were in the specimens initially. An initial outline is suggested. As being broken, its original shape can only be estimated by marginal curves. Bit is on the left, and has one straight margin which shows usage. Initially, the specimen probably exceeded 200 mm.

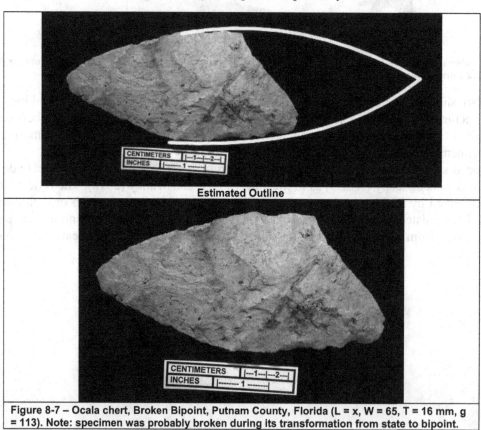

Estimated Outline

Figure 8-7 – Ocala chert, Broken Bipoint, Putnam County, Florida (L = x, W = 65, T = 16 mm, g = 113). Note: specimen was probably broken during its transformation from state to bipoint.

Section 10 - South American Bipoints

This section provides bipoint examples from South America which indicate the widespread Western Hemisphere distribution of the bipoint. This section argues that the El Jobo pointmakers spread from South to North America in paleo-times.

South American bipoints indicate a considerable antiquity (Lavallee 2000 and Roosevelt, et al. 2002, Watanake, et al. 2003, and Roosevelt, et al. 2002)). The major bipoint site in the New World is the controversial Taima Taima in Venezuela (Ochsinius and Gruhn 1979 and Gruhn and Brayan 1989). It has a bipointed El Jobo point with a radiocarbon date of 33 K (?) and 13.8 YBP (+/- 120 years) and is associated with a megafauna kill site. Brazil has an ovate bipoint like the one shown above (Lavallee 1995) and a suggested date of 36,000 YBP (Watanake, et al. 2003). Also, Lavallee (1995) reports a Peru bipoint that shows blade manufacture and is identical to the uniface specimen in Figure 10-1. South America is not an easy place for archaeological investigations; however, it supports numerous dates that are older than the Clovis in the U.S.

The major sites in South America containing bipoints are: Muaco site, Venezuela (Royo 1960), El Jobo site, Venezuela (Cruxent and Rouse 1956), El Inga site, Ecuador (Bell 1960), Lauricocha site, Peru (Cardich 1958), Intihuasi Cave, Argentina (Gonzales 1952), Chico Midden site, Argentina (Vignati 1927), Englefield Island site, Chile, needing the boat (Emperaire and Laming 1961), and Patagonian Marine Terraces sites with round base bipoints (Menghin 1952). The origin for South American bipoints is probably Africa, but this hypothesis is suggested.

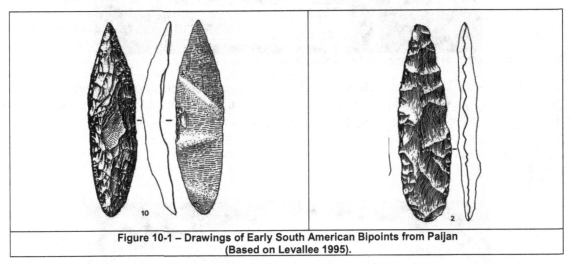

Figure 10-1 – Drawings of Early South American Bipoints from Paijan (Based on Levallee 1995).

Another early site in South America is the Flea Cave at Ayacucho, Peru. Artifacts associated with the sloth (megatherium) were found by MacNeish (1976) that date 14,150+/-180 years. The cave could date to 20,000 years. While not a bipoint, a pointed, parallel sided tool was discovered. The bipoint may start around 10,000 YBP.

One of the first archaeological proofs of transpacific migration was by Megger, et al. (1965). They sourced pottery from Japan to Ecuador which indicates long-distance ocean travel.

With good/bad dates for extremely early sites in the New World being common place (for one 36,000 YBP example, see Watanake, et al. 2003), the prehistory picture is left open to everyone who wants to forecast a prehistoric calendar. With this perspective, the following discussion provides insights to the Euro-Africa connection for the Americas. Numerous bipoints have dates prior to 12,000 YBP in South America (Levallee 1995).

Based on technology, there is a possible southern hemisphere migration to Florida. What are the cultural consequences and extent of the contacts also become a new topic in archaeology. Additionally, the South American point type – El Jobo – is found in the Southeast, but gets lost with types such as Lerma and Guilford. As argued, the bipoint has Old World direct connections, such as Solutrean and Aterian toolmakers. Figure 10-2 shows a bipoint that can easily be duplicated in eastern North America. With El Jobo points found in Mexico (MacNeish 1958) and the continental shelf providing easy almost walking distance from South America, the point type is suggested in the southeastern U.S., especially into the Gulf Coast states. The bipoint here has a biface lanceolate point which was found with the bipoint. Both were made from chert and have similar patinations. However, the bipoint flake scars are not as sharp as the lanceolate's scars; may be a consequence of usage.

BIPOINT SPECIMEN
BIPOINT MORPHOLOGY MODEL

Date: Legacy 1.
State: Pointed ends.
Mode: Knife.

Figure 10-2 – El Jobo Point from Venezuela with Lanceolate Point.

Figure 10-3 shows a bipoint example from Belize. This point does not show the high quality of most Maya points, but does present bipoint technology from outside the U.S. This Mesoamerican technology was probably transferred to the mound-building Mississippian people of the Southeast.

BIPOINT SPECIMEN
BIPOINT MORPHOLOGY MODEL

Date: Legacy 1.
State: Pointed ends.
Mode: Knife.

Figure 10-3 – Chert Bipoint from Belize (L = 126, W = 50, T = 12 mm, R = 30.24).

Figure 10-4 shows a non-continental shelf entrance into the Southeast. This suggests that countless migrations occurred from South America into the U.S. The shortest distance across the Atlantic is from western Africa to eastern Brazil.

218

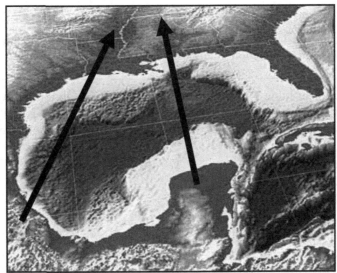

Figure 10-4 – Continental Shelf in the Gulf of Mexico. Arrows show possible routes into the U.S. from South America. With the continental shelf, humans could practically walk from South to North America (United States Geological Survey).

El Jobo Ancestry

The El Jobo bipoint sometimes in the U.S. is called a Lerma point; however, this bipoint made it into the U.S. It has various morphologies as do most bipoints. Thus, it is difficult to identify. Is it the ancestral form that led to Cumberland? Cumberland dates 5000 years older than Clovis (Hranicky 2011). Numerous sites in Alabama, Kentucky, Tennessee, and Ohio are highly suggestive of early technologies that are not Clovis. See Gramly 2012 for a Cumberland tradition, and he suggests that two recently discovered artifacts are El Jobo-like in Alabama.

Two complete bipoints and two midsections of the El Jobo bipoint were found at the type site in the Rio Pedregal valley. A midsection was found nearby at the Taima site in the body cavity of a juvenile mastodon (Gruhn and Bryan 1989). These specimens are bipoints. They have a convex or near diamond cross-section. They are long narrow spike-like points; they date from 14 to 11 YBP. However, the site dates 30,000 YBP by geologists. Bryan (1983) published a drawing of the El Jobo bipoint (shown earlier). Bryan (1983:143) suggested that humans reached South America prior to 20,000 years. Quero (1998) also provides data on the El Jobo. For Venezuela El Jobo presentation, see Cruxent and Rouse (1956).

Chile Bipoints

Chile's Huentelauquen culture complex has bipoints. Resharpened bipoints are in Jackson, et al. (2010). This complex probably dates to 13,000 YBP.

Andean Bipoints

Canales (2009) reports flint bipoints in central Andean area. However, he has not established a date, but places them in the Holocene at 13,000 to 5000 YBP.

Section 11 - Bipoint Mechanics

> This section provides an insight to the manufacture and use of prehistoric bipoints in the Americas. This section discusses basic bipoint production methods, performs, symmetry, resharpening bits, and bipoint hafting.

The bipoint is the most efficient lithic tool invented by humans. It has a cutting leverage that can be caused by its being hand-held or hafted. It is the oldest readily identifiable tool and is found throughout the world. The basic bipoint is considered as a representative of the Bipoint Morphology Model (BMM) which consists of:

- Having dual pointed ends
- Thin with a flat length-wise cross section
- Well made, usually out of fine grain stones
- Having excurvate lateral margins
- Pressure flaking of a prepared long blade
- Often having face-to-face flake scars.

However, the bipoint is a complicated tool when all the various morphological features are considered, such as:

- Dual pointed ends or straight/rounded base
- Parallel (curved length-wise) lateral margins
- Non-symmetric sides (Iberian curve)
- Hafting (chassis) vs. bit (workend) areas
- Possible use by turning the specimen around and re-hafting it
- Size (primary, secondary, tertiary forms)
- Lithic material
- Different bit resharpening methods
- Variation in manufacturing workmanship.

As further examples of resharpening, Figure 11-1 shows bipoints from Ohio, New Jersey, and Tennessee. The Ohio bit is semi-V-shaped and one lateral margin was used in addition to the bit. The specimen is a classic example of bipoint resharpening morphology. The Tennessee specimen is a classic Legacy 3 bipoint. It also shows resharpening and is probably an expended bipoint. These specimens demonstrate the range of attributes that can be found in bipoint technology.

220

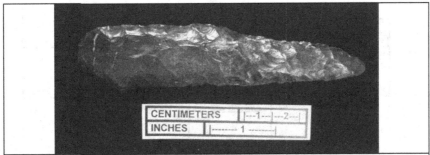

Figure 11-1 – Top: Flint, Benton County, Tennessee (L= 81, W = 32, T = 6.5 mm, R = 16.45, g = 17), Middle: Black Coshocton Flint, Perry County, Ohio (L = 114, T = 25, T = 10 mm, R = 45.60, g = 33), All are Legacy 3 bipoints.

And as a major concern, once resharpening occurred on the bit (workend), it is virtually impossible to define it as an originally-shaped bipoint. Each end varies but, overall, it has a general bipoint shape. At the modified stage, it becomes a V-shaped stemmed knife. In prehistory, once the cutting blade was exhausted, it was discarded and becomes archaeologically an expended knife which is relatively common nationwide. As a suggestion, the expended bipoint was sometimes turned around, re-hafted; thus, doubling the life of the tool. The Chesapeake diamond type in tidewater Virginia suggests this process (Hranicky and Painter 1989).

Bipoint States and Modes

The first act in the manufacture of a bipoint is selecting stone and formulating into the necessary piece from which a bipoint can be made. There are probably numerous shapes, most of which will never be discovered because the piece was modified away from its initial stone state. The manufacture of stone tools is a straightforward process…to produce a bipoint.

Selecting Stone>>>Initial Shaping (State)>>>Intending a Tool (Mode/Industry)

Stone State>>>Transformation (Mode)>>>Bipoint

The manufacture of a bipoint is the practice of producing a tool based on its physical shape or its mode. Mode can be considered the mental template which starts with a state initiation stone.

Bipoint Morphology Production

As suggested, the shape of a bipoint is relatively simple; the implement is composed of *two pointed ends* and dual cutting edges. The blade edges are excurvated with a biconvex or D-shaped cross section. It is made from a long blade, but large flaked biface versions occur. However, the bipoint's manufacture starts with a specific state which is intended to become a bipoint. Figure 11-2 shows the basic bipoint structure with resharpening and basal styles. While not proven, the bipoint is usually hafted. Importantly, it is not necessary to have an exact point at each end to be classified as a bipoint.[68] Other than the Solutrean, the point's end style varies within societies making bipoints. Basic bipoint morphology that is used for the model is based on Clark (1969), Brantingham, et al. (2004), and de Heinzelin de Braucourt (1962). When studying the variety of bipoints worldwide, the form has various shapes, which is collectively a synethic type. The synethic form is a mental image of a bipointed-shaped knife.

---

[68] The rounded base is suggested as the means that kept the pointed base from cutting into the hand during hand-held usage.

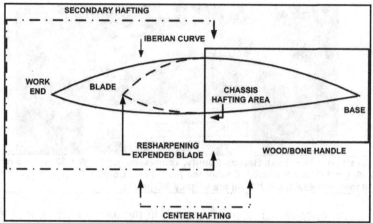

Figure 11-2 – Basic Bipoint (V-shaped Stemmed Knife) Model. The resharpened form is also referred to as a legacy bipoint. Once resharpened, as mentioned, they are rarely dual pointed. As drawing versions were shown earlier, it is the basic Bipoint Morphology Model (BMM).

Bipoint Knapping Methods

Once the toolmaker intends to manufacture a bipoint, stone is selected, tested, and shaped into the beginning process. The processing could be the start of having pointed distal/proximal ends. The stage is called its state. Now the piece is manufactured into a bipoint.

Based on collected samples for the U.S. Atlantic coast, there are two manufacturing methods used to produce the bipoint, which are:

- Pure blade,[69] spall, or flake technology
- Biface reduction technology from an elongated cobble.

Both hard and soft hammer percussion flaking techniques were used to shape the bipoint. Finalizing was accomplished by pressure flaking. One technique involved removing a large blade/flake from a large boulder or quarry outcrop. This spall is flaked into the bipoint form (Figure 11-3). This technique often produces a distal-to-proximal interior curve. This curve is present on East Coast specimens. This method is the alternative of the biface-produced bipoint.

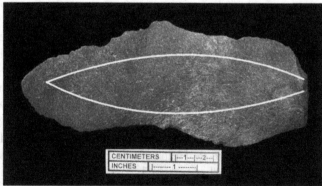

Figure 11-3 – Bipoint Outline on a Large Rhyolite Blade/Flake (Newly Made). It shows the striking platform and bulb scar which is often present on bipoints. (Drawing after Bordes 1956) This raw material form is often called a blank which is usually struck off a flake core. Is classified here as the bipoint initial state.

---

[69] Once the blade is flaked on both faces, it becomes a biface.

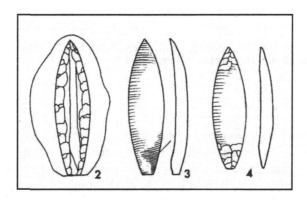

The above flake is the bases for numerous knives, but once the flake is shaped into a tool, its archaeological identification goes numerous ways, all of which depend on the researcher and his/her methodologies. Figure 11-4 shows a flake tool from northern Georgia which has the bulb scar remaining. The striking platform is present, and the blade has been pressure-flaked into the classic bipoint shape. Does it pre-date the bipoint like blades pre-date Solutrean bipoints? Of course, there is no answer, but the example argues the problems in the basics of tool identification, classification, and chronology in American prehistory archaeology.

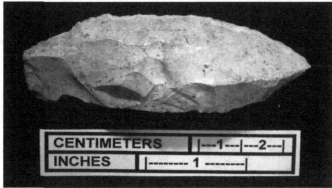

Figure 11-4 – An Ocala Chert Flake Knife from Northern Georgia (L = 73, W = 28, T = 13 mm, R = 33.89). Note the ridge going to the bit's point.

For an experimental study of bipoint manufacture, see Aubrey, et al. (2008) and de Boe and Pelegrim (1985).

Tool Mechanics

A salutation of lithic technology should be with the mechanics of the tools that were used. It allows humans the understanding of the immutable forces in Nature that they knew and used. Their tool designs facilitated Nature's forces and human-generated energies. While one may stretch it to say that Galileo and Newton led to our understanding of primitive technology, they were the first to insist on the importance of making observations in Nature and combining experiments with these observations. Historically, their careful thought and logical conclusions are part of what became the scientific process. Still, some use an Aristotelian philosophy that all knowledge comes from thought alone, which has its uses in science.

Many of Galileo's experiments were published in a book entitled *Two New Sciences*, which, written in dialogue form, is still worthy of reading today – his literary style might be seen in this publication. And as another enlightenment if you read Galileo's book, you may as well read Newton's book entitled *Principia* or officially *The Mathematical Principles of Natural Philosophy*. Aside from these readings, the study of mechanics in physics can make a tremendous contribution to lithic technology. They provide a philosophical beginning for science. This physical focus is what was previously presented as *dynamics as applied to lithic technology*.

As lithic scientists, we examine technology as it was used to work stone. It involves the American version of humanity's knowledge of relevant forces in Nature, sources of materials, mechanics of tool construction, and the ability to use the appropriate tools and implements for daily survival. Additionally, the term **Human technology** means prehistoric skills of knowing and doing; but of greater importance, it means they had the ability to reason the Mechanical Advantage (MA) of tools and predict future tool usage and social needs. For archaeology, technology is an abstract study with an emphasis on application – the study of technological processes in manufacturing, natural forces, chemistry of natural stones, and cultural aspects of all lithic objects. (From: Hranicky 2004).

Bipoint Preforms

The bipoint (laurel leaf) production in eastern Europe suggests a preform for the Solutrean bipoint (Aubrey, et al. 2003). The problem with American bipoints is that many of them are crudely made so to call it a preform becomes a subjective assessment on the part of the investigator. They would certainly not qualify as *high-tech foragers*. Perhaps a thick cross-section is the key. The preform can be made by either a uniface- or biface-reduction knapping method.

Asymmetrical Procedure

Bruce Bradley (2008) suggests another way of making a bipoint which is his asymmetrical manufacturing method. The Solutreans used a large flat boulder and reduced it to the bipoint. The technique produces a flat-sided bipoint. This procedure is contrary to the BMM legacy definition.

Bipoint Symmetry

The bipoint is a consistent technology that produced symmetrical implements over a 100,000 year time span. No attempt for a discriminant analysis was performed in this study primarily because there are few multi-specimen locations from which to draw data (Figure 11-5). However, specimens presented have L(length) divided W(width) times T(thickness) or the LWT Radio.

Figure 11-5 – Bipoint, Hood County, (L = 72, W = 30, T = 5 mm).

Bipolar Procedure

The bipolar method is basically the blade technique, but is a bed-based on removing a long piece from half of a medium-sized cobble. The method produces a flat-side bipoint. It prevents the length-wise curve that is sometimes obtained in the blade/flake method. The method is suggested, but not proven.

Haft vs. Bit Area

In classifying the bipoint, the determination of the hafting area vs. the cutting (bit) area is difficult. This is due to its usage, life cycle, and material. Bipoints were hafted (Holdaway 1989). Figure 11-6 shows a probable distinction of bit and stem.

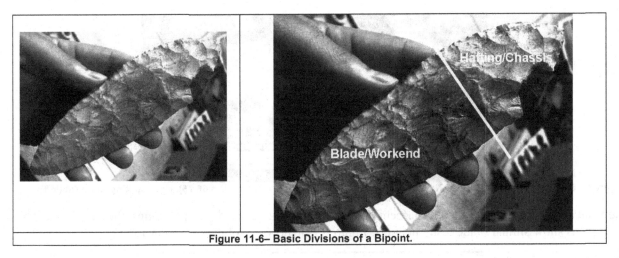

Figure 11-6– Basic Divisions of a Bipoint.

Once the cutting blade area has been resharpened to its becoming expended, the initial bipoint form is difficult, if not impossible, to determine. In many cases, other knife forms using various stems for hafting and blade expention will occasionally resemble bipoint technology. The V-shaped/stem on knives was used the same way that bipoints were. They usually have a different blade form (Figure 11-7) and, as such, are not initially bipoints, as suggested numerously. The V-shaped stem should be classified as bipoint technology, but there is too little data and examples to define them correctly. The figure below has a heavily resharpened blade. It is suggested that it was initially a large flint bipoint which was struck off a large boulder; the striking platform remains (right). The bipoint is suggested as its initial form, but depending on the viewer's archaeological perspective, this assessment will be argued.

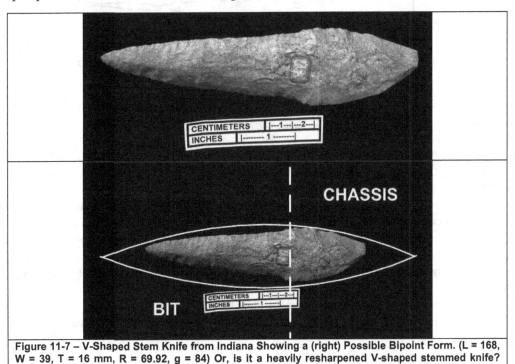

Figure 11-7 – V-Shaped Stem Knife from Indiana Showing a (right) Possible Bipoint Form. (L = 168, W = 39, T = 16 mm, R = 69.92, g = 84) Or, is it a heavily resharpened V-shaped stemmed knife? Note: striking platform right end.

Comparative example: Figure 11-8 shows a bipoint similar to the above specimen that has an expanded stem. The bit has been resharpened which causes the stem to appear larger. Note: striking platform (left).

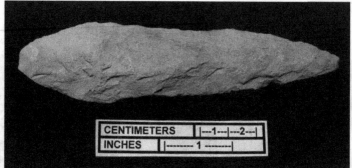

Figure 11-8 – Slate, Johnson County, North Carolina (L = 190, W = 37, T = 13 mm, R = 66.75). Note striking platform (left).

Comparative example: Blade resharpening often produces unusual morphologies; however, the above specimens show similar blade resharpenings. Figure 11-9 shows a Solutrean similar form.

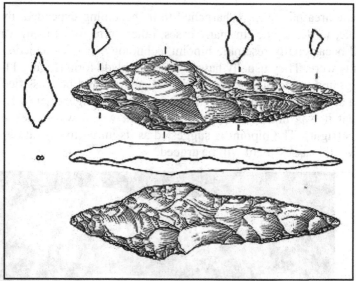

Figure 11-9 – Solutrean Blade Resharpening (after Miller 1962).

As mentioned, resharpening destroys the basic bit form, and the small blade area left over is frequently mis-classified as a stem. If these specimens are examined closely, the expended part (stem) often has sharp or beveled edges. Also, striations are usually visible under the microscope. They are classified here as V-shaped stemmed knives. They have beveled expended bits (workends). In both cases, archaeologists would generally classify them as stemmed points, which is the bit here; however, if they were stemmed points, there is no wear on the supposed blades. Far too many of these specimens are often mis-classified. Without the original specimen design by the knapper, the specimens would be classified as stemmed points which illustrate the problems with V-shaped stemmed knives. This problem will only be resolved using microscopic wear pattern analysis.

Andrefsky (2006) offers a Hafting Retouch Index, but applies it to the wrong end of the biface; Figure 11-10 shows his example. Densmore (2007) makes the same mistake with Gary points.

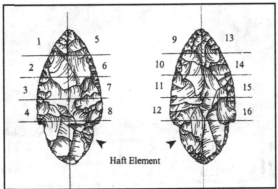

Figure 11-10 – Biface Indexing (after Andrefsky 2006). Note the resharpening on the bit in his right drawing.

The above drawing shows a common mistake with these knives. Andrefsky (2005) argues the use of microscopic instruments. Figure 11-11 shows two examples which were probably bipoints initially.

Florida, chert, with sharp bit

Florida, chert, with sharp bit

Figure 11-11 – V-shaped Stemmed Knife Examples Showing Expended Bits (Workends).

Comparative example: Figure 11-12 shows a bit-resharpened bipoint from Missouri. It is a tertiary bipoint. These small resharpened bipoints occur all over the eastern U.S.

Figure 11-12 – Flint, Expended Bipoint from Missouri (L = 63, W = 29, T = 8 mm, R = 17.38 resharpened). **Note the resharpening on bit (lower left).**

Comparative example: The expended V-shape stemmed knife is common, but it rarely receives attention in archaeology. The specimens often have residue(s) remaining and striations will often demonstrate function. Figure 11-13 shows this attribute. As mentioned previously, this form of bit resharpening dates to the Solutrean age.

Figure 11-13 – Quartzite, Johnson County, North Carolina (L = 66, W = 34, T = 11mm, R = expended, g = 17). **Bit has an opposite-side bevel and is sharp on its lateral margins.**

Comparative example: Figure 11-14 shows a resharpened bipoint that is often classified as an Adena beavertail (Hranicky 2011). It has a sharp bit which has striations from usage; tip is acutely pointed. The lateral margins show no usage-wear patterns. It is well made and has parallel lateral margin scars. Its cross section is biconvex. The surface has light polish suggesting that it was hafted.

Figure 11-14 – Chert Resharpened Bipoint, Ohio River Valley (L = 134, W = 41, T = 10 mm, R = 32.68, g = 47). **Lower photographs show lateral margin, surface, and bit close up analysis.**

Comparative example: Figure 11-15 shows a bit-resharpened bipoint from Pittsylvania County, North Carolina. It is a tertiary bipoint. These small resharpened bipoints occur all over the eastern U.S.

228

Figure 11-15 – Rhyolite, Expended Bipoint from North Carolina (L = 67, W = 35, T = 10 mm, R = expended).

Lateral Chassis Margins

Generally, the bipoint has curved margins, especially the early specimens. V-shaped stemmed knives are found with straight lateral margins which, again, compound analysis. Unless the bit is sharp and has wear patterns, it is probably a true stem for hafting the implement. Figure 11-16 shows such an example. This specimen is well made from banded rhyolite. Bit has parallel, diagonal flake scars. It is a surface find, and its age cannot be presently determined. Perhaps in this case, the small V-shaped extension is the stem? Both faces at the tip (left) have a built up short medial aris suggesting an increased tensile strength. The specimen definitely indicates the analytical difficulty with V-shaped knives. It was probably made by the biface reduction method. Overall, it is a well-made knife that initially was a bipoint.

Figure 11-16 – Slate, Mecklenburg County, Virginia (L = 132, W = 46, T = 12 mm, R = 34.43, g 30). It has relatively straight lateral margins.

Thick Bipoints

Most American bipoints have a thickness under 12 mm. However, late Archaic bipoints can be up to 30 mm in thickness. Figure 11-17 shows several examples. Since these specimens are surface finds, there is no way to date them. However, the bold flake scars and material seem to suggest the flaking of the Savanah River pointmakers. Both have flat faces.

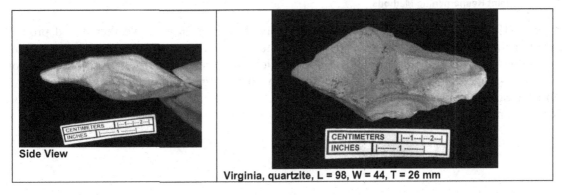

Side View

Virginia, quartzite, L = 98, W = 44, T = 26 mm

229

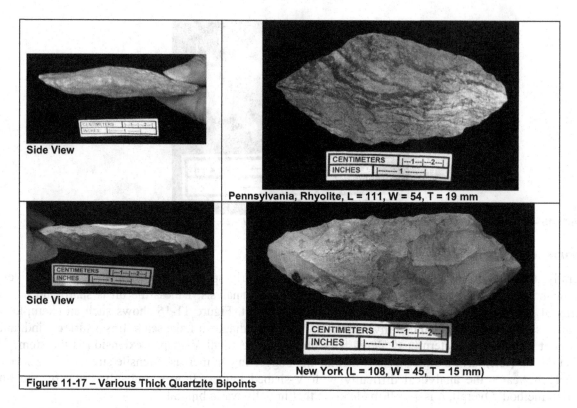

Side View

Side View

Pennsylvania, Rhyolite, L = 111, W = 54, T = 19 mm

New York (L = 108, W = 45, T = 15 mm)

Figure 11-17 – Various Thick Quartzite Bipoints

Bipoint Resharpening

As suggested in Section 2, the early bipoints are based on the distal-to-proximal resharpening method. While the bit shape varied with each user, the classic V-shaped bit is preferred archaeologically for determining the Solutrean association, or as having the closest legacy form. Later versions were resharpened laterally (Figure 11-18). The bipoint was resharpened by two methods:

- Distal end bit resharpening (mainly the Pleistocene). Legacy 1 and 2 bipoints.
- Lateral side bit resharpening (mainly the Holocene). Legacy 3 bipoints.

Area next to the bit end (or shoulder) often has a large circular flake removed which produces a sharp cutting edge. This method was used by the Solutreans.

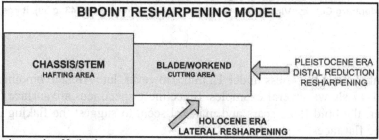

Figure 11-18 – Bipoint Resharpening Methods.

Figure 11-19 shows an example which is extremely thin. It is heavily weathered and probably has considerable antiquity. However, the specimen is used to show its bipointed base and has a medial ridge which is worn down. As a major attribute, it has parallel sides which are rare but do occur in Solutrean bipoints. The V-shaped bit and pointed stem suggest a primary stage bipoint. It is a thin piece (T = 8 mm) and below the Solutrean bipoint average thickness of 11.25 mm (author data, n = 31). It was made using the blade reduction method.

230

Figure 11-19 – Rhyolite Bipoint from Maryland's Eastern Shore (L = 93, W = 34, T = 8 mm, R = 21.88).

Comparative example: The following specimen has similar dimensions, but it is broken and was probably over 120 mm (Figure 11-20). It has a V-shaped stem (post-Indian breakage). It is probably a late Archaic specimen.

Figure 11-20 – Quartzite, Greenville County, Virginia (L = x, W = 42, T = 9 mm, R = broken) Specimen was heat treated.

Additionally, bit modification is discussed in Hranicky (2008b). Based on these specimens in this study with specimens shown previously, Figure 11-21 shows sample bipoint bit shapes.

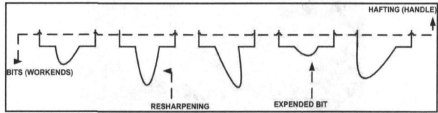

Figure 11-21 – Suggested Bit Modification on Bipoints or V-Shaped Stemmed Knives. These are Legacy 3 bipoint bits.

Figure 11-22 shows a North Carolina knife that has an expended bit. The bit is sharp and what is remaining has a steep taper to its end. There is very little remaining of the bit. Most archaeologists would drastically argue that it is a Morrow Mountain point. It does not match any description in Coe (1964) and Hranicky (2011), namely material, form, and flaking. The hafting V-shaped stem has no evidence of being used as a cutting tool. Based on the model discussed previously, this bipoint could have been initially 250 mm long. As the blade was reduced through resharpening, various bit styles were created. The process continued until the blade was expended, and the knife was discarded. Coe's (1964) Morrow Mountain shows a few of these variations in blade stem (narrow and wide). Note: Coe's specimens all have the same triangle *blade* form (stem) with no usage on the edges, only the point's assumed bases vary in shape.

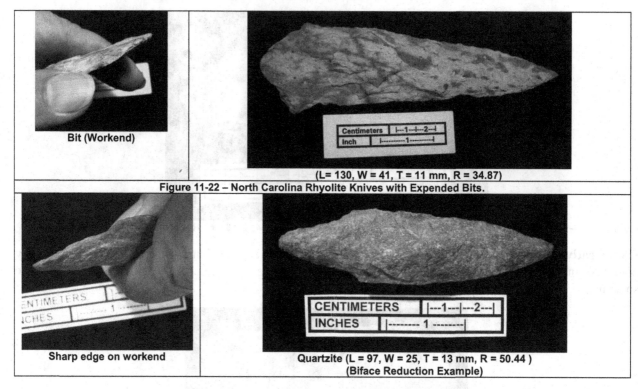

Bit (Workend)	(L= 130, W = 41, T = 11 mm, R = 34.87)

Figure 11-22 – North Carolina Rhyolite Knives with Expended Bits.

Sharp edge on workend	Quartzite (L = 97, W = 25, T = 13 mm, R = 50.44) (Biface Reduction Example)

Assuming the Old World assumption is correct, expended Solutrean bipoints offer examples for resharpening and expended forms. This publication starts identifying a tool class that has not received attention in American archaeology. Projectile points usually served as prehistoric knives and are the primary subject of most archaeological investigations and analyses. Knives are generally not analyzed; this industry has numerous forms and styles in prehistory.

Comparative example: Figure 11-23 shows a classic bit form. This specimen probably dates to the late Woodland era. It has a narrow V-shaped bit (right in photograph). The bipoint was used; therefore, it is not a preform.

Figure 11-23 – Kentucky Bipoint with an Extensive Bit (L = 109, W = 40, T = 15 mm, R = 40.87, g = 43).

The Iberian Curve

This hypothesis is based on bipoints from the Middle Atlantic area. Numerous specimens do not have symmetrical curved sides (lateral margins). The curve was named after this curve on Old World bipoint specimens. This attribute may have Old World implications and associations. The specimens under study are all surface finds, which, in itself, is a problem. The Iberian curve has one relatively straight lateral margin and the other margin has a pronounced curve (Figure 11-24).

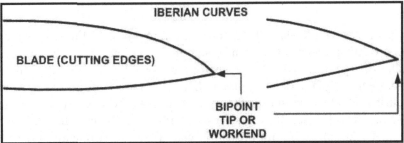

Figure 11-24 – Iberian (Solutrean) Edge Curve.

The following V-shaped Stemmed (expended) bipoints show this curve (Figure 11-25). They are numerous and often classified as Morrow Mountain points. The bit on both specimens is sharp, but the knife is expended. They are usually well made averaging 10.5 mm in thickness.

Quartzite, Halifax County, Virginia (L = 111, W = 41, T = 10 mm, R = resharpened, g = 47)

Slate, Mecklenburg County, Virginia (L = 95, W = 36, T = 11mm, R = resharpened, 28) Note the incurvate lateral margin. These specimens may be Legacy 2 bipoints.

Figure 11-25 – Expended Knives Showing the Iberian Curve.

Comparative examples: Figure 11-26 shows examples and a drawing of the variation on the chassis. These specimens have expended bits (right).

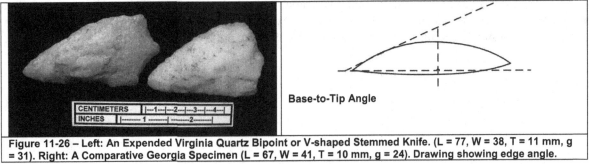

Base-to-Tip Angle

Figure 11-26 – Left: An Expended Virginia Quartz Bipoint or V-shaped Stemmed Knife. (L = 77, W = 38, T = 11 mm, g = 31). Right: A Comparative Georgia Specimen (L = 67, W = 41, T = 10 mm, g = 24). Drawing showing edge angle.

Mega Bifaces

Mega bifaces are large knives with V-shaped stems that are found in the Middle Atlantic coastal plain. They are classified as Large Cutting Tools (LCT). And, they are suggested as butchering knives that were used exclusively on kill sites. They are expedient tools that were probably a single-time knife and discarded after usage. These specimens generally have a LWT greater than 1:75 ratio.

There is a size attribute that occurs on mega bifaces that have the same style of manufacture as smaller bipoints (Figure 11-27). Mega bifaces are argued as Before-Clovis butchering tools for megafauna in the Middle Atlantic (Hranicky 2011). LCTs are present in central Africa (Braham 2007). Other than form, the relationship between mega bifaces and smaller bipoints remains to be established; for the present, age seems to be the connection. The mega biface has the same stem angle as the two previous expended knives. The obvious problem is classifying them as expended; many readers will call them simply knives, not having an initial bipoint form. Of course, this may be the case and for this reason, once bit resharpening occurs, the specimen must be called a V-shaped stemmed knife.

Figure 11-27 – Left: Jasper, Southwest Virginia (L =98, W = 52, T = 10 mm, R = resharpened) Right: Rhyolite Mega Biface. It is from North Carolina (L = 159, W = 62, T = 21 mm, R = 53.85). Note: Stem angles.

Rhyolite Mega Biface Knife from Mecklenburg County, Virginia, L = 179, W = 56, and T = 14 mm. Right end is the bit and left end is the hafting area. Bit is sharp and tapered. It was percussion flaked with minor distal edge trimming. Note: slight curve in the body of the knife.

Bipoint Quality

As with variation of size and form, the bipoint has a range of manufacture from high-quality to poorly made specimens all of which vary over time. The following example may be preforms which would have been pressure flaked into small bipoints. Figures 11-28 and 11-29 show poorly-made examples.

Figure 11-28 – Flint, Jackson County, Indiana (L = 128, W = 42, T = 16 mm, R = 48.76).

The above specimen was not placed into service; below specimen shows lateral edge resharpening. Both have relatively the same physical dimensions.

Figure 11-29 – Rhyolite, Randolph County, North Carolina (L = 129, W = 44, T = 13 mm, R = 38.11).

Bipoint Size

As mentioned earlier, the basic assumption here is that large bipoints are indicative of butchering large game while smaller forms were used for tasks, such as cutting branches, skins, etc. This morphology is assigned an algometric dimension. Equating non-sharpened lengths with chronology is impossible presently due to no site contexts. Figure 11-30 shows mid-sized bipoints that probably date to the Middle Archaic era. Most archaeologists would classify this specimen as Morrow Mountain projectile points, but the words *projectile point* would be false. They are knives and, by size/shape, are secondary stage bipoints. The U.S. bipoint can measure over 2000 mm; however, most specimens average 200 mm.

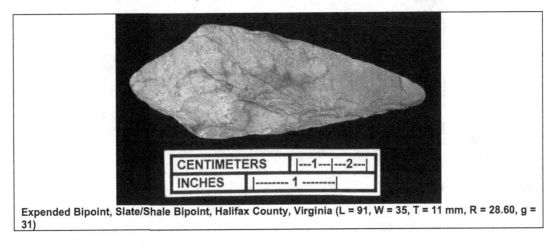

Expended Bipoint, Slate/Shale Bipoint, Halifax County, Virginia (L = 91, W = 35, T = 11 mm, R = 28.60, g = 31)

Rhyolite, Burke County, Pennsylvania (L = 116, W = 45 , T = 12 mm, R = resharpened, g = 47)

Figure 11-30 – Archaic Era Bipoints (Legacy 3). Note the bits are on the left in the photographs.

While most bipoints are approximately 150 mm in length, shorter versions do occur. These are mostly Legacy 3 bipoints which are usually made from flint or chert. The western versions are usually made from obsidian. Figure 11-31 shows a small specimen from Kentucky. It was made off a small blade as the platform remains.

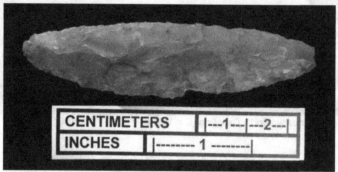

Figure 11-31- Flint, Glasgow area, Kentucky (L = 78, W = 19, T = 6.5 mm, R = 26.68)

The mega bipoint is discussed that argues for large bipoint knives in the lower middle Atlantic coastal and piedmont plains. Figure 11-32 shows an example. Question: Did it initially have a pointed workend?

Figure 11-32 – Slate, Mega Biface (Bipoint?), Stanly County, North Carolina (L = 146, W = 54, T = 15 mm, R = 109.65). Note V-shaped stem (chassis).

Bipoint Lithic Materials

The choice of high quality stones is simply a feature of the technology carryover from the Old World. Once hominids learned that stones varied in knappability, they made all efforts to obtain these stones, even if it meant traveling extreme distances to obtain them. Stone acquisition was a factor in human migrations and, as such, this factor was a technology carryover from the Old World. It is not surprising that a coastal bipoint, the Cinmar, is made from inland Pennsylvania rhyolite.

The number of true early bipoints on the Atlantic coast is limited presently to approximately 50 known specimens (author and Smithsonian collections). To establish a lithic preference can only be estimated, which is based on author observations:

- Rhyolite (highest)
- Slate (moderate)
- Flint (low)
- Chert
- Quartzite (lowest)
- Quartz (few expended specimens).

Adams and Blades (2009) provide an overview of stone procurement and usage in the Paleolithic. There are no American studies on stones for bipoints; naturally, data are needed. A scale of mobility is needed which involves spatial networks vs. chronology of band-oriented societies.

Quartz may actually have the highest frequency, but due to not recognizing expended forms, this material is probably under counted. Old World stone preferences would be the first choices in the New World but not necessarily available to the new immigrants. Inland quarry sites were discovered, as with the Cinmar bipoint, but the current bipoint sample does not present archaeometric data for analysis.

Figure 11-33 shows a crystal quartz specimen for North Carolina. The bit is thicker than the stem and is expended.

Figure 11-33 – Crystal Quartz, Pittsylvania County, Virginia (L = 64, W = 28, T = 12 mm, R = 27.42).

As such, rhyolite appears to be the preferred material of eastern bipoint knappers. For the Middle Atlantic rhyolite overview, see Stewart (1987), and rhyolite in the Northeast, see Strauss and Hermes (1996). The remaining areas are the rhyolite in North Carolina; other minor outcrops do occur, but were they exploited? Since most quarry outcrops were used throughout prehistory, finding a Pleistocene quarry source is impossible.

Does material indicate an age assessment? The answer is probably yes. But sites, contexts, and dates are obviously needed. Quartzite and slate appear to indicate an Archaic era form of the bipoints. Flints and cherts indicate the Woodland era.

Bone Bipoints

Obviously, the organic nature of bone implements greatly inhibits their preservation. Coastal occupations provide the suggestion of a bone bipoint. The Daisy Cave site in California has bone artifacts. Figure 11-34 shows specimens from Sandia Cover, New Mexico (Hibben 1941). Also, the Blackwater Draw site has bipointed bones (Hester 1972).

A tip of a bone projectile point was found in a cut-up mastodon at the Manis site which dated 13,800 YBP. While probably not a bipoint, it was an osseous projectile point, common to the Beringian Upper Paleolithic and Clovis, which were made and used during pre-Clovis times in North America (Waters, et al. 2010). It provides evidence that people were hunting proboscideans at least two millennia prior to Clovis.

The Ichetuckness River in Florida has produced numerous bone harpoon-like implements (Milanich 1994:68 and Dumbar and Vojnovski 2007).

Figure 11-34 – Sandia Cave Artifacts, Top is a Bone Bipoint. Lower is made from ivory. Photograph: Smithsonian, Washington, DC.

Bipoint Hafting

The bipoint has three ways to haft it, one of which is simply a hand-held implement (Figure 11-35). The others are:

- Blade inserted into a handle
- Blade chassis is wrapped with leather or sinew
- Or, it was simply hand held.

An experimental knife using bipoint technology is shown in Figure 11-32 (Hranicky 2004 and 2007 and Walker, et al. 2000). The bipoint's blade was made from obsidian. One of the pointed stems is used to drive the blade into the bone handle. Handle is an Elk rib bone. Once the blade is inserted by force into the bone, it is removed and coated with a glue, such as pine tar, to secure the blade in the handle. One method was wrapping the handle with sinew which increases the strength of the knife and keeps sharp margins from cutting the user's hand. For an experimentation study prehensile wear, see Rots (2004).

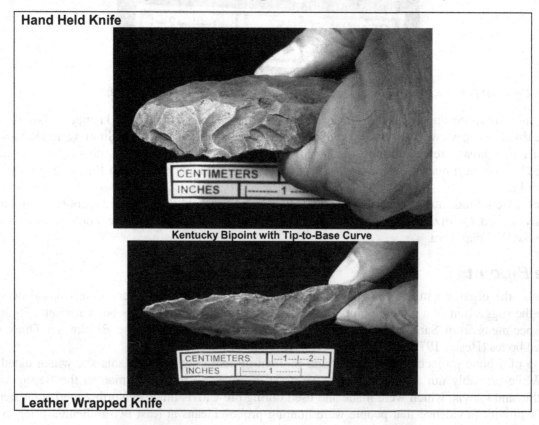

238

Newly-Made Bipoint Showing Experimental Hafting of a Prehistoric Bipoint with a Straight Base (Hranicky 2007b)

Bone Handle Knife

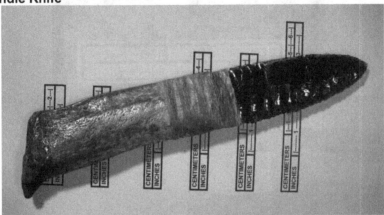

Newly-Made Knife Showing Bipoint in a Bone Handle

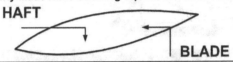

HAFT

BLADE

Figure 11-35 – Various Experimental Hafting Examples for Bipoints (Modern Specimens).

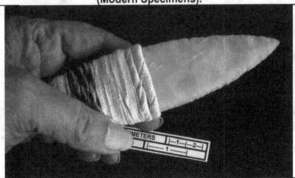

Daniel Firehawk Abbott made this bipoint out of Arkansas Novaculite which he heat treated. The hafting preparation is a strip of oil tanned buckskin with an inner dogbane that has black walnut dying. (L 170, W = 40, T = 8 mm, R = 34.00).

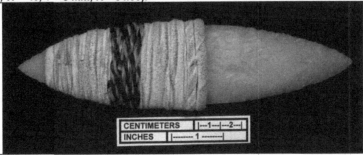

Biface Bipoints

The biface bipoint is not common, but it does occur especially during the Woodland era. They are usually thick and have a biconvex cross section. They are assumed as late prehistoric knives (Legacy 3) and are not restricted to any specific geographic region. Figure 11-36 shows a Florida specimen. Figure 9-37 shows a crudely-made flint specimen from Kentucky.

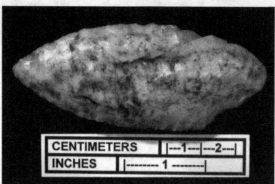

Figure 11-36 – Chert, Biface Bipoint from Northern Florida (L = 81, W = 33, T = 14 mm, R = 34.36). Note the off-set re-sharpening.

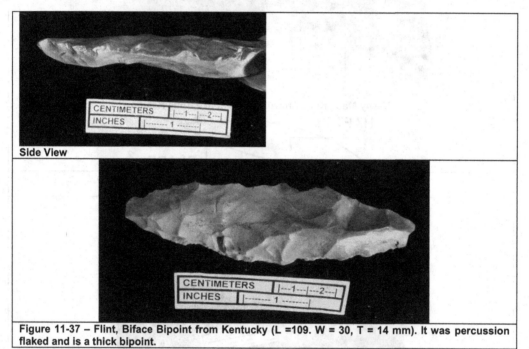

Side View

Figure 11-37 – Flint, Biface Bipoint from Kentucky (L =109. W = 30, T = 14 mm). It was percussion flaked and is a thick bipoint.

Expended Bit Shapes and Styles

As argued above, expended bits are difficult to determine what the general resharpening method or usage was. Figures 11-38 and 11-39 show two specimens with similar bits that suggest that they were last stage resharpenings. Both bits are tapered to a sharp edge.

Figure 11-38 – Northern Florida specimen made from Coastal Plain chert. Bit (left) is sharp even in the final stage of the knife. Chassis is thick with a major fracture (lower right). Top (right) margin has edge sharpening suggesting it was a hand-held tool. (L = 67, W = 57, T = 12 mm, R = expended blade) It has a short hafting stem.	Figure 11-39 – Southern Virginia made from North Carolina rhyolite. Bit (left) and adjacent margins are sharp even in the final stage of the knife. Chassis is thick. Top margin has a sharp edge. (L = 62, W = 55, T = 12 mm, R = expended blade). This specimen suggests that it may have been hafted (left).

These similar specimens are separated by 500+ miles and are made from different materials. They demonstrate a knife form that has:

- Manufacturing V-stemmed style
- Similar bit shapes suggesting similar knife function and usage
- Similar expention form for the southeastern U.S.

This style and material suggest the eastern Archaic Period, but without context, the date remains speculative on the part of the author. Both specimens were maxed-out for a final stage before discarding them.

As with the Morrow Mountain specimens shown in Coe (1964) and Hranicky (2011), there are various forms of bit resharpening. The major assumption is that the bit was long enough to be resharpened. Knives in Figure 11-40 show this variety; there is no way to determine how much of a blade was used-up in the tool's usage. The areas on both sides of the bit are usually sharp suggesting a wide cutting margin; dual functions?

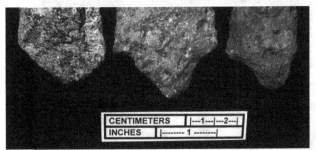

Figure 11-40 – Various Rhyolite Bits. Notice bit shift to one of the lateral margins; implies this bit increased the leverage with the knife. Right specimen suggests that it may have been hafted (bottom). They may be Legacy 2 bipoints.

The bit variation continues with quartzite-made specimens. For the Middle Atlantic, this material suggests the eastern Late Archaic Period knives (Figure 11-41). These are expended bits.

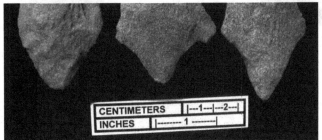

Figure 11-41 – Various Quartzite Bits. Each bit tapers off the chassis to form a sharp bit. Note the V-shaped bit. Material suggests that they are from the late Archaic. They are Legacy 3 bipoints.

Size is only a factor in bipoint manufacture; the expended form depended on the prehistoric user (Figure 11-42). Once into the eastern Woodland and as a suggestion, the bipoint becomes smaller, such as the northeastern Poplar Island and Piscataway points (as in Hranicky 2011).

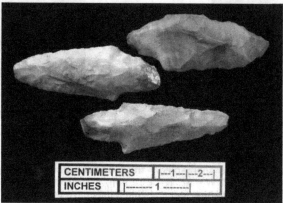

Figure 11-42 – Flint, Louisiana, Probably Expended Forms.

V-Stemmed Anomalies

While the V-shaped stem is a consequence of bipoint resharpening, this style/shape occurs in other tool classes. Thus, the V-shaped stem does facilitate hafting. These specimens are not classified as having initially been bipoints (Figure 11-43). The only parallel is the stem.

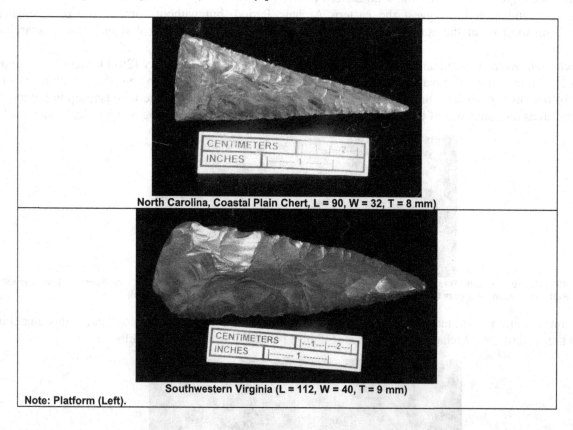

North Carolina, Coastal Plain Chert, L = 90, W = 32, T = 8 mm)

Southwestern Virginia (L = 112, W = 40, T = 9 mm)

Note: Platform (Left).

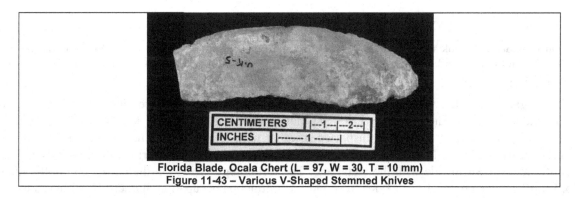

Florida Blade, Ocala Chert (L = 97, W = 30, T = 10 mm)

Figure 11-43 – Various V-Shaped Stemmed Knives

Expended Bipoints

Again, assuming a Solutrean bipoint legacy exists in the Middle Atlantic coastal area, numerous expended forms are found. Hranicky and Painter (1988) called the knives the Chesapeake Diamond point. They are consistently made from rhyolite or slate. They note that one point on the diamond was usually broken off. It is evidence of the knife being made off a blade. Figure 11-44 shows several examples from tidewater Virginia.

Not Chesapeake points; note round base.

Similar form, but not Chesapeake points.

Figure 11-44 – Expended Chesapeake Diamond Bipoints.

243

Section 12 – Bipoint Conclusion

This section provides the book's conclusion. The summary argues the book's contents for bipoints dating at least 35,000 BYP in the U.S. and, of course, greater time depth. The bipoint is present in the U.S. Before Clovis and is found to Contact times.

Some archaeologists argue the various bipoint technologies around the world are *simply* local inventions (discovery) of a basic knife. The argument has been that bipoint technology is a technological continuum which had its origins in Africa and was transported to other parts of the world, namely the Solutreans of Europe which transported it to North America. By 15k YBP, the bipoint has world-wide distribution. The bipoint was terminated worldwide with the metal age. The technology arrived in the U.S. around 50-35,000 years ago. While there is no genetic evidence to support a continuous occupation, numerous artifacts support the Solutreans (or any Old World population) as first peoples on the American Atlantic coast.

Perhaps, or most likely, the most colorful character in American archaeology is George F. Carter. He was so revered by his colleagues that they named an entire artifact industry after him – Carterifacts. His book ***Earlier Than You Think*** in 1980 makes interesting reading – there is more than one viewpoint (opinion and theory) about any time, space, or artifact in antiquity. Aside from his insistence on mankind being in the New World for 100,000 years or more, his scholarly approach and understanding of the human nature of scientists bears quoting in this conclusion (Carter 1980):

> *When a new idea is advanced, it necessarily challenges the previous idea. This disturbs the holders of the previous idea and threatens their security. The normal reaction is anger. The new idea is then attacked, and support of it is required to be of a high order of certainty. The greater the departure from the previous idea, the greater the degree of certainty required, so it is said. I have never been able to accept this. It assumes that old order was established on high orders of proof, and on examination this is seldom found to be true. Some of what we believe in science is habitual: we have learned it in our academic infancy and repeated it ad nauseum and so believe it implicitly and have never questioned its validity.*

For the present in archaeology, the American bipoint technology has:
- A suggested basic blade manufacturing method
- No stone preference, but rhyolite is suggested for early specimens
- Varies with length/thickness ratios, size may equal antiquity
- Various resharpening causes bit variations, no standard identification
- No consistent width or thickness, but they parallel Solutreans of Europe
- Has no land-based radiometric carbon dates, but the Cinmar dates of 24,000 YBP
- Has a Raman laser date of 16,000 YBP in Florida?
- Specimens that vary from well to poorly-made specimens which is common with Solutrean bipoints
- No consistent structural forms/shapes, but bits are similar with European specimens
- Material that can be traced to France (to be found)
- Early bipoints are found from Maine to Florida.

Hypothesis on the Americas

This publication absolutely supports any-and-all migrations into the Americas, and at any particular time during the Pleistocene era. As such, five hypotheses are suggested:

Hypothesis One: the Paleolithic Europeans made the shores of eastern U.S. 50,000 YBP

Hypothesis Two: the Paleolithic Africans made the eastern shores of South America 35,000 and the U.S. Southeast 25,000 YBP

Hypothesis Three: the Asians made the western shores of North America 25,000 YBP

Hypothesis Four: the Asians made Alaska 35,000 YBP

Hypothesis Five: the Australians made the western shores of South America 30,000YBP.

Most archaeologists are beginning to accept early migrations into the Western Hemisphere.

Many of east coast bipoints are of Solutrean design, but they still lack definitive archaeological contexts. Dates and preferred stones are still suggestive, but they are beginning to foster a *notion* Solutrean presence on the Atlantic coast which, of course, opens more questions than they presently answer. All specimens in this publication reflect a bipoint technological continuum which was shared subsequently as cross-cultural and chronological artifacts.

The eastern bipoint can be classified as a primary legacy (Solutrean-related specimen) that dates to the Pleistocene or as a secondary legacy (only shares the Solutrean legacy) specimens that dates to the late Pleistocene or early Holocene. The remainder bipoints are tertiary level bipoints which cover the entire U.S. There are numerous specimens found in the U.S. which should be re-appraised for the blade-made[70] manufacture technique.

Far too many archaeologists still use the term **pre-Clovis** for this era in American prehistory. They assume that all *early technology* leads to Clovis which is totally unproven. These archaeologists still do not know where Clovis came from, let alone that it does share a legacy with Solutrean. If this is the case, why does the bipoint not appear in Clovis toolkits? Furthermore, the Clovis lanceolate is a biface technology and the Solutrean bipoint is a blade technology; each for their main implements (points) that show different manufacturing techniques. Naturally, Clovis blade technology presents another window of toolmaking.

And, most prehistoric archaeologists are projectile point-oriented; that is: if a site does not contain a point, then it is simply a lithic scatter and ignored. What if a Solutrean-like site is found and has an expended bipoint with a few small blades? It would now be investigated!

Altogether, the specimens discussed provide numerous Solutrean attributes and properties on American coast bipoints. An excavated site with levels having bipoints is needed to define or identify American tools that can be associated with the European or Asian occupation. Bipoints will be subject to archaeometrical methods of stone analyses but, presently, the discovered bipoints are *simply* surface finds. Leaving the question: Did Solutreans die out and the bipoint was re-introduced by subsequent colonizers? Is there a second introduction of the bipoint on the Pacific coast?

50,000 Years and Counting

Providing that the southeastern bipoint is not simply a technological coincidence to the Old World, it represents an Atlantic crossing to the Southeast that must have occurred prior to 12,000 years ago. Other Old World tool forms are present in the Southeast that collaborate the technological relationship as argued here (Hranicky 2005). Throughout the archaeological literature, old dates for the New World have been published, some of which, by chance, are correct. Regardless, the time depth available for the Solutrean migration to the New World is evidenced by the Cinmar and Marion County bipoints. The illustrated specimens throughout this publication cannot be dated other than by relative dating and the tools' morphology. Naturally, morphology is the poorest form of an archaeological proof, but if it is not convincing, certainly this proposition should haunt archaeological thinking in American prehistory.

As a reminder, technology is viewed here as a continuum. New technologies are rarely created from nothing – Oldowan choppers are the initiating exception. Technology is constructed from a knowledge base, mostly trial and error events, and what is created leads to new technologies. Basically, technology is driven by hominid needs and environmental requirements (or restrictions) for the social unit. From a historical perspective and archaeological methodologies, defining technology is not a matter of counting artifacts. It is a process of collecting technological properties and tracking their change processes over time.

African Content in American Prehistory

The African prehistoric influence in the Americas cannot be overly emphasized. The bipoint was introduced into Africa and spread throughout the world...eventually the Americas. The shortest distance across the Atlantic is Africa to South America. This travel factor remains a major problem in archaeology. The easiest sailing is from west Africa to east Brazil.

---

[70] Still can be called a flake-made process.

Now for Clovis

Stanford and Bradley (2012 a&b) have convinced many, many archaeologists of the Solutrean-Clovisian connection; however, a few archaeologists will insist the relationship is impossible due to:
- Time depth – 19 vs. 13 k YBP
- Missing genetic connection to Europe.

But, the high-quality biface and blademaking in the Late Pleistocene remains ruminative on the body of the professional archaeological discipline. Who is correct? Does this publication argue for the connection? Yes and No. However, this publication was intended as a treatise on the universality of the bipoint.

One final word – what about the origins of the Clovis fluted lanceolate? If it is not a sudden invention in the Southeast, then its origins are most likely Europe. The Clovis has ancestry that as a product of the lithic continuum dates to the Moustrean of Europe. The Moustrean is the technology that was carried across the Atlantic 40-50,000 years ago, namely present at the Topper site in South Carolina and Arkfeld site in Virginia.

Late Prehistoric Bipoints

As illustrated, bipoints are found throughout the U.S. They share the bipoint legacy from the Old World. The hafting/blade separation is obvious. It dates to the Mississippian era. It has edge-to-edge flaking and is an extremely thin specimen which has high quality resharpening.

Prehistorically speaking, the Western Hemisphere is a child landform to the Old Worlds of Europe, Africa, and Asia. People migrated to this New World so many years remotely removed from this past that, until recently, the New World archaeological thinking paid little attention to what are ancestral homelands for New World prehistoric inhabitants. The presence of humans in the U.S. prior to Clovis is slowly being accepted (as in Waters and Strafford 2007). Also, the total Solutrean connection is dying slowly. Other cultures, namely the Aterians and Lupembans, probably made sea voyages to the New World. The bipoint probably is the key to world-wide human migrations, but how do you classify it?

Numerous examples of knife bits have been illustrated with variations that make it impossible to classify as an established form. Resharpening varied with each knife user; thus, specimens cannot be typed other than expended V-shaped stemmed knives.

The Solutrean culture of Iberia has its legacy in preceding technologies and cultures and left its influence on the New World. For the present, we cannot ascertain exactly whose bipoints are found where and when. The bipoint should be a major focus in archaeology in the Western Hemisphere. But it is not. This technology is the oldest continually made tool in the world, and it has the largest distribution of any *classifiable* form in the world. Proving both culture and time for this tool will be a challenge for archaeology.

The bipoint technological introduction into the New World in terms of place and time is highly controversial in American archaeology. And repeating, the bipoint is probably the most mis-classified implement in prehistoric archaeology because of its resharpening by its prehistoric users. Once resharpening and expention occur, the basic bipoint morphology is difficult to discern, identify, and classify. Additionally, it lacks datable contexts, so the tool's chronological position is also impossible. In many eastern surface surveys, an expended form is often classified as an eastern Morrow Mountain type or simply a stemmed point; thus, the implied date can be off by 1000s of years. All in all, the U.S. form of bipoint technology is present, but it dates to whatever archaeological perspective the researcher has. Somewhere, probably the Middle Atlantic coast, a land-based site[71] will be excavated that will produce early bipoint dates.

For the present in archaeology, American bipoint technology has:
- No identified basic manufacturing method
- No stone preference
- Varies with length/thickness ratios
- Various resharpening causes bit variations, no standard identification
- No consistent width or thickness
- Has no land-based radiometric carbon dates

---

[71] Best location possibility is the Dismal Swamp of Virginia and North Carolina.

- Specimens that vary from well-made to poorly-made specimens
- No consistent structural forms.

The conclusion is: a bipoint out of an archaeological site-context cannot be dated or attributed to any specific culture. It is a knife that by design has considerable antiquity. The sources for this technology in the New World are too *early* (archaeologically) to determine. The *when* for bipoints in the Americas is suggested after 50,000 YBP (presently); the *where* is the Lower Middle Atlantic (presently), and the *where from-first* is Africa (author's opinion). However, Europe is the key in popular news medias. Unless by lithic fingerprinting of an Old World stone found in the Americas, we will probably never know the *who was first*. And, on the Pacific side of the Americas the bipoint probably dates 30 k YBP.

As we move forward in the 21st century, each archaeologist will have access to a hundred years of work of countless people who had one focus – archaeology. In all, from all past events, it is a study of time; and a postword, written 100 years ago (Thomas 1898):

> *The work of archaeology in its broad sense is to revivify the dead, to put life into the past, and, so far as possible, to bring before the mind the ancient people with their activities, characteristics and customs. In other words, the chief object in view in the study of archaeology is the man of bygone ages.*

Conclusion: Technology – Coincidence or Legacy

The Solutrean culture of Iberia has its legacy in preceding technologies and cultures and left its influence on the New World. For the present, we cannot ascertain exactly whose bipoints are found where and when. The bipoint will (may) be a major focus in archaeology in the Western Hemisphere. This technology is the oldest continually made point in the world and it has the largest distribution of any *typeable* form in the world. Proving both culture and time for this tool will be a challenge for archaeology.

Based on the Iberian curve argument, how would the reader classify the broken blade in Figure 12-1? By using the curved edges for an estimate, the implement would have been approximately 210 mm with an average thinness of 14 mm. Who in Atlantic Coast prehistory is making tools this large? Obviously, there is no proof it was a bipoint. And, no proof it is Solutrean, or has an Old World legacy?

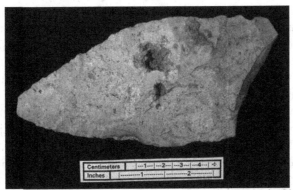

Figure 12-1 – Broken Blade Made from Ocala Chert (Putnam County, Florida). Chert is normally white, but the surface has grayed, and mineral crystallization has occurred. Crystals were present when the piece was knapped. Numerous flake scars cross the medial axis. The specimen is absolutely flat.

Finally, Don Crabtree told this author back in the 1970s: there are just so many ways to make stone tools – most human societies discovered all of them. And, Joffre Coe (1980s) at a Southeastern Archaeological Conference also provided the author with this philosophy: stone technology is simply a long technological continuum with divisions mostly arbitrary on the part of archaeologists. And, added here: tool morphology is the poorest form of an archaeological proof. All of which leaves archaeology only one long-time-tested way to study prehistory, namely the excavation. However, the excavation provides only a momentary view of time at a specific place. Technology never provides a momentary process in prehistory. Not everything is excavated; not every technology process is stationary; then archaeology may (probably never) put everything back together in order to write the true history book on the human experience on planet earth.

Eastern Atlantic Coast of Yesterday

Few archaeologists can, or for that matter need to, define the Atlantic Coast in terms of what the coastline was (or where) during the Late Pleistocene. The actual physical shape and corresponding data will never be known completely; however, parts of the shelf had flora and fauna lifeforms and social remains that can still be investigated. The earlier map from the U.S. Geological Survey's coastal physical surveys is a starting reference.

Lots of land – most of the Atlantic Coast study area for the Before Clovis into the Paleoindian time period is now under water. The exception is coastal Delmarva. How many archaeological sites does the area contain? The answer is: Quite probably thousands; these sites would hold keys to understanding early American prehistory. But, the total number will never be known. For this area, teeth of mastodons and mammoths have been recovered by fishermen from at least 40 sites on the continental shelf as deep as 120 meters. Also present are submerged shorelines, peat deposits, lagoonal shells, and relict sands (Whitmore, et al. 1967 and Wylie 1978). These and other large mammals ranged this region during the glacial stage of low sea level of the last 20,000 years. And, humans were found there, at least part of the time. Once again, the Big Game Tradition arises in American archaeology, but is being side-tracked by pre-Clovis.

Today, this area is continuously being subject to deposition from river runoffs and coastal deposition. As a consequence, early sites are deeply buried and were/are subject to sea bottom current movements which destroy cultural remains. Underwater archaeology would be a trying, expensive task to identify sites, let alone recover artifacts.

Fortunately for archaeology, the coastal plain (shelf) populations explored and moved onto what is now the coastal plain. The main objective for the inland exploration was lithic materials. Supplemental dieting procurement was also a factor. For this lithic reason, there are inland sites, but the now watered area is the real cultural plains. Inland occupations were temporary campsites for quarry procurements which explain the difficulty in finding sites. Also, for finding edible foods, people who stay only a night at a particular site and the next day move to another location leave few artifacts. However, given the total coastal geography, artifacts are found which do suggest cultures and their occupations. Archaeology faces a real challenge for adjusting its methodologies and database for the Atlantic coast investigations. A few artifacts discussed here may show the real appreciation of Mother Nature's saving something from the past.

For this coastal shelf, did it provide the paleodiet (carrying capacity) needed for human survival, or was inland exploitation needed? The paleodiet consisted of meat, fowl, fish, eggs, fruit, berries, nuts, and roots, some of which were not available on the exposed shelf. This diet is one requirement needed for human evolution and is encoded in the DNA (Hranicky 2006). How much of a factor was this in motivating world-wide migrations? The answer remains an open archaeological concern for the future.

Landfall for Old World immigrants assumes basic coastal explorations. Actual habitation areas would be based on the ancient population's need, expectations, desperations for places to live, and local curation possibilities for food- and natural-stuffs needed for survival. The coastal plain easily provided food, fresh river water, and a comfortable environment 20 to 10,000 years ago. The major problem was *fresh* lithic resources. They soon learned that the North Carolina-Virginia area provided fine grain quartzite, rhyolite, chalcedony, and slate/shale for toolmaking. The coastal plains of Florida and Georgia provided high quality chert and flint for toolmaking. For a landfall overview, see Hranicky (2007a). As a freshwater supply, the Chesapeake Bay is called the prehistoric Chesapeake River. Due to glacial melting at its headwaters, the river had a sufficient flow to ensure fresh water for coastal Virginia and North Carolina.

Do artifacts disappear...?

Yes, artifacts are discovered whether by surface pickups or excavations and temporarily become part of the public realm. Regardless of their curation, probably 90% of them lose their historic provenance, or simply get destroyed. If they get published, then there is a record of their acquisition, but un-marked ones simply become relics of the past. Archaeology cannot keep up with these discoveries; thus, the past becomes truly a thing of history. Fortunately, something gets into the records of history.

Finally – A Conclusion

Numerous examples of knife bits have been illustrated with variations that make it impossible to classify as an established form. Resharpening varied with each knife user; thus, specimens cannot be typed other than expended V-shaped stemmed knives.

The Solutrean culture of Iberia has its legacy in preceding technologies and cultures and left its influence on the New World. For the present, we cannot ascertain exactly whose bipoints are found where and when. Let alone attribute everything to the Solutreans. The bipoint should be a major focus in archaeology in the Western Hemisphere. This technology is the oldest continually made point in the world, and it has the largest distribution of any *classifiable* form in the world. Proving both culture and time for this tool will be a challenge for archaeology.

As a final bipoint, the following rhyolite specimen is from Princess Anne County, now the city of Suffolk (Figure 12-2). This tidewater area of Virginia is now under concrete, etc. While the continental shelf and city are almost gone for archaeology, they hold a romance as the port of entry for the eastern U.S.

Figure 12-2 - Rhyolite, Princess Anne County, Virginia (L = 100, W = 47, T = 15 mm, R = 31.91, E = 2.13, g = 71).

The *bipoint* is the only continuously and consistently made tool throughout prehistoric humanity. And, hominids have been in the Americas for 50,000 years...or more.

Appendix A – Properties and Concepts in Toolmaking

Once the archaeologist recognizes stone toolmaking as a lithic continuum that starts at Olduvai Gorge in Africa and continues to the global beginning of the metal age, there are factors for human cognition worldwide. All tools are based on human cognitive processes which are composed of primitive concepts which identify first humans millions of years ago. Once primates learned speech and how to make tools, humanness had its beginnings. The culture/tool divisions that archaeologists are used to accepting are not readily oblivious in prehistory; therefore, a long world-wide continuum is difficult to process sites, excavational elements, and data. But when one examines all the archaeological artifacts, information, and data, numerous material interpretations are presented over and over to the point that redundancy of material culture obscures the identification of regional, set-in time cultures. The following suggest factors and conditions for studying the human cognition of the physical tool world. For another similar viewpoint, see Kleindienst (1962).

1 - Primitive (Lithic Technology) - physical actions to create stone implements or physical properties in stone that are resistant to physical actions; all of which are basic to every stone implement. Any lithic artifact starts with an initial mental template of the toolmaker. These concepts can be classified as:

- Primitive structure (structor) - that are used to shape stone from its initial source
- Primitive function (functor) - that are present in the stone for manufacturing a tool for a specific usage.

►The structor is the state of a stone piece from which a tool can be manufactured. Its state stays with the knapping process to the finished tool which has recognizable structure. Structor is a basic state property. This is the equivalent to a tool's structural axis.

►The functor is the intended purpose of the state through manufacturing and continues via actual use of the tool to perform a specific task. Functor is a basic state property. Functor is the mode of a bipoint. This is the equivalent to a tool's functional axis.

2 - Primitives - in lithic technology, basic and natural function of any human activity that uses a tool to perform that function. It is operant behavior via a tool; and extension of the hand in tool form. For example, a fist for pounding which is replaced by the hammerstone for pounding. Pounding is the primitive. Also, set of basic technological functions that are found in Nature. Often, rocks can be found which perform as basic tools.

The use of primitives is not a new concept, as Raymond Dart's (1957) Ostedontokeratic Industry consisted of bone, tooth, and antler tools (weapons) for the australopithecines (his A. prometheus). Later, Mary Leakey (1971) defined the Olduvai tool technology of hammerstone, unifacial chopper, bifacial chopper, discoid, polyhedron, scraper, protobiface, spheroid, and awl. These beginnings are the start of the lithic technology continuum. Another important work is Schick and Toths (1993) study of early tools. They suggest a techno-organic evolution of:

- Stone flake. Analog: Carnivore flesh cutting as carnassial teeth.
- Hammer and anvil. Analog: Hyena bone crushing as with jaw-teeth.
- Digging stick. Analog: Bushpig snout and tusks, scratching with the animal foot.
- Missile. Analog: Natural motion.
- Club. Analog: Striking with limbs.
- Container. Analog: wooden skewer, large shells, skin bag.
- Anvil. Analog: Cracking teeth, platform.
- Fire. Analog: Natural fires.
- Lever. Analog: Tree limb to move an object.

3 – Primitive Concepts - All the above are natural extension of animal actions. They led to tool-using hominids. As Schick and Toth (1993) comment:

We cannot escape the biological, organic nature of our existence, but it is now bound up inextricably in the technological realm we have created.

A primitives (algorithm) - is created by the recognition of lithic primitives, which is defined as:

$$P_N = \zeta \{F_1, F_2..., F_N\} \{S_1, S_2..., S_N\}$$

whereas:

P = primitives
F = defined functions
S = design structure.

All F and S entities are characteristic of a specific primitive. We assume that all F and S values belong in the primitive and are always < 1. A primitive therefore must equal 1, or:

$$P_T \, \varepsilon \, F_N + S_N$$

whereas:

P_T = complete primitive
F_N = number of functions
S_N = number of structures.

4 - Primitive Forms - Presenting basic primitive forms for the development of all tool classes may be the most speculative part of this publication – an attempt is made. During the course of primate development, the hominid was able to classify its object-oriented world). As the brain developed, probably in parallel with language, objects could be manipulated by class and associated with their physiological primitives. The object then became an extension of the hands/feet capabilities. The wedge was probably the first primitive – a sharp-edged object that was used to split or cut another object. The simple flaked core having a sharp edge is the archaeological example of this primitive. The cone (1/2 of a sphere) and pyramid (diagonal 1/2 of a cube) are the first derivatives in ancient tools. Any one of the primitives, except the wheel could be the first primitive to have been hafted. The suggestion here is the sphere was the first hafted primitive which became the club. The wheel is discovered in the metal age and is the last primitive discovered. See Drawing A-1.

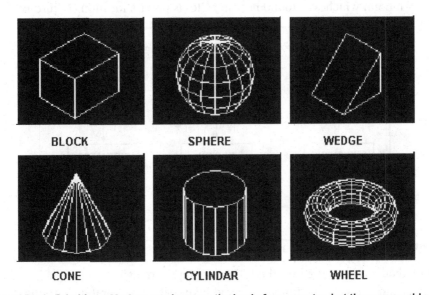

BLOCK SPHERE WEDGE

CONE CYLINDAR WHEEL

Drawing A-1 - Shapes of Basic Primitives. Modern versions are the basis for geometry, but they are as old as humanity.

Table A-1 presents briefly some of the factors that can be used in studying primitives. This concept is similar to the Platonic solids of tetrahedron, cube, octahedron, dodecahedron, and isosahedron shapes.

Table A-1 - Tool Primitives in Nature		
Basic Form (Primitive)	**Shape (Structure)d**	**Process (Function)**
Spheroid	Round	Hammering
Discoid	Irregular	Cutting
Polyhedron	Linear/ Rectangular	Perforating
Trianguloid	Irregular	Chopping
Broken	Leaf-Shaped	Cutting
Elongoid	U-Shaped	Cleaving
Flatoid	Thin/Flat	Scraping

Appendix B – Raman Laser-Induced
Luminance Dating

Without the radiocarbon dating method being available, archaeologists have turned to another method called the Optical Stimulate Luminance (OSL). The actual measurement on an artifact's surface is based on Miller (1985). Hranicky (1972) has an early proof of the luminance method. Since then, artifact and soil-contexts has advanced greatly. As such, these dates are becoming common in prehistoric archaeology.

The Raman laser technology and analytical methods have been used in many government and academic laboratories for approximately 10 years (Rong, et al. 2005 and Gramly and Walley 2012). It has been used in numerous technological applications, but, as per usual, archaeology is the last science to use the method. One application is to measure the reflected luminescence induced by the Raman laser on a prehistoric artifact. This light reflection is compared to a known dated sample: in the above case, an Ocala chert Clovis point from Marion County, Florida. The specimen is from Ben Waller's collection (#7794) which was assigned a date of 13,000 years before present (YBP). It produced a luminescence value that was compared to the Ocala chert Marion County bipoint which was found near the Clovis point's location (Figure B-1).

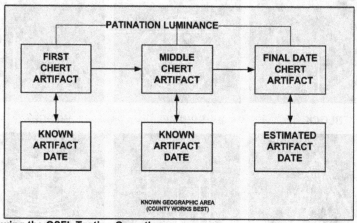

Figure B-1 – Flowchart Showing the OSFL Testing Operations.

This Raman laser method has been used for the following applications:
- Art and archaeology (determination of real and fake objects, restorations, pigment identification, luminescence reflection, etc.)
- Chemical education (for qualitative and quantitation courses, sample compositions)
- Gemology (determination of real and fake materials, origin determination, restoration, etc.)
- Geology (inclusion analysis, chemical and mineral identification)
- Treasury applications (identification of inks, pigments, and paper)
- Food sciences (identification and quantitation of unsaturation, fat content, etc.)
- SERS (Surface Enhanced Raman Spectroscopy) for trace surface wear detection
- Environmental determination of components from fraction of a percent to percent levels
- Glass and porcelain (composition, glasses, pigments, etc.).

In order to obtain an artifact's true luminescence value, 10 measurements are made on both faces (Figure B2). These values are averaged to produce a single value, then the following is calculated:

$$\frac{\text{Dated Artifact Sample } (A_S)}{\text{Artifact's Known Date } (A_D)} = \frac{\text{Test Sample Measurement } (T_s)}{\text{Test Sample Date } (T_D)}$$

The method is coined here as: Raman Infrared Laser Spectroscopy (R-ILS). The technique only works on fine-grain cherts and flints. While not tested, heat-treated materials probably will not produce valid results.

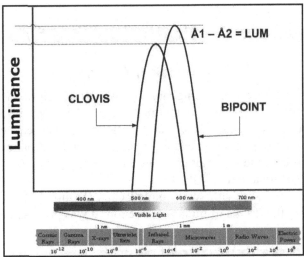

Figure B-2 – Light Spectrum for Luminance Test for the Marion County Bipoint.

Figure B-3 shows the paleopoint used in the test.

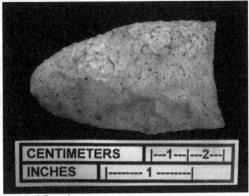

Figure B-3 – A Florida Paleopoint as a Control Specimen.

This analytical method for old stone absolutely will determined flake Clovis point from true points. The Ramam technique can *see* under a specimen's patination for ancient molecular activity. Finally, there is a method to eliminate bad paleopoints, especially the ones that have made their way into museum collections.

The following is an example of the equipment needed for the Raman laser technique.

Raman References:

Gramly, Richard M. and David Walley
(2012) Ft. Payne Chert: Inferred Laser Spectroscopy (ILS) Dating of Palaeo-American Artifacts and Trace Element Characterization. Paper: Society for American Archaeology, Annual Meeting, Memphis, TN.

Rong, Haisheng, Richard Jones, Ansheng Liu, Oded Cohen, Dani Hak, Alexander Fang, and Mario Paniccia
(2005) A Continuous-Wave Raman Silicon Laser. Nature, Vol. 433. pp. 725-728.

Appendix C – North Carolina Bifaces

The Rankin Cache

The following specimens were found in Rockingham County, North Carolina as a cache by Dr. Pressley Rankin. Their variations represent a possible functional usage. They may be simple a ceremonial cache; however, they are suggested as examples of the Nansemond knife. The cache is named after the finder. While the cache has a similar morphology, several specimens have pronounced V-shaped stems. These specimens are included because of the ovate or elongated state form. This cache represents a single toolkit that was probably used on megafauna in the East.

This specimen has an ovate shape with semi-pointed ends (Figure C-1). The entire edge margins are sharp; however, this is possibly the results of bifacial reduction. It was percussion flaked with probably a soft (antler) hammer.

Figure C-1 – Blade #1, Rankin Cache, Rhyolite (L = 119, W = 65, T = 16 mm, R = 29.29).

This specimen is the largest biface in the cache (Figure C-2). It has a V-shaped bit that has been used. It was percussion flaked with probably a soft (antler) hammer. It is classified as a mega biface. The bit (workend) is V-shaped and sharp.

Figure C-2 – Blade #2, Rankin Cache, Rhyolite (L = 179, W = 54, T = 14 mm, R = 46.40).

This specimen has an off-center shape (Figure C-3). The right blade is V-shaped and sharp. It was percussion flaked with probably a soft (antler) hammer.

Figure C-3 – Blade #3, Rankin Cache, Rhyolite (L = 127, W = 56, T = 14 mm, R = 31.74).

This specimen has a round sharp bit (Figure C-4). Noticeably, it has two cross face, diagonal flake scars. It was percussion flaked with probably a soft (antler) hammer. It is classified as a rounded-bit mega biface. Its size suggests that it was used for butchering large game.

Figure C-4 – Blade #4, Rankin Cache, Rhyolite (L = 131, W = 62, T = 13 mm, R = 27.46).

Comparative specimen: This French specimen has a V-shaped stem with a used rounded bit. It argues that is morphology is worldwide.

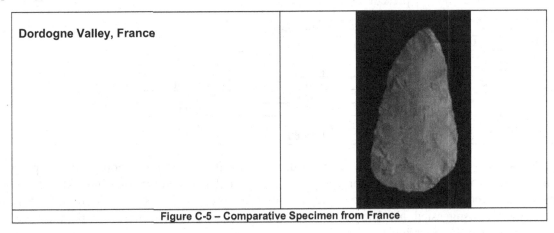

Dordogne Valley, France

Figure C-5 – Comparative Specimen from France

This specimen has a wide (left) sharp bit (Figure C-6). The V-shaped stem is short compared to the other specimens. It was percussion flaked with probably a soft (antler) hammer.

Figure C-6 – Blade #5, Rankin Cache, Rhyolite (L = 157, W = 75, T = 17 mm, R = 35.58).

This specimen is also an ovate-shaped specimen (Figure C-7). The length-wise margins are sharp. It was percussion flaked with probably a soft (antler) hammer. It is classified as a copper.

Figure C-7 – Blade #6, Rankin Cache, Rhyolite (L = 104, W = 61, T = 15 mm, R = 25.57).

The V-shaped stem varies, but the stem angle is similar for all specimens. The width varies but falls within 65 to 75 mm. Table C-1 present the cache's data.

Blade	Length	Width	Thickness	Notes
#1	119	65	16	Ovate
#2	179	54	14	Length
#3	127	56	14	Heavy duty
#4	131	62	13	Flaking
#5	157	75	17	Large Bit
#6	104	61	15	Ovate
Average	136.16	62.16	14.83	

Table C-1 – Rankin Cache Data

The Rankin cache represents a *working* toolkit. As such, it is probably a non-projectile point toolkit which is early in North Carolina prehistory. It has a variety of shapes and working bits. All bits have sharp margins, but the amount of wear needs to be determined. This presentation is only based on morphology. A multi-style toolkit is suggested. No date can be determined archaeologically, presently, but the suggestion is that the cache dates to Before Clovis.

Appendix D - Rounded-Bit Bipoints

The round-bit bipoint form probably dates to the eastern Ft. Ancient. The basic morphology is the V-stem that is the same as a bipoint. The round bit is probably a form that is early in its manufacture as a stemmed tool (Figure D-1). The V-shaped stem suggest a bipoint legacy and is simply a product of resharpening.

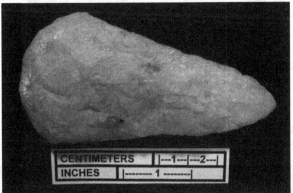

Figure D-1 – White Quartz, Yakin County, North Carolina (L = 94, W = 48, T = 16 mm, R = 31.33, g = 60).

Figure D-2 shows another example from Georgia. It is made from chert and has a sharp, finely retouched bit. It does not appear to be an expended round-bit bipoint.

Figure D-2 – Chert, Houston County, Georgia (L = 102, W = 52, T = 11 mm, R = 21.57, g = 36).

Figures D-3 and D-4 show specimens from Macon County, Florida. They illustrate the southeastern distribution of the rounded bit V-stemmed tool.

Figure D-3 – Chert, Macon County, Florida (L = 96, W = 65, T = 10 mm, R = 14.77, g = 57).

Figure D-4 – Chert, Macon County, Florida (L = 86, W = 44, T = 10 mm, R = 19.55, g = 38).

Comparative example: Figure D-5 shows a narrow form with a round bit. These tools are common in the eastern U.S. Their function and purpose remains to be proven.

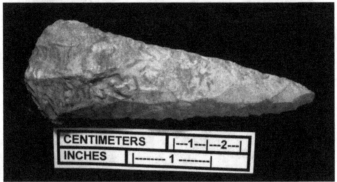

Figure D-5 – Chert, Yakin County, North Carolina (L = 97, W = 35, T = 11 mm, R = 30.48, g = 30).

Figure D-6 shows a rhyolite form which suggests it is earlier than the Ft Ancient specimens. It is heavily patinated. All round bit specimens are surface finds. As a note: this tool occurs in form and shape in European and Aterian toolkits (Hranicky 2007). It has one flat face.

Figure D-6 – Rhyolite, Sussex, Virginia (L = 90, W = 37, T = 10 mm, R = 24.32).

Comparative example: Figure D-7 shows both faces of a V-shaped stem tool. This tool is sometimes called a Limande in the U.S. (Hranicky 2007). It is another technological relationship with the Old World. It has one flat face.

Figure D-7 – Coastal Plain Chert, Northern Florida (L = 80, W = 47, T = 14 mm, R = 23.82).

Appendix E - Morrow Mountain Resharpened Bipoints

The eastern U.S. Archaic period has few bipoints or expended forms that could be classified as bipoints. The rhyolite Morrow Mountain (I & II) type is not readily accepted as a bipoint form. Rhyolite usually dates to the middle Archaic era for the Middle Atlantic area. The later Archaic period also has a large component known as the Savannah River culture. The major stone type for these toolmakers is quartzite. As argued, the bipoint form is found throughout prehistory.

The Archaic period has problems for identifying the bipoint, especially since these types are basically an undefined knife. And, resharpened forms often show expended bits which are not always sharp. These bipoints are classified as Legacy 3 bipoints.

Relying on the initial sole source, Coe (1964) does indicate that he had a high number of surface finds, namely the Guilford type; all of which could confuse classification. We cannot tell which specimens were surface-collected or excavated specimens. This applies to both Morrow Mountain (MM) and the Savannah River (SR) types.

The Morrow Mountain V-Shaped point by Coe (1964) in the Middle Atlantic area is the most mis-classified point type in the U.S. Coe's (1964) publication shows various morphologies, such as the stem shapes which are actually bits. The so-called blades (triangle-shaped) parts are actually the hafting (chassis) part.

Morrow Mountain I Points

Morrow Mountain Point Distribution

Morrow Mountain I [Stemmed] Point - named by Joffre L. Coe in 1964 after a mountain in North Carolina. It is a wide-bladed point with a short tapering stem. Base is rounded. Type dates 6700 to 5500 BP and is found all over the eastern U.S. Coe (1964) suggests: ... small triangular blade with a short pointed stem.

As a Type: it is a large resharpened bipoint – an expended point with a trianguloid blade which was originally the hafting area.

Flintknapping: average quality.

Major attribute: small pointed stem.

Type validity: traditional.

Type frequency in area: high as common.

Archaeological timemarker: yes.

Similar to: ?

Comment: for point dimensions, see Coe (1964).

1 - Reference: Coe, Joffre Lanning (1964) The Formative Cultures of the Carolina Piedmont. Transactions, American Philosophical Society, Philadelphia, PA.

2 - Reference: Hranicky, Wm Jack (2001) Projectile Point Typology for the Commonwealth of Virginia. Virginia Academic Press, Alexandria, VA.

3 - Reference: Brennan, Louis A. (1975) Artifacts of Prehistoric America. Stackpole Books, Harrisburg, PA.

4 - Reference: Sherwood, Sarah C., Boyce N. Driskell,, Asa R. Randall, and Scott C. Meeks (2004) Chronology and Stratigraphy at Dust Cave, Alabama. American Antiquity, Vol. 69, No. 3, pp. 533-554.

5 - Reference: Hranicky, Wm Jack (2002) Lithic Technology in the Middle Potomac River Valley of Maryland and Virginia. Kluwer Academic/ Plenum Publishers, New York, NY.

6 - Reference: Hranicky, Wm Jack (2011) Prehistoric Projectile Points Found Along the Atlantic Coastal Plain. Universal Publishers, Boca Raton, FL.

7 - Reference: McReynolds, Theresa E. (2005) Spatial and Temporal Pattering in the Distribution of North Carolina Projectile Points. North Carolina, Vol. 54, pp. 1-33.

8 - Reference: Hranicky, Wm Jack (2011) Projectile Points from Prehistoric Virginia. AuthorHouse, Bloomington, IN.

9 - Reference : Meeks, Scott (2000) The Use and Function of Late Archaic Projectile Points in the Midsouth. Report of Investigations77, University of Alabama Museums, Moundville AL.

10 - Reference: Carr, Kurt W. and Roger W. Moller (2015) First Pennsylvanians. Pennsylvania Historical & Museum Commission, Harrisburg, PA.

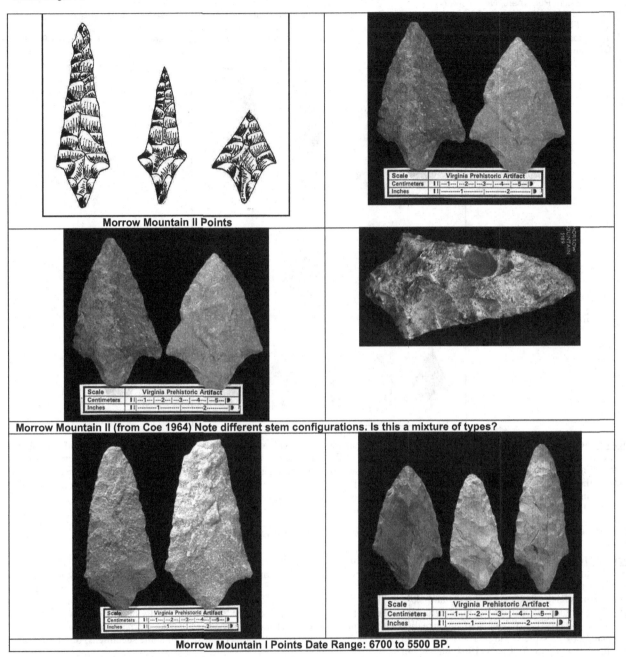

Morrow Mountain II Points

Morrow Mountain II (from Coe 1964) Note different stem configurations. Is this a mixture of types?

Morrow Mountain I Points Date Range: 6700 to 5500 BP.

Morrow Mountain II [Stemmed] Point

Morrow Mountain II [Stemmed] Point - named by Joffre L. Coe in 1964 after a mountain in North Carolina. It is a narrow-bladed point with a short tapering stem. Base is pointed. Type dates 6700 to 5500 BP and is found all over the eastern U.S. Coe (1964) suggests: … long narrow blade with a long tapered stem.

As a Type: it is a narrower version of the Morrow Mountain I point; it is also an expended point.

Flintknapping: average quality.

Major attribute: broad blade.

Type validity: traditional.

Type frequency in area: high as common.

Archaeological timemarker: yes.

Similar to: Rossville.

Comment: for point dimensions, see Coe (1964).

1 - Reference: Coe, Joffre Lanning (1964) The Formative Cultures of the Carolina Piedmont. Transactions, American Philosophical Society, Philadelphia, PA.

2 - Reference: Hranicky, Wm Jack (2001) Projectile Point Typology for the Commonwealth of Virginia. Virginia Academic Press, Alexandria, VA.

3 - Reference: Brennan, Louis A. (1975) Artifacts of Prehistoric America. Stackpole Books, Harrisburg, PA.
4 - Reference: Hranicky, Wm Jack (2002) Lithic Technology in the Middle Potomac River Valley of Maryland and Virginia. Kluwer Academic/ Plenum Publishers, New York, NY.
5 - Reference: Hranicky, Wm Jack (2011) Prehistoric Projectile Points Found Along the Atlantic Coastal Plain. Universal Publishers, Boca Raton, FL.
6 - Reference: McReynolds, Theresa E. (2005) Spatial and Temporal Pattering in the Distribution of North Carolina Projectile Points. North Carolina, Vol. 54, pp. 1-33.

Morrow Mountain II - A long, broad (formally defined as narrow) blade with a long tapering stem. Blade edges are usually straight or sometimes very slightly excurvate. Some specimens tend to flare outward at the shoulder giving the impression of a crude cross. The relatively short blade of some specimens appears to be the result of resharpening. Base is pointed. The stem is long and tapered. Although the shoulder curves onto the stem, there is more of a break than in Type I. The stem longer than Type I. Type II does not show grinding or smoothing, but was made the same may as Type I. See figure for classic Coe (1964) narrow-bladed points. The large Type II points are probably earlier than the narrow points.

Morrow Mountain I (from Coe 1964) Note different stem configurations. Is this a mixture of types?

Morrow Mountain I: A large (initially defined as short), broad triangular blade with a short pointed stem. Blade edges are slightly rounded, but a few specimens are straight or slightly incurvate. Serrations are faint and irregular. The greatest width of the point is at the shoulder. Base is rounded (initially defined as pointed). Stem is short and tapered (initially defined as frequently forming an equilateral triangle). Shoulders are wide and sloping. The shoulder is usually curved onto the stem without a noticeable break or angle. Larger points were made by direct percussion; therefore, they are sometimes crudely made. Initially defined as: smaller points were made by pressure flaking and are usually better made and symmetrically shaped (now smaller points are the result of resharpening by pressure flaking). There is slight grinding along the edge of the shoulder and stem of some specimens, but it is never pronounced. See figure for Coe's (1964) classic points.

Some archeologists have argued size as the basic difference between Morrow Mountain I and I types. While it may be true, generally size is a lithic consequence of the amount of stone that the knapper had initially and the amount of resharpening. The major difference is the stem/hafting technology of each type. Type I may have functioned primarily as a knife/scraper; whereas, the narrow Type II points functioned as a spearpoint. The wider Type II varieties may have been nultifunctional. This text shows two large Morrow Mountain I points found in Virginia. However, while not guide as broad, text shows very large Morrow Mountain I points. Both types were broadspears when initially made.

Note: The major problem with the Morrow Mountain type is the inconsistencies with the basic morphology.

The quartzite bipoint form is generally a large tool with a large bit. Coe's (1964) selection of points does not show any forms of a bipoint; he was projectile point-orientated. Numerous surface finds in an area of a high concentration of SR points suggest other tools. The key here is the use of quartzite which is indicative of this technology (Hranicky 2011). The bipoints shown are suggested as being late Archaic; there is an assumption that the SR pointmakers actually had the bipoint, but this remains to be proven archaeologically. Otherwise, the quartzite version is difficult to classify.

Figure E-1 has straight lateral margins and has polished sides, round bit. It appears to be an expended knife. However, the lower bit margin still retains some sharpness. It has hinges, and the specimen is not well made.

Figure E-1 – Quartzite, Prince George County, Virginia (L = 94 broken, W = 51, T = 10 mm, R = broken). Note left is the bit.

Figure E-2 has a prehistoric break on the stem. The bit may have formed a spoke shave which has wear usage along the curve's edge. The other side of the bit's lateral margin still retains sharpness, though worn. While it has hinges, the specimen is well made. The bit suggests that it was a multi-functional knife. Also, it has a large legacy flake removal from the upper bit area which produced a sharp cutting edge.

Figure E-2 – Quartzite, Prince George County, Virginia (L = 104 broken, W = 53, T = 10 mm, R = broken). Note: left is the bit. It has a large legacy sharpening flake (upper flake over the bit).

Savannah River Bipoints

The Savannah River (SR) toolmakers are classic late Archaic culture and date around 4000 YBP in the East (Hranicky 2011). They are not generally equated with the bipoint, but quartzite specimens do occur. Expended forms are suggestive of the bipoint which is assumed here. They are classified as Legacy 3 bipoints. Numerous round bit quartzite bipoint-like artifacts occur in the Middle Atlantic area.

Appendix F – Quantum Styles in Lithic Technology

Style – Quantum Classification Method

Projectile points are classified by their generalized shape; their basic morphology. There are numerous ways to divide them, such as by blade style, stem shape, material, or size (Figure F1). The Quantum Classification Method (QCM) divides all projectile points (Hranicky 1987) into:

1 – Lanceolate forms (L)
2 – Notched forms (N)
3 – Stemmed forms (S)
4 – Bifurcate forms (B)
5 – Triangle forms (T)
6 – Bipoint forms (Bp).

These six divisions are used throughout prehistory as the basic morphology schema for any projectile point/knife. Each point type that is listed begins with one of these styles in its title.

The QCM is based on a basic design principle that went into each point when it was knapped. While the pointmaker may or may not have been aware of all the possible styles that he could select from for making his point, the American Indians, for the most part, used one of the above five basic shapes for projectile points, which are described as:

Lanceolate Form – reference to a large parallel-edged point that does not have waisting, notching, or shouldering. QCM examples are: Clovis, Golondrina, Hells Gap, Hi-Lo, Agate Basin, Beaver Lake, Nebo Hill, Pee Dee, Pelican, Copena, Cumberland, Folsom, Guilford, Quad, and Plainview. The lanceolate form points are usually long slender points with no proximal area that shows any hafting designs. For Virginia, the major lanceolate forms are the Clovis, Whites Ferry, and Fox Creek types.

Notched Form – reference to point that has circular indentations cut into the lower edges or corners. QCM examples are: Hardaway, Besant, Big Creek, all Turkey- and Dove-tail points, Cache River, Cupp, Desert, Cahokia, Lost Lake, Palmer, Pine Tree, Big Sandy, and Dalton. The notched point is usually a medium triangular-shaped point that has notches cut into the side or corner areas of the proximal end of the point. For Virginia, the major notched forms are the Big Sandy, Vosburg, Susquehanna, St Charles, Snyders, and Kirk types.

Stemmed Form – reference to a point that has a downward extension from the blade at the proximal end. QCM examples are: Cotaco Creek, Duncan, Eden, Flint Creek, Godar, Holland, Morrow Mountain, Pryor, Johnson, Kramer, Pontchartrain, Rio Grande, Stanly, Alberta, Dallas, Kirk, LeCroy, Adena, Savannah River, Sandia, and Scottsbluff. The stemmed point has an obvious extension at the base of the point, which makes the stemmed area noticeably different from the blade part of the point. For Virginia, the major stemmed forms are Morrow Mountain, Adena, Savannah River, Snook Kill, Bare Island, and Koens-Crispin types.

Bifurcate Form – reference to a point that has bilobes. QCM examples are Nottoway River, St Albans, LeCroy, Fox Valley, Susquehanna Valley, and Rice. The larger the lobes, probably the older the point. Points are often found as expended points (less than 25 mm). The bifurcate probably was invented in the Carolinas and reflects a technological continuum of the Hardaway and Quad technologies. For Virginia, the major bifurcate forms are St Albans, Culpeper, and LeCroy.

Triangle Form – reference to a point that has three straight sides. QCM examples are: Madison, Clarksville, Garza, Levanna, Yadkin, Fort Ancient, Frazier, Fresno, Hamilton, Maud, Talco, and Tortugas. The triangle point is a medium to small point that does not have a stemmed area and does not have any notching. The sides are usually straight, and the base width is usually the same as the blade's length. For Virginia, the major triangle forms are the Madison, Levanna, and Potomac types.

Bipoint Form – reference to a dual tipped point. This style occurs from the Paleoindian to Woodland Period. The bipoint was not used as projectile point, but is included as a QCM.

Note: The QCM is used here for the entire U.S., and types listed are not necessarily found everywhere in the U.S. See Figure 4.

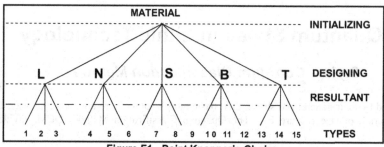

MATERIAL — INITIALIZING

L   N   S   B   T — DESIGNING

RESULTANT

1 2 3   4 5 6   7 8 9 10 11 12 13 14 15 — TYPES

Figure F1 - Point Knapper's Choice

Postword

While bipoints is the major focus on this publication, the *where/when* of Clovis remains an interesting, but controversial topic in American archaeology. The following paper was published on French materials over 145 years ago in the journal Archaeologia. Theses specimens could be placed in any Clovis contexts, especially Gault in Texas, and would get lost in the artifacts for the site. Fluting on a lancelet is not an American invention. The channel was present on ancient tools long before Clovis. For the following specimen, the center groove is a remnant flake scar. Is Clovis lithic technology a continuation of Old World lithic technology? Yes, indeed, but the Clovis culture is missing the bipoint!

Wm Jack Hranicky RPA

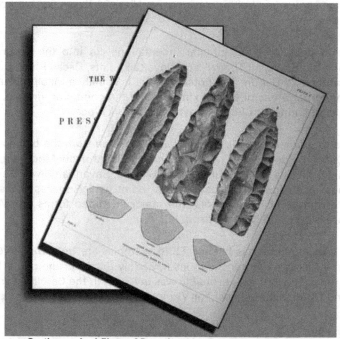

On the worked flints of Pressigny Le Grand (Indre Et Loire)
By John Evans
Archaeologia, Volume 40, 1867.

266

References

Abbot, Charles C.
(1881) Primitive Industry. Peabody Academy of Science, Salem, MA.

Adams, Bryan
(2009) The Impact of Lithic Raw Material Quality and Post-Depositional Processes on Cultural/Chronological Classification: The Hungarian Szeletian Case. In: B. Adams and B. Blades (eds.), Lithic Materials and Paleolithic Societies. Wiley-Blackwell, Chichester, West Sussex, UK.

Adams, Bryan and Brooke S. Blades (eds.)
(2009) Lithic Materials and Paleolithic Societies. Wiley-Blackwell, Chichester, West Sussex, UK.

Adams, Jonathan
(2002) Global Land Environments Since the Last Interglacial. Environmental Sciences Division, Oak Ridge National Laboratory, Oak Ridge, TN.

Adams, W. Y. and E. W. Adams
(1991) Archaeological Typology and Practical Reality: A Dialectical Approch to Artifact Classification and Sorting. Cambridge University Press, Cambridge, UK.

de Acosta, Joseph
(1590) The Natural and Moral Histories.

Adovasio, J. M.
(1993) The Ones that will not go away – A ba\iased view of Pre-Clovis populations in the New World. In: From Kostenki to Clovis, O. Soffer and N. Passlov eds., Plenum Press, New York, NY.

Adovasio, J. M., and R. C. Carlisle
(1988) The Meadowcroft Rockshelter. Science 239:713–14.

Adovasio, J. M, J. Donahue, and R. Stuckenrath
(1990_ The Meadowcroft Rockshelter Radiocarbon Chronology 1975–1990. American Antiquity 55:348–54.

Adovasio, J., J. Donahue, J. Gunn, and R. Stuckenrath
(1975) Excavations at Meadowcroft Rockshelter: 1973-1974: A Progress Report. Pennsylvania Archaeologist, Vol. 45, No. 3, pp. 1-30.

Adovasio, J. M. and David Pedler
(2016) Strangers in a Land – What Archaeology Revels about First Americans. Firefly Books, Buffalo, NY.

Adovasio, J., O. Soffer, and B. Klema
(1996) Upper Paleolithic Fiber Technology: Interlaced Woven Finds from Pavlov I. Czech Republic, c. 26,000 years ago. Antiquity, Vol. 70, pp. 526-44.

Advasio, J. M. and Jake Page
(2002) The First Americans – In Pursuit of Archaeology's Greatest Mystery. The Modern Library, New York, NY.

Agenbroad, Larry D.
(1989) Hot Springs, South Dakota – Entrapment and Taphonomy of Columbian Mammoth. In: Martin and Klein (eds.) Quaternary Extinctions – A Prehistoric Revolution. University of Arizona Press, Tucson, AZ.

Aitchison, J.
(2000) The Seeds of Speech: Language Origin and Evolution. Cambridge University Press, Cambridge, UK.

Aitken, M.J.
(1985) Thermoluminescence Dating. Academic Press, London, pp. 359.
(1998) An Introduction to Optical Dating. Oxford University Press. London, pp. 267.

Alan L. Bryan , Rodolfo M. Casamiquela , Jose M. Cruxent, Ruth Gruhn, and Claudio Ochsenius
(1978) An El Jobo Mastodon Kill at Taima-Taima, Venezuela. Science, Vol. 200, No. 4347. pp. 1275-127.

Alimn, H.
(1965) Prehistoire – Tome I: Generalities – Methodes en Prehistoire. Editions N. Boubee & Co. Paris.

Allsworth-Jones, P.
(1986) The Szeletian and the Transition from the Middle to the Upper Paleolithic in Central Europe. Oxford University Press, Oxford, Eng.

Alley, R. B.
(2004) GISP2 Ice Core Temperature and Accumulation Data. IGBP Pages, World Data Center for PaleoclimatologyData Contriution Series #2004-013. NOAA/NGDC Paleoclimatology Program, Boulder, CO.

Amante, C. and B. W. Eakins

(2009) ETOPO1 Arc-Minute Global Relief Model: Procedures, DataSources and Analysis. NOAA Technical Memorandum NESDIS NGDC-24, National Geophysical DataCenter, Boulder, CO.

Ambrose, Stanley H.

(2001) Paleolithic Technology and Human Evolution. Science, Vol. 291, No.5509, pp. 1748-1753.

(1998) Late Pleistocene Human Population Bottlenecks, Volcanic Winter, and Differentiation of Modern Humans, Journal of Human Evolution, Vol. 34, No. 6, pp. 623-651.

Amick, Daniel S.

(2004) A Possible Ritual Cache of Great Basin Stemmed Bifaces from the Terminal Pleistocene – Early Holocene Occupation on NW Nevada, USA. Lithic Technology, Vol. 29, No. 2, pp. 119-145.

Anderson, David G. and J. Christopher Gillam

(2000) Paleoindian Colonization of the Americas: Implication from an Examination of Physiography, Demography, and Artifact Distribution. American Antiquity, Vol. 65, No. 1, pp. 43-66.

Anderson, David G., and Kenneth E. Sassaman

(1996) The Paleoindian and Early Archaic southeast. University of Alabama Press, Tuscaloosa, AL.

Anderson, David G., Stephen J. Yerka, and J. Christopher

(2010) Employing High-Resolution Bathymetric Data to Infer Possible Migration Routes of Pleistocene Populations. Current Research in the Pleistocene, Vol. 27, pp. 55-59.

Andrefsky, William

(2006) Experimental and Archaeological Verification of an Index of Retouch for Hafted Bifaces. American Antiquity, Vol. 71, No. 4, pp. 743-757.

(2005) Lithics: Microscopic Approaches to Analysis, 2nd ed. Cambridge University Press, Cambridge, MA.

Andrew, Frank Sr.

(2008) Paitarkiutenka – My Legacy to You. Translations by Alice Rearden and Marie Meade. University of Washington Press, Seattle, WA.

Anderson, Adrian D. (ed.)

(1984) The Cooperton Mammoth: An Early Man Bone Quarry Great Plains, Journal, Vol. 14. In: Early Specialized Hunters, in The Prehistory of Oklahoma, ed., Robert E. Bell, Academic Press, NY.

Anderson, David G., Stephen J. Yerka, and J. Christopher

(2010) Employing High Resolution Bathymetric Data to Infer Possible Migration Routes of Pleistocene Populations. In: Current Research in the Pleistocene, T. Goeblet ed, pp. 55-59.

Anderson, David G., Thaddeus G. Bissett, and Stephen J. Yerka

(2013) The Late-Pleistocene Human Settlement of Interior North America: The Role Physiography and Sea-Level. In: Paleoamerican Odyssey, eds. K. Graf, C. Kenton, and M. Waters, Center for the Study of the First Americans, Department of Anthropology, Texas A&M, College Station, TX.

Arnold, Brigham

(1957) Late Pleistocene and Recent Changes in Land Forms, Climate and Archaeology in Central Baja California. University of California Publications in Geology, Vol. 10, No. 4.

Arnold, Jeanna E. and Michael R. Walsh

(2010) California's Ancient Past – From the Pacific to the Range of Light. The SAA Press, Society for American Archaeology.

Arsuga, Juan L. and Igracio Martinez

(1998) The Chosen Species – The Long March of Human Evolution. Blackwell Publishing, Malden, MA.

Aubry, Thierry, Miguel Almeida, Maria Joao Neves, and Bertrand Walter

(2003) Solutrean Laurel Leaf Point Production and Raw Material Procurement During the Last Glacial Maximum in Southern Europe: Two Examples from Central France and Portugal. In: Soressi, Marie and Harold L. Dibble (eds.) Multiple Approaches to the Study of Bifacial Technologies. University of Pennsylvania Museum of Archaeology and Anthropology, Philadelphia, PA.

Aubry, Thierry, Bruce Bradley, Miguel Almeida, Bertrand Walter, Maria Joaˇo Neves, Jacques Pelegrin, Michel Lenoir and Marc Tiffagom

(2008) Solutrean laurel leaf production at Maıˆtreaux: an experimental approach guided by techno-economic analysis. World Archaeology Vol. 40, No. 1, pp. 48–66.

Austin, Robert J.

(2006) Knife and Hammer: An Exercise in Positive Deconstruction – The I-75 Project and Lithic Scatter in Florida. Publication No. 16, Florida Anthropological Society.

Aveleyra, A. de Anda, Luis

(1956) The Second Mammoth and Associated Artifacts at Santa Isabel, Iztapan, Mexico. American Antiquity, Vol. 22, No. 1, pp. 12-28.

268

Babits, Lawrence E. and Hans Van Tilbury
(1998) Maritime Archaeology – A Reader of Substantive and Theoretical Contribution. Plenum, New York, NY.

Bada, Jeffery L., Roy A. Schroeder, and George F. Carter
(1974) New Evidence for the Antiquity of Man in North America Deduced from Asparatic Acid Recemization. Science, Vol. 184, No. 4138, pp. 791-793.

Bandelt, Hans-Jurgen, Martin Richards, and Vincene Macauly
(2006) Human Mitchondrial DNA and the Evolution of Homo Sapiens. Springer-Verlz, Heildelbery, Ger.

Bailey, G. N.
(1978) Shell Middens as Indicators of Post-Glacial Economies: A Territorial Perspective. In: The Early Postglacial Settlement of Northern Europe, ed., P. Mellar, pp. 37-63, University of Pittsburgh Press, Pittsburgh, PA.

Bailey, G. N. And P. Callow
(1986) Stone Age Prehistory – Studies in Memory of Charles McBurney. Cambridge University Press, Cambridge, UK.

Balter, Michael
(2011) Was North Africa the Lanch Pad for Modern Human Migrations? Science, Vol. 331, pp. 20-23.

Bandi, Hans-Georg
(1969) Eskimo Prehistory. University of Alaska Press, Fairbanks, AK.

Barbujani, Guido and David B. Goldstein
(2004) Africans and Asians Abroad: Genetic Diversity in Europe. Annual Review of Genomics in Human Genetics, Vol. 5, pp. 119-150.

Barham, Lawrence.
(2007) Modern Is as Modern Is? Technological Trends and Thresholds in the South-central African Record. In: Rethinking the Human Revolution, eds. P. Mellars. K. Boyle, O. Bar-Yosef, and C. Stringer, McDonald Institute Monographs, Oxbow Books, Oxford, UK.

Barham, Lawrence and Peter Mitchell
(2008) The First Africans. Cambridge World Archaeology, Cambridge University Press, New York, NY.

Bar-Yosef, Ofer and Steven L. Kuhn
(1999) The Big Deal about Blades: Laminar Technologies and Human Evolution. American Anthropologist, Vol. 101, Issue 2, pp. 322-338.

Bandelt, Hans-Jurgen, Martin Richards, and Vincene Macauly
(2006) Human Mitchondrial DNA and the Evolution of Homo Sapiens. Springer-Verlz, Heildelbery, Ger.

Banks, William E. and Marvin Kay
(2003) High-Resolution Cast for Lithic Use-Wear Analysis. Lithic Technology, Vol. 28, No. 1, pp. 27-34.

Barton, C. M.
(1990) Beyond Style and Function: A View from the Middle Paleolithic. American Anthropologist, Vol. 92, pp. 57-72.

Beaton, J. M.
(1991) Colonizing Continents: Some Problems from Australia and the Americas. In: The First Americans: Search and Research, pp. 209-230, eds., T. Dillehay and D. Meltzer, CRC Press, Boca Raton, FL.

Bednarik, Robert G.
(1997) The Earliest Evidence on Ocean Navigation. International Journal of Nautical Archaeology, Vol. 26, pp. 183-91.
(1995) Seafaring Homo Erectus. Artefact, Vol. 18, pp. 91-92.
(1989) On the Pleistocene Settlement of South America. Antiquity, 63: 101-111.

Bell, Robert E.
(1960) Evidence of a Fluted Point Tradition in Ecuador. American Antiquity, Vol. 26, No. 1, pp. 102-106.

Bell, Robin E.
(1998) Gravity Gradiometry. Scentific American, Vol. 278, No. 6, pp. 74-79.

Binford, Lewis R.
(1983) In Pursuit of the Past. Thames and Hudson, New York, NY.
(1980) Willow Smoke and Dogs' Tails: Hunter-Gatherer Settlement Systems and Archaeological Site Formation. American Antiquity, vol. 45, pp. 4-20.
(1979) Organization and Formation Processes: Looking at Curated Technologies. Journal of Anthropological Research, Vol. 35, pp. 255-273.

Binford, Lewis R. and Sally R. Binford
(2009) A Preminiary Analysis of Functional Variability in the Mousterian of Levallous Faces. American Anthropoligst, Vol. Vol. 68, Is. 2, pp. 238-295.

Bini, C., F. Martini, G. Pitzalis & A. Ulzega.
(1993) Sa Coa de Sa Multa e Sa Pedrosa Pantallinu: due 'Paleosuperfici' clactoniane in Sardegna. Atti della XXX Riunione Scientifica, 'Paleosuperfici del Pleistocene e del primo Olicene in Italia, Processi si Formazione e Interpretazione', Venosa ed Isernia, 26-29 Ottobre 1991, pp. 179-197. Firenze: Istituto Italiano di Preistoria e Protostoria.

Bird, Junis B.
(1967) The Physiography of Arctic Canada. Johns Hopkins Press, Baltimore, MD.
(1946) The Archaeology of Patagonia, Bur. Of America Ethnography Bul. 143, Vol. 1, pp. 17-24.

Birket-Smith, Kia
(1947) Recent Achievements in Eskimo Research. Journal of the Royal Anthropological Institute of Great Britain, Vol. LXXVII, p. 145.

Bischoff, J. L., J. L. Shelenon, R. J. Ku, and R. D. Simpson, R. J. Rosenbauer, and F. E. Buclinger
(1981) Uranium-series and Soil-geometric Dating of the Calico Archaeological Site, California. Geology, Vol. 9, pp. 576-582.

Blades, Brooke S.
(2003) End Scraper Reduction and Hunter-Gatherer Mobility. American Antiquity, vol. 68, pp. 141-156.

Blockley, S., M. Blockley, R. Donahue, C. Lame, J. Love, and A. Pollard
(2006) The Chronology of Abrupt Climate Change and Late Upper Palaeolithic Human Adaptation in Europe. Journal of Quaternary Science, Vol. 21, pp. 575-84.

Blue, Lucy, Fred Hocker, and Anton Englert (eds.)
(2006) Connected by Sea. Oxbow Books, Oxbow, UK.

de Boe, E. and Pelegrin, J.
(1985). Approche expe´rimentale des amas de Marsangy. In Les amas lithiques de la zone N19 du gisement magdale´nien de Marsangy: approche me´thodologique par l'expe´rimentation. Beaune: Association pour la Promotion de l'Arche´ologie en Bourgogne, pp. 19–36.

Boldurian, Anthony T. and John L. Cotter
(1999) Clovis Revisited – New Perspectives on Paleoindian Adaptations from Blackwater Draw, New Mexico. University Museum, University of Pennsylvania, Philadelphia, PA.

Bolus, Michael and Nicholas J. Conard
(2001) The Late Middle Paleolithic and Earliest Upper Paleolithic in Central Europe and Their Relevance for the Out of Africa Hypothesis. Quaternary International, 75(1): 29-40.

Bonatto, S.L. and Salzano, F.M.
(1997) Diversity and age of the four major mtDNA haplogroups, and their implications for the peopling of the New World. American Journal Human Genetics. 1997 Dec;61(6):1413-23.

Bond, G., W. Broecker, S. Johnen, J. McManus, L. Labeyrie, J. Jouzel, and G. Bonani
(1993) Correlations Between Climate Records from North Atlantic Sediments and Greenland Ice. Nature, Vol. 365, pp. 143-147.

Bonnichsen, Robson (ed.)
(1999) Who Were the First Americans? Center for the Study of the First Americans, Oregon State University, Corvallis, OR.
(1977) Models for Discovering Cultural Information from Stone Tools. Canada Paper 60, National Museum of Canada, Ottawa, Can.

Bonnichsen, R. B., D. Lepper, D. Stanford, and M. Waters, (eds.)
(2005) Paleoamerican Origins: Beyond Clovis. Texas A&M Press, College Station, TX.

Bonnichsen, R. and K. L. Turnmire
(1991) Clovis: Origins and Adaptations. Center for the Study of First Americans, Oregon State University, Corvallis, OR.

Boorstin, D. J.
(1983) The Discoverers. Random House, New York, NY.

Borden, Charles E.
(1952) An Archaeological Renaissance of Tweedsmuir Park, British Columbia. Vancouver City Museum, Museum and Art Notes, ser. 2, Vol. 2, No. 2, pp. 9-15.

Bordes, Francois
(1968) The Old Stone Age. McGraw-Hill, New York, NY.
(1968) Emplacements de tentes du Perigordien superieur evolue a Corbiac. Quartia, Bd. 19, pp. 251-262.
(1967) Considerations sur la typologie et les techniques dans le Paleolithique. Quartia, Bd. 18, pp. 25-27.
(1965) A propos de typologie. L'Anthropologis, Vol. 69, pp. 369-377.
(1961) Typogie du Paleolithique ancient et moye. Delmas, Bordeaux, France.
(1953) Notules de typologie Paleolithik, II: Pointes Levalloisiennes et pointes pseudo-Levalloisiennes. Bulletin de la Prehistorique Francais, Vol. 50, pp. 311-313.
(1950) Principes d'une methode d'etude des techniques de debitage et al la typologie du Paleolithique ancient et moyan, L-Anthropologie, Vol. 54, pp. 19-34.
(1947) Etude comparative des differentes techniques de taille du silex et des roches dures. L'Anthropologie, Vol. 51, pp. 1-29.

Bordes, F. and M. Bourgon
(1951) Le complexe Mousterian: Mousterien, Levalloisien st Tayacian, L' Anthropologie, Vol. 55, pp. 1-23.

Bordes, F. and D. Sonneville-Bordes
(1970) The Significance of Variability in Paleolithic Assemblages. World Archaeology, Vol. 2, pp. 61-73.

Bordaz, Jacques
(1970) Tools of the Old and New Stone Age. The American Museum of Natural History, Natural History Press, Garden City, NY.

Bouzouggar, A., et al.
(2007) 82,000-Year Old Shell Beads from North Africa and Implications for the Origins of Modern Human Behavior. Proceedings of the Natural Academy of Sciences, Vol. 104, No. 24, pp. 9964-9969.

Boyle, Kathrine V., Clive Gamble, and Ofer Bar-Yosef
(2010) The Upper Palaeolothic Revolution in Global Perspective – papers in honour of Sir Paul Mellars. McDonald Institute Monographs, University of Cambridge, Cambridge, UK.

Bowen, D. Q.
(1978) Quarternary Geology. Pergamon Press, Oxford. Eng.

Brantingham, P. Jeffrey
(2010) The Mathematics of Chaines Operatories. In: New Perspectives on Old Stones – Analytical Approches to Paleolithic Technologies, S. Lycett and P. Chauham, eds.,183-206, . Springer, New York, NY.

Brown, Robin C.
(1994) Florida's First People. Pineapple Press, Inc. Sarasota, FL.

Bradley, Bruce
(2008) Flintknapping Featuring Solutrean Technology. CD, INTERpark, Inc.
(1975)

Bradley, Raymond S.
(1999) Paleoclimatology – Reconstructing Climates of the Quaternary. International Geophysics Series, Vol. 68, Academic Press, New York, NY.

Bradley, Bruce and Dennis Stanford
(2004) The North Atlantic Ice-edge Corridor: A Possible Paleolithic Route to the New World. World Archaeology, Vol. 36, pp. 459-78.

Bradley, Bruce A., Michael B. Collins, and Andrew Hemmings
(2010) Clovis Technology. International Monographs in Prehistory, Archaeological Series 17, Ann Arbor, MI.

Brantingham, P. Jeffrey, Steven L. Kuhn, and Kristopher W. Kerry (eds.)
(2004) The Early Upper Paleolithic beyond Western Europe. University of California Press, Berkley, CA.

Bratlund, Bodil and Breit V. Eriksen, eds.
(2002) Recent Studies in the Final Palaeolithic of the European Plain. Jutland Archaeological Society Publications, Aarhus University Press, Aarhus, Denmark.

British Museum
(1956) Flint Implements. Trustees of the Bristih Museum, London, UK.

Brown, Allen
(1942) Indian Relics and Their Values. Lightner Publishing Co., Chicago, IL.

Brown, Robin C.
(1994) Florida's First People. Pineapple Press, Inc., Sarasota, FL.

Brown, M. D., S. H. Hosseini, A. Torroni, H. Bandelt. J. Allen, T. G. Schurr, R. Scozzari, F. Cruciani, and D. C. Wallace
(1998) MtDNA Haplogroup X: An Ancient Link Beteen Europe.Western Asia and North America? American Journal of Human Genetics, Vol. 63, pp 1852-61.

Broyles, Bettye J.
(1971) Second Preliminary Report: The St Albans Site, Kanawha County, West Virginia. Report of Archaeological Investigations, No. 3, West Virginia Geological and Economic Survey, Morgantown, WV.

Broughton, J. M.
(1999) Resource Depression and Intensification during the Late Holocene, San Francisco Bay: Evidence from the Emeryville Shellmound Vertebrate Fauna. University of California Anthropological Records, No. 32, University of California Press, Berkeley, CA.

Browman, David L. and David A. Munsell
(1969) Columbia Plateau Prehistory: Cultural Development and Impinging Influences. American Antiquity, Vol. 34, No. 3, pp. 249-264.

Brown, M., S. Hosseini, A. Torroni, H. Bandelt, J. Allen, T. Schurr, R. Scozzari, F. Crucini, and D. Wallace
(1998) MtDNA Haplogroup X: An Ancient Link Between Europe/Western Asia and North America? American Journal of Human Genetics, Vol. 63, pp. 1852-61.

Bryan, Alan L.
(1986 ed.) New Evidence for the Pleistocene Peopling of the Americas. Center for the Study of Early Man, University of Maine, Orono, ME.
(1983) South America. In: Early Man in the New World, ed. R. Shutler, Sage Publications, Beverly Hills, CA.
(1978) Early Man in America from a Circum-Pacific Perspective. Occasional Paper 1, pp. 306-327, Department of Anthropology, University of Alberta, Archaeological Researches International, Edmonton, Can.
(1969) Early Man in America and the Late Pleistocene Chronology of Western Canada and Alaska. Current Anthropolgy, Vol. 10, pp. 339-367.
(1965) Paleo-American Prehistory. Occasional Papers, Idaho State University Museum, No. 16.

Bryan, Alan Lyle and Ruth Gruhn
(1964) Problems Relating to the Neothermal Climatic Sequence. American Antiquity, Vol. 29, No. 3, pp. 307-315.

Buchanan, William and Randolph M. Owen
(1981) The Browning Farm Site, Charles City County. ASV Quarterly Bulletin, Vol. 35, No. 3, pp. 139-158.

Buchanan, Briggs and Mark Collard
(2010) As Assessment of the Impact of Resharpening on Paleoindian Projectile Point Blade Shape Using Geometric Morphometric Techniques. In: New Perspectives on Old Stones – Analytical Approches to Paleolithic Technologies S. Lycett and P. Chauhan eds., pp. 255-273,. Springer, New York, NY.

Burchell, J. P. T.
(1934) The Middle Mousterian Culture and Its Relation to the Coombe Rock of Post-Earlt Mousterian Times. Antiquaries Journal, Society of Antiuaries of London, Vol. XIV, No. 1, pp. 33-39.

Bush, Andrew B. C. and S. George H. Philander
(1999) The Climate of the Last Glacial Maximum: Results from Coupled Atmospheric-ocean Circulation Model. Journal of Geophysical Research, 104(D20): 24,509-24,525.

Butler, B. Robert
(1961) The Old Cordilleran Culture in the Pacific Northwest. Occasional Papers of the Idaho State Museum, No. 5.

Butzer, Karl W.
(1971) Environment and Archaeology – An Ecological Approach to Prehistory. Aldine-Atherton, New York, NY.

Byers, Douglas
(1957) The Bering Bridge - Some Speculations. Ethnos, Vol. 22, pp. 20-26.

Campbell, Lyle.
(1997) American Indian Languages: The Historical Linguistics of Native America. Oxford Univ. Press, UK.

Cambron, James W. and David C. Hulse
(1964 to 1975) Handbook of Alabama Archaeology, Part 1, Point Types. Archaeological Research Association of Alabama, Inc., Moundville, AL.

Cambron, James and Spencer Waters
(1959) Flint Creek Rock Shelter (Pt 1&2). Tennessee Archaeologists, Vol. XV, No. 2, p. 49.

Camps, G.
(1974) Les civilization prehistoriques de l'Afrique du Nord et du Sahara. Doin, Paris, France.

Cann, Rebecca L.
(2001) Genetic Clues to Dispersal in Human Populations: Retracing the Past from the Present. Science, Vol. 291, No. 5509, pp. 1742-1748.

Callahan, Errett
(1979) The Basics of Biface Knapping in the Eastern Fluted Point Tradition – A Manual for Flintknappers and Lithic Analysts. Vol. 7, Archaeology of Eastern North America.

Callahan, Errett and Jan Apel
(20110 The Flint Daggers of Denmark, Vol. 1. Piltdown Production, Lynchburg, VA.

Campbell, Elizabeth W. C.
(1936) Archaeological Problems in the Southern California Deserts. American Antiquity, Vol. 1, No. 4, pp. 295-300.

Camps, G.
(1974) Les Civilisation Prehistoriques de l'Afrique du Nord et du Sahara. Doin, Paris.

Camps, Marta and Parth R. Chauhan (eds.)
(2011) Sourcebook of Paleolithic Transitions. Springer, New York, NY.

Canales, Elmo Leon
(2009) Central Andean Lithic Techno-Typology at the Terminal Pleistocene-Early Holocene Transition. In: Sourcebook of Paleolithic Transitio, M. Camps and P. Chauhan eds., pp. 527-536, Springer, New York, NY.

Capes, K.H.
(1964) Contributions to the prehistory of Vancouver Island. Occasional Papers of the Idaho State University Museum, No. 15: 143 pp.

Capitan, L. and D. Peyrony
(1927) La Madeleine, son gisement – son industrie, ses oeuvres d'art. Publications de 1'Institut International d'Anthropologie, 2 Paris, FR.

Cardich, Augusto
(1958) Los Yacimientos de Lauricocha, Nuevas Interpretaciiones de la Prehistoria Peruana. Centro Argentine de Estudios Prehistoricos, Studia Praehistorica I. Buenos Aires.

Carlson, Roy L.
(1983) The Far West. In: xxx

Carr, Phillip J., Andrew P. Bradbury, and Sarah E. Price (eds.)
(2012) Comtemporay Lithic Analysis in the Southeast. University of Alabama Press, Tuscaloosa, AL.

Carter, George F.
(1980) Earlier then You Think. Texas A&M University Press, College Station, TX.
(1958) Archaeology in the Reno Area in Relation to Age of Man and the Culture Sequence in America. Proceeding of the American Philosophical Society, Vol. 102, No. 2, pp. 174-192.
(1957) Pleistocene Man at San Diego. Johns Hopkins Press, Baltimore, MD.
(1951) Man in America: A Criticism of Scientific Thought. Scientific Monthly, Vol. 73, pp. 297-307.
(1950) Evidence for Pleistocene Man in Southern California. Geog. Rev., Vol. XL, pp. 84-102.

Cartwright, John
(2001) Evolution and Human Behavior: Darwinism Perspective on Human Nature. Bradford Books, w/ Macmillam Press. UK.

Cassell, Mark S.
(1988) Farmers of the Northean Ice: Relations of Production in the Traditional North Alaskan Inupiat Whale Hunt. Research in Economic Athropology, Vol. 10, pp. 89-116.

Casson, L.
(1995) Ships and Seamanship in the Ancient World. Johns Hjopkins University Press, Baltimore, MD.
(1994) Ships and Seafaring in Ancient Times. University of Texas Press, Austin, TX.

Castellanos, Alfredo
(1943) Antiquedad Geologica del Yacimiento de los Restos Humano de la Gruta de Candonga (Cordoba). Publ. Inst. De Fisiografia y Gl eol., University Nac. De Litor, 14 Rosario.

Cavalli-Sfora, Luigi Luca and Francesco Cavalli-Sfora
(1995) The Great Human Diasporas – the History of Deversity and Evolution. Persus Books, Cambridge, MA.

Chang, Kwang-chih
(1960) New Light on Eary Man in China. Asian Perspective, Vol. 2, No. 2.

Chandler, James M.
(2001) Clovis and Solutrean: Is There a Common Thread? Mammoth Trumpet, Vol. 16, No. 3.

Chase, Philip G., Andre Debenath, Harold L. Dibble, and Shannon P. McPherron
(2009) The Cave of Fontechevade – Recent Excavation and their Paleoanthropological Implication. Cambridge University Press, Cambridge, UK.

Chard, Chester and Harumi Befu
(1960) Precermanic Cultures of Japan. American Anthropologist, Vol. 62, No. 5, pp. 815-850.

Chatters, James C., Steven Hackenberger, Anna M. Prentiss, and Jayne- Leigh Thomas
(2012) The Paleo Indian to Archaic Transition in the Pacific Northwest In Situ Development or Ethnic Replacement?
www.cwu.edu/anthropology/sites/cts.cwu.edu.anthropology/files

Chazan, Michael
(2001) Bladelet Production in the Aurgnacian of La Ferrassie (Dordogne, France). Lithic Technology, Vol. 26, No. 1, pp. 16-28.

Cherry, J. F.
(1990) The First Colonization of the Mediterranean Islands: A Review of Recent Research. J. Medit Archaeology, Vol. 3, No. 2, pp. 145-221.

Childress, William A.
(1989) A Unique Bipoint: Possible Evidence of a Deeply Stratified Paleo-Indian Component in the Southwestern Virginia Piedmont. ASV Quarterly Bulletin, Vol. 44, No. 4, pp. 177-200.

Chomsky, Norman
(1972) Language and Mind. Jovanovich Press, New York, NY.

Churchill, Steven E. and Fred H. Smith
(2001) Makers of the Early Aurignacian of Europe. American Journal of Physical Anthropology, 113(S31): 61 – 115.

Clark, A. Geoffrey
(2011) Accidents of History: Conceptual Frameworks in Paleoarchaeology. In: Sourcebook of Paleolithic Transitions, eds. M. Camps and P. Chauhan, Springer, New York, NY.

Clark, Grahame
(1969) World Prehistory – A New Outline. University of Cambridge Press, Cambridge, UK.

Clark, J. Desmond
(1970) The Prehistory of Africa. Praeger Publishers, New York, NY.
(1967) The Middle Acheulian Occupation Site at Latamne, Northern Syria. Quaternaria, Vol. 9, pp. 1-68.
(1963) Prehistoric Cultures of Northeast Angola and Their Significance in Tropical Africa. Companhia de Diiamantes de Angola, Lisbon.
(1954) Excavations at Star Carr: An Early Mesolithic Site at Seamer near Scarborough, Yorkshire. Cambridge, UK.

Clark, John E. and Michael B. Collins (eds.)
(2002) Folsom Technology and Lifeways. Special Publication No. 4, Department of Anthropology, University of Tulsa, Tulsa, OK.

Clarke, David L.
(1978) Analytical Archaeology. Methue Publisher, London, UK.

Clarkson, Chris
(2002) An Index of Invasiveness for the Measurement of Unifacial and Biface Retouce: A Theoretical, Experimental and Archaeological Verification. Journal of Archaeological Science, Vol. 29, pp. 65-75.

Cockrell, W. A. and Larry Murphy
(1978) Pleistocene Man in Florida. Archaeology of Eastern North America, Vol. 6, pp. 1-13.

Coe, Joffre L.
(1964) The Formative Cultures of the Carolina Piedmont. Transactions of the American Philosophical Society, New Series, Vol. 54, Part 5, Philadelphia, PA.

Coles, J.M. and E.S. Higgs
(1969) The Archaeology of Early Man. Frederick A. Praeger Publishers, New York, NY.

Collins, Henry B.
(1943) Eskimo Archaeology and Its Bearing on the Problem of Man's Antiquity in America. Proceedings of the Americal Philosophical Society, Vol. 86, No. 2, pp. 220-235.

Collins, Michael B.
(2012) Personal Communication, and Paper: Preliminary Geographic Patters in Older-Than-Clovis Assemblages in North America, SAA Meeting, Memphis, TN.
(1999) Clovis Blade Technology. University of Texas Press, Austin, TX.

Collins, Michael, and Tom Dillehay
(2011) Early Cultural Evidence from Monte Verde in Chile. Nature, Vol. 332, pp. 150-152.

Coon, Carlton S.
(1971) The Hunting Peoples. Atlantic Monthly Press Book, Little, Brown, and Company, Boston, MA..
(1957) The Seven Caves. Alfred A. Knoft, New York, NY.

Combier, J.
(1967) Le Paleolithique de l'Ardeche dans son cadre paleoclimatique. Delmas, Bordeaux, France.
(1955) Pointes levalloisiennes retouches sur la face plane (pointes type Soyons). Bulletin de la Societe Prehistorique Francaise, Vol. 52, pp. 432-434.

Commont, V.
(1909) L'industrie mousterrienne dans le Nord de la France. In; Congres Prehistorique de France, pp. 115-197, 5eme session, Beauvais.

Cook, H. J.
(1926) The Antiquity of Man in America. Scientific American, Vol. 137, pp. 334-336.

Cotes, M., V. E. Munoz, J. L. Sanchidrian, and M. D. Simon (eds.)
(1996) El Paleolitico en Andalucia. La Dinamica de los Grupos Predaores en la Prehistoria Andaluza Ensayo de Sintesis. Universidad de Cordoba, Cordoba, Spain.

Cremaschi, Mauro, Savino Di Lernia, and Elena A. A. Garcea
(1998) Some Insights on the Aterian in the Libyan Sahara: Chronology, Environment, and Archaeology. African Archaeological Review, Vol. 15, No. 4, pp. 261-286.

Crabtree, Don E.
(1972) An Introduction to Flintknapping. Occasional Papers, No. 28, Idaho State University, Pocatello, ID.

Cressman, Luther S.
(1960) Cultural Sequences at the Dalles, Oregon. American Philosphical Society, Vol. 50, Part 10.
(1948) Odell Lake Site: A New Paleo-Indian Campsite in Oregon. American Antiquity, Vol. 14, No. 1, pp. 57-58.
(1940) Early Man in Oregon. University of Oregon Studies in Anthropology, No. 3.
(1939) The Wikiup Damsite No. 1, Knives. American Antiquity, Vol. 3, No. 1, pp. 53-67.

Crock, John G., James B. Peterson, and Ross Anderson
(1993) Scalloping for Artifacts: A Biface and Plummet from Eastern Blue Hill Bay, Maine. Archaeology of Eastern North America, Vol. 21, pp. 179-192.

Crothers, George M. (ed.)
(2004) Hunters and Gatherers in Theory and Archaeology. Occasional Paper No. 31, Center for Archaeological Investigations, Southern Illinois, Carbondale, IL.

Cronl, Lee, Napoleon Chagon, and William Irons
(2000) Adaptation and Human Behavior – An Anthropological Perspective. Aldine de Grunter, Wawthrone, NY.

Cross, Dorothy
(1939) The Indians of New Jersey. Leaflet No. 7, Archaeological Society of New Jersey.

Crowley, Thomas J., and Gerald R. North
(1991) Paleoclimatology. Oxford University Press, Clarendon Press, New York, NY.

Cruxent, J. M. and Irving Rouse
(1956) A Lithic Industry of Paleo-Indian Type in Venezuela. American Antiquity, Vol. 22, No. 2, pp. 172-179.
Dalton, Rex
(2007) Blast in the Past? Nature, 447: 256-257.
(2005) Caveman DNA Hints at Map of Migration. Nature, Vol. 436, No. 162.

Dancey, William S.
(1994) The First Discovery of America – Archaeological Evidence of the Early Inhabitants of the Ohio Area. The Ohio Archaeological Council, Inc. Columbas, OH.

Davies, J. L.
(1969) Landforms of Cold Climates. MIT Press, Cambridge, MA.

Debenath, Andre and Harold L. Dibble
(1994) Handbook of Paleolithic Typology. University Museum, University of Pennsylvania, Philadelphia, PA.

De Braucourt, Jean de Heinzelin
(1962) Manual de Typologie des Industries Lithiciques. L'Institut Royal des Sciences Naturellis de Belique, Bruxelles.

de Heinzelin de Braucourt, Jean
(1962) Manual de Typologie des Industries Lithiques. Bruxelles.

Deller, D. Brian and Christopher J. Ellis
(2011) Crowfield (AfHi-31) – A Unique Paleoindian Fluted Point Site from Southwestern Ontario. Memoirs of the Museum of Anthropology, No. 49, University of Michigan, Ann Arbor, MI.
(1992) Thedford II – A Paleo-Indian Site is the Auusable River Watershed of Southwestern Ontario. Memoirs of the Museum of Anthropology, No. 24, University of Michigan, Ann Arbor, MI.

Dennell, Robin
(2009) The Paleolithic Settlement of Asia. Cambridge University Press, Cambridge, UK.

Densmore, Julie A.
(2007) A Detailed Analysis of the Variation in Morphology of the Gary Dart Point. Lithic Technology, Vol. 32, No. 1, pp. 7-16.

Denton, G. H. and T. J. Hughes (eds.)
(1981) The Last Great Ice Sheets. Wiley & Sons, New York, NY.

Derev'anko, Anatoliy, Demittr B. Shimkin, and W. Roger Powers
(1998) The Paleolithic of Siberia. University of Illinois Press, Urbana, IL.

DeSalle, Tob and Ian Tattersall
(2008) Human Origins: What Bones and Genomes Tell Us About Oursleves. Texas A&M Press, College Station, TX.

Des Lauriers, Matthew Richard
(2010) Island of Frogs. University of Utal Press, Salt Lake City, UT.
(2005) The Watercraft of Isla Cedros, Baja California: Variability and Capabilities of Indigenous Seafaring Technology Along the Pacific Coast of North America. American Antiquity, Vol. 70, pp. 342-363.

Dillehay, Thomas
(2000) The Settlement of the Americas. Perseus (Basic Books) Group, New York, NY.

Dibble, Andre D. and Harold L. Dibble
(1994) Handbook of Paleolithic Typology (Volume One). University Museum, University of Pennsylvania, Philadelphia, PA.

Dibble, Harold L. and Ofer Bar-Yosef
(1995) Preface. In: The Definition and Interpretation of Levallois Technology, ed. Dibble and Bar-Yosef, pp. ix-xiii, Monographs in World Archaeology, No. 23, Prehistory Press, Madion, WI.

Dibble, H. and A. Monet-White (eds.)
(1988) Upper Pleistocene Prehistory of Western Eurasia. University of Pennsylvania Museum, Philadelphia, PA.

Dikov, N. N.
(1978) Ancestors of Paleo-Indians and Proto-Eskimo-Aleuts in the Paleolithic of Kamchatka. In; Early Man in America from a Circum-Pacific Perspective. A. Bryan ed. Pp. 68-69, Occasional Paper 1, pp. 306-327, Department of Anthropology, University of Alberta, Archaeological Researches International, Edmonton, Can.

Dilleyhay, Tom D.
(2017) Where the Land Meets the Sea – Fourteen Millenna of Human History at Huaca Prieta, Peru. University of Texas Press, Austin, TX.
(1997) Monte Verde: a late Pleistocene settlement in Chile, Vol. 2, The Archaeological Context and interpretation. Smithsonian Institution Press, Washington, DC.
(1989) Monte Verde: a late Pleistocene settlement in Chile, Vol. 1, Palaeoenvironment and research, eds. T. Tillehay and D. Meltzer, pp. 231-64, CRC Press, Boca Raton, FL.

Dincauze, D. F.
(1984) An Archaeological Evaluation of the Case for Pre-Clovis Occupations. Advances in World Archaeology 3:275-323.
(1968) Cremation Cemeteries in Eastern Massachusetts. Papers of the Peabody Museum of Archaeology and Ethnobotany, Harvard University, Vol. 59, No. 1.

Dixon, E. James
(1999) Bones, Boats, & Bison – Archaeology and the First Colonization of Western North America. University of New Mexico, Albuquerque, NM.

Doyle, Rodger
(1998) U. S. Werlands. Scientific American, Vol. 278, No. 6, pp. 24-25.

Drew, D. L.
(1979) Early Man in North America and Where to Look for Him: Geomorphic Contexts. Plains Anthropologist Vol. 24, pp. 269-281.

Dugan, B. and P. B. Flemings
(2002) Fluid Flow and Stability of the U.S. Continental Slope Offshore New Jersey from the Pleistocene to the Present. Geofluids, Vol., 2, No. 2, pp. 137-146.

Dumond, Don E.
(1987) The Eskimos and Aleuts. Thames and Hudson, New York, NY.

Dunbar, James S.(1991) Resource Orientation of Clovis and Suwannee Age Paleoindian Sites in Flordia. In: Clovis: Origins and Adaptations, eds. R. Bonnichsen and K. Turnmire, pp. 185-213, Center for the Study of the First Americans, Dept. Anthro, Oregon State University, Corvallis, OR.

Dunbar, James S. and Pamela K. Vojnovski
(2007) Early Floridians and Late Megamammals – Some Technological and Dietary Evidence from Four North Floruda Paleoindian Sites. In: Forgers of the Terminal Pleistocene inNorth America, R. Walker and B. Driskell, eds., pp. 167-202, Unoversity of Nebraska Press, Lincoln, NE..

Ebert, James I.
(1992) Distributional Archaeology. University of Utah Press, Salt Lake, UT.

Edwards, Robert L. and Arthur S. Merrill
(1997) A Reconstruction of the Continental Shelf Areas of the Eastern North American for the Times 9,500 BP and 12,500 BP. Archaeology of Eastern North America, Vol. 5. pp. 1-42.

Ellis, C. and J. Lothrop (eds.)
(1989) Eastern Paleoindian Lithic Resourse Use. Westview Press, Boulder, CO.

Emiliani, C.
(1955) Pleistocene Temperatures. Journal of Geology, Vol. 63, No. 6, pp. 538-578.

Emperaire, Jose and Annette Laming
(1961) Les Gisements des Iles Englefied et Vivian dans la Mer D'Otway,Palagonie Australe. Jounal Societe des Americanistes, Vol. 50, pp. 7-75.

Engelbrecht, William E. and Carl K. Seyfert
(1994) Paleoindian Watercraft: Evidence and Implication. North American Archaeologist, Vol. 15, No. 3, pp. 221-234.

Eriksen, Berit and Bodil Bratlund
(2002) Recent Studies in the Final Palaeolithic of the European Plain. Proceedings of a U.I.S.P.P. Symposium, Jutland Archaeological Society, Moesgaard Museum, Hojbjerg, DK.

Erlandson, Jon M.
(2002) Anatomically Modern Humans, Maritime Voyaging, and the Pleistocene Colonization of the Americas. In: The First Americans, ed., N. Jablonski, Menorirs, California Academy of Sceinces, No. 27, pp. 59-92, San Francisco, CA.
(2001) The Archaeology of Aquatic Adaptations: Paradigms for a New Millennium. Journal of Archaeological Research,, Vol. 9, pp.287-350.

Erlandson, Jon M., Torben C. Rick, Todd J. Braje, Molly Casperson, Brendan Culleton, Brian Fulfrost, Tracy Garcia, Daniel A. Guthrie, Nicholas Jew, Douglas J. Kennett, Madonna L. Moss, Leslie Reeder, Craig Skinner, Jack Watts, and Lauren Willis
(2011) Paleoindian Seafaring, Maritime Technologies, and Coastal Foraging on California's Channel Islands. Science, Vol. 331, No. 6021, pp. 1181-1185.

Evans, John
(1867) On the worked flints of Pressigny Le Grand (Indre Et Loire), Archaeologia, Vol. 40, France.

Facchni, F. and G. Giusberti
(1992) Homo Sapiens Sapiens Remains from the Island of Crete. In: G. Brauer and F. Smith, eds., Continuity or Replacement: Conversation in Homo Sapiens Evolution, A. A. Balkema, Rotterdam.

Farrington, Oliver C. and Henry Field
(1929) Neanderthal (Mousterian) Man. Geology Leaflet 11, Field Museum of Natural History, Chicage, IL.

Fiedel, Stuart J.
(1999) Older Than We Thought: Implications of Corrected Dates for Paleoindians. American Antiquity Vol. 64, No. 1, pp. 95-115.
(2000) The Peopling of the New World: Present Evidence, New Theories, and Future Directions. Journal of Archaeological Research Vol. 8, No. 1, pp. 39-103.

Field, Henry
(1956) Ancient and Modern Man in Southwest Asia. University of Miami Press, Coral Gables, FL.

Figgins, J. D.
(1927) The Antiquity of Man in America. Natural History, Vol. XXVII, No. 3, pp. 229.

Fitzhugh, William W.
(1972) Environmental Archeology and Cultural Systems in Hamilton Inlet, Labrador. Smithsonian Contributions to Anthropology, No. 16.

Fladmark, Knut R.
(1979) Routes: Alternate Migrations Corridors for Early Man in North America, American Antiquity, 44(1) 55-69.

Fleming, N.C., G. N. Bailey, V. Courtillot, G. King, K. Lambeck, F. Ryerson and C. Vita-Finzi
(2003) Coastal and Marine Paleo-Environments and Human Dispersal Points Across the Africa-Eurasia Boundary.Maritime Heritage. WIT Press, Southampton.

Flennoken, J. J. and A. W. Raymong
(1986) Morphological Projectile Point Typology: Replication Experimentation and Technological Analysis. American Antiquity, Vol. 51, pp. 603-614.

Fladmark, Knut R.
(1979) Routes: Alternate Migration Corridors for Early Man in North America, American Antiquity, 44(1): 55-69.

Ford, J. A.
(1969) A Comparison of Formative Cultures in the Americas: Diffusion or the Psychic Unity of Man. Smithsonian Institution, Washington, DC.

Foss, Robert V.
(1986) Carney Rose Site (28Me106), Data Recovery Report 5. Trenton Complex Archaeology: Report 6, Louis Berger & Associates, East Orange, NJ.

Freeman, L. G.
(1975) Acheulian sites and stratigraphy in Iberia and the Maghreb. In K. W. Butzer and G. I. Isaac (eds), After the Australopithecines, pp. 661-743. Mouton Publishers, Hague/Paris.

Frison, George and Bruce Bradley
(1999) The Fenn Cache, Clovis Weapons and Tools. One Horse Land and Cattle Company, Santa Fe, NM.

Gamble, Clive
(1999) The Palaeolithic Societies of Europe. Cambridge World Archaeology, Cambridge University Press, Cambridge, UK.

Geikie, James
(1974) Great Ice Age – Its Relation to the Antiquity of Man. D. Appleton & Company, New York, NY.

Gerasimov, M. M.
(1928) New Sites of the Stone PeriodMan near Khabarocsk. News of the East Siberian Department of the Russian State Geological Society, LIII, p. 141..

Giddings, J. L.
(1963) Some Artic Spear Points and Their Counterparts. Anthropological Papers of the University of Alaska – Early Man in the Western American Artic – A Symposium, Vol. 10, No. 2, pp. 1-12.

Gladilin, N. V. and V. Sitlivy
(1990) Aszel Centralnoy Evropy, Kiev.

Goebel, T.
(1999) Pleistocene Human Colonization and Peopling of the Americas: An Ecological Approach. Evolutionary, Anthropology, Vol. 8, pp. 208-26.

Goebel T, Waters M. R. and D. H. O'Rourke
(2008) The Late Pleistocene Dispersal of Modern Humans in the Americas. Science, Vol. 319, pp.1497-1502.

Gonzales, Alberto Rex
(1952) Antiquo Horizonte Preceramico en las Sierras Centrales de la Argentina. RUNA, Vol. 5, pp. 110-133.

Gramly, Michael F.
(2012) Bifaces of the Cumberland Tradition. American Society for Amateur Archaeology, Andover, MA.
(1992) Prehistoric Lithic Industry at Dover, Tennessee. Presimmon Press, Monographs in Archaeology, Buffalo, NY.

Gardner, William A.
(1989) An Examination of Cultural Change in the Late Pleistocene and Early Holocene (circa 9200 to 6800 BC) In: Paleoindian Research in Virginia – A Synthesis. ASV Special Publication No. 19.

Gardner, James V., Michael E. Field, and David C. Twichell (eds.)
(1996) Geology of the United States Seafloor. Cambridge University Press, Cambridge, UK.

Garrod, D.
(1926) The Upper Paleolithic Age of Britian. Clarendon, Press, Oxford, UK.

Gibbons, Ann
(1997) Monte Verde: Blessed But Not Confirmed. Science, Vol. 275, No. 5304, pp. 1256-1257.

Gidley, James W.
(1927) Investigating Evidence of Early Man in Florida. Smithson Institution, Explorations and Field Work in 1926, Smithsonian Miscellaneous Collections, Vol. 79, No. 7, pp. 168-174.

Gilbert, M. Thomas P., Dennis L. Jenkins, Anders Götherstrom, Nuria Naveran, Juan J. Sanchez, Michael Hofreiter, Philip Francis Thomsen, Jonas Binladen, Thomas F. G. Higham, Robert M. Yohe II, Robert Parr, Linda Scott Cummings, Eske Willerslev
(2008) DNA from Pre-Clovis Human Coprolites in Oregon, North America. Sceince DOI: 10.1126/Science 1154116 (online website).

Gildey, J. W. and F. B. Loomis
(1926) Fossil Man in Florida. American Journal of Science, Vol. 12, pp. 254-264.

Gillespie, Rachard
(2002) Dating the First Australians. Radiocarbon, 44(2): 455-472.

Goebel T, M. R. Waters, and D. H. O'Rourke
(2008) The Late Pleistocene Dispersal of Modern Humans in the Americas. Science, Vol. 319, pp. 1497-1502.

Goebel, T.
(1999) Pleistocene Human Colonization and Peopling of the Americas: An Ecological Approch. Evolutionary Anthropology, Vol. 8, pp. 208-26.

Goebel, Ted, Michael R Waters, Ian Buvit, Mikhail V. Konstantinov and Aleksander V. Konstantinov
(2000) Studenoe-2 and the origins of microblade technologies in the Transbaikal, Siberia. Antiquity, Vol. 74, pp. 567-575.

Golson, Jack
(1977) Simple Tools and Complex Technology. In: Stone Tools as Culture Markers: Change, Evolution, and Complexity, ed. R. Wright, pp. 189-194, Australian Institute of Aboriginal Studies, Canberra.

Goodyear, A.C.
(2011) Personal communication.
(2005) Evidence of Pre-Clovis Sites in the Eastern United States. In Paleoamerican Origins: Beyond Clovis, pp. 103-112 edited by R. Bonnichsen, B. Lepper, D. Stanford, M. Waters. Texas A&M University Press, College Station, TX.
(2000) The Topper Site 2000: Results of the 2000 Allendale Paleoindian Expedition. Legacy 5 (2):18–25. Newsletter of the South Carolina Institute of Archaeology and Anthropology, University of South Carolina, Columbia.
(1999) Results of the 1999 Allendale Paleoindian Expedition. Legacy,4 (1-3):8–13. Newsletter of the South Carolina Institute of Archaeology and Anthropology, University of South Carolina.
(1999) The Early Holocene Occupation of the Southeastern United States: A Geoarchaeology Summary. In Ice Age Peoples of North America, edited by R. Bonnichsen and K. L. Turnmire, pp. 432–81. Oregon State University Press, Corvallis.

Goodyear, A. C., and T. Charles
(1984) An Archaeological Survey of Chert Quarries in Western Allendale County, South Carolina. Research Manuscript Series 195. Institute of Archaeology and Anthropology, University of South Carolina, Columbia.

Goodyear, A. C., and K. Steffy
(2003) Evidence for a Clovis Occupation at the Topper Site, 38AL23, Allendale County, South Carolina. Current Research in the Pleistocene 20:23–25.

Goodyear, Albert C., Keith Derting, D. Shane Miller, and Ashley M. Smallwood
(2009) Exotic Clovis Stone Tools from the Topper Site, 38Al23, Allendale County, South Carolina. Current Research in the Pleistocene, Vol. 26, pp. 60-62.

Gould, Richard A., G. A. Clark, and Mary C. Stiner
(1999) Paleolithic Population Growth. Science, 284(5419): pp. 1465.

Gramly, Richard M.
(2012) Presonal communication.
(2012) Phil Stratton Site Report. In preparation.
(2012) Bifaces of the Cumberland Tradition. Persimmon Press Monographs in Archaeology, Buffalo, NY.
(2009) Origin and Evolution of the Cumberland Palaeo-American Tradition. Persimmon Press Monographs in Archaeology, Buffalo, NY.
(2009) Palaeo-American & Palaeo-Environment at the Vail Site, Maine. Monographs in Archaeology, Persimmon Press, Andover, MA.
(1992) Prehistoric Lithic Industry at Dover, Tennessee. Persimmon Press Monographs in Archaeology, Buffalo, NY.
(1982) The Vail Site: A Paleo-Indian Encampment in Maine. Buffalo Society of Natural Sciences, Bul. 30, Buffalo, NY.

Gramly, Richard M. and David Walley
(2012) Ft. Payne Chert: Inferred Lasert Spectroscopy (ILS) Dating o0f Palaeo-American Artifacts and Trace Element Characterization. Paper: Society for American Archaeology, Annual Meeting, Memphis, TN.

Greenhill, Basil
(1976) Archaeology of the Boat. Wesleyan University Press, Middletown, CT.

Grigorieva, G. V.
(1983) Palynological and Radiocarnen Data for the Multilevel Site of Korpatch. In: Pervobytnye drevnosti Moldavii, N. Ketrau ed., pp. 202-206, Shtiintsa, Kisinev.

Grigor've, Gennadii P.
(1993) The Kostenki-Avdeevo Archaeological Culture and the Willendorf-Pavlov-Kostenki-AvdeevoCultural Unity. In: From Kostenki to Clovis, O. Soffer and N. Passlov eds., Plenum Press, New York, NY.

Grootes, P. M. and M. Stuiver
(1997) Oxygen 18/16 Variability in Greenland Snow and Ice with 10^{-3} to 10^3 Year Time Resolution. Journal of Geophysical Research, C102:26455-26470.

Grote, Aug R.
(1877) The Peopling of America. American Naturalist.

Groube, L., J. Chappell, J. Muke, and D. Price
(1986) A 40,000 Year Old Human Occupation Site at Huon Penninsula, Papua New Guinea. Nature, Vol. 324, pp. 453-435.

Grace, Roger
(1989) Interpretating the Function of Stone Tools: The Quantification and Computerisation of Microwear Analysis. BAR International Series 474, Archaeopress, Oxford, UK.

Griffin, James B.
(1966) The Fort Ancient Aspect. Anthropological Papers, No. 28, Museum of Anthropology, University of Michigan, Ann Arbor, MI.

Griffin, John W.
(1974) Investigatings in Russell Cave. Publication in Archaeology, No. 13, National Park Service, Department of the Interior, Washington, DC.

Grote, Aug R.
(1877) The Peopling of America. American Naturalist.

Gruhn, Ruth
(1998) Linguistic Evidence in Support of the Coastal Route of Earliest Entry into the New World. Man, 23(1): 77-100.

Gruhn, Ruth and Alan L. Bryan
(1989) The Record of Pleistocene Megafaunal Extinction at Taima-taima, Northern Venezula. In: Martin, and Klein (eds.) Quarterary Extinctions – A Prehistoric Revolution. University o0f Arizona Press, Tucson, AZ.

Guidon, Niède y G. Delibrias
(1986) Carbon-14 Dates Point to Man in the Americas 32 000 Years Ago. Nature, Vol. 321, pp. 769-771.

Gustafson, C.
(1979) The Manis Mastodon Site: Early Man on the Olympic Penninula. Canadian Journal of Archaeology, Vol. 3, pp. 157-164.

Guslitzer, Bosis I. and Pavel Y. Pavlov
(1993) Man and Nature in Northeastern Europe in the Middle and Late Pleistocene. In: From Kostenki to Clovis, O. Soffer and N. Passlov eds., Plenum Press, New York, NY.

Hall, Don A. and George Wisner
(2000) Texas Site Suggests Link with European Upper Paleolithic. Mammoth Trumpet, Vol. 15, No. 1.

Hall, Stephen S.
(2008) Last of the Neanderthals. National Geographic, Vol. 214, No. 4, pp. 34-59.

Hall, Roberta, Diana Roy, and David Boling
(2004) Pleistocene Migration Routes into the Americas: Human Biological Adaptations. Evolutionary Anthropology, Vol. 13, No. 4, pp. 132-144.

Harrington, C. R., Robert Bonnichsen, and Robert E. Morlan
(1975) Bones Say Man Lived in Yukon 27,000 Years Ago. Canadian Geographical Journal, Vol. 91, Nos. 1&2, pp.42-48.

Harrington, M. R.
(1933) Gypsum Cave, Nevada. Southwest Museum Paper, No. 8, p. 190.

Harrington, M. R. and R. O. Simpson
(1961) Tule Springs , Nevada with other Evidences of Pleistocen Man in North America. Southwest Museum Papers, No. 18, Los Angles, CA.

Harris, Ron
(2011) Part Two: The Reverend Douglas Right Collection. Central States Archaeological Journal, Vol. 58, No. 2, pp. 74-75.

Haynes, Gary
(2002) The Early Settlement of North America. Cambridge University Press, Cambridge, UK.
(1986) Geochronology of Sandia Cave. Smithsonian Contributions to Anthrolopogy, No. 32, Washington, DC.

de Heinzelin de Braucourt, Jean
(1962) Manuel de Typologie des Industries Lithiques, Edite par la Commission Administrative du Patrimoine de l'institut Royal des Sciences Naturelles de Belgique, Bruxelles.

Hemmingway, Mark F.
(1980) The Initial Magdalenian in France. BAR International Series 90 (Part ii), Brishish Archaeological Reports, Oxford, UK.

Hemmings, C. A., J. S. Dunbar, and S. D. Webb
(2004) Florida's Early-Paleoindian Bone and Ivory Tools. In: New Perspectives on the First Americans. Lepper and Bonnichsen, eds., pp. 87-92, Center for the Study of the First Americans, Texas A&M, College Station, TX.

Henry, Donald O., Harold J. Hietala, Arline M. Rosen, Yuri E. Demidenko, Vitality I. Usik, and Teresa L. Armagan
(2004) Human Behavioral Organization in the Middle Paleolithic: Were Neanderthals Different? American Anthropologist, 106(1): 17-31.

Hester, Jim J.
(1972) Backwater Locality No. 1 – A Stratified, Early Man Site in Eastern New Mexico. Fort Burgwin Research Center, No. 8, Southern Methodist University, Dallas, TX.
(1960) Late Pleistocene Extinction and Radio Carbon Dating. American Antiquity, Vol. 26, No. 1, pp. 58-77.

Hibben, Frank C.
(1941) Association of Man with Pleistocene Mammals in the Sandia Mountains, New Mexico. American Antiquity, Vol. 2, No. 4, pp. 260-263.

Hibben, Frank C. and Kirk Bryan
(1941) Evidence of Early Occupation in Sandia Cave, New Mexico. Smithsonian Miscellaneous Collections, Vol. 99, No. 23.

Higgs, E. S. and J. M. Coles
(1969) The Archaeology of Early Man. Frederick A. Preager, Publishers, New York, NY.

Hill, K.
(2011) A Story of Ancient Mariners. Mammoth Trumpet, Vol 26, No. 4, pp. 12-19.

Hirth, Kenneth G. (ed.)
(2003) Mesoamerican Lithic Technology – Experimention and Interpretation. University of Utal Press, Salt Lake, UT.

Hoffman, C. Marshall
(1985) Projectile Point Maintenance and Typology: Assessment with Factor Analysis and Canonical Correlation. IN For Concordance In: Archaeological Analysis: Bridging Data Structure, QuantitativeTechnique, and Theory. C. Carr, ed. Pp. Westport Publishers,, Kansas City.

Hoffman, Jack L.
(2003) Tethered to Stone or Freedom to Move: Folsom Biface Technology in Regional Perspective. In: Soressi, Marie and Harold L. Dibble (eds.) Multiple Approches to the Study of Bifacial Technologies. University of Pennsylvania Museum of Archaeology and Anthropology, Philadephia, PA.

Holbrook, W. S., G. M. Purdy, R. E. Sheridan, L. Glover III, M. Talwani, J. Ewing, and D. Hutchinson
(1994), Seismic Structure of the U.S. Mid-Atlantic Continental Margin, J. Geophys. Res., 99(B9), 17,871–17,892.

Holdaway, S.
(1989) Were There Halfted Projectile Points in the Mousterian? Journal of Field Archaeology, Vol. 16, pp. 79-85.

Holen, Stephen
(2012) Evidence for a Mid-Western Human Presence in the Americas. Paper: Society for American Archaeology Annual Meeting, Memphis, TN.

Holmes, William H.
(1918) On the Antiquity on Man in America. Science, Vol. 47, pp. 561-562.
(1903) Flint Implements and Fossil Remains from a Sulphur Spring at Afton, Indian Territory. Report of the U.S. National Museum, Smithsonian Institution, Washington, DC.
(1899) Review of the Evidence Relating to the Auriferous Gravel Man in California. Annual Report, Smithsonian Institution, Washington, DC.

Hoernes, Moriz
(1903) Diluviale Mensch In Europa. Braunschweig Verlag Von Friedrich Vieweg Und Sohn.

Hough, W.
(1898) The Lamp of the Eskimo. In: Report of the U.S. National Museum for 1896, pp. 1025-57, Washington, DC.

Hovers, Erella and Steven Kuhn (eds.)
(2006) Transition Before the Transition – Evolution and Stability in the Middle Paleolithic and Middle Stone Age. Springer Science+Business Media, Inc., New York, NY.

Howard, Edgar B.
(1935) Evidence of Early Man in North America. Museum Journal, University of Pennsylvania, Vol. XXIV, Nos. 2-3.
(1930) An Outline of the Problem of Man's Antiquity in North America. American Anthropologist Vol. 38, pp. 394-415.

Hranicky, Wm Jack
(2018) North American Projectile Points. AuthorHouse, Bloomington, IN.
(2018) Prehistoric Tools from Virginia. Virginia Academic Press, Alexandria, VA.
(2017) Clovis Points in Virginia. Virginia Academic Press, Alexandria, VA.
(2016) Pleistocene Archaeology in Virginia : The Arkfeld Site. Virginia Academic Press, Alexandria, VA.
(2013 – updated 2004) An Encyclopedia of Terminology and Concepts for American Prehistoric Lithic Technology. AuthorHouse, Bloomington, IN.
(2012) Bipoints Before Clovis. Universal-Publishers, Boca Raton, FL.
(2011) Material Culture in Prehistoric Virginia (Vol. 1 and 2). AuthorHouse, Bloomington, IN.
(2011 3rd edition) Projectile Points found along the Atlantic Coast. Universal Publishers, Boca Raton, FL.
(2011) Paper: The Norfolk Bipoint, Eastern States Archeological Frederation, Annula Meeting, Mt. Larual, New Jersey.
(2011) Projectile Points from Prehistoric Virginia. AuthorHouse, Bloomington, IN.
(2010) Pre-Clovis in Virginia: A Matter of Antiquity. Archaeology of Eastern North America, Vol. 38, pp. 53-62.
(2010) Recording Clovis Points - Techniques, Examples, and Methods. AuthorHouse, Bloomington, IN.
(2008) The Eastern U.S. Continental Shelf: A Late Pleistocene and Early Holocene Focus in Virginia. Journal on Middle Atlantic Archaeology, Vol. 24, pp. 45-55.

(2008) Mount Olive, North Carolina Cache: Points, Knives, or Bifaces? North Carolina Archaeology, Vol. 57, pp. 108-116.
(2008) McCary Fluted Point Survey of Virginia – Point Numbers 1 to 1055. Authorhouse, Bloomington, IN/
(2007) North African Aterian Tools in Virginia. ASV Quarterly Bulletin, Vol. 62, No. 2, pp. 61-85.
(2007) A Solutrean Landfall on the U. S. Atlantic Coast? Middle Atlantic Journal of Archaeology, Vol. 23, pp. 1-15.
(2007) Experimental Archaeology - A Science for Studying Native American Prehistoric Technology. AuthorHouse, Bloomington, IN.
(2005) A Model for a Paleoindian Fluted Point Survey. Authorhouse, Bloomington, IN.
(2004) An Encyclopedia of Terminology and Concepts for American Prehistoric Lithic Technology. AuthorHouse, Bloomington, IN.
(2004) Encyclopedia of Concepts and Terms for American Lithic Technology. Authorhouse, Indianapolis, IN.
(2004) Blade Technology: Earliest Dimension in American Toolmaking. Journal of Middle Atlantic Archaeology, Vol. 20, pp. 125-135.
(2004) Encyclopedia of Concepts and Terms for American Lithic Technology. Authorhouse, Indianapolis, IN.
(1992) Patination: A Poor Determinant of Age. Ohio Archaeologist, Vol. 42, No. 4, pp. 13-15.
(1987) The Quantum Projectile Point Classification. Ohio Archaeologist, Vol. 37, No. 4, pp. 28-29.
(1972) Thermoluminescent Dating of Pottery. Anthropology: UCLA. Vol. 4, No. 1, pp. 73-81.

Hranicky, Wm Jack and Larry Higgins
(2018) The Higgins Site, Clarke County, Virginia – A View of a PaleoAmerican Site in Virginia. Virginia Academic Press, Alexandria, VA.

Hranicky, Wm Jack, and Floyd Painter
(1989) A Guide to the Identification of Virginia Projectile Points. Archeological Society of Virginia, Special Publication 17, Richmond.

Huckell, Bruce B. and J. David Kilby
(2009) Beach: A Clovis Cache in Southwestern North Dakota. Current Research in the Pliestocene, Vol. 26, pp. 68-70.

Hudjashov, Georgi, Toomas Kivisild, Peter A. Underhill, Phillip Endicott, Juan J. Sanchez, Alice A. Lin, Peidong Shen, Peter Oefner, Colin Renfrew, Richard Villems, and Peter Forster
(2007) Revealing the Prehistoric Settlement of Australia by Y Chromosome and mtDNA Analysis. Proceedings of the National Academy of Sciences, Washington, DC.

Huntington, Ellsworth
(1919) The Red Man's Continent: A Chronicle of Aboriginal America, pp. 31-35.

Ikawa-Smith, Fumiko
(1978) Lithic Assembleges from the Early and Middle Upper Pleistocen Formation in Japan. In: Early Man in America from a Circum-Pacific Perspective, Bryan ed. Pp. 42-53, Occasional Paper 1, pp. 306-327, Department of Anthropology, University of Alberta, Archaeological Researches International, Edmonton, Can.

Imbril, John
(1985) Theoretical Framework for the Pleistocene Ice Ages. Journal of the Geological Society; 1985; 142(3): 417-432.

Ingold, Tim, David Riches, and James Woodland
(1991) Hunters and Gatherers, Vol. 2. Berg, London and Washington, DC.

Iovita, Radu
(2010) Comparing Stone Tool Resharpening Trajectories with the Aid of Elliptical Fourier Analysis. In: New Perspectives on Old Stones – Analytical Approches to Paleolithic Technologies S. Lycett and P. Chauhan eds., pp. 235-254, Springer, New York, NY.

Irwin-Williams, C.
(1967) Association of Early Man with Horse, Camel, and Mastondon at Hueyatlaco, Valsequillo (Puebla, Mexaco). In: Pleistocene Extnction, P. Martin, ed, pp. 337-347, New Haven, CT.

Irving, W. N. and C. R. Harrington
(1973) Upper Pleistocene Radiocarbon Dated Artifacts from the Northern Yukon. Science, Vol. 179, pp. 335-340.

Izagirre, N. and C. de la Rua
(1999) An mtDNA Analysis in Ancient Basque Populations: Implications for Haplogroup V as a Marker for a Major Paleolithic Expansion from Southwestern Europe. American Journal of Human Genetics, Vol. 65, pp. 199-207.

Jablonski, Nina G. (ed.)
(2002) The First Americans. Memoirs of the California Academy of Sciences, No. 27, San Francisco, CA.

Jackson, Donald, Cesar Mendez, and Antonia Escudero
(2011) Coastal-Inland Mobility during the Early Holocene in the Semiarid North Chile: La Fundicion Site. Current Research in the Pliestocene, Vol. 28, pp. 102-104.

Jett, Stephen C.
(2017) Ancient Ocean Crossings. University of Alabama Press, Tuscaloosa, AL.

Jeske, Robert J.
(1992) Energetic Efficiency and Lithic Technology: An Upper Mississippian Example. American Antiquity, Vol. 57, No. 3, pp. 467-481.

Jelks, A. E.
(1936) Pleistocene Man in Minnsota. University of Minnsota Press, p.197.

Jelinek, Author J.
(2013) Neanderthal Lithic Industries at La Quina. University of Arizona Press, Tuscon, AZ.
(1971) Early Man in the New World: A Technological Perspective. Arctic Anthropology, Vol. 8, pp. 15-21.

von Jelinek, J.
(1972) Das grobe Bilderlexikon des Manschen in der Vorzert Alk Rechte der deulschsprachigen Ausgaber bel Verlagsgruppe Bertelsman Gah H Gulersloh Grafishe Gaslaltung Fratilsek Prokel.

Jenkins, Dennis L.
(2011) NGBPP Research at the Paisley Caves. Museum of Naturral and Culture History, OR.

Jennings, Jessie D.
(1989) Prehistory of North America, 3rd edition. Mayfield Publishing Co., Mountain View, CA.

Jenning, J. and E. Norbeck (eds.)
(1964) Prehistoric Man in the New World. Chicago, IL.

Jolly, N.
(1894) Man Before Metal.D. Appleton and Company, New York, NY.

Jones, Terry L., Fitzgerald, Douglas J. Kennett, Charles H. Miksick, John L. Fagan, John Sharp, and Jon M. Erlandson
(2002) The Cross Creek Site (CA-SLO-1797) and Its Implications for New World Colonization. American Antiquity, vol. 67, No. 2, pp. 231-230.

Johnson, Michael F.
(2012) Blueberry Hill (44SX327): Replicating Again the Cactus Hill Paleoamerican Model in the Nottoway River Valley of Southeastern Virginia. Paper: Middle Atlantic Archaeological Conference, March 23-25, Virginia Beach, VA.
(1997) Additional Research at Cactus Hill: Preliminary Description of Northern Virginia Chapter-ASV 1993 and 1995 Excavation. In: Archaeological Investigations of Site 44SX202, Cactus Hill, Sussex County, Virginia by J. McAvoy. DHR Research Report Series, No. 8, Richmond, VA.

Johnstone, P.
(1980) The Sea-craft of Prehistory. London and Henley: Routledge & Kegan Paul.

Johnson, Frederick
(1951) Radiocarbon Dating. Memoirs of the Society for American Archaeology, Vol. XVII, No. 1, Pt. 2,

Josselyn, Daniel W.
1967 More on America's "Crude Tool." Tennessee Archaeologist, 23(1). 1-11.

Justice, N. D.
(1987) Stone Age Spear and Arrow Points of the Midcontinental and Eastern United States. Indiana University Press, Bloomington, IN.

Kashani BH, Perego UA, Olivieri A, Angerhofer N, Gandini F, Carossa V, Lancioni H, Semino O, Woodward SR, Achilli A, Torroni A.
(2011) Mitochondrial haplogroup C4c: A rare lineage entering America through the ice-free corridor? American Journal of Physical Anthropolgy. 2011 Oct 24.

Kay, Marvin
(1996) Microwera Analysis of Some Clovis and Experimental Chipped Stone Tools. In: Stone Tools – Theoratical Insights into Human Prehistory, G. Odell, ed., pp. 315-344, Plenum Press, New York, NY.

Keeley, L. H.
(1980) Experimental Determination of Stone Tool Uses: a Microwear Analysis. University of Chicago Press, Chicago, IL.

Kelly, R. L.
(1988) The Three Sides of a Biface. American Antiquity, Vol. 53, pp. 717-734.

Kelly, R. L. and L. C. Todd
(1988)Coming into the Country: Early Paleoindian Hunting and Mobility. American Antiquity, Vol. 53, pp. 231-244.

Kidder, Alfred V.
(1932) The Artifacts of Pecos. Yale University Press, Hartford, CT.

Kivieild, Toomas
(2007) Complete MhDNA Sequences – Quest on "Out-of-Africa" Route Complete? In: Rethinking the Hman Population – New Behavioral and Biological Perspectives of Modern Humans, eds. P. Mellars, K. Boyle, O. Bar-Yonsf, and C. Stringer. The McDonald Institute Monographs, Oxbow Books, UK.

Klein, Richard G.
(1993) Culture in the Paleolithic. Science, (262)5140: 1751-1752.

Kleindienst, M. R.
(1962) Components of the East African Acheulian Assemblage: An Analytical Approach. In: C. Mortelmans and J. Nenquin, eds., Acts du 4e Congres Panafrican de Prehistoire et de l'Etude du Quarternaire, pp. 81-105, Tervuren, Belguim.

Klien, Zdenek
(2000) The Ethnological Approach to the Syudy of Human Behavior. Neuroendocrinology Letters, Vol. 21, No. 6, pp. 477-481.

Knight, Veron J.
(2010) Mound Excavations at Moundville. University of Alabama Press, Tuscaloosa, AL.

Kornfeld, Marcel and Andrei Tabarev
(2009) The French Connection? Or Is It? Current Research in the Pliestocene, Vol. 26, pp. 78-81.

Kozlowski, Janusz K.
(2003) From Bifaces to Leaf Points. In: Soressi, Marie and Harold L. Dibble (eds.) Multiple Approches to the Study of Bifacial Technologies. University of Pennsylvania Museum of Archaeology and Anthropology,Philadephia, PA.

Krantz, Grover S.
(1977) The Populating of Western North America. Society for California Archaeology – Occasional Paper in Method and Theory in California Archaeology, pp. 1-64.

Krieger, Alex D.
(1962) Comments on "The Paleo-Indian Tradition in Eastern North America" by R. J. Mason. Current Anthropology, Vol. 3, No. 3, pp. 256-259.
(1960) Archaeological Typology in Theory and Practice. In: Men and Culture, University of Pennsylvania Press, pp. 141-151, Philadelphia, PA.
(1957) Early Man in the New World. American Antiquity, Vol. 22, pp. 434-436.

Kraus, Mary J.
(1997) Lower Eocene alluvial paleosols: Pedogenic development, stratigraphic relationships, and paleosol/landscape associations. Palaeogeography, Palaeoclimatology, Palaeoecology, Vol. 129, Issues 3–4, April 1997, pp. 387–406.

Kurten, Bojorn and Elaine Anderson
(1980) Pleistocen Mammals of North America. Columbia University Press, New York, NY.

Kuzmin, Y. V.
(2004) Origin of the Upper Paleolithic in Siberia. In: The Early Upper Paleolithic Beyod Western Europe, J. Brantingham, S. Kuhn, and K. Kerry, eds., pp. 196-206, University of California Press, Berkeley, CA.

Laguens, Andres G., Eduardo A. Pautassi, Gisela M. Sario, and G. Roxana Cattaneo
(2007) Els1, a Fistail Projectile-Point Site from Central Argentina. Current Research in the Pleistocene, Vol. 24, pp. 55-57.

Lambeck, K. T., M. Esat, and K. Potter
(2002) Links Between Climate and Sea Levels for the Past Three Million Years. Nature, Vol. 419, pp. 199-206.

Largent, Floyd
(2010) Human Migration into the New World – A New Look at the Genetic Evidence. Mammoth Trumpet, Vol. 25, No. 4, pp. 8-11.

Lasca, Norman P. and Jack Donahue
(1990) Archaeological Geology on North America. Centennial Special, Vol. 4, Geological Society of America, Boulder, CO.

Laub, Richard S.
(2000)A Second Dated Mastodon Bone Artifact from Pleistocene Deposit at the Hiiscock Site(Western New York State. Archaeology of Eastern North America, Vo. 28, pp. 141-154.

Lavallee, Daniele
(1995) The First South Americans. University of Utah Press. Salt Lake, UT.

Leakey, L. S. B.
(1935) The Stone Age Races of Kenya. Oxford University Press, Oxford, UK.

Leplace, G.
(1968) Les niveaux Aurignaciens et l'hypothese du syntheotype. In L'Homme de Cro-Magnon, pp. 141-163, Arts et Metiers Graphiques, Paris.

Leroi-Gourhan A. and M. Brezillion
(1972) Fouilles de Pincevent Essai d' anaalyse ethnographique d' un habitat Magdalenien. La Section 36, Gallia Prehistoire Supplement VIII, Center National, de la Recherche Scientifique, Pasis.

Lepper, Bradley T. and Robson Bonnichsen
(2004) New Perspectives on the First Americans. Center for the Study of the First Americans, Texas A&M University, College Station, TX.

Leveque, Francois, Anna Mary Backer, and Michael Guilbaud
(1993) Context of a Late Neandertal. Monographs in World Archaeology, No. 16, Prehistory Press, Madison, WI.

Lewis, D.
(1972) We the Navigators. University of Hawaii Press, Honolulu, HI.

Lister, Adrain and Paul Bahn
(2007) Mammoths – Giants of the Ice Age. University of California Press, Berkeley, CA.

Lively, Matthew
(1965) The Lively Complex: Preliminary Report on a Pebble Tool Complex in Alabama. Special Report of the Archaeological Society, Birminghan, AL.

Lorenzo, Jose Luis and Lorena Mirambelll
(1999) The Inhabitants of Mexico During the Upper Pleistocene. In *Ice Age People of North America*. ed. by Robson Bonnichsen and Karen Turnmire, pp. 482-496. Oregon State University Press, Corvallis, OR.
(1986) Preliminary Report on Archaeological and Paleoenvironmental Studies in the Area of El Cedral. San Luis Potosi, Mexico 1977-1980. In: New Evidence for the Pleistocene Peopling of the Americas, Bryan ed., Center for the Study of Early Man, University of Maine, Orono, ME.

Losco, Russell L., Willian Stephens, and Martin F. Helmke
(2010) Periglacial Features and Landforms of the Delmarva Peninsula. Southeastern Geology, Vol. 47, P. 85-94.

Lowery, Darrin L.
(2010) A Geological Understanding of Archaeological Landscapes in the Central Zone: Specific Examples in the Middle Atlantic Region. Paper, Eastern States Archeological Federation's Annual Meeting, Williamsburg, VA.
(2009) The Loess and Archaeological Record of the Late Pleistocene through Early Holocene on the Northwestern Section of the Delmarva Peninsula, USA. Paper given at the Eastern States Archeological Federation Annual Meeting, November, Johnstown, PA.
(2008) Archaeological Survey of the Chesapeake Bay ShorelinesAssociated with Mathews Cunty, Virginia: An Erosion Threat Study. Virginia Department of Historic ResourcesSurvey and Planning Report Series, Rochmond, VA.

Lowery, Darrin and Dennis Stanford
(2012) Coastal Plain Geology, Marine Transgression, and Geochemistry: An Understanding of Archaeological Patterns along the Delmarva Peninsula, USA. Paper: Annual meeting, Society of American Archaeology, Memphis, TN.

Lowery, Darrin L., Michael A. O'Neal, John Wah, Daniel P. Wagner, and Dennis J. Stanford
(2010) Late Pleistocene Upland Stratigraphy of the Western Delmarva Peninsula, USA. Quarterly Science Reviews, Vol. 29, pp. 1472-1480.

Lucas, Frederick A.
(1899) The Truth about the Mammoth. Annual Report, Smithsonian Institution, Washington, DC.

Lumley-Woodyear, de Henry
(1969) Le Paleolithique Inferieur et Moyan du Midi Mediterraneen Dans Son Cadre Geologique.Editions du Centre National de la Recherche Scientique, Paris, France.

Lumley, de H. and B. Bottet
(1960) Sur l'evolution des climates et des industries au Riss et au Wurm d'apres le remplissage de la Baume Bonne (Quinson, Basses Alpes). In: Restschriff fur Lothar Zotz, pp. 271-301, Steinzeitfragen der Alten und Neuen Welt, Ludwig Rohrscheid Verlag, Bonn, Germany.

Lycett, Stephen J. Parth R. Chauhan
(2010) New Perspectives on Old Stones – Analytical Approches to Paleolithic Technologies. Springer, New York, NY.

Lynch, T. F.
(1980) Guitarrero Cave: Early Man in the Andies. Academin Press, New York, NY.

MacCurdy, George Grant
(1929) Old-World Prehistorybin Retrospect and Prospect. American Philosophy Society, Vol. 68, No. 2, pp. 95-106.

Macgrail, Sean, and Paul Johnston
(1980) The Sea-Craft of Prehistory. Routledge, London, UK.

MacGowan, K.
(1950) Early Man in the New World. Macmillan, New York, NY.

MacGowan, Kenneth and Joseph A. Hester, Jr.
(1962) Early Man in the New World. American Museum of History Natural History, Doubleday & Company, New York, NY.

Macgrail, Sean, and Paul Johnston
(1980) The Sea-Craft of Prehistory. Routledge, London, UK.

MacKendrick, Paul
(1960) The Mute Stones Speak. W. W. Norton & Company, New York, NY.

MacNeish, R. S.
(1983) Mesoamerica. In: Shutler, R (ed.), Early Man in the New World. Sage Publication, Beverly Hills, CA.
(1976) Early Man in the New World. American Scientist, Vol. 63, pp. 316-327.
(1976) Early Man in the Andes. In: Avenues of Antiquity, W. H. Freeman and Company, San Francisco, CA.
(1971) Early Man in the Andes. Scentific American, Vol. 224, pp. 36-46.
(1963) The Early Peopling of the New World – as seen from Southwestern Youkon. Anthropological Papers of the University of Alaska – Early Man in the Western American Artic – A Symposium, Vol. 10, No. 2, pp. 93-106.
(1959) A Speculative Framework of Northern North American Prehistory as of April 1959. Anthropologica, n.s., Vol. 1, Nos. 1-2,, Ottawa, CAN.
(1958) Preliminary Archaeological Investigations in the Serria de Tamaulipas, Mexico. Ameriican Philosophical Society, Vol. 48, No. 6, pp. 1-120.

MacNeish, Richard S. and Jane G. Libby
(2003) Pendejo Cave. University on New Mexico Press, Albuquerque, NM.

Magne, Martin P. R.
(2004) Technological Correlates of Gwaii Haanas Microblades. Lithic Technology, Vol. 29, No. 2, pp. 91-118.

Magoffin, R. V. D. and Emily C. Davis
(1929) The Romance of Archaeology. Garden City Publishing Company, Inc., Garden City, NY.

Mahan, E. C.
(1955) ASurvey of Paleo-Indian and Other Early Flint Artifacts from Sites in Northern, Western, and Central Alabama, Part I. Tennessee Archaeologist, Vol. X, No. 2.

Malhi, Ripan S., Jason A. Eshleman, Jonathan A. Greenburg, Deborah A. Weiss, Beth A. Schultz Shook, Frederika A. Kaestle, Joseph G. Lorenz, Brian M. Kemp, John R. Johnson, and David G. Smith
(2002) The Structure of Diversity within New World Mitochondrial DNA Haplogroups: Implication for the Prehistory on North America. American Journal of Human Genetics, Vol. 70, pp. 905-919.

Marean, Curtis W.
(2010) When the Sea Saved Humanity. Scientific American, Vol. 303, No. 2, pp. 54 -61.

Markewich, H. W., R. J. Litwin, M. J. Pavick, and G. A. Brook
(2009) Late Pleistocene Eolian Features in Southwestern Maryland and Chesapeake Bay Region Indicate Strong WNW-NW Winds Accompanied Growth of the Laurentide Ice Sheet. Quartenary Research, Vol. 71, No. 3, pp. 409-425.

Martin, Paul S. and Richard G. Klein (eds.)
(1989) Quarterary Extinctions – A Prehistoric Revolution. University 0f Arizona Press, Tucson, AZ.

Martini, I. Peter, Michael E. Brookfield, and Steven Sadura
(2001) Principles of Glacial Geomorphology and Geology. Prentice Hall, Englewoods, NJ.

Mayer-Oaks, W.
(1963) Early Man in the Andes. Scientific American, No. 5, pp. 117-128.

McAvoy, Joseph M. and Lynn D. McAvoy
(2003) The Williamson Clovis Site, 44DW1, Dinwiddie County, Virginia: An Analysis of Research Potential in Threatened Areas. Research Report Series No. 13, Virginia Department of Historic Resources, Richmond, VA.

McBreaty, Sally
(1988) The Sangoan-Lupembon and Middle Stone Age Sequence at the Muguruk Site, Western Kenya. World Archaeology, Vol. 19, No. 3, pp. 388-420.

McBrearty, S. A.
(1988) The Sangoan-Lupenban and Middle Stone Age Sequence at the Muguruk Site, Western Kenya. World Archaeology, 19:379-420.

McBrearty, S and A. Brooks
(2000) The Revolution that wasn't: A New Interpretation of the Origin of Modern Human. Journal of Human Evolution, Vol. 39, pp. 453-463.

McBurney, C. B. M.
(1960) The Stone Age of Northern Africa. Penguin Books, Harmondsworth.

McCary, Ben C.
(1983) The Paleo-Indian in Virginia. ASV Quarterly Bulletin, Vol. 38, No. 1, pp. 43-70.
(1951) A Workshop Site of Early Man in Dinwiddie County, Virginia. American Antiquity, Vol. 17, pp. 9-17.

MacCord, Howard A.
(1967) An Unusual Jasper Knife from Warren County, Virginia. ASV Quarterly Bulletin, Vol. 22, No. 2.

McCown, Theodore
(1939) That Magic Word Solutrean. American Antiquity, Vol. 5, No. 2, pp. 150-152.

McDonald, Jerry N.
(2000) An Outline of the Pre-Clovis Archeology of SV-2, Saltville, Virginia, with Special Attention to a Bone Tool Dated 14,510 yr BP. Jeffersonia Contributions from the Virginia Museum of Natural History 9:1-59.
(1985) Late Quaternary Deposits and Paleohydrology of the Saltville Valley, Southwest Virginia. Current Research in the Pleistocene, Vol. 2, pp. 124-124.

McDonald, Jerry N. and James E. Wiederhold
(2009) Microwear on a Probable Burnishing Tool of Pre-Clovis Age from SV-2 (44Sm37), Saltville, Virginia. Current Research in the Pleistocene, Vol. 26, pp. 132-135.

McGee, W. J.
(1889) An Obsidian Implement from Pleistocene Deposits in Nevada. American Antrhropologist, Vol. II, No. 4, pp. 301-312.

McGuire, Joseph D.
(1896) Classification and Development of Primitive Implements. American Anthropologist, Vol. IX, No. 7, pp.227-236.

McLearn, Douglas and Michael Fokkem
(1986) White Horse West Site (28Me119), Data Recovery. Trenton Complex Archaeology Report 4. Trenton Complex Archaeology: Report 6, Louis Berger & Associates, East Orange, NJ.

McNutt, Charles
(2012) Personal Communication, Memphis State University, Memphis, TN.

McNutt, Charles, James Cherry, and David Walley
(2010) A Double-Blind Test of the Walley IR Raman Laser Technique for Relative Dating of Lithics. Report: Museum of the Native American Artifacts, Bentonville, AR.

McPhillips, M.
(1998) Hair Analysis, New Laboratory Ability to Test for Substance Abuse. British Journal of Psychiarty, Vol. 173, pp. 287-290.

Meggers, Betty, J. Cliffor Evans, and Emilio Estrada
(1965) Early Forative Period of Coastal Ecuador: the Valdivia and Machililla phases. Smithsonian Contributions to Anthropology, No. 1, Washington, DC.

Mellars, P. A.
(1969) Thhe Chronology of Mousterian Industries in the Perigord Region of South-West France. Proceeding of the Prehistoric Society, Vol. 35, pp. 134-171.

Mellars, P. A. and C. B. Stringer (eds.)
(1989) The Human Revolution: Behavioral and Biological Perspectives on the Origins of Modern Humans. Princeton University Press, Princeton, NJ.

Mellars, P. A. and C. B. Stringer (eds.)
(1989) The Human Revolution: Behavioral and Biological Perspectives on the Origins of Modern Humans. Princeton University Press, Princeton, NJ.

Meltzer, David J.
(2009) First Peoples in a New World. University of California Press, Berkeley, CA.
(1993) Search for the First Americans. Smithsonian Books, Washington, DC.
(1993) Is There a Clovis Adaptation? In: From Kostenki to Clovis, O. Soffer and N. Passlov eds., Plenum Press, New York, NY.

Menghin, D. F. A.
(1952) Fundamentos Chronologieos de la Prehistoria de Palagonia. Runa, Vol. 5, pp. 23-43.

Mercati, Michael
(1717) Metallotheca, Opus Postumum.

Merriwether, D. Andrew
(2002) A Mitochondrial Perspective on the Peopling of the /new World. In: The First Americans. Memoirs of the California Academy of Sciences, Jablonski ed., No. 27, San Francisco, CA.

Milanich, Jerld T.
(1994) Archaeology of Precolumbian Florida. University Press of Florida, Gainsville, FL.

Miller, Carl F.
(1962) Archaeology of the John H. Kerr Reservoir Basin, Roanoke River Virginia-North Carolina. Bul. 182, Smithsonian Institution, Washington, DC.

Miller, D. S. and A. C. Goodyear
(2008) A Probable Hifted Uniface from the Clovis Occupation at the Topper Site, 38Al23, Allendale County, South Carolina. Current Research in the Pleistocene, vol. 25, pp. 118-120.

Miller, Frederic P., Agnes F. Vandome, and John McBrewster, eds.
(2009) Clovis Culture. Alphascript Publishing, Mauritus.

Miller, J. N.
(1985) Luminescence Measurement on Surfaces. Pure and Applied Chemistry, Vol. 57, No. 3, pp. 515-522.

Minkel, J. R.
(2007) Paleoanthropology – Food for a Thought. Scientific American 289(1):30.

Mithen, Steven
(2006) The Singing Neanderthais: The Origins of Language, Mind, and Body. Harvard University Press, Cambridge, MA.

Mochanov, I. Alekseevich
(1978) Stratigraphy and Absolute Chronology of the Paleolithic of Northeast Asia, According to the Work of 1963-1973. In: Early Man in America from a Circum-Pacific Perspective, Bryan A. ed., pp. 54-76,. Occasional Paper 1, pp. 306-327, Department of Anthropology, University of Alberta, Archaeological Researches International, Edmonton, Can.

Mochanov, Yari A. and Suetlana A. Fedoseeva
(1969) Verkhne-Troitskaya. In: American eginnings, West (ed.) University of Chicago Press, Chicago, IL.

de Mortillet, A.
(1869) Essai d'une classification des caverns et des stations sous abri, fondee sur les produits de l'industrie humaine. C. R. Acad.. Sci., Paris, pp. 553-555.

Montane, J.
(1968) Paleo-Indian Remains from Laguna de Tagua-Tagua, Central Chile. Science, Vol. 161, pp. 1137-1138.

Montet-White, Anta
(1973) Le Malpas Rockshelter. Publication in Anthropology, No. 4, University of Kansas, Lawrence, KA.

Montet-White, A., L. R. Binford, and M. L. Papworth
(1963) Miscellaneous Studies in Typology and Classification. Museum of Anthropology, University of Michigan, Anthropological Paper, No. 19, Amm Arbor, MI.

Moorehead, Warren K.
(1900) Prehistoric Implements. Robert Clark Publishers, Cincinnatti, OH.

Morales-Muniz, Arturo and Eufrasia Rosello-Izquierdo
(2008) Twenty Thousand Years of Fishing in the Strait. In: T, Rick and J. Erlandson (eds.), Human Impacts on Ancient Maine Ecosystems – A Global Prespective, pp. 243-277,. University of California Press, Berkely, CA.

Morin, Eugène
(2008) Evidence for Declines in Human Population Densities during the Early Upper Paleolithic in Western Europe. Proceedings of the National Academy of Sciences, 105(1): 48-53.

Morrow, Juliet E. and Cristobal Gnecco
(2006) Paleoindian Archaeology – A Hemispheric Prespective. University Press of Florida, Gainsville, FL.

Morwood, M. J., P. B. O'Sullivan, F. Aziz, and A. Raza
(1998) Fission-track Ages of Stone Tools and Fossils on the East Indonesian Island of Flores. Nature, Vol. 392, pp. 173-176.

Mourant, A. E.
(1954) The Distribution of the Human Blood Groups. Blackwell Scientific Publications, Oxford, UK.

Mourre, V, P. Villa, and C. Henshilwood
(2010) Early Use of Pressure Flaking on Lithic Artifacts at Blombos Cave, South Africa. Science, Vol. 330, pp. 659-662.

Movius, Hallam L. Jr.
(1960) Radiocarbon Dates and Upper Paleolithic Archaeology in Central and Western Europe. Current Athropolgy, Vol. 1, Nos. 5-6, pp. 355-375.
(1953) Old World Prehistory: Paleolithic. Anthropology Today, pp. 163-192, In: A. L. Krober, University of Chicago Press, Chicage, IL.
(1949) Lower Paleolithic Archaeology in Southern Asia and the Far East. Studies in Physical Anthropology, No. 1, Early Man in the Far East.
(1949) Excavations at the Prehistoric Rock-Shelter of La Colombiere. Archaeology, Vol. 2, No. 1, pp. 22-30.
(1947) The Lower Paleolithic Cultures of Southern and Eastern Asia. Transactions of the American Philosophical Society, Vol. 38, No. 4, Philadelphia, PA.

Movius, Hellam L. and Shelton Judson
(1956) The Rock-Shelter of La Colombiere. American School of Prehistoric Research, Peabody Museum, Harvard University, Bul. 19, Cambridge, MA.

Mulvaney, D. J.
(1961) The Stone Age of Australia. Proceeding of the Prehistory Society, Vol. 27, pp. 56-107.

Munsell
(1994) Munsell Soil Color Charts. GretagMacbeth, New Winsor, NY.

Munro, Robert
(1912) Paleolithic Man and the Terramare Settlement in Europe. Macmillan Company, New York, NY.

Nance, Jack D.
(1971) Functional Interpretations from Microscopic Analysis. American Antiquity, Vol. 36, pp. 361-366.

Neill, Wilfred T.
(1958) A Stratified Early Site at Silver Springs, Florida. Florida anthropologist, Vol. 11, No. 2, pp. 33-52.

Nelson, Margaret C.
(1991) The Study of Techological Organization. In: Archaeological Method and Theory, Vol. 3, ed. H. Schiffer, pp. 57-100. University of Arizona Press, Tucson, AZ.

Nelson, R.
(1969) Hunters of the Northern Ice. University of Chicage Press, Chicage, Il.

Nelson J.R. Fagundes, Ricardo Kanitz, Roberta Eckert, Ana C.S. Valls, Mauricio R. Bogo, Francisco M. Salzano, David Glenn Smith, Wilson A. Silva Jr., Marco A. Zago, Andrea K. Ribeiro-dos-Santos, Sidney E.B. Santos, Maria Luiza Petzl-Erler, and Sandro L. Bonatto
(2008) Mitochondrial Population Genomics Supports a Single Pre-Clovis Origin with a Coastal Route for the Peopling of the Americas. American Journal of Human Genetics, Volume 82, Issue 3, pp. 583–592.

Neves, W. A.
(2001) Paleoindian Skeletal Remains from Santana do Riacho I, Minas Genais, Brazil: Archaeological Background, Chronological Context and Comparative Crainal Morphology. Seventieth Annual Meetinf of the American Association of Physical Anthropolists, March, Kansas City, KA.

Newman, T. M.
(1966) Cascade Cave. Occassional Papers of the Idaho State University Museum, No. 18, Pocatello, ID.

Newman, Walter S. and Bert Salwen (eds.)
(1977) Amerinds and Their Paleoenvironments in Northeastern North America. New York Academy of Sciences, Volume 288, New York, NY.

Noble, Marlene, Bradford Butman, and Redward Williams
(1983) On the Longshelf Structure and Dynamics of Subtitle Currents on the Eastern United States. Vol. 13, No. 12, pp. 2125-2147, Journal of Physical Oceanography.

Oakley, Kenneth P.
(1959) Man the Tool-Maker. Phoenix Books, University of Chicage Press, Chicago, IL.

O'Brian, Michael J.
(2010) The Future of Paleolithic Studies: A View from the New World. In: New Perspectives on Old Stones – Analytical Approches to Paleolithic Technologies S. Lycett and P. Chauhan eds., pp. 311-334,. Springer, New York, NY.

Ochsenius, C. and R. Gruhn (eds.)
(1979) Taima-taima - A Late Paleo-Indian Kill Site in Northernmost South America--Final Reports of the 1976 Excavations. CIPICS/South American Quaternary Documentation Program. Printed in the Federal Republic of Germany.

Odell, George H. (ed.)
(2009) Archaeological Lithic Analysis: Readings from American Antiquity and Latin American Antiquity. Society for American Archaeology, Washington, DC.
(1996) Stone Tools – Theoratical Insights into Human Prehistory. Plenum Press, New York, NY.

Okladnikov, A. P.
(1950) The Neolithic and Bronze Ages of the Baikal Area (In Russian), Pt 1. Materialy I Issledovaniya po Arkheologii SSSR 18, Moscow-Leningrad.

Olson, Steve
(2003) Mapping Human History. Houghton Mifflin Company, New York, NY.

Osborn, A.
(1977) Strandloopers, Mermaids, and Other Fairy Tales: Ecological Determinants of Marine Resource Utilization – the Peruvian Case. In: For Theory Building in Archaeology, ed., L. Binford. Pp. 157-205, Academic Press, New York, NY.

Osborn, Henry Fairchild
(1922) Men of the Old Stone Age. Charles Scribner's Sons, New York, NY.

Oswalt, W. H.
(1976) An Anthropological Analysis of Food Getting Technology. Wiley Interscience, New York, NY.

Otte, M.
(2004) The Aurignacian in Asia. In: The Early Upper Paleolithic Beyod Western Europe, J. Brantingham, S. Kuhn, and K. Kerry, eds., pp. 114-150, University of California Press, Berkeley, CA.
(2002) The Pitfalls of Using Bifaces as Culture Markers. In: Multiple Approaches to the Study of Bifacial Technologies, ed. M. Soressi and H. Pibble, pp. 183-92, University of Pennsylvania Museum of Archaeology and Anthropology, Philadelphia, PA.

Ousley, Steve D.
(1985) Relationships between Eskimos, Indians, and Aleuts: Old Data, New Perspectives. Human Biology, Vol. 67, pp.:427-458.

Owsley, Douglas W. and Richard L. Jantz (eds.)
(2018) Kennewick Man. Texas A&M Press, College Station, TX.

Owsley, Douglas W. and Sally M. Walker
(2012) Their Skeletons Speak. Carolrhoda Books, Minneapolis, MN

Palmer, Jack A. and Linda K. Palmer
(2002) Evolutionary Psychology: The Ultimate Origins of Human Behavior. Allyn and Bacon Publishers, Boston, MA,

Parfit, Michael
(2000) Hunt for the First Americans. National Geographic, Vol. 198, No. 6, pp. 41-67.

Parveer, Juliette M.
(2004) The Djies Hunters. A.A. Balkema Publishers, London, UK.

Pastra, Alejandro and Kenneth G. Hirth
(2003) Biface Production and Craft Specialization. In: Mesoamerican Lithic Technology, K. Hirth, ed., University of Utal Press, Salt Lake, UT.

Paunescu, A.
(1993) Ripiceni-Izvor paleolitic si mezolitic. Editura Academei Romane, Bucharest, Romainia.

Pavesic, Max G.
(1985) Cache Blades and Turkey Tails – Piecing Together the Western Idaho Archaic Burial Complex. In: Stone Tool Analysis – Essays in Honor of Don. E. Crabtree, M. Plew, J. Woods, and M. Pavesic (eds.), pp. 55-89, University of New Mexico Press, Albuquerque, NM.

Peake, Harold and Herbert John Fleure
(1927) Hunters & Artists. Clarendon Press, Oxford, UK.

Pendleton, Elizabeth A., E. Robert Thieler, and S. Jeffress Williams
(2005) Coastal Vulnerability Assessment of Cape Hatteras National Shore (CHNS) to Sea-Level Rise. USGS Open-File 2004-1064, Reston, VA.

Perazio, Philip
(1986) Abbott's Lane site (28Mel-I), Data Recovery. Trenton Complex Archaeology Report 7. Louis Berger & Associates, East Orange, NJ.

Perego U.A., Achilli A., Angerhofer N., Accetturo M., Pala M., Olivieri A., Kashani B.H., Ritchie K.H., Scozzari R., Kong Q.P., Myres N.M., Salas A., Semino O., Bandelt H.J., Woodward S.R., Torroni A.
(2009) Distinctive Paleo-Indian migration routes from Beringia marked by two rare mtDNA haplogroups. Current Biology,. Jan 13, Vol. 19, No. 1, pp. 1-8.

de Perthes, Boucher
(1847) Not available.

Pewe, Troy L.
(1954) The Geological Approach to Dating Archaeological Sites. American Antiquity, Vol. 20, No. 1, pp. 51-61.

Peyrony, D., P. Bourrinet, and A. Darpeix
(1930) Le burin mousterien. In: Congres International d'Anthropologie et d'Archeologie Prehistorique, pp. 310-315, 15eme session, Portugal.

Phillipson, David W.
(2005 – 3rd) African Archaeology. Cambridge University Press, United Kingdom.

Pinker, S.
(1997) The Language Instinct: The New Science of Language and Mind. Penquin, London, UK.

Pirsson, Louis V. (Vol. 1) and Schuchert, Charles (Vol. 2)
(1915 and 1920) Introductory Geology. John Willey and Sons, Inc., New York, NY.

Pitulko, V. V., et al.
((2004) Yana RHS Site: Humans in the Arctic Before the Last Glacial Maximum. Science, Vol. 303, No. 5654, pp. 52-56.

Pitulko, V. V., E. Y. Pavlova, and P. A. Nikolskiy
(2015) Mammoth Ivory Technologies in the Upper Palaeolithic Archaic Siberia: A Case Study Based on the Materials from the Yana RHS Site. World Archaeology, Vol. 447, Is. 3, pp. 333-389.

Poag, C. W.
(1978) Stratigraphy of the Atlantic Continental Shelf and Slope of the United States. Vol. 6, pp. 251-280, Annual Review of Earth and Planetary Sciences.

Pradel, L.
(1963) La pointe Mousterienne. Bulletin de la Societe Prehistorique Francaoise, Vol. 60, pp. 569-581.

Pringle, Heather
(2011) The 1st Americans. Scientific American, Vol. 205, No. 5, pp. 36-45.

Purdy, Barbara A.
(2012) The Mammoth Engraving from Vero Beach, Florida: Ancient or Recent? Paper, SAA Meeting, Memphis, TN.
(2008) Florida's People During the Last Ice Age. University Press of Fllorida, Gainsville, FL.
(1986) Florida's Prehistoric Stone Technology. University Presses of Florida, Gainesville, FL.
(1981) Florida's Prehistoric Stone Technology. University Press of Florida, Gainsville, FL.

Purdy, B. A., K. Jones, J. Mecholsky, G. Bourne, R. Hulbert, B. MacFadden, K. Church, M. Warren, T., Jorstad, D. Stanford, M. Wachowiak, and R. Speakman
(2011) Earliest Art in the Americas: Incised Image of a Proboscidean on a Mineralized Extinct Animal Bone from Vero Beach, Florida. Jounal of Archaeological Science, Vol. 38, pp. 2908-2913.

Putnam, F. W.
(1906) Evidence of the Work of Man on Objects from Quaternary Caves in California. American Anthropologist, Vol 8, No. 2, pp. 229-235.

Pyle, David M., Graham D. Ricketts, Vasiliki Margari, Tjeerd H. van Andel, Andrei A. Sinitsyn, Nicolai D. Praslov and Sergei Lisitsyn
(2006) Wide dispersal and deposition of distal tephra during the Pleistocene 'Campanian Ignimbrite/Y5' eruption, Italy. Quaternary Science Review, 25(21-22): 2713-2728.

Quero, A. S.
(1998) El Vano, Venezuela: El Jobo Traditions in a Megathere Kill Site. Current Research in the Pleistocen, Vol. 15, Corvallis, OR.

Rapp, George and Christopher L.
(2006) Geoarchaeology – The Earth-Science Approch to Archaeological Interpretation. Yale University Press, New Haven, CT.

Redman, C. L.
(1999) Human Impact on Ancient Environments. University of Arizona Press, Tucson, AZ.

Reeder, Leslie A., Torben C. Rick, and Jon M. Erlandson
(2008) Forty Years Later: What Have We Learned about the Earliest Human Occupations of Santa Rose Island, California? North American Archaeologist, Vol. 29, No. 1, pp. 37-64.

Reidle, M., T. Kivisild, E. Metspalu, K. Kaldma, K. Tambets, H. Tolk, J. Parik, E. Loogvali. M. Derenko, B. Malyarchuck, M. Bremishevam S. Zhadanov, E. Pennarun, M. Gubina, M. Chaventre, E. Khusnutdinova, L. Osipova, V. Stepanov, M. Voevoda, A. Achilli, C. Rengo, O. Richards, G. De Stefano, S, Papiha, L. Beckman. B. Janicijevic, P. Rundan, N. Anagnou, E. Michalodimitrakis, S. Koziel, E. Usanga, T. Geberhiwot, C. Herrnstadt, N. Howell, A. Torrini, and R. Villems
(2003) Origin and Diffusion on meDNA Haplogroup X. American Journal of Human Genetics, Vol. 73, pp. 1178-90.

Renfrew, C.
(1973) The Explanation of Culture Change: Models in Prehistory. Duckworth, London, UK.

Report
(2002) Abrupt Climate Change: Inevitable Surprises. Sponsors: Ocean Studies Board (OSB), Polar Research Board (PRB), Board on Atmospheric Sciences and Climate (BASC), and Earth and Life Studies (ELS). National Research Council, National Academy Press, Washington, DC.

Retallack, Gregory
(2007) Paleosols. In: Handbook of Paleoanthropology, pp 383-408. Springer, New York, NY.

Richardson, J. B.
(1998) Looking in the Right Places: Pre-5000 BP Maritime Adaptations in Peru and the Changing Environment. Revista de Arqueologia Americana, Vol. 15, pp. 33-56.

Richarson, Peter J. and Robert Boyd
(2005) Not by Genes Alone. University of Chicago Press, Chicago, IL.

Rick, John W.
(1996) Projectile Points, Style, and Social Process in Peru. In: Stone Tools – Theoratical Insights into Human Prehistory, G. Odell, ed. Pp. 245-278, Plenum Press, New York, NY.

Rick, Torben C. and Jon M. Erlandson (eds.)
(2008) Human Impacts on Ancient Maine Ecosystems – A Global Prespective. University of California Press, Berkely, CA..

Rivet, P.
(1943) Les Origines de Phomme American. L'Arbre, Montreal, Canada.

Robinson IV, Francis W.
(2011) The Thurman Station Site: A Probable Late Paleoindian Ceremonial Artifact Deposit in the Lake George Region of New York. Archaeology of Eastern North America, Vol. 39, pp. 67-92.

Roberts, Frank H. H., Jr.
(1943) A New Site. American Antiquity, Vol. 8, No. 3, p. 300.
(1951) The Early Americans. Scientific American, Vol. 184, No. 2, pp.15-19.
(1937) New World Man. American Antiquity, Vol. 12, No. 2, pp. 172-177.

Roger, Malcolm J.
(1930) Preliminary Report of Archaeological Work on Pacific Coast Shell-Middens During 1929. MS on file, San Diego Museum of Man, Scientic Library.
(1929) The Stone Art of the San Dieguito Plateau. American Anthropology, Vol. 31, pp. 454-467.

Rogers, David Banks
(1929) Prehistoric Man of the Santa Barbara Coast. Santa Barbara Museum, CA.

Rogers, R. A., L. A. Rogers, and L. D. Martin
(1992) How the Door Opened: The Peopling of the New World. Human Biology, Vol. 64, No.3, pp.:281-302.

Roosevelt, A. C., John Douglas, and Linda Brown
(2002) The Migration and Adaptations of the First Americans – Clovis and Pre-Clovis Viewed from South America. In: The First American, ed. Nina Jablonski, Memoirs of the California Academy of Science, No. 27, pp. 159-235.

Rong, Haisheng, Richard Jones, Ansheng Liu, Oded Cohen, Dani Hak, Alexander Fang and Mario Paniccia
(2005) A Continuous-Wave Raman Silicon Laser. Nature, Vol. 433, pp. 725-728.

Rosen, Steven A.
(1997) Lithic afterbthe Stone Age. AltaMira, Walnut Creek, CA.

Rots, Veerle
(2004) Prehensile Wear on Flint Tools. Lithic Technology, Vol. 29, No. 1, pp. 7-32.

Rouse, Irving
(1976) Peopling of the Americas. Quarternary Research, Vol. 6, pp. 567-612

Rousse, S., C. Kissel, C. Laj, J. Eiríksson, and K. L. Knudsen
(2006) Holocene centennial to millennial-scale climatic variability: Evidence from high-resolution magnetic analyses of the last 10 cal kyr off North Iceland (core MD99-2275). Earth and Planetary Science Letters, Vol. 242, Nos. 3-4, pp. 390-405.

Royo y Gomez, Jose
(1960) Venezuela Note. Society of Vert. Paleon, News Bul., Vol. 58, pp. 31-32.

Ruddimate, William F.
(2007) Earth's Climate – Past and Future (2nd edition) W. H. Freemam and Company, New York, NY.

Ruspoli, Mario
(1986) The Cave of Lascaux. Harry N. Abrams, Publishers, New York, NY.

Ruhlen, Merritt
(1984) The Origin of Language: Tracing the Evolution of the Mother Tongue. John Wiley & Sons, Hoboken, NJ.

Russell, I. C.
(1885) The Geologic History of Lake Lahontan. Monograph, No. 11, U.S. Geological Survey

Rutherford, A.A., J. Wittenberg, and R. Wilmeth
(1981) University of Saskatchewan Radiocarbon Dates IX. Radiocarbon, Vol. 23, No. 1, pp. 94-135.

Saltzman, Barry
(2002) Dynamical Paleoclimatology. Academic Press, New York, NY.

Santos F. R., et al.
(1999) The Central Siberian Origin for Native American Y-chromosomes. American Journal of Human Genetics 64, pp. 619-628.

Santos, G. M., M. I. Bird, F. Parenti, L. K. Fifield, N. Guidon, and P. A. Hausladen
(2003) A Revised Chronology of the Lowest Occupation Layer of Pedra Furada Rock Shelter, Piaui, Brazil: the Pleistocene Peopling of the Americas. Quaternary Sciences Reviews, Vol. 22, Iss. 21-22, pp. 2303-2310.

Sarnthein, Michael, Thorsten Kiefer, Pieter M. Grootes, Henry Elderfield, and Helmut Erlenkeuser
(2006) Warmings in the Far Northwestern Pacific Promoted pre-Clovis Immigration to America During Heinrich Event 1. Geology, Vol. 34, No. 3, pp. 141-144.

Sauer, Carl P.
(1944) A Geographic Sketch of Early Man in America. Geographic Review, Vol. 34, pp. 529-573.

Schofield, A. J.
(1995) Lithic in Context. Lithic Studies Society Occasional Paper No. 5, London, Eng.

Schulz, Michael and Andre Paul
(2002) Holocene Climate Variability on Centennial-to-Millennial Time Scales: Climate Records from the North-Atlantic Realm. In: Climate Development and History of the North Atlantic Realm, Berger and Jansen (eds.), Springer Books, Heidelberg, Ger.

Sellards, E. H.
(1952) Early Man in America, University of Texas Press, Austin, TX.
(1917) On the Association of Human Remains and Extinct Vertebrates at Vero, Florida. Journal of Geology, Vol. 25, pp. 4-24.
(1916) Human Remains and Associated Fossils from the Pleistocene of Florida. Florida Geological Survey, 8th Annula Report, pp. 123-160, Tallahassee, FL.

Semenov, S. A.
(1964) Prehistoric Technology. Cory, Adems & Mackay, London, Eng.

Service, E. R.
(1966) The Hunters. Prentice-Hall, Englewood Cliffs, NJ.

Shafer, Harry J. and Thomas R. Hester
(1983) Ancient Maya Chert Workshps in Northern Belize. Central America. American Antiquity, Vol. 48, No. 3, pp. 519-543.

Shlemon, Roy J. and Fred E. Budinger
(1990) The Archaeological Geology of the Calico Site, Mojave Desert, California. In: Lasca P. and J. Donahue, eds, pp. 301-313, Archaeological Geology on North America. Centennial Special, Vol. 4, Geological Society of America, Boulder, CO.

Shiner, Joel L.
(1961) The McNary Reservoir: A Study in Plateau Archeology. River Basin Surveys Papers, No. 23, Bul. 179, Smithsonian Institution, Washington, DC.

Shippee, J. Mott
(1948) Nebo Hill, A Lithic Complex in Western Missouri. American Antiquity, Vol. 14, No. 1.

Short, John T.
(1882) The North Americans of Antiquity. Harper & Brothers, Publishers, New York, NY.

Shaffer, Brian S. and Barry W. Baker
(1997) How Many Epidermal Ridges per Linear Centimeter? Comments on Possible Pre-Clovis HumanFriction Skin Prints from Pendejo Cave. American Antiquity, Vol. 62, No. 3, pp. 559-560.

Shennan, Stephen
(1988) Quantifying Archaeology. University of Iowa Press, Iowa City, IA.

Shott, Michael J.
(2007) The Role of Reduction Analysis in Lithic Studies. Lithic Technology, Vol. 32, No. 1, pp. 131-142.
(2007) Chaine Operatoire Reduction Sequence. Lithic Technology, Vol. 32, No. 2, pp. 95-106.
(1993) The Leavitt Site – A Parkhill Phase Paleo-Indian Occupation in Central Michigan. Memoirs of the Museum of Anthropology, No. 25, University of Michigan, Ann Arbor, MI.

Short, John T.
(1882) The North Americans of Antiquity. Harper & Brothers, Publishers, New York, NY.

Shutler, Richard Jr. (ed.)
(1983) Early Man in the New World. Sage Publication, Beverly Hills, CA.

Siegert, M. J.
(2001) Ice Sheets and Late Quarternary Environmental Change. John Wiley and Sons, New York, NY.

Simpson, Ruth D.
(1978) The Calico Mountains Archaeological Site. In: Early Man in America from a Circum-Pacific Perspective, ed A Bryan, pp.. Occasional Paper 1, pp. 218-220, Department of Anthropology, University of Alberta, Archaeological Researches International, Edmonton, Can.
(1960) Archaeological Survey of the Eastern Calico Mountains. Masterkey, Vol. 34, No. 1, pp. 25-35.

Simpson, Ruth D., Leland W. Patterson, and Clay A. Singer
(1986) Lithic Technology of the Calico Mountains Site, Southern California. In: New Evidence for the Pleistocene Peopling of the Americas, Bryan ed., Center for the Study of Early Man, University of Maine, Orono, ME.

Smallwood, Ashley M. and Albert C. Goodyear
(2009) Reworked Clovis Biface Distal Fragments from the Topper Site, 38AI23: Implications for Clovis Technological Organization in the Central Savannah River Region. Current Research in the Pleistocene, Vol. 26, pp. 118-120.

Smith, Carlyle, S. and Roger T. Grange
(1958) The Spain Site (39LM301), a Winter Village in Fort Randall Reservoir, South Dakota. River Basin Surveys Papers, No. 11, Bul. 169, Smithsonian Institution, Washington, DC.

Smith, Kevin E. and Michael C. Moore
(1999) Through Many Mississippian Hands: Late Prehistoric Exchange in the Middle Cumberland Valley. In: Raw Materials and Exchange in the Mid-South, E. Peacock and S. Brooks, eds, pp. 95-115, Archaeological Report No. 29, Mississippi Department of Archives and History, Jackson, MS.

Smith, E. L. Philip
(1972) The Solutrean Culture. In: Old World Archaeology – Foundations of Civilization, Readings from Scientic American, W. H. Freeman and Compant, San Francisco, CA.
(1962) Upper Paleolithic France, Solutrean. Dissertation, Harvard University, Boston, MA.

Smith, Julian
(2011) Polynesian Contact? American Archaeology, Vol. 15, No. 3, pp. 38-43.

Smith, P. E. L.
(1964) The Solutrean Culture. Scientific American, Vol. 112, No. 2, pp. 86-94.

Soffer, Olga and N. D. Praslov (eds.)
(1993) From Kopstenki to Clovis – Upper Paleolithic-Paleo-Indian Adaptations..Plenum Press, New York, NY.

Sollas, W. J.
(1924) Ancient Hunters. London, UK.

Sondaar, P. Y., G. D. Van Denbergh, B. Mubroto, F. Aziz, J. De Vos and U. L. Batu
(1994) Middle Pleistocene faunal turnover and colonization of Flores (Indonesia) by Homo erectus. Comptes Rendus de l'Academie des Sciences Paris 319: 1255-62.

Sorensen, Mikkel and Pierre Desrosiers (eds.)
(2008) Technology in Archaeology. National Museum Studies in Archaeology & History, Vol. 14, Copenhagen.

Soressi, Marie and Harold L. Dibble (eds.)
(2003) Multiple Approches to the Study of Bifacial Technologies. University of Pennsylvania Museum of Archaeology and Anthropology,Philadephia, PA.

Spiess, Arthur and Deborah Brush Wilson
(1987) Michaud – A Paleoindian Site in the New England – Maritime Region. Ocassional Publications in Maine Archaeology, No. 6, Maine Historic Preservation Commission, Augusta, ME.

Stanford, Dennis
(2018) The Point of the Story. In: Kennewick Man, eds. Owsley and Jantz, Texas A& Press, Collecge Station, TX.
(2012) Personal communication, Smithsonian, Washington, DC.
(2011) Origins of the First Americans: New Discoveries in the Chesapeake Basin. Paper given: Friends of Fairfax Archaeology Spring Symposium, Falls Church, VA.
(1999) Paleoindian Archaeology and Late Pleistocene Environments in the Plains and Southwestern United States. In *Ice Age People of North America*. Edited by Robson Bonnichsen and Karen Turnmire, pp. 281-339. Oregon State University Press, Corvallis, OR.

Stanford, Dennis and Bruce Bradley
(2012a) Across Atlantic Ice: The Origin of America's Clovis Culture. University of California Press, Los Angeles, CA.
(2012b) Special Lecture: Coming to North America. Smithsonian Associates, Smithsonian Institution, Washington, DC.
(2005) Clovis in the Southeast Conference, Southeastern Paleoamerican Survey, October 26, 29, Columbia, SC.

(2004a) America's Stone Age Explorers. PBS Broadcast, Date: November 9, 2004.
(2004b) The North Atlantic Ice-Edge Corridor: A Possible Paleolithic Route into the New World. World Archaeology, Vol. 36, No. 4, pp. 459-478.
(2004) Ocean Trails and Prairie Paths? Thoughts about Clovis Origins. In: The First Americans: The Pleistocene Colonization of the New World, ed. N. Jablonski, Memoirs of the California Academy of Sciences, Vol. 27, pp. 255-71.
(2002) Ocean Trails and Prairie Paths? Thoughts about Clovis Origins. In: The First Americans: the Pleistocen Colonization of the New World, N. Jablonski, ed., pp. 255-271, Memoir of the California Academy of Sciences, No. 27, San Francisco, CA.
(2000) The Solutrean Solution. Scientific American Discovering Archaeology, Vol. 2, pp. 54-55.

Stanford, Dennis, Darrin Lowery, Margaret Jodry, Bruce Bradley, Marvin Key, Tom Stafford, and Robert Speakman
(2011) New Evidence for the Paleolithic Occupation of the Eastern North American Outer Continental Shelf at the Last Gacial Maximun. To be published.

Straight, Melanie J.
(1990) Archaeological Sites in the North America Continental Shelf. In: Lasca P. and J. Donahue, eds, pp. 439-465, Archaeological Geology on North America. Centennial Special, Vol. 4, Geological Society of America, Boulder, CO.

Steele, D. Gentry and Joseph F. Powell
(2002) Facing the Past: A View of the North American Human Fossil Record. In: The First Americans. Memoirs of the California Academy of Sciences, Jablonski ed., No. 27, San Francisco, CA.

Steward, Julian H.
(1937) Ancient Caves of the Great Salt Lake Region. Bulletin, Bureau of American Ethnology, No. 116.

Stewart, Tamara Jager
(2018) Of Mastodons and Men. American Archaeology, Vol. 22, No. 3, pp. 40-45.

Stewart, T. Dale
(1960) A Physical Anthropologist's View of the Peopling of the New World. Southwestern Journal of Anthropology, Vol. 16, No. 3.

Stix, Gary
(2008) Traces of a Distant Past. Scientific American, Vol. 299, No. 1, pp. 56-63.

Strasser, T., E. Panagopoulou, C. Runnel, P. Murray, N. Thompson, P. Karkana, F. McCoy, and K. Wegmann
(2010) Stoneage Age Seafaring in the Mediterrannean Evidence from Plakias Region for Lower Paleolithic and Mesolithic Habitation of Crete. Hesperia, Vol. 79, pp. 145-90.

Straus, Lawrence Guy
(2011) Has the Notion of Transition in Paleolithic Prehistory Outlived Its Usefulness? The European Record in Wider Context. In: Sourcebook of Paleolithic Transitions, eds. M. Camps and P. Chauhan, Springer, New York, NY.
(1993) Saint-Cesaire and the Debate on the Transition from the Middle to Upper Paleolithic. In: Context of a Late Neanderthal, ed. F. Leveque, et al., Monographs in World History, No. 16, Prehistory Press, Madison, WI.
(1977) Thoughts on Solutrean Concave Base Point Distribution. Lithic Technology, Vol. 6, pp. 32-35.

Straus, L. G. and G. A. Clark (eds.)
(1986) La Riera Cave: Stone Age Hunter-Gatherer Adaptation in Northern Spain. Arizona State University Anthropological Research Papers, No. 36, Tempe, AZ.

Straus, L., F. Bernaldo Dequiros, V. Cabrera, and G. Clark
(1978) Solutrean Chronology and Lithic Variability. Zephyrus, Vol. 28-29, pp. 109-112.

Straus, L. G. and O. Bar-Yosef
(2001) Out of Africa in the Pleistocene: An Introduction. Quaternary International, Vol. 75, No. 1, pp.1-3.

Strauss, Alan E. and O. Don Hermes
(1996) Anatomy of a Rhyolite Quarry. Archaeology of Eastern North America, Vol. 24, pp. 159-172.

Straus, Lawerence Guy, David J. Melzter, and Ted Goebel
(2005) Ice Age Atlantis? Exploring the Solutrean-Clovis "Connection." World Archaeology, Vol. 37, No. 4, pp. 507-532.

Stewart, R. Michael
(1987) Rhyolite Quarry and Quarry-Related Sites in Maryland and Pennsylvania. Archaeology of Eastern North American, Vol. 15, pp. 47-58.
(1986) Lister Site (28Mel-), Data Recovery.Trenton Complex Archaeology: Report 6, Louis Berger & Associates, East Orange, NJ.

Suarez, Rafael
(2009) Unifacial Fishtail Points: Consideration About the Archaeological Record on Paleo South Americans. Current Research in the Pleistocene, Vol. 26, pp. 12-15.

Stumpf, Michael P. H. and David B. Goldstein
(2001) Genelogical and Evolutionary Inference with the Human Y Chromosome. Science, Vol. 291, No. 5509, pp. 1738-1728.

Surovell, Todd A.
(2012) Toward a Behavioural Ecology of Lithic Technology.University of Arizonia Press, Tucson, AZ.

Surovell, Todd, Nicole Waguespack, and P. Jeffrey Brantingham
(2005) Gobal Archaeological Evidence for Proboscidean Overkill. PNAS., Vol. 102, No. 17, 6231-6236.

Svoboda, Jiri A. and Olfer Bar-Yosef, eds.
(2003) Stranska skala – Origins of the Upper Paleolithic in the Brno Basin, Moravia, Chech Republic. Dolni Vestonice Studies, Vol. 10, Peabody Museum, Harvard University, Cambridge, MA.

Sykes, Bryan (ed.)
(1999) The Human Inheritance, Genes, Language, and Evolution. Oxford University Press, Oxford, UK.

Tankersley, Kenneth
(2002) In Search of Ice Age Americans. Gibbs Smith, Publisher, Salt Lake City, UT.

Tallerman, Maggie (ed.)
(2005) Language Origins: Perspectives on Evolution. Oxford University Press, Oxford, UK.

Tattersall, Ian
(2009) The fosil Trail. Oxford University Press, Oxford, UK.

Tattersall, Ian, Eric Delson, and John Van Couvering (eds.)
(1988) Encylopedia of Human Evolution and History. Garland Publishing, New York and London.

Templeton, A.
(2002) Out of Africa Again and Again. Nature, Vol. 416, pp. 45-51.

Theler, James L. and Robert F. Boszhart
(2003) Twelve Millennia – Archaeology of the Upper Mississippi River Valley. University of Iowa Press, Iowa City, IA.

Thompson, Jessica C., Nawa Sugiyana, and Gray S. Morgan
(2008) Taphonomic Analysis of the Mammalian Fauna from Sandia Cave, New mexico and the Sandia Man Controversy. American Antiquity, Vol. 73, No. 2, pp. 337-360.

Thulman, David K.
(2009) Freshwater Availability as the Constraining Factor in the Middle Paleoindian Occupation of North-Central Florida. Geoarchaeology: An International Journal. Vol. 24, No. 3, pp. 243-276.

Toggweiler, J. R. and Joellen Russell
(2008) Ocean Circulation in a Warming Climate. Nature, Vol. 45, pp. 286-288.

Tolstoy, Paul
(1958) The Archaeology of the Lena Basin and its New World Relationships, pts I and II. American Antiquity, Vol. 23, No. 4, pp. 397-418 and Vol. 24, No. 1, pp. 63-81.

Torben C. Rick, Jon M. Erlandson and René L. Vellanoweth
(2001) Paleocoastal Marine Fishing on the Pacific Coast of the Americas: Perspectives from Daisy Cave, California. American Antiquity, Vol. 66, No. 4, pp. 595-613.

Tixier, J.
(1961) Les Pieces Pedoncules de L'Aterian, Libya, pp. 6-7.

Treat, Ida
(1931) Sailing Forbidden Waters. National Geographic Magazine, Vol. LX, No. 3, pp. 357-386, Washington, DC.

Trustees of the British Museum
(1956) Flint Implements. Published by the Trustees of the British Museum, London, Eng.

Tryon, Christian, Sally McBrearty, and Pierre-Jean Texier
(2005) Levallous Lithic Technology from the Kapthurin Formation, Kenya: Acheulian Origin and Middle Stone Age Diversity. African Archaeological Review, Vol. 22, No. 4, pp. 199-229.

Turner, Christy G.
(2002) Teeth, Needles, Dogs, and Siberia: Bioarchaeological Evidence for the Colonization of the New World. In: The First Americans. Memoirs of the California Academy of Sciences, Jablonski ed., No. 27, San Francisco, CA.
U.S. Forest Service
(2012) Website: http://www.fs.fed.us/r10/tongass/forest_facts/resources/heritage/onyourknees.shtml

Van Peer, Philip
(1992) The Levallois Reduction Strategy. Monographs in World Archaeology, Prehistory Press, Madison, WI.

Vegnati, M. A.
(1927) Arquelogia y Antropologia de los Conchales Fuetinos. Revista del Museo de la Plata, Vol. 30, pp. 70-143.

Vento, F.J., H.B. Rollins, A. Vega, J.M. Adovasio, P. Stahlman, D.B. Madsen, and J.S. Illingworth
(2008) Development of a Late Pleistocene-Holocene Genetic Stratigraphic Framework for the Mid-Atlantic Region: Implications in Archaeology. Paper presented at the 73rd Annual Meeting of the Society for American Archaeology, Vancouver, BC.

Vertes, L.
(1964) Tata-Eine Mittelpalaolithische Travertinsiedlung in Ungarin. Archeologia Hungarica 43. Budapest: Akademiai Kiado.
(1955) Neure Ausgrabungen und Palaolithische Funde in der Hohle von Istallosko. Acta Archaeologica Academiae Scientiarum Hungaricae, Vol. 3/4 pp. 111-131.

Veth, Peter
(2011) The Dispersal of Modern Humans into Australia. In: The Upper Paleolithic Revolution in Global Perspective, K. Boyle, C. Gamble, and O. Bar-Yosef, eds., MacDonald Institue Monographs, University of Cambridge, Cambridge, UK.

Wadley, Lyn
(2010) The Effect of Organic Preservation on Behavioural Interpretation at the South African Stone Age Sites of Rose Cottage and Sibudu. In: The Upper Paleolithic Revolution in Global Perspective, K. Boyle, C. Gamble, and O. Bar-Yosef, eds., MacDonald Institue Monographs, University of Cambridge, Cambridge, UK.

Walker, Elizabeth A., Francis Wenban-Smith, and Frances Healy (eds.)
(2000) Lithic in Action. Oxbow Books, Lithic Studies Society, Occasional Paper No. 4, Oxford.

Wagner, Friederike, J. Sjoerd, P. Bohncke, David L. Dilcher, Wolfram M. Kürschner, Bas van Geel, and Henk Visscher
(1999) Century-Scale Shifts in Early Holocene Atmospheric CO_2 Concentration. Science, Vol. 284, No. 5422, pp. 1971-1973.

Waguespack, Nicole M. and Todd A. Surovell
(2003) Clovis Hunting Strategies, or How to Make Out on Plentiful Resources. American Antiquity, Vol. 68, No. 2, pp. 333-252.

Walker, Elizabeth A., Francis Wenban-Smith, and Frances Healy
(2004) Lithics in Action, Lithic Studies Society, Occasional Paper No. 8, Oxbow Books, Oxford, UK.

Walker, Renee B. and Boyce N. Driskell (eds.)
(2007) Foragers of the Terminal Pleistocene in North America. University of Nebraska Press, Lincoln, NE.

Wall, Jeffrey D. and Molly Przeworki
(2000) When Did the Human Population Size Start Increasing? Genetics (155) pp. 1865-1874.

Warren, C. N., Alan L. Bryan, and Donald R. Tuohy
(1963) The Galdendale Site and Its Place in Plateau Prehistory. Tegiwa, Vol. 6, No. 1, pp. 1-21.

Waselkov, G. A.
(1987) Shelfish Gathering and Shell Midden Archaeology. Archaeological Method and Theory, Vol. 10, pp. 93-210.

Watanake, S., Feria Ayta, Guidon Hamaguchi, Maranca La Salvia, and Baffer Filho
(2003) Some Evidence of a Date of First Humans to Arrive in Brazil. Journal of Archaeological Science, Vol. 30, pp. 351-354.

Waters, Mickael
(2012) The Emerging Archaeological Pattern in North America from 13,000 to 15,000 cal yr. B.P. – A viewpoint from the the Debra L. Friendkin Site, Texas and Manis Site in Washington. Paper: Society for American Archaeology Annual Meeting, Memphis, TN.

Waters, Michael R., Charlotte, D. Pevny, and David L. Carlson
(2011) Clovis Lithic Technology. Texas A&M Press, College Station, TX.

Waters, Michael R., and Thomas W. Stafford, Jr.
(2007) Redefining the Age of Clovis: Implications for the Peopling of the Americas. Science, Vol. 315, No. 5815, pp. 1122-1126.

Waters, Michael R., Thomas W. Stafford, Jr., H. Gregory McDonald, Carl Gustafson, Morten Rasmussen, Enrico Cappellini, Jesper V. Olsen, Damian Szklarczyk, Lars Juhl Jensen, M. Thomas P. Gilbert, and Eske Willerslev
(2010) Pre-Clovis Mastodon Hunting 13,800 Years Ago at the Manis Site, Washington. Science, Vol. 334, No. 6054, pp. 351-353.

Watson, William
(1960) Archaeology in China. Max Parrish, London, UK.

Waters, M.R., Forman, S.L. Jennings, T.A., Nordt, L.C., Driese, S.G., Feinberg, J.M., Keene, J.L., Halligan, J., Lindquist, A., Pierson, J., Hallmark, C.T., Collins, M.B., and Wiederhold, J.E.
(2011) The Buttermilk Creek complex and the origins of Clovis at the Debra L. Friedkin Site, Texas. Science, Vol. 331, pp.1599-1603.

Weaver, Kenneth F.
(1985) The Search for Our Ancestors. National Geographic, Vol. 168, No. 5, pp. 560-623.

Weaver, Timothy D. and Charles C. Roseman
(2008) New Developments in Genetic Evidence for Modern Human Origina. Evolutionary Anthropology, Vol. 17, pp. 69-80.

Webb, S.G.
(2006) The First Boat People. Cambridge Studies in Biological and Evolutionary Anthropology, Vol. 47, Cambridge University Press.

Weedman, Kathryn J.
(2002) On the Spur on the Moment: Effects of Age and Experience on Hafted Stone Scraper Morphology. American Antiquity, Vol. 67, pp. 731-744.

Wells, Spencer
(2010) Pandora's Seed. Random House, New York, NY.
(2007) Deep Ancestry – Inside the Genographic Project. National Geographic, Washington, DC.
(2003) The Journey of Man. Random House, New York, NY.

Wendorf, Fred
(1966) Early Man in the New World: problems of migration. American Naturalist, Vol. 100, pp. 253-270.
(1961) Paleoecology of the Llano Estacado, publication No. 1, Fort Burgwin Research Center, Inc., Museum of New Mexico Press, Santa Fe, NM.

Wendorf, F. A., A. D. Krieger, C. C. Albritton, and T. Dale Stewart
(1955) The Midland Discovery: A Report of the Pleistocen Human Remains from Midland, Texas. University of Texas Press, Austin, TX.

Wendorf, Fred and James J. Hester
(1962) Early Man's Utilization of the Great Plains Environment. American Antiquity, Vol. 28, No. 2, pp. 159-171.

West, Frederick H., ed.
(1969) American Beginnings. University of Chicago Press, Chicago, IL.

Westfall, Tom
(2011) A Keosho Knife from the South Platte River. Central States Archaeological Journal, Vol. 58, No. 2, p. 81.

Westley, K. L. C., and J. K. Dix
(2006) Coastal Environments and Their Role in Prehistoric Migrations. Journal of Maritime Archaeology Vol.1, No. 1, pp. 1-20.

Wheat, Amber, D.
(2012) Survey of Professional Opinions Regarding the Peopling of the Americas. The Archaeological Record, Vol. 12, No. 2, pp. 10-14.

Wheat, Joe Ben
(1953) An Archeological Survey of the Addicks Dam Basin, Southeast Texas. River Basin Surveys Papers, No. 4, Bul. 154, Smithsonian Institution, Washington, DC.

White, J. Peter and James F. O'Connell
(1982) A Prehistory of Australia, New Guinea, and Sahul. Academic Press, New York, NY.

Whitehead, Donald R.
(1972) Developmental and Environmental History of the Dismal Swamp. Ecological Monographs, Vol. 42, No. 3, pp. 310-315.

Whitmore, Frank C., K. O. Emery, H. B. S. Cooke, and Donald J. P. Swift
(1967) Elephant Teeth from the Atlantic Continental Shelf. Science, Vol. 156, No. 3781, pp. 1477-1481.

Wild, Eva M., Maria Teschler-Nicola, Walter Kutschera, Peter Steir, Erik Trinkaus, and Wolfgang Wanel
(2005) Direct Dating of Early Upper Palaeolithic Human Remains from Mlade. Nature, Vol. 435, pp. 332-335.

Williams, Stephen
(1957) The Island 35 Mastodon: Its Bearing on the Age of Archaic Cultures in the East. American Antiquity, Vol. 22, No. 4, Pt. 1, pp. 359-372.

Wilson, Thomas
(1899) Arrowpoints, Spearheads, and Knives of Prehistoric Times. Rep. U. S. National Museum 1897, Pt. 1, pp. 811-988.
Willey, Gordon R.
(1971) An Introduction to American Archaeology, Volume Two – South America. Prentice-Hall, Inc., Englewood Cliffs, NJ.

Willoughby, Pamela R.
(2007) The Evolution of Modern Humans in Africa: A Comprehensive Guide. AltaMira Press, Lanham, MD.

Wong, Kate
(2012) First of Our Kind. Scientic American, Vol. 306, No. 4, pp. 30-39.

Wormington, H. Marie
(1963) The Paleo-Indian and Meso-Stages of Alberta, Canada. Anthropological Papers of the University of Alaska – Early Man in the Western American Artic – A Symposium, Vol. 10, No. 2, pp. 107-114.
(1962) A Survey of Early American Prehistory. American Scientist, Vol. 50, No. 1, pp. 230-242.
(1957) Ancient Man in North America. Denver Museum of Natural History, Popular Series 4.

Wright, George F.
(1892) Man and the Glacial Period. D. Appleton and Company, New York, NY.

Wyckoff, Don G., James L. Theler, and Brian J. Carter (eds.)
(2004) The Burnham Site in Northwestern Oklahoma: Glimpses Beyond Clovis? Sam Noble Oklahoma Museum of Natural History, University of Oklahoma and the Oklahoma Anthropological Society, Memoir 9.

Wylie, Alison
(2002) Thinking from Things – Essays in the Philosophy of Archaeology. University of California Press, Berkeley, CA.

Wylie, Poag C.
(1978) Stratigraphy of the Atlantic Continental Shelf and Slope of the United States. Annual Review of Earth and Planetary Sciences, Vol. 6, p.251.

Wymer, J.
(1982) The Palaeolithic Age. St. Martin's Press, New York, NY.

Yamaoka, Takuya
(2009) Broken Projectile Points from Mattobara, and Leaf-Shaped Points Assemblages During the Late Upper Paleolithic in Japan. Current Research in the Pleistocen, Vol. 26, pp. 27-30.

Yesner, David R.
(1987) Life in the Garden of Eden: Constraints of Maritime Diets for Human Societies. In: Food and Evolution, ed., M. Harris, pp. 285-310, Temple University Press, Philadelphis, PA.
(1984) Population Pressure in Coastal Environments: An Archaeological Test. World Archaeology, Vol. 16, pp. 108-127.

Zakhariov, A.
(1999) Indmiustrii s Bifasami i Perekhod ot Mustie k Pozdnemy Paleolitu v Evopie. Arkbeologicheski Almananakb, Vol. 8, pp. 197-206.
(1999) Industries with Bifaces and the Middle to Upper Paleolithic Transmission in Europe. Arkheologichesky Almanackh (Donetsk), Vol. 8, pp. 197-206.

Zarikian, Carlos, A. Alvarez, Peter Swart, John Gifford, and Patricia
(2005) Holocene Paleohydrology of Litter Salt Spring, Floriad, Based on Ostracod Assemblages and Stable Isotopes. Palaeography, Palaeoclimatology, Palaeoecology, Vol. 225, pp. 134-156.

Zhong, Hua, Hong Shi, Xue-Bin Qi, Chun-Jie Xiao, Li Jin, Runlin Z Ma and Bing Su
(2010) Global distribution of Y-chromosome haplogroup C reveals the prehistoric migration routes of African exodus and early settlement in East Asia. Journal of Human Genetics, Vol. 55, pp. 428-435.

Zimmer, Carl
(2005) Smithsonian Intimate Guide to Human origins. Smithsonian Books, Madison Press Books, New York, NY.

Zorich, Zack
(2018) A long was to eat rhino. Archaeology, Vol. 71, No. 5, p. 22.

Index

14th Street Bipoint, 106
44FK731, 111
Acheulian era, 173
Adena, 58, 129
Adena Culture, 141
Africa, 56, 217
Africa bipoint, 189
African Factor, 182
African points, 172
African routes, 83
African source, 182
Agate Basin, 43
Alabama, 64, 157
Alaska, 70, 75, 86
Andean Bipoints, 219
Anderson bipoint, 194
Antholithic form, 8
Archaic Period, 260
Arkansas, 161
Artform, 22
Artifact, 16
Asia, 70, 187
Asian Factor, 187
Asymmetrical method, 224
Aterian bipoints, 184
Aterian example, 171
Aterian legacy, 80
Aterian tanged tool, 183
Aterians, 71, 168
Atlantic coast, 72
Atlantic coastal area, 77
Atlantic Maritime, 78
Atlantic seaboard, 68, 70
Australia, 188
Aztec, 164
Baja California, 164
Base, 8
Basic Bipoint, 18
Basic design, 31
Basic model, 48
Beavertails, 58
Before Clovis, 1, 67
Before Clovis dates, 67
Belize, 218
Biconvex, 221
Biface bipoint, 240
Biface tools, 40
Bifaces, 9
Bifacially or unifacially flaked, 61
Bipoint, 1, 8, 51, 166
Bipoint Axis, 13
Bipoint chronology, 169
Bipoint continuum, 145
Bipoint Cortex, 29
Bipoint culture areas, 72
Bipoint Dart, 9
Bipoint definition, 19
Bipoint definition, 20
Bipoint era, 61
Bipoint factors, xi
Bipoint knives, 236
Bipoint Legacy Model, 41

Bipoint material, 237
Bipoint mechanics, 220
Bipoint Mechanics, 220
Bipoint model, 12, 221
Bipoint Model, 12
Bipoint morphology, 221
Bipoint Morphology Model, 12, 13, 19, 220
Bipoint Origins, 173
Bipoint Patination, 197
Bipoint production, 220
Bipoint Resharpening, 61, 230
Bipoint Size, 235
Bipoint technology, 48, 68, 170
Bipoint technology, 33, 189
Bipoint/blade index, 25
Bipoints, 111
Bipolar method, 224
Bit end reduction, 39, 59
Bit modification, 231
Bit styles, 62
Blackwater Draw, 44
Blade, 7
Blade Bipoints, 34
Blade framework, 171
Blade tools, 40
Blademaking, 173
Blademaking, 186
Blombos Cave, 189
BMM, 13, 39, 59, 220
Bone bipoints, 237
Borneo, 188
Brazil, 217
British Columbia, 74
Burins, 71
Butchering, 235
Cactus Hill site, 67
California, 75, 149
Canada, 74, 162
Cascade Point, 74
Cascade type, 73, 151
Chaine operatoire approach, 60
Change, 67
Channel Island, 74, 149
Chassis (stem), 191
Chesapeake diamond, 53
Chesapeake Diamond, 243
Chile Bipoints, 219
China, 188
Chronology, 70
Cinmar, 202
Cinmar bipoint, 76, 199
Cinmar Bipoint, 202
Circum-Pacific, 167, 187
Circum-Pacific, 75
Circum-Pacific coastal area, 73
Class, 16
Classic Bipoint, 190
Classic Solutrean, 189
Classification, 40
Clovis, 1, 32, 40, 67, 68, 90, 97, 116, 168, 170, 178, 185, 190, 210, 211, 212, 217, 234, 245, 246, 276
Clovis and bipoints, 42

Clovis blade, 186
Clovis contexts, 42
Clovis lanceolates, 42
Clovis LWT, 24
Coastal Old World people, 78
Coastal vs. Inland technology, 39, 59
Cobble tools, 40
Colorado, 150
Columbia Cache, 93
Composite tool, 8
Connecticut, 124
Continental shelf, 75, 76, 194
Continuum, 40
Cordilleran Tradition, 73
Cross Creek, 74
Cross-face flaking, 19
Crowfield, 42
Cryptocrystalline materials, 20
Crystal pocket, 53, 163
Crystal pockets., 163
Crystal quartz, 237
Crystals, 163, 216
Cumberland, 219
Cutting edge, 62
Cutting leverage, 220
Cutting margin, 45
Danish daggers, 169
Dates, 68
Dates, 40, 67
Defining a bipoint, 18
Definition, 20
Delaware, 120
Diagonal Bipoint, 35
Diamond-shaped, 53
Diamond-shaped knife, 53
Dismal Swamp, 203
Distal end resharpening, 230
Distal/Proximal, 61
Distal-to-proximal curve, 222
Distal-to-proximal resharpening, 230
D-shaped cross section, 221
Dual workends, 53
Duck River Cache, 137
Duty function, 57
Early dates, 68
Early Man, 68
Eastern chronology, 68
Eastern Europe, 177
Economics, 55
El Cedral, 204
El Jobo, 217, 219
El Jobo bipoint, 82
El Jobo points, 172
Elliptical shape, 55
Elongate bipoint, 18
Eskimo, 78
Eskimos, 77
European plain, 176
European Solutrean, 33
Expended bipoint, 45, 51
Expended bipoints, 243
Expended forms, 45
Exploring inland, 76
Failed colonization, 68
First Americans, 66, 67

First artifact, 71
First principal tool, 7
Flake, 8
Florida, 58, 81, 86, 212, 240, 257
Florida bipoints, 212
Foliace, 175
Folsom, 43
Frank Andrew, 78
Ft Ancient, 124, 128, 129
Ft. Ancient, 257
Function, 7, 8
Functional axis, 11
Functor, 250
Georgia, 87, 91, 93, 257
Green Island bipoint, 194
Guilford type, 101
Hafting, 224, 238
Hafting area, 49
Hand-held knife, 54, 57
Heat treated, 157
Heavy duty function, 57
High-quality bipoints, 27
Human cognition, 250
Iberian bipoint, 190
Iberian curve, 232
Iberian Curve, 232
Idaho, 162
Ideological Interaction Sphere, 27
Illinois, 144, 167
Indented base, 19
Indiana, 133, 158
Indo-China, 188
Industry, 16
Infinite wedge, 19
Initial Manufactured Form, 15
Iowa, 144
Japan, 217
Java, 188
Kennewick Man, 74
Kennewick Man., 172
Kentucky, 54, 138, 139, 232
Knife, 51, 54
Knowledge base, 30
Labrador, 167
Landfall, 194
Landfall hypothesis, 210
Landfall Model, 178, 198
Large Cutting Tools, 234
Last stage resharpenings, 240
Late Archaic Period, 241
Lateral margins, 229
Lateral margins, 61
Lateral side resharpening, 230
Laurel leaf, 166
Laurel leaf classification, 168
Lcts, 234
Leaf-shaped knives, 167
Legacy, 8, 66
Legacy 1 and 2 bipoints, 230
Legacy Bipoint Definition, 40
Legacy implement, 170
Legacy resharpening, 62
Legacy Solutrean Tools, 181
Length-wise curve, 32
Lerma point, 124, 219

Lerma Point, 75
Levallois blades, 173
LGM, 186
Life cycle, 60
Lithic continuum, 7, 30
Lithic determinism, 41
Lithic materials, 7
Lithic sourcing, 107, 196
Louisiana, 242
Lupembans, 71, 168
LWT ratio, 25
Maccord Bipoint, 107
Magdalenian, 185
Magdalenian Factor, 185
Magdalenians, 71
Maine, 42
Maine discovery, 194
Maine specimens, 195
Maine to Florida occupation, 77
Mammoth bones, 212
Manufacturing, 31
Manufacturing process, 32
Manufacturing technique, 190
Maryland, 115
Maya, 164
Meadowcroft site, 67
Measurements, 25
Mega bifaces, 25
Mega bifaces, 234
Mexico, 46, 163
Michigan, 86
Middle Atlantic area, 78
Middle Atlantic coast, 178
Mississippi, 148
Missouri, 142
Mode, 221
Mode, 16
Model, 48
Monte Verde, 189
Morrow Mountain, 231, 260
Mounds, 144
Mousterian Factor, 175
Mousterian technology, 177
Mousterian-age burins, 71
Mousterians bipoints, 175
Neanderthalensis, 176
Nebraska, 150
Needle bipoint, 54
Nevada, 155
New Brunswick, 163
New Jersey, 121
New Mexico, 43, 159
New York, 123
Norfolk bipoint, 199
North America, 84
North America bipoints, 84
North Atlantic Ice, 77
North Carolina, 57, 97, 210
North Dakota, 150
Ohio, 129
Old World bit, 62
Old World connection, 166, 169
Old World microtool, 179
Oldovai Gorge, 169
Opequon Complex, 111

Opequon Creek, 111
Oregon, 53, 151
Outré passé, 87, 90, 116, 195
Ovate biface, 55
Ovate bipoint, 55, 83
Ovate form, 55
Overshot flaking, 190
Pacific coast, 72, 75, 81
Pacific Occupation, 73
Paleoamerican, 72
Parson's Island, 119
Pedra Furada, 82, 204
Pennsylvania, 53, 57, 124, 126
Pinnacle Point, 189
Popular bipoint name, 77
Ports-of-entry, 72
Pre-Clovis toolkits, 207
Primary legacy, 40
Projectile point, 191
Pure blade bipoints, 36
Pure Blade Bipoints, 37
Racloir, 81
Ratios, 25
Red ocher, 30, 71, 189
Resharpened specimens, 63
Resharpening, 39, 59, 191, 221, 230
Resharpening, 60
Resharpening Standards, 65
Rhode Island, 120
Rights cache, 210
Rights Cache, 210, 211
Round-bit bipoint, 257
Russia, 188
Saltville site, 67
Sandia point, 43
Sangoans, 71
Savannah River, 264
Secondary legacy, 40
Shouldered Bipoint, 114
Siberia's Paleolithic, 187
Side bit reduction, 39, 59
Social organization, 39, 59
Soft hammer percussion, 222
Solutrean, 20, 77
Solutrean argument, 190
Solutrean attributes, 169
Solutrean bipoints, 166
Solutrean factor, 182
Solutrean Factor, 177
Solutrean form, 191
Solutrean Hypothesis, 21, 207
Solutrean Technique, 178
Solutrean toolkit, 178
Solutrean tools, 180
Solutrean vs. Clovis, 170
Solutreans, 71, 168, 178
South America, 82, 217
South American, 217
South Carolina, 90
Southeastern Asia, 188
Spiro Mounds, 27
Stage, 15
Stage of resharpening, 60
Standard cutting implement, 7
State, 19, 221, 222

State, 15
State forms, 16
State-derived, 19
Status item, 191
Stem, 52
Stem (chassis), 8
Stemmed projectile point, 63
Stone continuum, 30
Striking force, 32
Striking platform, 31
Structor, 250
Structural Axis, 11
Structural definitions, 190
Suffolk bipoint, 199, 204
Sumatra, 188
Symmetry, 61
Synethic form, 8
Synethic type, 221
Synetic attributes, 34
Taima, 204
Taima Taima, 190, 217
Taxonomy, 30
Technological coincidence, 67
Technological continuum, 169
Technology continuum, 30
Technology's wings, 173
Tennessee, 90, 134
Tertiary legacy, 40
Texas, 43, 65, 156, 167
Thick Bipoints, 229
Tidewater Virginia, 198
Timeline, 41
Toca rockshelter, 82
Toldense complex, 82
Tool logic, 7, 173
Tool Organization, 39
Tool resharpening, 39, 59

Toolkit, 8
Topper site, 67, 190, 209
Trade item, 191
Transatlantic migrations, 68, 166
Transatlantic Migrations, 181
Transpacific migration, 217
Transverse Bipoint, 37
Tribute items, 191
Two pointed ends, 12
Type, 16
Uniface Bipoints, 35
Uniface specimens, 32
Unifaces, 9
Universal toolkit, 169
Upper Paleolithic cultural, 185
Vail site, 42
Venezuela, 217
Virginia, 45, 80, 103, 198, 204, 206
Virginia discovery, 194
Virginia specimens, 195
V-shaped, 226
V-shaped bit, 103, 191, 192, 193
V-Shaped Knife, 115
V-shaped stem, 193, 242
V-shaped stemmed, 166
V-stemmed tool, 51
Washington, 75
Wear pattern analysis, 49
Wear patterns, 49
West Virginia, 128
Western Hemisphere, 71
Wetlands, 199, 212
Wisconsin, 161
Woodland, 139
Workend, 61
Yup'ik Eskimo, 78

Arkfeld Site (44FK731) in the Opequon Quarry Complex of Frederick and Clarke Counties on Opequon Creek at Clear Brook, Virginia
Wm Jack Hranicky

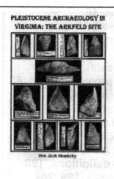

The Arkfeld site in Clarke and Frederick Counties, Virginia presents a study of Pleistocene material culture that has not been discovered on the Atlantic seaboard. While many of the tools resemble the Paleoindian toolkit, most artifacts are tools not present in Clovis technology. Also, many of the tools at the site seem to imply a heavy duty function, namely megafauna hunting and butchering. The site has produced numerous large (300+ mm) knives.

The Higgins Site, Clarke County, Virginia – A View of a PaleoAmerican Site in Virginia Jack Hranicky, RPA and Larry Higgins

The Higgins site is located in Clarke County, Virginia. It is a Pleistocene era jasper occupation on the Shenandoah River. Microtools were recovered with have an Old World legacy. The site is a pure blade technology occupation. The basic tool classes are punching, graving, drill, scraping, and cutting tools. These site implements are illustrated and discussed along with other area similar tools. The basic argument here is these artifacts have a one-to-one comparative and similar morphology with Paleolithic artifacts of Europe.

The Spout Run Site (44CK151): An Early American Stone Circles and Dual Solstice Site by Wm Jack Hranicky

The Spout Run site is located in Clarke County, Virginia. The site investigation was conducted by the author with the cooperation and assistance of the landowners. Standard archaeological methods were used, and the basic hypothesis for the site is:

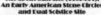

The Spout Run site is a prehistoric occupation that was used by Virginia's early Americans as a ceremonial location. Further, the site layout by them provided a calendar for observing both solstices and the equinoxes. This calendar was used for timing the seasonal visits to the area for exploiting natural resources and performing social ceremonies. Also, features allowed for daily measurement of the sun's positions – a day clock.

The site has concentric stone rings, solar clock, and numerous blade tools which reflect an Old World legacy.

Clovis Points in Virginia

Based on: the McCary Fluted Point Survey of Virginia

by
Wm Jack Hranicky RPA

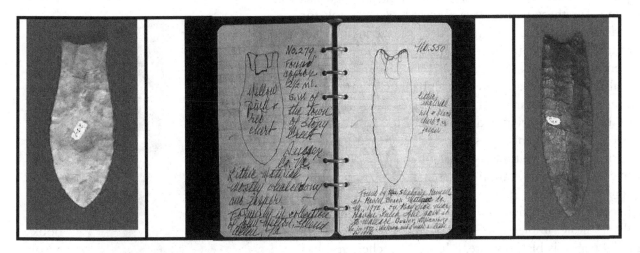

The publication provides a history of Clovis investigations in Virginia. With over 1000 point illustrations, it describes the Clovis technology in Virginia and the surrounding areas. The book is based on the McCary Fluted Point Survey which is the basic source for Virginia Clovis projectile points. The Williamson (44DN1), Cactus Hill (44SX202) and Thunderbird (44WR11) site investigations are discussed. Text is 8½ by 11 inches, black and white, indexed, and 225 pages with a comprehensive set of references. This book is an effort to organize Paleoindian data collected by the Survey and other sources into meaningful and useful information for the archaeological community and the interested general public.

Order by going to:

www.amazon.com\books

Then type in the title of this book…
Best projectile point reference source…

North American Projectile Points

Wm Jack Hranicky RPA

This book is now in its 8th edition and covers the entire North American prehistory of projectile points, which are commonly called arrowheads. There are over 2000 point types listed. Each listing contains point photographs, brief description, where it is found, who named it, its general dates, distribution maps, and references. There are numerous photographs and drawings for these points. It is a basic look-up book for American projectile points. Also, it contains an introduction, how to identify projectile points, and numerous other book examples that the reader may wish to consult. The points are listed in alphabetical order. The common points are marked which makes them easier to find. The book is a tremendous asset to professional archaeologists and collectors who are interested in stone tools. One of its major features is a list of most of the point types in the U.S. This publication represents 75 years of point typing in the U.S. It was written by a professional archaeologist with over 40 years of investigating and studying lithic implements of Native Americans. The book has **600** pages, is black&white, 8 ½ by 11 inches, and has a soft cover.

Order from:

AuthorHouse
(888-519-5121)
https://www.authorhouse.com
1663 Liberty Drive
Bloomington, Indiana 47403

The author at the Gault Site in Texas with dates 15,000 YBP. Photograph taken after the April 2012 excavation at this loci was by Michael Collins.

PaleoAmerican Archaeology in Virginia
By Wm Jack Hranicky

- **Number of Pages:** 256
- **ISBN-10:** 1627341102
- **ISBN-13:** 9781627341103
- **Publisher:** Universal-Publishers
- **Year:** 2017
- **Category:** History & Biography, Social Science
- **Cost:** $69.95 (Full Color)

View First 25 Pages: (free download)

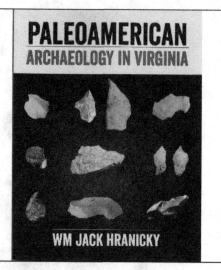

This book is a full-color study of over 500 pre-Clovis stone artifacts of Virginia. With the 22K-year date of the Cinmar bipoint in Virginia, there is ample evidence of artifact classes that are older than Clovis. Over 50 tool types are illustrated and discussed. Artifact single-site collections are documented. The book argues the differences between Holocene biface technology with the blade and core technology of the Pleistocene era. The requirements for identifying Pleistocene artifacts is presented, such as platforms, remaining cortex, and invasive retouch. They are presented in a tool model. Major stones, namely jasper, are discussed as a lithic determinism. The east coast distribution is presented for various tool types. Additionally, as a major focus, cross-Atlantic flake/blade identical tools from Europe are illustrated with Middle Atlantic artifacts. Artifact ergonomics, such as right-left handed tools, hypothetical tool center, are argued. Structural and functional axes are shown and described on how to identify them on tools. Overall, this book presents an initiating view of the archaeology needed to study Pleistocene era artifacts on the American east coast.

Order from the website:

Universal-Publishers, Inc.
www.universal-publishers.com
Boca Raton, Florida USA

Printed in the United States
By Bookmasters